John Spring's Arizona

This junior high school at North Main and West Second Street, Tucson, was named after John Spring in 1951 as a memorial to the pioneer educator.

John Spring's Arizona

Edited by

A. M. GUSTAFSON

THE UNIVERSITY OF ARIZONA PRESS
TUCSON

About the Editor . . .

A.M. GUSTAFSON since 1964 has been Director of Guidance Services for the public schools in Tucson, where he has been a resident since 1935— as a school principal both prior to and following World War II. He is author of "Schools for a Frontier State" which appeared in the *Arizona Teacher*, and is continuing his research on early Arizona schoolmasters. He holds a B.A. degree in history from Wheaton College, Illinois; his M.A. in history and his Ph.D. in education, both from the University of Arizona.

The University of Arizona Press
www.uapress.arizona.edu

Printed in the United States of America
21 20 19 18 17 16   7 6 5 4 3 2

ISBN-13: 978-0-8165-0046-8 (cloth)
ISBN-13: 978-0-8165-3524-8 (Century Collection paper)

L.C. Catalog Card No. 65-25159

♾ This paper meets the requirements of ANSI/NISO Z39.48-1992
(Permanence of Paper).

CONTENTS

A Word of Appreciation

Grateful acknowledgement is made to all those whose help has made possible the publication of this volume. Appreciation is expressed to Mrs. Tony Urías for the information that she gave me and for the use of the pictures painted by her grandfather. To the family of Mrs. Braulio Elías, sincere acknowledgement is made for first-hand recollections by Mrs. Elías of her father, John Spring, before her death in 1963.

Without the encouragement of Dr. Jack Cross, Mr. Douglas Peck, and Mrs. Elizabeth Shaw of the University of Arizona Press, the assistance of the staff of Arizona Pioneers' Historical Society in the use of filed materials, and the help of Mrs. Lutie Higley of the Library of the University of Arizona in securing microfilms from the Library of Congress, the completion of the project would not have been possible.

Appreciation is also expressed to Mrs. Florence Reece, Pima County Superintendent of Schools, for the use of old school records and letters written by John Spring when he was the teacher of the public school on the northwest corner of Meyer and McCormick streets.

A. M. Gustafson

The following symbols are used throughout to indicate annotation by two different individuals: for the editor, A. M. Gustafson (†), and for the author, John Spring (*).

John Spring's Arizona

INTRODUCTION

W<small>HILE SEARCHING</small> for material on early Arizona education at the Arizona Pioneers' Historical Society, I came across two nearly forgotten writings of John Spring published in serial form in *The National Tribune* of Washington, D.C., in 1902 and 1903. Bearing the titles, *With the Regulars in Arizona in the Sixties* and *Troublous Days in Arizona,* these accounts gave the readers of the nation's capital near the turn of the century a glimpse of the early days of a far western territory little known to most of them.

Readers today will find these accounts of equal appeal. Nearly one hundred years have gone by since Spring in the company of fellow soldiers was on his way to Tucson from California trudging along the dusty road which the Spanish of a bygone day called El Camino Real or the King's Highway. Writing lucidly and with good descriptive style and often with humor, he brings to life again the happenings in and around the Old Pueblo. His narrative is autobiographical in nature, and he adds a personal touch as he views events through his own eyes. Intrigued by the study of nature, he has included a number of excellent descriptions of the flora and fauna of the Southwest.

In the first serial, *With the Regulars in Arizona in the Sixties,* he relates as a member of Company "E," Third Battalion, Fourteenth U. S. Infantry (later replaced by the Thirty-Second Infantry) the story of the long journey in 1865 and 1866 from Hart's Island, New York, to the army posts of southern Arizona by way of the Isthmus of Panama, and later experiences and observations of military life while protecting the lives and property of early settlers from Apache raids. As seen through the eyes of Sergeant Spring, the days at Camp Wallen and other military sites were filled with interest and adventure which did much to relieve the monotony of camp life.

In the second serial, *Troublous Days in Arizona,* Spring continues the story of the early frontier, still in danger of attack by the Apache. After three years with the army in southern Arizona, he turned to various pursuits and at different times was a storekeeper, farmer, clerk, brewer, school teacher, federal court translator, artist, and writer. From a wealth of experience, Spring was able to narrate in an interesting manner a portion of Arizona history.

[1]

Thun, Switzerland, the birthplace of John Spring, eighteen and a half miles southeast of Bern, has been described as "a quaint old town, charmingly situated on the rapid green Aare." The Alps with snow-covered peaks of the Blümlisalp and the Doldenhorn may be seen in all their grandeur, and there are exceptionally fine views from the walk around the castle of Zähringen-Kiburg built in 1182 and from the bold square tower of the castle itself. An even finer view, it is said, may be seen from the parish church erected in 1732.

In these surroundings on May 8, 1845 was born Johann Arnold Spring who was to become one of the earliest educators in Arizona. He was the third of a family of four boys all native to Thun. The eldest was Gottlieb followed by Rudolf Samuel, and the fourth, younger than Johann, was Emil Arnold.

Johann's parents were both born in Steffisburg, a "considerable village" one and one-half miles to the north of Thun. Delightful walks in the vicinity led to mineral springs and baths, for the area was one of the health resorts of Switzerland. Christian Spring, Johann's father, was born May 28, 1810 and died August 20, 1872. Spring received word of his father's death on September 30. At that time a teacher in the little adobe earthen-floor school on the corner of South Meyer and McCormick streets in Tucson, he wrote the following to the board of trustees:

Tucson, A. T.
October 1st, 1872

To The Hon.
  The Board of Trustees
    School District No. 1
      Tucson, A. T.

Gentlemen,
  Having received last night the distressing news of my father's death, I have taken the liberty of dismissing school for today.
  I doubt not that the Hon. Board will appreciate my feelings of sorrow & excuse my nonattendance for this day.

Most respectfully,
John Spring
teacher

Spring's mother, Anna Marie Buchler von Steffisburg was born some time in 1814 and died June 25, 1875. She and Christian Spring were married in Muri, Switzerland, February 18, 1836, and made their home in Thun where Christian became a notary public and police inspector.

Spring, writing years later of the time that he left Switzerland, implied that he was of "good family." A review of his family record bears this out. His father's position in the city government of Thun was one to command

The family residence and birthplace of John Spring in Thun, Switzerland; in the background the castle of Zähringen-Kiberg, built in 1182. Spring's border decoration is typical of late nineteenth-century floral painting.

the respect of his fellow citizens. His eldest brother Gottlieb was a merchant in Thun; his next brother was a lawyer and superior judge (Oberrichter); and his younger brother, Emil Arnold, was a goldsmith in the city of Vienna.

As for Spring himself, the occupation listed on his Civil War records was that of merchant. At the time of his enlistment in the United States Regular Army, September 15, 1865, he was listed as clerk. In his own writings he makes no mention of his early vocations except to say that he left a very lucrative position when he embarked for America with several other youths of good family to enlist in the Union Army.

His family standing is indicated also by the vocations of his forebears on his mother's side. His grandfather, Christian Buchler von Steffisburg, was a farmer, judge, and legislative councilman, and his great grandfather, whose name was also Christian Buchler von Steffisburg, was a farmer and judge.

Comparatively little is written of Spring's boyhood, but it is known that he at times visited his Grandfather Buchler's farm. Such visits were undoubtedly memorable occasions. Half a century later he wrote that while he was yet of a tender age, he had been lifted upon one of his grandfather's farm horses during harvest.

He also enjoyed shooting. From his early youth he had become accustomed to firearms, and in his own words "having been trained to marksmanship from the age of twelve years." Perhaps it was on hunting expeditions in the Swiss Alps that he became acquainted with the chamois with which he later compared the skill of the Apaches in "leaping from rock to rock."

In Switzerland, too, he observed the marmot. Some years later he was reminded of it when he saw the great number of prairie dogs between Camp Wallen and Camp Crittenden. "The prairie dog," wrote Spring, "bears a great likeness to the marmot of the Swiss Alps."

That Spring was well educated there can be little doubt. On no less than two occasions, he referred to his college days. It was not unusual for young men of good middle-class families to attend school, for at the time that he resided in Thun there were no fewer than six institutions of higher learning in Switzerland, three of which were called universities.

Further evidence of his education was his employment as a school teacher in Tucson in 1872 and his appointment in 1885 by the Mexican government for the purpose of establishing schools in Sonora.

Spring had a natural inclination for travel. Language was not a barrier, and, always a keen observer of details, he acquired interesting information to which he made reference in later years. His travels as a youth took him to French North Africa, Egypt, and Palestine, as well as several countries of Europe. Of his trip to Egypt and the Holy Land he stated that he was "with a small college contingent." It is likely that the visit to French North Africa was made at the same time.

It was not uncommon for Spring to refer to his experiences in the old world and include them in his writings. In North Africa he found the same prickly pear cactus that he saw later growing in Arizona. He learned that it there was called *figue de Barbarie* and was used to make poultices to relieve the enflamed limbs of horses. Again the old world was brought to mind when he first entered Tucson in 1866. He wrote: "The aspect of the town reminded me forcibly of the small hamlets I had seen in the Holy Land, the more so as the women, all half-breeds, wore about the same dress as the Palestine women and carried upon their heads water-jars of the exact pattern of use in the Orient." There the similarity ceased for he hastened to add: "We soon discovered, however, that the languid state of inactivity and silence prevailing in the villages about Jerusalem did not exist here."

One can easily surmise that Spring was an excellent traveling companion. He was always at ease and sure of himself, easy to get along with, and "full of fun at all times." He was very sociable and had a good sense of humor, and by his own admission was good looking. He described himself as an ardent admirer of feminine beauty, a possessor of poetic vision, and much petted by the ladies.

When Spring arrived in America, according to his own statement, he had a fluent knowledge of three modern languages and Latin. Like so many other Swiss, the three tongues he spoke readily were German, French, and Italian. He, himself, mentioned specifically his ability with the first two, but it was his daughter, Mrs. Amelia Elías, who confirmed for me his knowledge of Italian. At least on one occasion, she told me, he visited Italian friends of his son, Arnold, in Bisbee, Arizona, and conversed with them with great enjoyment and sociability.

It was, however, to his knowledge of Latin that he attributed the ease with which he learned English and Spanish. That he had an excellent command of English is shown by his mastery of grammatical construction, evidence of which is found in the quality of his writings published in newspapers and journals.

A physical description of Spring would include his own words that he had a "healthy physique and a superabundance of energy." On muster roll records of 1864 at the time of his enlistment in the Union Army the following may be read: "Eyes *Brown*; Hair *Dark*; Complexion *Fair*; Height *5 ft 6 in.*" It is possible that the record of his height was in error for on the Register of Enlistments for September 1865 he is described as being 5 feet 8½ inches, and on his application for pension in 1907 he gave his height as 5 feet 9 inches. Members of his family remembered him as having a ruddy complexion. His weight in later years was estimated by those who knew him as approximately 175 pounds.

A rather remarkable young man was Johann Spring who by the time he was nineteen had completed his education, traveled widely in the old world, and held a good position. Added to his many interests was the great struggle between the North and South. In early June, 1864, scarcely a month following his nineteenth birthday, he and a group of his young Swiss friends set sail for New York to enlist in the Army of the North.

On June 29, 1864, Hans Spring walked down the gang plank of a ship in New York Harbor. It was as Hans that he had come to enlist in the Union Army. Probably he had been called that more than Johann, and naturally enough for it was the short form of Johann or Johannes.

Spring lost little time in finding his way to the recruiting office, most likely the one on Chatham Street where a little more than a year later he was to enlist in the United States Regular Army. Before the day was over he had given to Lieutenant Davason (sic.), the recruiting officer, the information that he was twenty-one, born in Switzerland, spoke German, and that he was a merchant by occupation. The enlistment, for three years, was actually for the duration of the war. Spring at the time knew no English and was assigned to the German-speaking Seventh New York Infantry Regiment with which he was to serve for the remainder of the war except for the time spent in various military hospitals.

Spring enlisted as a substitute for William E. Dodge Jr. Twentieth Ward, Eighth Congressional District, New York State, under the Act of February 24, 1864. Little did it matter to him that another was to escape the rigors of war.

It must have been with singleness of purpose that he sought out the recruiting office. Although amply provided with funds, sufficient to see the city and surrounding country, he volunteered immediately in spite of his natural inclination to see new lands and people. His desire to serve the cause of the North seemed genuine. He wrote that "when the fearful losses incident to the bloody Wilderness campaign became known, many young Swiss declared their intention to abandon everything to cross the ocean and take service in the Union Army."

Service as a private in the New York Seventh Regiment was his first military experience. Because of his youth, he had not been in the army in Switzerland. Swiss law restricted membership in the military to the inclusive ages of twenty to thirty-four.

During the Civil War, Spring's name appeared on the records in three different ways: as Hans Spring, Carl Hans Spring, and John Spring. He apparently enlisted as Hans, but a little more than two weeks later his

—Courtesy the National Archives

Muster rolls of the N. Y. Seventh Regiment, 1864, carried Hans Spring, Carl Hans Spring, and John Spring. All were variations of the author's original name, Johann Arnold Spring.

name appeared on the Muster-In and Descriptive Roll of Company D as Carl Hans Spring. For the most part, only the name Hans Spring appeared on the company muster rolls, but Carl Hans seems to have been used on his discharge papers. Indicative of this was its appearance on a notation paper issued by the War Department in 1887 noting the furnishing of one certificate in lieu of a lost discharge.

Spring began using the name John the first year after arriving in the United States. It appeared thus on the muster rolls of the U.S.A. General Hospital, Beverly, New Jersey; the U.S.A. Depot Field Hospital, Second Army Corps, City Point, Virginia; and the Campbell U.S.A. General Hospital, Washintgon, D. C. Like many others who came to the shores of the New World, Spring changed his name to its English equivalent.

Much of the year that Spring was in the Union Army was spent in military hospitals. From September 1 to December 31, 1864, he was at the Army General Hospital in Beverly, New Jersey, where by October 18 he was assigned duty as a convalescent guard. No indication was given as to the nature of his disability. It is possible that he was hospitalized because of illness, as Spring himself mentions only the wound received at the assault on the Southside Railroad.

Following his release from the hospital in December, he rejoined the German-speaking Seventh New York Infantry under the command of Colonel George W. von Schaack. As a part of the Third Brigade, First Division, Second Army Corps, commanded by Major General Winfield Scott Hancock, the Seventh New York took an active part in the fighting around Richmond and Petersburg. One of the objectives of the North was to take the Southside Railroad, running from Petersburg to Lynchburg through Burkeville and Appomatox Station, and thus deal a crippling blow to this important supply and communication line of the South.

In the successful assault on the Southside Railroad on April 2, 1865, John Spring was wounded in the shoulder by a rifle ball. This meant his evacuation from the front lines to the field hospital at City Point, Virginia, arriving there on April 4.

In writing for *The Arizona Enterprize* in 1890, Spring gave the following interesting description of the military base at City Point:

> There probably never existed a military depot of such gigantic proportions like those found at City Point on the James River during the last year of our civil war. It was an immense city mainly of canvas. Not only was it the base of supplies of every kind for the Army of the Potomac around Petersburg and the Army of the James near Richmond, but it contained also the store houses of the Christian and Sanitary Commissioners, German Relief, State Reliefs of every State in the Union that had troops in the field, a library, innumerable sutler stores and a hospital which would accommodate

from three to four thousand sick and wounded until such time as the great steamers could carry them off to general hospitals situated in various parts of the Northern States. To these sufferers City Point was a haven of rest, peace and quiet. . . .

City Point was a haven of rest not only to the sick and wounded, but also to soldiers in line of duty sent there to escort prisoners of war from the front. Concerning them, Spring wrote as follows:

It is not always possible during fighting time, to provide a large army scattered over many miles of West Virginia clay with all the necessaries of life, so that our soldiers' clothing was quite often in sad plight, both as to the cleanliness and serviceableness and a visit to City Point was therefore a great boon, inasmuch as the mentioned commissions and reliefs would supply any petitioner most liberally with the creature comforts asked for, from a good suit of underwear to a pipe and tobacco, a good book to a so-called housewife, manufactured by somebody's "girl I left behind me," and containing needles, thread, buttons, etc., of every size and suited to every want. There were not less than forty places where the boy in blue could set himself comfortably down and pen a few lines to his anxious parents, brothers and sisters, to the weeping sweetheart and let them know, that once more he has escaped unscathed from the last terrific battle. Kind hands would furnish him gladly with the necessary materials and postage stamps and even attend kindly to the safe mailing of his loving missive to the dear ones at home.

The hospital at City Point became very crowded during the latter part of March and the early days of April, 1865. With the severe fighting at Five Points and the Southside Railroad, the wounded were brought in by the train load and assigned to hospital tents. Spring arrived April 4 and was placed in a tent with twelve beds, all of which were occupied. One male nurse was in attendance.

Vividly impressed upon the mind of Spring was the death of one of the wounded. He was a large man about forty years of age "with a silky beard and beautiful blue eyes," but due to his wounds was unable to speak or write his name. A bullet had penetrated his upper lip, lodging somewhere inside so that it was impossible for him to open his swollen mouth. It was necessary to feed him by means of a tube through the hole made by the bullet. Wounded also in his right hand he was unable to write even his name. The attending surgeon had no doubt that he would soon die of lockjaw. Apparently there were no remaining papers to identify him. Usually it was possible to place a soldier as to company, regiment, and state by means of his cap, but this too was missing.

Although unable to speak, "he was unquestionably a close observer and eager listener to what went on around him." His eyes were "mirrors of his intellect," and it was easy to see that he was very fond of music.

In the same tent was a young soldier who was almost a boy, coming from a Massachusetts regiment. He was slightly wounded in one of his ankles and was able to entertain the others with his singing whenever the opportunity afforded. It was evident by the eager looks of the unidentified man that he enjoyed the youngster's rather extensive repertoire of love and patriotic songs. His favorite was apparently "We are coming Father Abraham, three hundred thousand strong!" And whenever he would hear this song, he would "beat out the measure with his uninjured hand upon the counterpane and his eyes would — oh! how they would speak." But he was visibly becoming weaker from day to day.

President Lincoln came to visit the wounded at City Point. Spring described the visit to their tent in the following words:

> On the occasion of President Lincoln's visit to Richmond just after its surrender, he came to see us also; I think it was on April 9th. He shook hands with us all and addressed to us a few friendly words, reminding us to bear patiently our sufferings, that now the beginning of the end had come. When he touched our unknown's hand and said a few kindly words to him especially (he must have noticed his intense pain and pitiable condition) two great crystal drops started from the sufferer's eyes and fell slowly over his poor mutilated face.

Little wonder was it that the wounded at City Point were personally affected by the news of Lincoln's assassination. They remembered well his recent visit which brought him close to each of them. Spring wrote that it "was as if a great catastrophe had come upon each roof, each tent; as if a death blow had been dealt to each particular heart, thus did we feel, we boys in blue." A little later he continued, "There were no songs in our tent that day! Silent comings and goings of those who could walk or hobble on crutches for the latest dispatches only!"

The unknown soldier grew visibly worse that day and the surgeon privately told the nurse that he was sinking fast. In Spring's own words we read the following:

> Thus came the night. I do not think that many slept; still, silence, deep and unbroken, pervaded the whole tent which was dimly lighted by the night lamps. Towards midnight somebody came to the door and asked if our nurse could go, if he could be spared for a little while, to another tent near by to lend a helping hand with another man suddenly taken with a spasm; before the nurse went out he stepped to the bed of the unknown and bent over him; he found him breathing regularly, apparently asleep. A little more than half an hour later we were all startled by an occurrence as sudden as it was unexpected. We were all the victims of a magic spell. Could eleven men be at once and at the same moment under the same influence of optical and aureal delusion? No! it was a fact and

a most astounding fact. From the bed of the silent unknown came a strong sonorous, yet musical voice, singing correctly and distinctly the well known melody with these words: "I am coming, Father Abraha—." Here it broke off . . . sudden snap as if it were, of the last string, and there on the bed sat upright . . . the form of our long mute companion. He had joined the three hundred thousand gone before.

A little more than two weeks later on May 2, Spring was transferred to the Campbell U.S.A. General Hospital in Washington where he remained until he was mustered out of service July 3, 1865. His efforts to re-enlist, this time in the Regulars, were unsuccessful because his shoulder was not completely healed. Great numbers of soldiers were returning to civilian life with the result that employment was hard to secure, especially for a young man who had not mastered the English language. After performing a variety of odd jobs, he applied again for re-enlistment and this time was accepted. He described the medical examination at the recruiting office on Chatham Street, New York, as cursory with the possible inference that his wound was still giving him trouble.

The next three years with the Regular Army, spent for the most part, at military posts in Southern Arizona provided Spring with the experiences that he recounted later in the story, *With the Regulars in Arizona in the Sixties.*

It was in this period that lasting friendships were formed with Solomon Warner and Leslie B. Wooster. Warner is remembered by Tucsonans as the owner of Warner's Store on Main Street, the flour mill at the base of Sentinel Peak, and Warner's Lake, a reservoir on the Santa Cruz River created for the purpose of supplying water power for grinding flour from the grain brought in by the farmers of the valley. His wagon trains moving slowly along the historic Camino Real brought in goods for his store from both California and Mexico. During the Civil War, his original store and all his possessions were lost when Captain Sherod Hunter and his Confederate Cavalry occupied Tucson for a brief period. Like Estevan Ochoa, he was given the choice of either swearing allegiance to the Confederacy or having his property confiscated. Neither accepted the Southern cause and both left Tucson; Ochoa to join the Union Army at El Paso and Warner to go to Mexico.

Beginning life anew in Santa Cruz, Sonora, Warner married a wealthy widow, the owner of a large hacienda. Cattle grazed on the grasslands and servants and ranch hands cared for every need. His wagon trains once more moved along the old Spanish roads carrying merchandise and grain between Hermosillo and Tucson. A government contract to supply corn to Camp Wallen was his introduction to Quartermaster Sergeant Spring

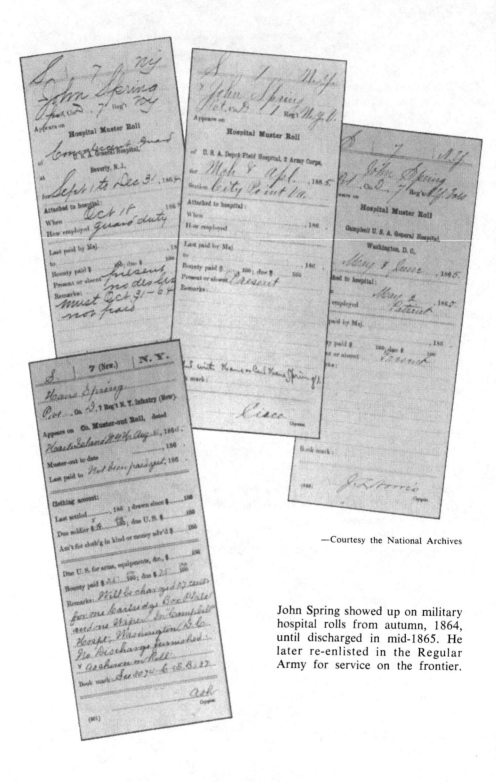

—Courtesy the National Archives

John Spring showed up on military hospital rolls from autumn, 1864, until discharged in mid-1865. He later re-enlisted in the Regular Army for service on the frontier.

whom he invited to visit his hacienda in Santa Cruz. It was there that Spring fell in love with the beautiful dark-eyed Eulalia, Solomon Warner's step-daughter who was destined to marry a Lieutenant Reyes of the Mexican Cavalry.

Warner's business ventures were to fail him again and when he died penniless in 1899 only Spring was with him to bid an old friend goodbye.

September 16, 1868 marked the close of John Spring's military career. His length of service consisted of somewhat more than a year with the Union Army and three years with the United States Regulars. With his discharge in his pocket he left the hospital in Tucson not yet completely recovered from dysentery, a disease prevalent at the time in southern Arizona.

He soon joined his friend Leslie Wooster with whom he had formed a partnership to deliver hay under government contract from the Babocomari Valley to Camp Wallen. They had become fast friends dating from the time that Wooster operated the sutler's store at the camp. In addition to the hay venture they were partners in a general store in Tubac and in farming in the Tubac Valley. After Spring had left him, Wooster and his housekeeper were killed in an Apache raid on the farm. *The Weekly Arizona Miner* of March 21, 1871, reported that "the Indians in strong force descended the Valley of Tubac and killed L. B. Wooster and Miss Trinidad Aguirre and destroyed property to the value of $1,500."

Spring was not suited to the lonely life of an isolated farm or settlement and ended his partnership with Wooster in 1869. He gave as his real reasons, however, the return of his recent illness and the low prices of farm produce caused by competitive bidding of newly established mercantile firms in Tucson. After a number of jobs of short duration – as a barkeeper in Tucson, as a clerk in the sutler's store at Fort Crittenden, a helping hand to Wooster with his hay camp in the Sonita Valley and at the *Palo Parado* farm, and as a quartermaster clerk in Tucson, by February 21, 1870 he was in the employ of A. Levin and Company, operators of the Pioneer Brewing Company in Tucson. A. Levin was Alexander Levin, a native of Prussia, who was soon to become John Spring's brother-in-law through marriage to sisters. A notice of Spring's connection with the firm appeared in *The Weekly Arizonian* of February 26 and March 12, 1870:

NOTICE

The undersigned hereby inform the public that they have formed a partnership under the firm name of A. Levin and Co.

John Spring, as agent for S. W. Hopkins, [sic] is hereby authorized to transact business in the name of the said firm.

A. Levin
S. W. Hopkins

In the transaction of business for the company, it seems that he performed the duties of clerk, bookkeeper, and general salesman. In the United States census of 1870 his occupation is listed as brewery clerk.

Somewhat earlier that year, January 20, 1870, along with Joseph Goldtree and Samuel H. Drachman, Spring became a naturalized citizen of the United States. A minute entry of the court in Tucson presided over by the Honorable John Titus, judge of the First Judicial District, reads as follows:

> Came into court with witnesses and made proof he was in service of U.S. for a term of four years and was honorably discharged; made renunciation of allegiance to Gov't of Switzerland, and was admitted into citizenship.

In a lighter vein, *The Weekly Arizonian* of January 29 stated "Jno. Spring, Joseph Goldtree, and Sam'l Drachman renounced their allegiance to the Faderland and are now running loose as naturalized children of Uncle Sam."

Spring was married June 22, 1870, to Miss Manuela Molina born in Sonora, Mexico, of a rather prominent family. A story in *The Weekly Arizonian* described the wedding in the newspaper style of the time:

> Hymeneal: Wednesday evening Mr. John Spring, a youth of some 26 summers, sacrificed his cherished batchelorhood (*sic.*) at the altar of affection by incorporating his being with that of a modest and very superior young lady, Miss Manuela Molina. Mr. Spring's highly social qualities, and the popularity of the young bride had the effect of calling together on the occasion a large and select attendance. After the marriage ceremony had been concluded the company adjourned to a grove on the premises where seats were arranged and tables spread to receive and provide for its enjoyment. Never having taken the pains to study female appearl (*sic.*) we dare not venture on a description of the attire of the numerous ladies present, and therefore inform the "posted" questioner on this point, that he or she cannot imagine any style of dress combining elegance, symmetry and real sterling beauty which might not have been witnessed there. The guests after largely enjoying themselves at dancing, drinking, toasting and thinking, took their departure at midnight after having first tendered their final congratualations to the happiest couple in Arizona.

Spring counted Samuel Drachman as one of his many friends. After leaving the employ of Levin and Hopkins and while he was engaged in the brewery business in Florence, he was visited by Drachman who made the following entry in his diary: "5 P.M. started for Florence, arrived at Florence at 7 A.M. took breakfast with Spring rec'd letter from the Maj, went with Spring to Sanford."

During his residence in Florence, he received a letter offering him the position of teacher of the public school to be opened in Tucson on the northwest corner of Meyer and McCormick Streets. In a few days Spring was on his way to the Old Pueblo to take the teacher's examination which would qualify him for the appointment. Passing the examination with ease which required proficiency in the common school subjects, he officially began his duties March 4, 1872.† The only other public school in Tucson prior to this time was the one taught by Augustus Brichta for six months in 1868.

An excellent description of the school taught by Spring is found in his story, *Troublous Days in Arizona*. Among his pupils was Ignacio Bonillas, the son of a blacksmith, who was to become Mexico's first ambassador to Washington. Many years later, January 2, 1926, Bonillas was interviewed by the press concerning his school days at the time when Tucson was the Territorial capital and A.P.K. Safford was governor. The governor was a frequent visitor at the school and Bonillas told of the interest that he had taken in him. On one occasion it was noted that he had been absent from school for a week or ten days and in answer to Safford's inquiry in regard to his absence, Spring explained that Ignacio was a poor boy and had to work to pay for his books. The governor then offered to buy his books, paper and anything else that was needed if he would remain in school. After talking the matter over with his parents, Ignacio agreed to accept the offer, but with the provision that he could work for anything that was give him. In Bonillas' own words, "The governor told me I could come over in the morning and feed his mules, black his boots, and sweep his office if I wanted to, "Safford continued to help by paying for private lessons from John Spring after the public school was closed and until it opened again in the court house. Today the Ignacio Bonillas Elementary School is named in honor of John Spring's former pupil.

Confirmation of Governor Safford's interest in the school is the note appended to the Quarterly Report of District School No. 1 for the quarter ending March 21, 1873:

> The school has during this quarter quite frequently been visited by citizens of this town. In the commencement of February Governor A.P.K. Safford while visiting the school promised the pupils to distribute among the most deserving the amount of $.20 on the end of the quarter. This money was divided into 3 prizes of $2- each & 14 prizes of $1- each and distributed by the donator to the best pupils on the afternoon of the 31st of March.

---

†*The Arizona Citizen* of March 2, 1872, stated that "next Monday [March 4, 1872] one [school] will be opened in Tucson."

Governor Safford as *ex officio* superintendent of schools reported on the success of Spring's teaching:

> At the commencement scarcely one could speak a word of the English language; now many of them can read and write very well and have rapidly advanced in arithmetic, geography and grammar. The teacher John Spring has been tireless in his efforts, and is entitled to much credit for his work.

The Arizona Citizen stated on June 1, 1872 that "the first three months had closed on the 21st ultimo. The progress the scholars have made is quite remarkable and great credit is due the teacher, John Spring." Again on May 3, 1873 in reporting the closing of school on May 1 the *Citizen* wrote that "Mr. J. Spring who has taught our school from the commencement and who has proved himself a most excellent teacher, will continue private school at his residence and will receive a limited number of pupils."

Spring had resigned his position of public school teacher effective May 1, 1873 and established in his own home the private school attended by Ignacio Bonillas. No information is available to determine how long he continued to give private lessons, but it is assumed that he continued at least until the school was opened in the court house.

Supplementing his income as a private school teacher, Spring in 1873 accepted the position offered him as interpreter and translator for the United States Court and District Court of the First Judicial District of Arizona. His duties began officially when the court convened September 1. His fluency with languages, especially his knowledge of Spanish, made him an ideal person for this type of work. He estimated that approximately seven-eighths of the people in Tucson spoke only this language. Several incidents which occurred in the court furnished him with interesting material for his later writings.

Although the Old Pueblo in the early days was a rough and ready town, Spring did not find it altogether lacking in cultural interests. "In 1873," wrote Samuel Drachman, "we established in Tucson the 1st Literary Society where we would pass pleasantly our evenings discussing the various topics of the day." It is not surprising to note that Spring's application for membership was received that same year on Sunday evening, December 7. Besides Drachman and Spring, the Society included the names of Albert Steinfeld, William Zeckendorf, L. C. Hughes, Carlos Tully, L. M. Jacobs, B. M. Jacobs, H. S. Stevens, and J. S. Vosburg.

A naturalist at heart, Spring was collecting in 1874 biological specimens for a museum in California and the following year for the Smithsonian Institution in Washington. A news item in the *Citizen* of November 28, 1874 described the nature of his work:

John Spring of this town is engaged in collecting specimens of all the botanical productions of Arizona, so far as he can get them, for the purpose of sending them to Professor Bolander of California. Mr. Spring sent some time ago, the professor some samples and their receipt called forth the request for a full assortment, and Mr. Spring is doing a good work in supplying the museum of so eminent a gentleman with them.

Correspondence with the Smithsonian Institution resulted in the following request: "Please gather whatever you can in the way of small snakes, lizards, etc." Work was commenced at once with the help of young Henry Buehman, a kindred soul from Germany. Buehman at the time was twenty-four years of age, an artist who later opened a photography shop in Tucson. His son Albert R. Buehman, also a photographer, has told me of his father's friendship with Spring and of his visiting him in California. *The Arizona Citizen* of June 5, 1875 reported:

> "They have shown great energy in the labor they have undertaken, and have already secured a very large collection. When their collection is completed we anticipate that it will be one of the most interesting furnished by any State or Territory in the Union. We wish that this collection could be used on exhibition at the Centennial (Philadelphia) before going into the Smithsonian.

The collection was duly sent to Washington and except for a mutilated specimen of a chaparral cock, commonly known as a road runner, it arrived in good condition. The brevity of the following entry in the Smithsonian annual report of 1875 does not detract from the significance of the undertaking:

> Spring, J. A. and H. Buschman (sic) birds, nests, and eggs: collection of plants: mutilated specimen of chaparral-cock (Geococcyx Californianus) from Arizona.

Another example of Spring's interest in natural science was his project to propagate fish in Warner's Lake. A news item in *The Arizona Enterprize* of June 2, 1888, stated "that about five or six years ago John Spring placed half a dozen small carp in Warner's Lake at Tucson, and they have multiplied so rapidly that 700 pounds of carp are sold every week in that city for 15c per pound."

It may be that Spring conceived the idea of planting carp in Warner's Lake from his visit in 1885 to the ranch of Peter Charouleau in the Santa Catalina Mountains. (This is a later date than indicated in the *Enterprize*.) In a story written for *The Arizona Daily Citizen* of July 7, 1885, Spring described his experiences as follows:

> Pursuant to a long standing invitation of Mr. Peter Charouleau to visit his ranch, reservoir, etc., situated in the Canyon del Oro to

examine the carp placed there about eighteen months ago and to make drawings of his new reservoirs for the information of the Fish Commissioners, together with other business, Mr. Charouleau called for me at 7 a.m. on Tuesday last and we started in his light wagon at a good round trot. About 10:00 we arrived at the ranch of Mr. George Pusch where we found his steam pump in full operation, fetching forth at every stroke a goodly quantity of delicious cool water as clear as a crystal. . . . From here one road leads to the left to the Mammoth Mine, one to the right to the ranch of Mr. Romero and to that of Mr. Charouleau while we kept on the middle road almost due north and arrived at half past 11 on the ranch of our destination, situated I should say about 28 miles from the city. . . . We saddled up and started for the big reservoir. . . . From here we begin to climb, climb climb, over rocks, under rocks, and between rocks to a considerable height until we arrive at another very small reservoir cut into the side of a hill, where a living spring of water comes out of the ground and after filling the basin discharges the precious fluid into a large wooden trough, where the roaming cattle quench their thirst. Into this small reservoir we threw some bran, and lo! in a few minutes rose five beautiful fat carp to the surface to feed. These are the survivors of the three inch seedlings from Washington in the month of January 1884, they are the only ones that arrived alive at the reservoir, and they have thrived wonderfully well, being now from fifteen to sixteen inches long and apparently in the best bodily and mental condition. If among these five are both male and female specimens, some progeny should be forthcoming in a very short time. Mr. Charouleau is going to take steps to stock his two large reservoirs with these fish during the coming winter.

Spring's efforts to propagate fish in Warner's Lake evidently were successful.

The Arizona Daily Star of May 4, 1889 carried the following story:

Allison & Sons are now supplying the market with fine fat carp from their carp lake [Warner's Lake] at the base of sentinel peak. During two days they took 700 hundred pounds each (sic) weighing from two to five pounds, all of which were taken at once by the hotels. They also made a shipment of 160 pounds. . . .

Fish had also been planted in Silver Lake, a reservoir on the Santa Cruz, a short distance south of Warner's Lake. A news item in the *Star* of July 29, 1890 stated that "Sunday the Santa Cruz overflowed its banks at Silver Lake, passing around the hotel. The overflow carried out a large number of carp, many of which Mr. Swart gathered up and found ready market for them in this city yesterday."

During the early days of Arizona, John Spring was in demand as a speaker. To him was given the honor of delivering the Centennial address, July 4, 1876, commemorating the one hundredth anniversary of the Declaration of Independence. A joint resolution of Congress on March 13 of that year stated that there should be a historical account of every town and county prepared and delivered and then filed away as a permanent record.

From his friend, Bishop Salpointe, Spring obtained the history of San Xavier del Bac and neighboring missions. From another friend, Francisco Léon, born in Tucson under Spanish rule in 1819, he obtained information about the city when it was a military garrison for the Mexican government. Spring quoted his friend in the following words:

> It was merely a military post with a garrison of eighty to ninety soldiers, and about three hundred inhabitants. All the grain raised was sold to the government and placed in a store-house situated where Mr. Fish's dwelling house now stands. The total number of houses or rather hovels could not have exceeded one hundred and forty, and . . . by no means were capable of affording any degree of comfort . . . barren surfaces met the eye everywhere, not one sign of beauty or strength; the interior matched the exterior in its prison-like and angular appearance, nothing but adobe walls, bare floors and ceilings, with perhaps a small table, a few cooking utensils and a roll of bedding.

It was Mr. Léon's opinion that the temperature had greatly changed since 1825, and positively asserted "that no late frosts were ever known to occur to the injury of trees in blossom, and that large quantities of grapes, peaches, pomegranates, quinces, apples, and apricots were raised in the Santa Cruz Valley west of Tucson."

Samuel Hughes was given the credit in Spring's address for his knowledge of the existence of an old town about three miles below Tucson, one mile due east of what is known as the *Casa de Padre,* but "I regret to say" said Spring, "notwithstanding my efforts I have entirely failed in obtaining the least clue as to its age, formation, and destruction."

In describing Tucson of 1876, Spring reminded his listeners:

> The telegraph now transmits our messages to their destination with the speed of lightning. A fine library is open to the inquiring mind. A delicious park with an extensive hop plantation and brewery offer shelter against the heat of noon day. Ice cream and soda water of excellent quality are manufactured. Thousands of acres have been brought under cultivation and furnish work for the three flouring-mills, while gardens furnish the table almost the year round with their savory produce. . . . If we take a retrospective look at the spot where twenty years ago a few old ruins, representing this town, passed into the power of the United States, we may well feel proud and bless American courage, perseverance, endurance, and industry.

The complete story of John Spring is difficult to piece together. Following his employment as a United States court interpreter, it is noted that he was a bookkeeper prior to 1880 in the firm of Zeckendorf and Staab. Beginning that year he worked in the same capacity for the A. Goodman's Grocery Store. During the summer of 1883 and for a short period in 1884 and 1885 he was engaged by Tucson attorneys to go to Hermosillo and Guadalajara to copy documents of Spanish and Mexican land grants which later became part of the United States and which had been purchased by American claimants who wished to establish clear title to their lands. In 1885 he was employed by the Mexican government to establish the public schools in the state of Sonora. After this little is known of his regular activity. Concerning this period he wrote, "I was not particularly anxious to enter anybody's employ at that time, as I had already entered the field of literature. I was the Arizona correspondent for the *Illinois Staatszeitung,* and wrote a weekly story for its Sunday supplement; also several articles for the *Globus,* an ethnological journal issued at Brunswick, Germany, and several descriptive articles of travel in Mexico for the *Journal des Voyages,* published at Paris, France." He explained that "these different languages never proved any serious obstacle to me, because in the high schools and colleges of Switzerland foreign languages are taught in such a manner as to stay with you for life." While in the soldiers' home and hospital in California he wrote his two serials which comprise this volume. During this period he was also a contributor to *The Wide World Magazine.* Previously while he was still in Tucson there is evidence that he published an article in *Chambers Journal* of London and Edinburgh. His services were also available professionally for people who required someone to write their personal and business letters or other matters of interest. "The Story of the Oatman Family" was written by Spring as told him by Sam Hughes and is now on file at The Arizona Pioneers' Historical Society in Tucson.

Of the several vocations that he followed during his life, that of an artist seemed to give him the greatest pleasure. An early resident of Tucson recalled for me that he had often seen Spring painting in front of his home at 221 North Court Street, dressed in artist's smock and smoking his pipe. He was always cheerful, had a good word for everyone, and enjoyed the experience of living.

To Spring we are indebted for the sketch of the ruins of one of the oldest monasteries in Arizona, once situated on the west bank of the Santa Cruz River at Simpson, six streets south of Congress. As late as 1920 the ruins which once stabled the livestock of Sam Hughes could still be seen. Since then they have completely disappeared into brick made by the kiln which still stands there today. From his own statements it is known that he liked taking along his sketch book on trips as he did when he took his wife to Fuller's Springs. He loved to paint desert and mountain

One of the oldest monasteries in Arizona, on the west bank of the Santa Cruz River south of Congress Street, Tucson, was in ruins when sketched by John Spring. These ruins later stabled Sam Hughes' livestock, and were eventually made into bricks at the nearby kiln.

landscapes. His services were for hire and apparently the brush and crayon became one of his means of livelihood.

During the 1870's Mrs. Spring was in poor health and for several years occasional trips were taken to Fuller's Springs, also known as Agua Caliente, fourteen miles from Tucson, and to the hot springs of Ymuris, Mexico, both reputed to have curative powers. Seemingly her condition improved, but her illness returned in May, 1881, and more severely than before. No further benefit was derived from the baths at Fuller's Springs and the prescriptions of three physicians. The decision was made to visit again the hot springs at Ymuris. Accompanied by two older sisters of Mrs. Spring, the group left in a commodious wagon on June 4. To their dismay the springs were gone. Dr. Brown, a graduate of Vienna, who happened to be in nearby Magdalena was consulted, but was unable to give the patient any relief. Not long after, on July 2, Mrs. Spring died.

With the care of four little ones it was not surprising that later the same summer Spring married his wife's sister, Refugia Molina, who became a second mother to the children. They were Ana María, Arnold, Manuela, and Amelia. Amelia, who had married Braulio Elías, lived in Tucson until her death in 1963. From her I was able to obtain firsthand knowledge of her father.

Grandchildren making their homes in the city are Mrs. Elías' son and daughter, Albert and Helen Elías; Mrs. Tony Urías, the daughter of Ana María; and Richard Spring Legarra, son of Manuela. Arnold Spring, Jr., a grandson, lives in Denver. Great grandchildren living in Tucson include Albert Elías, Jr., Aida Elías, Gilbert Urias, and Tony Urias, Jr. Living in Los Angeles are two great grandchildren, Yvonne and John Spring, grandchildren of Arnold Spring.

It was with his favorite granddaughter, Ana Barreda (Mrs. Urías), that he corresponded most when he was living at the Soldier's Home at Sawtelle, California. Several of his paintings and a hand-painted quilt are among her prized possessions. One picture of flowers bears on the back this inscription: "Painted for my darling grandchild, Ana Barreda, for her birthday, October 17th, 1908 (The actual date is October 12) by her grandfather, John Spring."

Most of Spring's later life was spent at Sawtelle, California. Apparently his first stay there was in 1892, although one official record from the Bureau of Pensions gives his residence as Tucson until 1894. It seems that occasional visits were made to his old home in Tucson, one occurring in 1899 at the time of Solomon Warner's death when only Spring was with him. Apparently his last and final visit was in 1902. Toward the close of his life, he was transferred to Hampton, Virginia, where he died December 6, 1924, at the age of 79.

PART I

With the Regulars in Arizona in the Sixties

John Spring, a well-educated Swiss youth, voluntarily became an American frontier soldier. While in the Army and later as a civilian, he gave readers of the *National Tribune* in Washington, D.C. vivid accounts of military life, Indian perils, hardships, adventures, and living conditions in the far West.

With the Regulars in Arizona in the Sixties

FROM HART'S ISLAND TO CALIFORNIA

A FEW DAYS after arriving at Hart's Island our first sergeant happened to see a letter written by me for a German member of our company, and taking a fancy to my writing, had me detailed as company clerk with the rank of lance corporal. This first sergeant was Max Lipowitz, a native of Prussia, a perfect martinet, who was of a very trying temper at times and at all times over-strict to men, a goodly number of whom were used to the less rigid discipline of the volunteer service. He was consequently most heartily disliked. It is a well-known fact that the Fourteenth Infantry of those days contained a great deal of nondescript material, recruited from the waterfront and rowdy element of New York City, at that time very prolific in the production of "tough" characters.

The commanding officer of the battalion, who was present at Hart's Island, was Major Chapin, a gentleman of the old school and every inch a soldier; the company commanders were for the greater part officers appointed from civil life, and with few exceptions hardly qualified for their military duties. The number of subalterns was very small, no company having more than one commissioned officer.

The life on Hart's Island was the humdrum everyday garrison life of recruits, varying between drill, fatigue, and dress parade, the guard duty being done by the regularly established garrison of the island. I remember to this day, partly with sad feelings, partly with grim humor, our parade uniforms, the stiff leather stock around the neck, the glittering brass scales upon the shoulders and the very tall black hat adorned with a single black feather of doubtful origin. There came, however, one incident to enliven the everyday routine of dullness and sameness, an incident which may not be overlooked, as it was the beginning of a sensational story, reading rather more like a romance than an actual occurrence, which latter, however, I beg my readers to believe it was, and happened as related from time to time, as its different phases developed themselves.

We had been at Hart's Island about three weeks when a battalion order was issued to the effect that all knapsacks, haversacks, and canteens should be plainly marked with letters and numbers in white oil paint, four inches high, preparatory to our departure. The first sergeant had gone to New York in order to purchase the necessary material, and I was alone in the room occupied with the descriptive lists and clothing accounts of the company. I may here remark that I had begun to apply myself seriously to the study of the English language; and, owing to my knowledge of Latin and three modern languages, was making steady and rapid progress, hearing nothing spoken but English. A gentle knock at the door interrupted my work; upon my calling out, "Come in" there entered a woman, to whom I offered a chair forthwith. She appeared to be about forty-five years of age, and bore unmistakable traces of former beauty. Although quite indifferently, I may almost say shabbily, dressed, she used excellent language, her manners were ladylike, her voice exquisite, and, as I especially noticed, the shape of her small feet and hands quite aristocratic. Imagine, then, my utter surprise at her statement that she had come to make application as a laundress to our company, knowing that we had but one laundress, although the army regulations allowed four laundresses to each company. She stated that she had a son in the Second Battalion, Fourteenth Infantry, then at Vancouver; that she wished to join her son, but had not the means to do so, and perhaps could obtain her end in the way indicated.

Of course, I knew full well that the laundress of a company must be the lawful wife of a member of said company, and the lady knew it also; but she begged very hard to be taken to the company commander. This I could not refuse, if I had wished to (which was far from being the case), and I accompanied her across the parade ground to the quarters of our Captain, W. Harvey Brown, brevet major, to whom I introduced her as Mrs. Mary Wilson, the name she had given to me. Here I left her and returned to my work. About half an hour later she returned bearing a slip of paper containing an order to admit to Company "E" Mrs. Mary Wilson as a regular laundress, to assign quarters to her, and to issue her soap, rations, etc. All this was done forthwith to the supreme astonishment of the first sergeant upon his return. I do not know how much washing Mrs. Wilson performed, if any, during our stay on Hart's Island; I only know that she had frequent visits from the more decent men of the company during all hours of the day and evening until "taps" sounded; at all events she never gave cause for complaint of any kind.

At last the order for our departure was issued, the rifles were packed away in the original gunchests, the non-commissioned officers retaining the swords carried in those days by all sergeants of Infantry, and we embarked about October 30 for Colon (then called Aspinwall), where we arrived six days later without any occurrences worthy of mention.

At this place some of our men, after descending from the steamer, slipped away unperceived and entered one of the many barrooms occupying a good part of the waterfront, the consequence of which was an almost immediate, and very noisy and promising "scrap" between them and some dark-skinned sailors. I had been made lance sergeant previous to our departure from New York, and happened to be in charge of the (unarmed) guard on that day. The noise of the fight having reached the ears of Brevet Major Brown, who was officer of the day, he ordered me to proceed forthwith with the guard to the place of combat, to arrest and bring away our men, if any were implicated. I arrived in the middle of a very lively scrimmage, and I succeeded in extricating our men, who were being pretty well mauled by the sailors, from the melee, from which I came out with a black eye, a broken sword, and a feeling of having many more bones in my body than necessary. One of our men was badly hurt, having sustained a fracture of the right kneecap, and had to be carried to the cars. Major Brown, meeting the carriers, asked one of them, "Was this man hurt in the fracas?" To which he received the reply: "No sir, he was hurt in the knee."

During our transit by rail across the isthmus, one Snyder of our company jumped from the cars during a temporary stop and disappeared in the high jungle surrounding the Chagres River. This deserter was the forerunner of many more to be recorded in due sequence. As the train could not be stopped for so insignificant a cause, no steps were taken to recapture the deserter, who, I afterward learned from reliable sources, managed to make his way down to Guatemala where he established a bakery and prospered.

We observed with some astonishment the scarcity of clothing indulged in by the natives, full-grown young and very pretty girls included. These surrounded the cars at every stopping place, offering for sale sweetmeats, cigars and cigarettes of good quality at astonishingly low prices.

We were greatly amused by the appearance of the Colombian soldiers drawn up in line on each side of the train when it reached Panama. They wore dark blue tunics with yellow facings made of heavy cloth, and wide red trousers; these habiliments were almost without exception ill-fitted and much mended. I think they were discarded uniforms of the French infantry of the line. A stiff, snow-white kepi or shako topped the heads of these warriors, whose complexions varied between the color of new leather and dark molasses, with here and there a sprinkling of chocolate brown and lampblack. The most ridiculous features of their looks, however, consisted in the circumstance that these showily-dressed and multicolored soldiers were, with the exception of the somewhat dandified officers, all barefooted.

The transfer of the army-chests, baggage, provisions, etc., delayed our progress for nearly a whole day, during which we enjoyed a good view, from the harbor, of the palm-embowered city of Panama. Soon after our start, thence rough weather set in; the steamer cut all sorts of capers, everything had to be fastened tight to something of a stable nature, and the much-crowded decks were strewn all over with men suffering with seasickness, causing many and repeated visits to the railing to relieve the rebellious stomachs of their contents. Mrs. Wilson, being in great distress, sent for me and set forth her pitiable condition in a manner that would have moved a stone to compassion. Through the kindness of Captain Brown I was able to procure for the suffering woman some ice, brandy, and lemons, all of which tended to lighten her sufferings and to increase our friendship.

I knew English pretty well by this time, and discovered now, to my astonishment, that our pseudo-laundress was well posted in classic literature, being able to quote Shakespeare by the hour, and not only to quote it, but to render the lines with all the feeling incident to a perfect dramatic understanding.

After a tempestuous, but otherwise uninteresting voyage, we arrived at San Francisco, and were marched at once to the military post called the Presidio, where we took quarters in the ugly, wooden barracks of those days about November 20. Here it became soon manifest that a great number of our men had simply enlisted for the purpose of obtaining a free passage to California, even then "the land of great promise," with the intention of deserting their colors as soon as possible after their arrival. We had started with a full complement of ninety enlisted men to each company. This number was now reduced by daily, or rather nightly desertions, to an average of about fifty men remaining with each company. By far the greater number of deserters took their rifles with them, as well as all the cartridges, selling these articles of warfare to outlying settlers, prospectors, and barrooms.

There being paid by the quartermaster a premium of thirty dollars for the apprehension and delivery of each deserter, many of them were arrested by the police of San Francisco, and the guardhouse at the Presidio was in consequence continually overcrowded with privates awaiting their courts-martial. The duties, troubles, annoyances, and worry of the officer in charge of the guard caused the duty to be abhorred by officers and sergeants alike more than any other, except perhaps that of being ordered on city guard, which was at least equally uncongenial. This city guard consisted of one sergeant, one corporal, and eight privates, and started for the city every morning after guard-mount to relieve the detachment of the previous day.

If I remember rightly, the quarters of the city guard were situated on the corner of Sansome and Market streets, in an old one-story building. They consisted of an office, a guardroom, and behind this a cellar-like lockup. The city guard was, taken all in all, not only a superfluous undertaking, but proved to be a downright nuisance, inasmuch as many members of the guard itself became drunk, while others pilfered from the market-wagons in the night, and committed all sorts of misdemeanors and even minor crimes.

The sergeant in charge of the guard took his seat in the little corner office, where his principal business during the day consisted in stamping the passes of all soldiers who were in the city on leave of absence (provided they reported there at all), and to arrest all such as should present themselves in an intoxicated condition, while the corporal had general supervision of the men and posted and relieved the sentry in front of the guardhouse.

When my turn came to command this guard, I was fortunate to have with me a good, sober corporal and a few good men; still when I was relieved and returned to the Presidio on the following morning my detail was diminished by five privates; one had been arrested by the police for taking from a little girl the few coins she carried for the purchase of medicine for her sick mother; two had been caught by the night watchman while purloining and carrying off from a market-wagon a sack of potatoes, and two others I found myself compelled to put in the lockup of the guardhouse because they were too drunk to march home.

Is it any wonder that the reputation of the Fourteenth Infantry of those days was most unsavory? Especially if we add to the above that the First Battalion, as well as the Second, in its transit to Vancouver, had already, by cutting similar capers and even stealing a burning-hot stove from the momentarily unguarded kitchen of a restaurant, laid the foundation for such ill-repute.

The moment has now arrived for resuming the history of our laundress, Mrs. Wilson. At our arrival at the Presidio, this lady was assigned a house in the quarters built for the laundresses, situated upon a ridge of high ground behind, but somewhat distant from the barracks. Several men began soon to make complaints to the first sergeant that Mrs. Wilson either refused point blank to take in any washing, or, if she did so at all, neglected to submit the same to the usual process of purification. Sergeant Lipowitz sent me to the lady's house to investigate the matter. She received me well enough at first, but at the mention of "washing for men," she burst out in great dramatic fury and gave me a message for Mr. Lipowitz which, although couched in classic language, made me feel very uncomfortable. It contained a condemnation, anathema, and fearful threat against the first sergeant in condensed form; I abstained from delivering it verbatim, but modified it to more temperate terms and reported that Mrs. W. desired to "tender her resignation." She left her quarters on the same day for parts unknown.

Now, on the day when I was in charge of the city guard, while I was sitting in the door in full regimentals, reading the *Daily Alta California,* with my back turned against the sidewalk, I felt a light tap on my shoulder, and heard a gentle, not unfamiliar-sounding voice saying: "Sergeant Spring I believe; good morning; I hope I see you well." Standing up and turning around I beheld before me a lady of middle stature, dressed in some rich black material, fashionably trimmed, daintily gloved and wearing a beautiful black velvet hat adorned with ostrich feathers, from which descended a rather thick veil of black dotted tulle, which latter circumstances prevented my recognition of her person at the moment. Perceiving my embarrassment, she stepped into the room, lifted her veil and smiling at me mischievously, said: "Do you know me now, sir?"

"Mrs. Wilson, I declare," I managed to utter as well as my astonishment would permit.

With a rapid motion she placed a dainty gloved finger upon my lips and whispered: "Pst, pst, Mrs. Wilson no longer, but Mrs. Crampton now."

Thereupon we sat down together and she began to explain to me her metamorphosis. She stated that she was really an actress, had been so for years, appearing on many a stage with great success, and had just then been engaged by the company performing at McGuire's Opera House; that the story of her son and the son himself were a myth; that in the ups and downs of her profession she had found herself without the necessary means for a journey to California, where she well knew that she soon would find an engagement, and — well, here she was, and on the following day, or rather the night of the following day, she would appear as Ophelia in Shakespeare's *Hamlet,* a performance in which she had always excelled and would undoubtedly earn new laurels from the as yet unsophisticated audiences of San Francisco. During her conversation her features had become quite animated and assumed once more much of the beauty which must have been hers in former years not very much remote either. She said she knew that after being relieved from city guard I would be entitled to two hours' leave of absence, during which she requested me to visit her at 12 midnight at her hotel, the Oriental, where she would write me an admission card to the dress circle for her first performance, the playbill for which she produced from a small hand-satchel. It was printed in very large letters, and bore the legend:

"Grand Reappearance
of
The Star of the East,
Mrs. Charlotte Crampton,
as Ophelia
in
Hamlet." etc., etc.

She also requested me to wait for her after the performance at the actor's entrance to the stage and thence to see her home in a hansom which would be ready to receive her. Upon my remarking I would have to be dressed in full regimentals with the ominous No. 14 on my plumed hat (only thus and with side-arms were we allowed to go on pass), she added that it made no difference to her, and after some hesitation and embarrassment, confessed to me that she had lately married one "Jim" Walsh, of my company. This was another stunner! This man Walsh was an altogether illiterate Irishman, and at the same time the most all-around worthless member of the company (which was saying a great deal), much addicted to inebriety. Physically considered, however, he was a splendid specimen of the genus man, fully six feet tall, well built, with fine, olive complexion, athletic development, curly black hair, and lovely gray eyes. His age was about twenty-eight years. He had deserted about a week previously, and been brought in by the police about five days later, a fact which was not yet known to Mrs. Crampton, to whom I communicated it. She was not much surprised thereat, and said she would soon come to the Presidio and have her "Jim" released. I may as well state here that three days later she did visit the Presidio, arriving there in a fine closed carriage and that from that time forward her "Jim" was seen no more.

Well, I called at Mrs. Crampton's apartments in the Oriental Hotel at the appointed hour of the day following my city guard, and received from her a written admission card to the dress circle at McGuire's Opera House. As to the performance of the play I must say that Mrs. Crampton's rendering of Ophelia, notwithstanding her advanced years, was very satisfactory indeed. I know whereof I speak, as I had seen many famous performers in large theatres all over Europe. She received and merited applause.

I found many young bloods of San Francisco standing at the stage entrance of the theatre after the performance, ready to receive and accompany the "Star of the East"; but she passed by them all, came straight to me, allowed me to hand her into the carriage and take a seat by her side; arrived at her hotel, we partook together of the usual late supper in which actors are wont to indulge after their work. It may easily be imagined that I was not a little proud over all this, and I hope it will not be set down against me as undue vanity, if I mention here, that I was in those days considered a very good-looking youngster (being not quite twenty years of age) and much petted by the ladies. — "Why don't they do so now?"

As soon as the balance of the companies making up the battalion and some troops of the First Cavalry regiment arrived, we were shipped to San Pedro Harbor, behind which lay the little town of Wilmington, composed for the most part of adobe houses; still farther inland was the military post officially called Drum Barracks, which we occupied. Here again we found a complete pandemonium to be the chronic state of the guardhouse lockup, which contained at times from sixty to eighty prisoners confined in a room not exceeding 24 x 24 feet. To this confined contingent contributed not only the Regulars en route for Arizona, but also the California Volunteers returning thence, who were mustered out at that place. This coming and going of troops made the town of Wilmington quite gay and lively, especially when the paymaster arrived and paid everybody off up to December 31, 1865.

Here I saw for the first time a Mexican dance-house, erroneously called by the soldiers a "fandango," which is the name of a Spanish dance. In this place, situated in an old adobe house with low, flat roof, could be found all day long the Mexican game of "monte" and the cosmopolitan game of "faro" in full blast. A motley crowd of miners, ranchmen, teamsters and loafers, all armed with knives and revolvers, and soldiers without arms, kept going and coming, or were sitting or standing around the gaming tables or drinking at the bar. The walls were bare, the floor of pounded dirt, the two small windows provided with wooden bars, and the aspect of the whole untidy, uninviting, and primitive in the extreme.

After nightfall the tables were moved towards the wall, in order to make space for the dancers, although the games never stopped, day or night. Presently a few candles were lighted and stuck up against the walls, along which ran rough wooden benches, part of one being occupied by the "orchestra" consisting of two cracked fiddles and a rheumatic guitar. As soon as these were tuned up, from six to eight females, dressed up in cheap finery, would put in their appearance, and dancing began.

No admission fee was collected for these nightly entertainments, but at the end of every dance each male dancer was expected to take his female partner to the bar and there stand treat; i.e., he was put to the expense of half a dollar, each drink or "take" (which in the case of the woman was quite often one cigaret), being charged for at the rate of twenty-five cents, or, in the vernacular of California, existing to this day, "two bits." No smaller coin than a quarter of a dollar was known, mentioned, exhibited, or handled. Greenbacks, at that time under a discount of

25 per cent, were seen only when distributed by the paymaster; the soldiers soon converted them into coin, which never ceased to be the currency of the State of California. From time to time the bank holders of the games would call for drinks for all the playing bystanders. A meal in any hotel or restaurant cost then one dollar, even though it left much to be desired, according to present views.

During our stay in this garrison, it being winter, the bay of San Pedro, the numerous small inlets of the sea, and the surrounding marshy ground was literally covered with immense flocks of wild geese and all sorts of wild ducks, which our officers hunted with great success, often returning after a day's sport with boatloads of game up to and above the gunwale. The whole country around was covered with little excavated hills containing the burrows of the prairie squirrels, and the low-lying places abounded with mushrooms produced by the winter rains. After dark the coyotes would assemble in great numbers, come to the very edge of the garrison grounds, and make night hideous with their howling. The garrison life here was dull and monotonous, consisting of guard duty, drill, and now and then patrol duty to hunt up the absent-without-leave men downtown.

A short time before beginning the march to Arizona our garrison was visited and inspected by Major-General McDowell, at that time commanding the Division of the Pacific.

On March 1, 1866, the writer was made sergeant by regimental orders, and thus started for Arizona occupying the position of ranking duty sergeant of Company E.

On March 15, 1866, a detachment consisting of companies "D" and "E," Third Battalion, Fourteenth U.S. Infantry, under command of Captain and Brevet Major W. Harvey Brown, left Drum Barracks, near Wilmington, Calif., and started on its march to Arizona, in order to relieve the California volunteers stationed in that territory. Other detachments had preceded us, and others were to follow, so as to gradually occupy all the military posts in Arizona then existing and to establish new ones. As each command was accompanied by a considerable number of draft animals, and the water along the road was known to be scarce at many halting places, the several detachments started at intervals of from two to three weeks.

THE MARCH TO ARIZONA

The route at that time from Drum Barracks to Yuma, as traveled by the army, led over Santa Ana, Richies, Temecula, Dutchman's Flat, Oak

Grove, Warner's Ranch, Vallecito, Carrizo Creek, Laguna (Indian Wells), New River, Alamo Wells, Cook's Wells and Pilot Knob to Yuma, making a total distance of 298 miles.

Everything went well at first; but as the daily distances increased in length and the road became more and more sandy, the officers found it somewhat tedious to keep pace in their ambulance with their marching soldiers, and would drive on ahead in order to reach the next halting place as soon as possible. Leaving their companies in charge of their first sergeants to tread along on their weary way. Consequently, after a while each followed his own inclination as to speed, and the two companies would at times stretch out into single travelers, pairs and trios, covering a space of several miles, some reaching camp several hours before others.

Up to the twelfth day of our marching nothing happened worthy of record; on the night of this day, however, the writer, together with several others, made a somewhat intimate acquaintance with the prairie wolves, called in California "coyotes." This was at New River Station, where a man had taken up a place under a tree, giving it the name just mentioned, and established himself as station keeper in a somewhat peculiar habitation constructed of poles, branches, bits of tin sheeting, and canvas. I remember distinctly that it was a very primitive concern, offering conspicuous advantages in the way of free air circulation.

Here I was detailed as sergeant of the guard and established my guardhouse under a group of trees somewhat distant from the main camp. During the earlier part of the night a dismal howling emanating from the throats of what seemed to be several thousand coyotes made night hideous and sleep an utter impossibility. About 2 a.m. the moon came out and shone brightly over the sandy plain. As I was resting with my knapsack for a pillow, this useful article of soldierly travel was suddenly snatched from under my head. Jumping up I saw a lean coyote dragging my earthly belongings by an appendant strap. I reflected in a moment that by firing my piece I would unnecessarily alarm the whole camp; so I ran forward and, having nothing else at hand, threw my rifle at the robber. This made him relinquish his hold and scamper off. By comparing notes in the morning it was ascertained that many others had had a like experience with these vagabonds of the desert; also, that about half a dozen haversacks and several harness straps were missing. The station keeper listened to our story of the missing property with the greatest coolness; winking with one eye he pointed with uplifted finger to a high branch of his dwelling tree where his enormous boots and Mexican saddle dangled in the rays of the rising sun in perfect security. He remarked that several sad experiences had taught him to hang his leathery belongings high up, adding: "I believe them critters ken climb some, boys; but they can't git up thar."

On March 13 we reached Alamo Wells, about 2 p.m., and met there some deserters from the French army in Mexico.

During the afternoon some of the men went to Max Lipowitz, first sergeant of Company "E" and acting sergeant-major of the detachment, with the request that he obtain permission from the commanding officer of the detachment to have us start for the next camp about nightfall, in order to avoid marching during the already quite oppressive heat of the day. The next station lying in an easterly direction was Cook's Wells, distant about twenty-seven miles. This permission was granted, and about twenty-six men (of both companies) set out about 8 p.m. First Lieutenat and Bvt.-Maj. Choisy, in command of Company "D," lent Lipowitz an old mare, and we started. The night was dark, but the road being well defined by wagon tracks was easily followed. A few minutes after our start, before we had traveled over 300 to 400 yards, a sandstorm came up suddenly, which, although of but short duration, for a little while enveloped us in clouds of dust and sand to such an extent as to blind our powers of vision. When it passed over, and we had rubbed our eyes, we proceeded on our way, and kept marching along the well-defined road for nearly eight hours, for we knew we had no expectation of water beyond that in our canteens until reaching Cook's Wells. At the end of that time Lipo-witz ordered a halt and proposed a rest of a couple of hours, after which, he said, we would make the remaining half-dozen miles in the cool of the morning. When the moon had risen the sky had been very cloudy and remained overcast during nearly the whole night. A little before daylight we took up the march; after covering about three miles we per-ceived that the road was becoming more and more indistinct; wagon tracks crossed it in all directions and started from it in all directions, and it soon became evident that we were certainly not on any army road. About this time the sun began to rise, and we discovered to our astonish-ment and disgust that it rose in our back and that we must have been traveling about southwest instead of due east, in which direction we knew (from the map), Cook's Wells and Yuma to lie.

After looking around and about us for some time, and finding that our road ceased altogether in a maze of crossing and recrossing wagon tracks upon a grassy plain, we came to the conclusion that while blinded by the sandstorm we had accidentally stumbled upon a road branching off from the main road, and that we had thus taken the road to the hay camp whence the stage horses at Alamo Wells had been supplied with hay for years. Lipowitz now addressed us, saying that as we had gone in a south-westerly instead of an easterly direction, the best and shortest way was for us to turn about and start out due east, in order to intercept the road leading from Alamo to Cook's Wells, which road we were bound to strike "sooner or later."

An experienced prairie man among the crowd ventured to criticize this undertaking, calling our attention to the circumstances that we knew absolutely nothing about the nature of the country thus to be traversed and to the fact that the distance must be nearer fifty than forty miles, in view of the great deviation made by our night march. He suggested that we return upon our tracks to Alamo Wells, and start anew on the right road. Two others gave it as their opinion that under the circumstances we had better go on westward, as we would strike the Colorado River before long, and could follow it up to Yuma, buying food from the Indian settlements on its banks; indeed, we could see a far off green line much resembling the course of a river bordered by trees.

Finally Lipowitz ordered us to follow him, and we started out through "terra incognito" in an easterly direction with the exception of the two last-mentioned men, who lagged behind and then started for the green river line "on their own hook." Our party came shortly to several water holes, but to everybody's great disappointment found the water so impregnated with alkali that its use was not to be thought of. Towards noon our march across country came to a sudden stop on account of a deep ravine which crossed our path diagonally; its steep banks prevented our crossing, so that we followed it in a southerly direction for about six miles before we found a crossing place. Once on the other side we resumed the easterly direction of our march, which by this time was carried on at a very slow gait; we were beginning to suffer from thirst and fatigue. Lipowitz ordered us to load our rifles and at the word of command we fired three volleys in quick succession like a funeral escort over the grave of a comrade. These were meant as signals of distress to whomsoever might hear us; but not even an echo did we awake on that blistering, arid, sandy plain. We made a halt here in the shade of some underbrush, with the intention of taking up our march again at sundown.

This we did, and presently we came to an immense field or tract of prairie grass of the nature and size of reeds or cane-brake, which lay directly across our path. To penetrate this thick growth proved to be a most laborious task; however, as it reached towards the right and left as far as the eye could see, there was no other way. Lipowitz, who was on horseback and whose head the stems of grass overtopped by a foot at least, led the way and we followed, one by one, in the small path made by the horse's hoofs; the dust and sand accumulated for years in this receptacle of the desert almost choked us and increased our thirst to incipient madness. Here it was that one Cavanaugh, of Co. E, showed the first sign of coming collapse.

Bringing up the rear of the single file column I heard several threats against the life of Lipowitz, and those from men who, I knew, would shrink from no acts of violence, especially as they were in a condition of mental despair and great physical suffering, and attributed their desperate condition mainly to his lack of perception. He, they said, had led them into this, and as he was a regular military martinet at all times, there was no love lost between him and the men.

After about two hours we reached the eastern border of the horrible grassy thicket and sank completely exhausted upon the ground. Before sleeping I went to Lipowitz and communicated to him the dangers that threatened his life.

Fortunately the night was cool, and we awoke somewhat refreshed and rested, but miserably thirsty. Cavanaugh was talking wildly, with eyes starting from their sockets; he appeared to see water everywhere. Lipowitz and his horse had disappeared during the night; the sergeant next in rank being under arrest, the command of the party now devolved upon me; but I knew there was little to command under such distressing circumstances. We held a consultation, and I advised an immediate return to Alamo Wells. By adopting this suggestion we knew exactly that we had only to retrace our steps upon the track made, we knew how far we had to go, and we knew for a certainty wither we were going, while, if we followed the direction taken there was blank uncertainty as to everything. The desert, as seen from a little knoll, looked endless. I would not order anybody to follow me; it was a matter of life and death, each could act according to his own inclination; but by keeping together we could mutually encourage each other, the stronger could assist the weaker, etc. They all approved of my view, and we started, after making a huge fire with dry grass. We threw upon it large bundles of green twigs in order to produce smoke, which might call the attention of searching parties towards our tracks.

A DESERT BURIAL

Our progress was necessarily slow; about noon we had recrossed the prairie grass and began making towards the crossing of the ravine, when the conduct of poor Cavanaugh brought us to a halt. This unfortunate man was a fearful sight to behold; his tongue was protruding from his mouth, black and swollen. He now began to utter inarticulate sounds, threw himself upon the ground, lapping sand, which he apparently took for water in his hallucination; his mind was evidently wandering, his eyes were bloodshot, his features distorted. For about half a mile farther we managed to lead him under the burning sun. All at once he made a lurch which freed him from his leader, then he fell like a log, gave one deep gasp, and expired. After a while we buried him in the sand as best we could, erecting a mound over his resting place and firmly fixing his musket into the top of the mound, with a strip of paper attached conveying the necessary information. The dragoons (California Volunteer Cavalry), attracted by our fire, as we learned latter (sic), found him shortly afterwards and gave him more decent burial than our distressing circumstances admitted.

You can better imagine than I can relate with what sad feelings we resumed our march, but we dragged slowly along, the stronger assisting the weaker, well knowing that our only salvation consisted in keeping steadily ahead. We were in a measure buoyed up by the hope that some of our people had seen our smoke and would hurry to our assistance. Shorty (sic) after nightfall we reached the waterholes previously mentioned. We all soaked a handkerchief or a rag to moisten our throats, necks and chests. One Scheller, a Belgian, could not resist the temptation to drink, and swallowed some of the brown alkali water; it made him miserably sick for a while. After a few hours' rest we resumed the march on the tracks leading to the hay camp and thence resumed the road towards Alamo Wells.

About midnight, as we were passing by some bushes, a man in soldiers' clothing stepped from behind them and challenged: "Hello! who comes there?" I answered immediately, and asked back: "Who are you and what are you doing here?"

"Oh," said the man, whom I recognized now, "I am only Shmidt (sic) of your company; I goes out mit you day before yesterday, but I no likes the looks of the road, so I stays pehint mit myself, 'cause I knows you comes back dis vay purty soon pyempy. I 'spects you vants one trink, hain't I?"

This was a godsend. I now remembered that Smith, a German youngster, had started with us, but in our general misery his absence had not been noticed. He had found a little lagoon hidden amongst some trees near the road and had stayed there "all mit mineself," as he said. The water was close by; but fearing the consequences of too hasty and too liberal drinking, I would not allow the men to go near it at once. For a wonder these men obeyed without a single exception. I sent Smith with another man to fill and fetch back 10 canteens. They returned in about fifteen minutes, and by coaxing, entreaty and threats I succeeded in distributing the water about equally; about half an hour later we all went to the lagoon, guided by Smith, who was prouder than any mandarin.

After we had satisfied our thirst we all began to notice simultaneously that we were very hungry. Smith could not help us in this emergency. He had killed a rabbit that same day and eaten it all up, together with his last cracker. But help was again near at hand. While we were sitting around the lagoon, we heard the rattle of wagon wheels coming in our direction, and directly two Mexicans drove up, sitting on an empty hay wagon coming from the station at Alamo Wells, en route to the hay camp. They had five days' rations each, and being told of our distress set immediately to work and cooked all their provisions for us. There was just one good meal for the crowd. Having been paid off shortly before leaving Drum Barracks, we were able to tender these two men a most liberal compensation. Then we slept, oh, yes, we slept "loud and long."

The haymakers having now no rations to pursue their work, had to return to Alamo Wells. They bid us mount upon the hay rick and took us to the station where we arrived towards sundown, just seventy hours after our unsuccessful but eventful start.

During the night two companies of the First California Volunteers arrived at the station on their way back to California. The captain in command immediately sent for me and offered me rations for my detachment, which I gladly accepted, giving a receipt therefor. He told me that Captain W. Harvey Brown was in a state of great anxiety about us; that the smoke of our fire in the desert had been seen apparently at a great distance from any traveled road, and that some cavalrymen and Indians were then searching the desert for us. He advised me to push ahead as fast as we might.

ARRIVAL AT YUMA

About midnight I called my men together and we started on the road to Yuma, where we arrived after two days almost uninterrupted marching, with blistered feet, burnt skin, and clothes in tatters. I reported our arrival immediately to Capt. W. Harvey Brown, who was visibly affected by the relation of our sufferings, so much so, that he failed to notice my exhausted condition. Capt. Guido Ilges (later on the captor of "Sitting Bull") saw that I was ready to faint; he gave me a chair and brought me a glass of wine.

Still, Lipowitz had not arrived. Where was he? During the evening the two men who had left us in the desert to "make for the river" were brought in by Yuma Indians who had found them wandering about and had taken good care of them. Four days later, just as the companies were drawn up for the evening call, a spectral horse appeared in the camp, led by an Indian; upon the spectral horse sat a spectral man, and that man was Lipowitz, or at least what there was left of him. Never before and never since have I seen such change in the physique of a human being in so short a time. He looked like one of the survivors of Andersonville. His tale of suffering and mental distress, which would fill a volume, I shall omit here. When I lifted him from his horse he cried like a child from sheer weakness and emotion.

Nothing of all this was ever reported officially to headquarters. In order to hush up all trace of the matter, poor Cavanaugh was set down as "deserted" in the monthly report to the Adjutant-General. And thus will that record stand until the grand day of reckoning, the last and mighty roll call, when a voice from that dreary desert will arise and give that infamous report the lie!

After reaching Yuma we (called now and for some time to come "lost children of the desert," and also for a variation, "babes in the woods," by our comrades) enjoyed a well-earned rest, after which we began to look about us. Our camp, where Company "A," of our battalion, had already arrived before us, was pitched in a low bottom about a half a mile distant from the Colorado River, in the midst of more or less dense groves of mesquite trees, known to the botanists as *"Prosopis juliflora,"* probably because it blooms in the month of July. This tree does not extend its habitat on the western, or California, side of the river more than about ten miles, where the sandy desert belt begins; it grows, however, all over Southern Arizona and Sonora, Mexico, where it attains considerable height in those low-lying places in which permanent moisture is retained; while on the dry, sandy tablelands (mesas) and upon the foothills it does not exceed ten or fifteen feet in height, and has rather more the appearance of a large bush than that of a tree. It belongs to the numerous natural order of the *'Mimosae,'*† the trunks of the trees are very crooked and gnarled, as well as the branches, and are therefore not suitable for building purposes; the wood is very heavy, tough, and hard, and susceptible of a fine polish, which brings out its grain to great advantage; as firewood it is unexcelled by any wood known, giving out a tremendous heat to such a degree that the mining smelters and ore mills using steam, which were established later on, along the San Pedro River in Arizona, refused to make use of it, claiming that it produced such a tremendous heat as to burn out the boilers much faster than other wood.

Whether tree or bush, it produces an abundance of pods not unlike the green beans of our vegetable gardens. These pods ripen toward the middle of August (in and about Yuma a full month earlier), turn gradually yellow, and some red, and when thoroughly dry have a pleasant sour-sweet taste, resembling that of weak lemonade. When in this condition they make excellent feed for horses and hogs, and the Indians of those regions — the Yumas, Pimas, Maricopas and Papagos—gather them in wooden mortars and with the coarse flour or meal thus obtained prepare by boiling a sort of mush for immediate consumption; while they also frequently make a

---

†Although highly literate and a keen observer, like many other educated laymen, John Spring did not always have his botanical names just right.

dough, which they bake into small cakes, about the size of our codfish balls; these they bake in hot ashes; they are quite palatable and may be kept a long while as a traveling or scouting ration, although to our stomachs they proved somewhat difficult to digest.

COLORADO RIVER

The Colorado River forms the dividing line between the state of California and the Territory of Arizona; it is a considerable river at all times, being navigable during the rainy seasons and periods of melting snow about 650 miles upwards from its mouth in the Gulf of California. It receives the waters of the Gila on its east side just above the grounds now occupied by the Territorial prison of Arizona. Both the Gila and Colorado are subject to heavy overflows during the spring, when the snow melts on the San Francisco and Mogollon ranges in Arizona and the mountains of Utah and Colorado. At these times the Colorado River is at its best, the swift current carrying large masses of water which form many inlets and sloughs on the western border, the bottoms of which, after the water recedes, remain covered with a heavy alluvial deposit not unlike that carried upon the lands of Egypt by the inundations of the River Nile. This natural fertilizer causes a rapid and luxurious growth from all seeds planted upon such land; the Yuma Indians know how to profit thereby, and raise large melons of fine flavor, immense pumpkins, squash, beans, and corn without the use of a plow, merely dropping the seeds into small cavities made with a stick. The rapidly developing heat proverbial to Yuma does the rest.

We saw these Yuma Indians quite frequently poling big loads piled upon rafts of their making, which they called "lanchas," along these sloughs toward the river, and even crossing the latter by swimming behind the float and pushing it across. We found the Yuma men, for the most part, tall and well built, as agile in the water as on the land, and fine marksmen with their bows and arrows, killing birds on the wing, rabbits on the run, and the fish in the shallow water of the sloughs, towards sunset, when they generally remain just below the surface. These fish we found to be very indifferent food, quite coarse with more bones than made their eating comfortable.

The young Yuma women were quite pretty, with small hands and feet. All Yumas paint their faces with red and white ocher in straight lines and round patches, interspersed with some blue-black spots produced by the juice of a berry. The women and many of the men wore anklets, bracelets, and heavy necklaces made up with a profusion of multi-colored beads and very pretty scarlet beans. All wore their hair long, the women's

falling somewhat below their shoulders, while the men wore theirs braided
into long strands falling over their backs, in some instances thirty-six inches
long, and interwoven with bits of red and white cloth. The young women
came into camp frequently at first, until prohibited from doing so; they
were very fond of coffee, which they drank from pretty little water-tight
baskets, neatly plaited from fine willow twigs and coarse grasses, and
painted in various tasteful designs or patterns. Captain and Brevet Lieut.
Col. Guido Ilges, who about ten or twelve years later surrounded and captured the Sioux under "Sitting Bull," near the Canadian frontier, was then
the captain of Company "A," and being the ranking officer present, was
in command of the detachment. He considered a caution given to the men
as to abstaining from intimate intercourse with these women quite timely.

Our camp, as well as the garrison and the quartermaster's building of
those days, was situated on the western side of the river on the hill where
the present Indian school is located; while a small town, called Yuma,
now much developed and reached by crossing the substantial railway
bridge of the Southern Pacific, of which it is a dining station, was then
called Arizona City, and did a thriving fandango and saloon business during the period of continual going and coming of troops and teamsters.

There was no bridge of any kind spanning the river at the time I speak
of, but a man named Jaeger had established a ferry between the two places,
and transported men, horses, wagons, stores, etc., from shore to shore by
contract with the government, charging a considerable fare to civilians. He
was also the beef contractor of the garrison and furnished all the fresh
meat to the troops in transit.

Although we were yet in early spring, and the intense heat proverbial
to Yuma had not yet begun, I noticed that a few hours after I had brought
our meat to camp in a cart from the slaughterhouse, it would already be
fly-blown, and by the following morning it would show fully developed
maggots. This was probably caused by the foul condition of the slaughterhouse, than which I had never seen an establishment of its kind more
filthy, malodorous, and disgusting; not even in the slums of the large Italian
cities, nor in Egypt or Palestine, countries which I had visited with a small
college contingent in 1863. This slaughterhouse was situated on the edge
of a river slough about two miles below our camp and swarmed with flies
and musketos (sic). Its stench poisoned the atmosphere to a great distance.

MARCH THROUGH THE APACHE COUNTRY

Our wagons, teams, rations, and camp equipage being at last ready,
we resumed our march towards Arizona on March 9, Company "A" going
with us. Being ferried across, we struck the road which in those days was

the old stage route used by the Butterfield overland mail coaches, and touched many points which are at the present day halting stations of the Southern Pacific Railway. It led over Gila City, Mohawk Station, Texas Hill, Antelope Peak, Oatman's Flat, Gila Bend, Maricopa Wells, Sacaton, Blue Water, Picacho, and Point of Mountain† to Tucson, a total distance of about 285 miles, the greater part of which was either heavy sand or alkali desert. This latter looked for all the world, where dry, like immense tracts of ground covered with fine salt, but when moisture was retained, like dirty snow, commonly called "slush."

Since the Apaches had broken out into hostility, the mail coaches had been abandoned, and were replaced by buckboards. Arriving at Oatman's Flat, we found the grave of the family from which the place received its name, marked by a small mound surmounted by a headboard and surrounded by a railing. The keeper of the mail stock told us the story of the murder of the family, who were among the first victims of the Apaches when they turned hostile about 1855, after having lived at peace with the whites. Reduced to the bare facts, the tragedy occurred as follows: Said Oatman with his family, consisting of his wife, a son aged about fourteen years, two girls of the ages of nine and eleven years, respectively, and a baby-in-arms, was on his way to California. He had with him two wagons loaded with agricultural implements and household goods, and drawn by two yoke of oxen each. Arriving at a steep hill thereabouts and finding that the loads were too heavy to be pulled up the steep incline as hitched up, he halted and began to double up his teams, during which occupation he was approached by some Indians who were apparently friendly and helped in the ascent of the wagons by pushing and manipulating the wheel spokes, for which service they received a liberal supply of tobacco, for which they had asked. While Mr. Oatman was unhitching the foremost oxen from the doubled-up team, one Indian stabbed him from the back through the heart with a lance, while another knocked the boy on the head with a war club. The father fell dead in his tracks and the still-moving boy was dispatched with lance thrusts. Then these fiends murdered the mother and baby and left, carrying off the two girls and driving off the oxen with them. Some years later the two girls, now grown women, were obtained through barter from a roving band of Indians, who had captured them from the Apaches, and were brought to Yuma. To all appearances they had become Indians themselves, in complexion, manners, and language; they no longer spoke or understood their mother tongue, and would have remained "Indians" forever, had not the blacksmith of the place, who had

---

†The site then called Point of Mountain is the northernmost tip of the Tucson Mountains.

known the Oatman family in Texas a short time before the tragedy and remained in Yuma all these years, thought he saw something familiar in the features of the girls. Lifting up the hair behind the ears where the skin had remained untanned by exposure to the sun, and noticing the hair itself as being different from all Indian hair, he investigated further, and by means of an interpreter, the whole story was brought to light. The girls were taken to Siskyou County and there placed with a family.

We had with us six drummer boys, two to each company, and it would be difficult, I think, to find anywhere in the universe a set of more mischievous, impudent and all-around rascally rapscallions than these youngsters. Before our start from Yuma they had been given in charge of one Dewitt of my company, a tall, much-freckled, very active Irish-American, whose principal merit, if such it was, consisted in having "the gift of the gab very galloping." I do not know through what representations he succeeded in obtaining the position and rank of lance drum-major of the detachment, for he was certainly not versed in the art of performing on the snare drum or, for that matter, on any drum whatever; he could, however, blow a feeble resemblance to a bugle call, and always carried a specimen of the infantry bugle of those days, an immense instrument constructed of copper, much adorned with blue cords and tassels, about with him.

At Gila Bend where we camped near the first Indians we had seen since leaving Yuma, the deviltry of our drum corps (whose instruments, by the way, were carried during the march in our baggage wagons together with our knapsacks) reached its climax. Some of the boys had obtained from the Indians a bow and some arrows, with which they forthwith proceeded to endanger the eyesight and general comfort of our men, even going to the extent of making a target of the old hospital steward accompanying the detachment. They succeeded in wounding him in the most fleshy part of his person, and were reported, several additional complaints being made at the same time from various sources. It was quite astonishing what amount of perforations these youngsters had succeeded in making with their arrows in a limited space of time. The drum major was sent for and ordered to prepare a goodly number of tough, pliant switches from the trees growing on the border of the river and to administer severe chastisement to the offenders on the following morning after breakfast, before the march was resumed. The adjutant of the detachment was requested to see this order well executed, and from the succeeding behavior of the young sinners, I had every reason to believe that such was the case.

Of Mr. Dewitt and his bugle we will hear more later on.

From Gila Bend to Maricopa Wells, a distance of forty-five miles, without water, we had to march in one stretch, with the interruption of only one hour for a meal on the way. Our men, and principally our draft animals, arrived at the latter place much exhausted by this continuous long march over a desert strongly impregnated with alkali, the dust of which entered our nostrils and parched our throats. We saw several fine mirages during this transit, some in the sky in our front, representing ships at sea in full sail; others of large cities with high walls, towers and turrets, like the fortifications of the Middle Ages, but upside down, and, worst of all, beautiful landscapes with lakes surrounded by lofty trees and dense foliage that appeared to be only a few miles ahead of us and directly in our path. As we were all very thirsty, I was strongly reminded of the tortures of Tantalus in Hades, as described in classic lore.

After resting a day at Maricopa Wells, we proceeded toward Sacaton. We were now in the country of the Pima and Maricopa Indians, the latter occupying a few villages upon the reservation set apart for the former, through which our road lay. These Indians, who at the present writing are allowed to suffer from starvation while they are receiving the varnish of civilization in substantial school buildings erected by the government, have at all times been friendly to the whites, rendering unpaid services against the hostile Apaches again and again. They always say with pride: "We do not know the color of the white man's blood." In those days their weapons consisted of bows and arrows with which they were great experts, like nearly all Indians; the war club, made of gnarled mesquite wood; and for defense they used a round shield of undressed oxhide.

These Indians sustained themselves then as now by agriculture, irrigating their fields by means of small ditches which carried the waters of the Gila through a larger ditch or canal upon their arable lands. These larger ditches were the common property of the different villages. In order to guide the water into them, the Indians constructed large dams on convenient spots of the river shore, which they built and renewed from year to year with rocks, tree trunks, willow branches, and rushes.

Because of complete lack of water at Picacho (a high steep cliff rising abruptly on the south side of the road), we had to make another forced march from Blue Water to Point of Mountain, which the mail rider said to be a distance of forty-eight miles, but which I should rather estimate at fifty-two miles. At all events, although we made no halt on the road and ate as we went along, we occupied seventeen hours in this march and arrived at our destination completely worn out with fatigue; for it must be remembered that on this whole route we traveled frequently for long stretches over heavy sand. Many of the men had blistered feet, while others were sadly chafed. Our wagons with their escort came to camp fully three hours later.

Here we rested again for one day and the following resumed the march toward Tucson, only eighteen miles away . . . next to Prescott, the most important town in Arizona — which was not saying much. After traveling about nine miles, we came into a valley where there was a house and small enclosure for animals, standing on a small wooded knoll, at whose foot gently flowed the Santa Cruz River, at that spot not larger in size than a creek; from here on we had the valley in sight all the time, and were not a little delighted at its aspect; here and there were small fields of grain clad in that soft, pale-green verdure which precedes the ripening of the ears, while the cottonwood trees standing along the borders of the river presented to the eye their beautiful foliage clad in vivid, brilliant emerald green.

We all experienced a feeling of great relief and almost delight as we beheld these signs of civilized life after encountering for so long a period nothing but sand, dust, rocks, cacti, thorns, greasewood, rattlesnakes and the enormous venomous lizards, there called Gila monsters *(Heloderma suspectum)*, road-runners (chaparral cocks), and now and then a tarantula lazily crossing the dusty road.

We arrived at Tucson on April 28 and went into camp in a grove of mesquite bushes about one-quarter of a mile south of town. Here we discharged our rifles and began to clean up.

TUCSON IN 1866

The Tucson of those days had but one regular street, now called Main Street. The buildings which deserved the name of houses were of adobe with flat mud roofs; those of the poorer class of Mexicans were constructed of mesquite poles and the long wands of the candlewood *(Fouquieria splendens)*, the chinks being filled in with mud plaster. With the exception of the soldiers and teamsters in transit, there were not over a dozen American men in the town, and not one American woman. The doors of many houses consisted of rawhide stretched over rough frames, the windows being simply apertures in the walls, barred with upright sticks stuck therein. The aspect of the town reminded me forcibly of the small hamlets I had seen in the Holy Land, the more so as the women, all half-breeds, wore about the same dress as the Palestine women and carried upon their heads water-jars of the exact pattern in use in the Orient.

We soon discovered, however, that the languid state of inactivity and silence prevailing in the villages about Jerusalem did not exist here. When I visited the town towards evening, in order to present our ration return to the Commissary of Subsistence (Captain Gilbert C. Smith) with a view of obtaining our rations, I found that the one street of Tucson was fairly bubbling with life and motion. Its whole length was taken up by a long train of army wagons and another of "prairie schooners," carrying flour from Sonora, Mexico, while heavily-loaded hay wagons were trying to make their way to the government corral, where numberless horses and mules were continually coming and going, as the quartermaster's department of this place was the chief depot of supplies for all the military posts of southern Arizona. Cursing teamsters, rollicking soldiers, rustling gamblers, and the usual nondescripts of a frontier town jostled each other in the narrow street, devoid of sidewalks.

As soon as I had received and loaded up our rations, of which the long-untasted and much-coveted fresh meat was the most desirable article, I started my ration wagon to camp, and looked for a store where I might purchase a much-needed paper of needles and some thread. The only store worthy of the name was quite easily found and the desired articles were produced. To my horror and to the great financial detriment of my purse, I found a paper of needles to cost seventy-five cents and a spool of thread twenty-five cents. As I gave vent to my astonishment at such exorbitant prices the storekeeper observed, somewhat sarcastically, I thought: "It isn't the value of the article, but the cash money on the freight, you know." Freight on needles, indeed! However, the thing worked both ways, as I found out later when I brought to this same store our surplus rations and received for them, per pound: For coffee, seventy-five cents (it was sold at $1); brown sugar, fifty cents; salt pork, fifty cents; and bacon, sixty cents, from all of which our company fund derived a substantial benefit. The utter absence of all vegetables caused me, although not a Catholic, to pay a visit to the priest of the place, a very sociable Frenchman, to whom I could speak in his own language. I knew that these missionary priests always brought with them all kinds of useful seeds; and I was not disappointed in my surmise that he might have some. He received me very kindly, treated me to a fine glass of Burgundy wine, presented me with a small collection of vegetable seeds and some fishhooks and lines, all of which came in very good stead later on. His home was a veritable oasis in the desert.

Before we leave Tucson, I will relate an incident, although it reflects but badly upon the writer, as a non-commissioned officer of the regular army, supposed to be a representative of military discipline. I hope, however, that at least some of my readers who have found themselves in similar circumstances during their service, may feel inclined to attenuate and forgive my breach of discipline committed under "a terrible temptation." I was in a measure punished on the spot by falling into the only waterhole existing in that dry region within a radius of about one hundred miles, excepting, of course, the Santa Cruz River, which had a few places where the water was perhaps a little over four feet deep.

As previously mentioned, we arrived at Tucson on April 28, and the day following the next would be muster day. I was assisting the first sergeant in the preparation of the muster rolls in a rickety wall-tent illuminated by two candles, when all at once, about 8:30 p.m., Private Lutje, our company tailor, protruded his broad German features through the tent flap, and announced in great agitation: "Sergeant, there is beer in this town: there is a brewery here!" Let a kind reader imagine the effect of this announcement upon a couple of Germans, whose national beverage is brought suddenly within their reach after protracted hardships, during which they had been entirely deprived of the precious fluid! Lutje went on to explain the exact location of the small brewery, only recently established, and stated that the price of the beer was only $1 a bottle! Lipowitz turned his pockets inside out, but in vain. "The needful" was not there. My last quarter had been spent in the purchase of the sewing material, and Lutje had expended the remnant of his cash at the beer shop when he came. He stated, however, that in a little grocery opposite the brewery, an Italian purchased cartridges at $1 per package. Now we had about 3000 rounds of these cartridges (the paper cartridges of the Springfield rifle), which we were lugging along, although we knew that we were soon to be provided with needle-guns and the accompanying metallic cartridges. In view of this latter fact, Lipowitz thought that we might spare about one hundred or so, wherewith to satisfy our desire for the coveted beverage.

In less than two minutes I was en route for town with ten packages of the cartridges tightly strapped under my belt, from which I had removed the sword. The night was very dark and the path through the surrounding bushes uncertain and uneven; but a solitary light in the direction of the town guided my steps. As I was nearing the first huts on the southern edge of the town, the ground suddenly gave away from under my feet and I toppled over, falling with a splash into a body of water whose dimensions I could not distinguish in the dark. The water was quite cold and reached up to my neck. After the first shock I began feeling for the shore which I soon touched and found to be a steep or rather perpendicular bank. While I was setting forth every effort toward reaching terra firma by climbing, a tremendous splash in my rear suddenly directed my attention thither. The splashing continued, intermingled with sundry profane exclamations. I soon perceived from the voice that my companion in misfortune, i.e., in the water, was no other than our commanding officer, Brevet Major W. Harvey Brown, who, coming from town, had struck a beeline for camp, taking as his guiding star the light shining in the tent of Lipowitz, and tumbled into the pond on the side opposite to mine. I loosened my belt and let my purchasing power, the ammunition now thoroughly soaked and worthless, drop to the bottom and resumed my climbing. The noise I made attracted the attention of the Major, who called out:

"Who is there?"

"Sergeant Spring," I answered.

"Please come and help me out of this infernal hole," said he; "the bank is so steep I can't get out."

"All right, Major," I made answer; "just wait one moment, I think I'm getting out."

In this latter undertaking I soon succeeded by taking hold of an overhanging willow branch. I then pulled out Major Brown and accompanied him to camp in order to put on dry clothing and renew the discarded ammunition. Then I started anew and taking great care to circumvent the waterhole, arrived safely in town, where I found the information of Tailor Lutje confirmed. The cartridges were disposed of; I purchased six bottles of beer (the less said about its quality the better), which I put in a barley sack for greater convenience in carrying, and arrived without accident at Lipowitz's tent, to his great relief, joy, and delectation. The muster rolls now progressed finely and were ready in good time. While on this night expedition I noticed three dance-houses with the customary game of chance in full swing in town and saw that Tucson was about as lively a town as a man wished to see, and some men had perhaps better avoid.

FORT BOWIE

We soon learned that our company had been assigned to garrison Fort Bowie, situated 120 miles to the east situated at the end of a spur issuing from the Chiricahua Mountains. We resumed our march on May 3, reaching the first day a swampy bottom called Cienega, now Pantano; the second day's march took us to the San Pedro crossing, a mail station now called Benson; on the third day we reached Sulphur Springs, now Willcox, and at sunset of the fourth day we arrived at Fort Bowie, where we found a company of California cavalry and a company of the First New Mexican Volunteer Infantry. These latter could vie in complexion with the Colombian soldiers encountered while crossing the isthmus. The California volunteers packed up at once and started west on the following morning, surrendering to us their quarters, which consisted of comfortable huts constructed by themselves of stones, boards, cactus sticks, mesquite branches, etc., and more or less fancifully furnished with articles of their own handicraft. One of them gave me a well-filled woolen mattress which outlasted my term of service.

The New Mexican Volunteers remained there for several days longer, during which our drum major, Dewitt, so as not to lose his job and rank, took their two buglers in hand, making the attempt to teach them the bugle calls. For this undertaking the commanding officer assigned to them a small canyon at a safe distance, whence our ear drums could not be penetrated nor our nervous systems endangered. From the time that we had reached the Pima villages, and principally during our stay at Tucson, quite a number of our men had enticed stray dogs away from their habitats and brought them to Bowie, where the New Mexican Volunteers were already the proud owners of a canine contingent as remarkable for breed and color as for ugliness and utter worthlessness. After a few days' practice with our own two drummer boys and the aforesaid bugles, our drum major announced to Maj. Brown that he could now undertake to perform with his band a creditable "retreat" at the close of the usual sunset dress parade. We were naturally all very much interested in the matter, and therefore anxious to witness the performance. As soon as the parade came to "parade rest" the music started to beat and blow the "retreat," but, alas! it was never finished, for as soon as the bugles started giving forth sounds that seemed to come from the subterranean caverns of the damned, all the dogs in the immediate vicinity, to the number of about 30, squatted on their haunches and broke forth in the most heart-rending howlings. The echo of their howls, coming back tenfold from the surrounding hills, combined with the accompaniment from the dogs taken up to as far a distance as the most remote canines could hear, made up a veritable pandemonium. Oh, it was grand! The commanding officer turned purple with fury, while we all laughed till our sides ached. For a moment I thought that Major Brown would throw his sword at the drum-major, or strangle him, or something.

That dress parade had two immediate results: In the first place, the drum corps was disbanded and the drum major relegated to the ranks, where he did his duty as a private henceforth, until — but we will come to that later. In the second place, a great slaughter of all the dogs, except two valuable hunting dogs and a fine mastiff, was put into effect by a detail of men selected for their marksmanship.

The officer's quarters and storerooms of the AQM and ACT being found in a leaking and otherwise unsatisfactory condition, I was placed in charge of a detail consisting of ten men, accompanied by three six-mule teams for the purpose of cutting and hauling some pine timbers from the neighboring mountains. The wagonmaster, who had come all the way from Wilmington, had charge of the teams, and he relieved the tedium of the road by relating many stories incident to the earliest days of California, i.e., the discovery of gold and its immediate results. The distance to the timber camp was about 35 miles, and we took with us three days' rations; we were, however, not able to accomplish our task, although the men and teamsters worked faithfully, until the fourth day while we needed one and a half days more for our return trip with the heavily loaded wagons. Of course when the rations were exhausted, hunger set in; but fortunately, the Mexican Volunteers which I had with me discovered on the borders of a mountain creek or rivulet a weed which they called *quelite,* and which they knew to be edible. We gathered and cooked a few camp kettles full of it, found it quite palatable, and appeased therewith the worst pangs of hunger.

COCHISE

Near the fort we were shown by this wagonmaster, Mr. Kate, what was generally considered a "historic" spot in those regions, as it was supposed to be the spot upon which had stood the tent whence the famous and wily Apache chief [Cochise] made good his escape in 1858, after being captured by our troops during a raid instituted to punish him for the murder of two teamsters, whom he was said to have put to death by fire on a projecting, inaccessible rock (from our side) in full view of but at a safe distance from a scouting party. It was related that during the night Cochise succeeded in untying the ropes that bound him and with a knife he carried hidden in his buckskin leggings, ripped open the rear of the tent while the sentry in front failed to observe his escape until the following morning, when the wily Indian must have been miles away. Mr. Kate did not take much stock in this story, and told us that many recitals then afloat about Cochise and his doings were much garbled and unreliable, in many cases made up for the purpose of entertaining and quizzing "tenderfeet." Later on I found that this was indeed the case, and it was a very difficult matter to sift the truth from falsehood, history from romance. It was undoubtedly true that Cochise was then, at the time of our reaching Arizona, a bloodthirsty murderer and robber, who perpetrated with his tribe generally divided into small bands, the greatest atrocities in the most cowardly manner of assassins, never daring to fight in the open, but always waylaying the unwary travelers from ambush in the road, stabbing the farmers suddenly from behind, with a lance from a convenient hiding place, and then murdering in cold blood his family and burning all his property that could not be carried off. All this was, indeed, so; but it was equally true, as I ascertained from many reliable settlers, that, up to the winter of 1857, Cochise had lived at peace with all the whites on the American side of the boundary line, which was established by stone monuments at certain distances from each other after the ratification of the Gadsden "Treaty."

What turned the peaceful Apache chief, Cochise, into a relentless murderer and robber, an implacable enemy to all whites, with whom he had lived at peace heretofore? In order to sift facts from rumor, history from romance, I made inquiries of several settlers (near whom I lived from 1868 to 1869, in the Santa Cruz valley when farming myself) who had lived and farmed near Calabazas "before the country broke up," from 1854 to 1857; also from the oldest inhabitants of the small town of Tubac, which was, in 1857, a flourishing little place on account of the silver mines worked west of Tubac on a large scale by the Cerro Colorado Company. Later on I became well acquainted with Col. Charles D. Poston, who was superintending the work at these mines. He told me that, although the Apaches were forever at war with the Pima and Maricopa Indians and unmercifully murdered and robbed the Mexicans south of the boundary line, they respected the lives and property of all settlers on the American side of the boundary line; that he himself employed as laborers in the mines near Tubac, as herders of stock and drivers of ore wagons, many Apaches, who afterward became veritable fiends in murder, rapine and robbery; that he had known Cochise personally and had several conversations with him. More than that, we had at Camp Wallen, from 1866 to '68, an Indian guide or scout employed by the government and named Marigildo Grijalba, a half-breed, who until lately had been, and perhaps is at this present writing, connected with the Indian reservation at San Carlos. This man had been captured by one of Cochise's bands when a boy near a small town (I believe "Bagauche") in Sonora, about one hundred miles south of the American line, established later. This man stated to me that when United States Dragoons occupied Fort Buchanan (later named Camp Crittenden), in 1857, at the foot of the Santa Rita Peaks, the Apaches, with whom he then was, were in the habit of making frequent raids into Mexico for the purpose of stealing stock, etc.; but that they had strict orders from Cochise never to lay hands on anybody or anything within the boundary of the United States; that he, Marigildo, witnessed the fact of Cochise's stabbing to the heart with a lance one of his best Apache warriors, when the latter brought to Cochise's camp several horses bearing the U. S. brand, which Cochise knew belonged to the Dragoons stationed at Fort Buchanan.

I have also gathered information of like nature from men who worked in the Mowry mines in the Patagonia Mountains from 1856 to 1858, and having now given the sources of my information, I shall proceed, interrupting my narrative for a short space, with what I, together with my informants, take and know to be the real and true cause of the Apache outbreak, so pregnant with terrible consequences, demanding the lives of hundreds of people, and making for a period of thirty years constant heavy demands upon the treasury.

The Gadsden Treaty, by which the United States acquired from

Mexico by purchase for the sum of $10 million all that territory of modern Arizona lying south of the Gila River and not included in the treaty of 1848, was concluded by James Gadsden Dec. 30, 1853. In June, 1854, the treaty was ratified and the money paid. The population of Tucson at that time was about 760 inhabitants, with very few exceptions, all Mexican; Tubac had a population of about 250, also Mexicans with the exception of a few American mechanics, who worked in the Cerro Colorado mines. The United States took military possession of its newly-acquired territory in 1856, sending thither a detachment consisting of four companies of Dragoons, which force was at first stationed at Tucson, and later on at Calabazas. In 1857 a permanent station was selected and Fort Buchanan established on the Sonoita about twenty-five miles east of Tubac.

Soon after the ratification of the Gadsden Treaty there arrived at Tucson, mainly from Texas, a number of immigrants in search of farming and grazing lands. The Mexican settlers around Tucson and along the whole Santa Cruz Valley were not disturbed; by virtue of the treaty, they retained possessions of their farms and irrigating ditches, while their herds enjoyed free pasture in the uncultivated bottomlands and upon the hills. A number of the newly-arrived squatters followed the Santa Cruz River upward as far as Calabazas and Huebabe and settled there, while a party of about eighteen, including women and children, stayed at a place named then, as now, "La Canoa," so called because a Mexican settler already there had built a large canoe, or flat-bottomed boat, upon which he crossed the river whenever the lower, or western, road leading to Tubac became flooded by the summer rains, in which case the eastern road was chosen, as it led over the high ground along the ever-present foothills. Here they erected log houses, began to cultivate the virgin soil, raising cattle at the same time. We have already mentioned Cochise's orders to his men directing them to abstain from all depredations north of the boundary line which ran from east to west fully forty miles south of the Canoa. On the other hand, all newcomers were cautioned again and again, never, under any circumstances, to interfere with the Apaches in their doings across the line. These conditions were accepted and observed in the whole newly-acquired region like an unwritten law.

Now, it happened toward the end of 1857 that a large band of Apaches belonging to Cochise's tribe, made a raid deep into the adjoining Mexican state of Sonora, and there captured a numerous herd of horses and cattle. In all such cases the Apaches stampeded the herd, nearly always successfully driving the stock in the direction desired. A stampeded herd will run until the animals drop from utter exhaustion; this renders them stiff and sore, making travel quite slow for the next few days. The owners of the stolen stock, following with their herders in the tracks of the stampeded herd, soon discovered it was headed for the boundary line. The band of Apaches being quite numerous, the former dared not to attack them, but contented themselves with observing from a safe distance the direction in which the animals were being driven. They soon found that the direction taken would bring the stolen herd, after crossing the line, toward the neighborhood of Tubac. About three miles above that town stood the old ruins of the Tumacacori Mission; about two miles below, a canyon, known as Turkey Canyon, which is about twelve miles in length.

As soon as the owners of the herd had ascertained that their animals were headed toward the southern entrance of this canyon they rode to the settlement at the Canoa (having previously applied for help, but unsuccessfully, to the inhabitants of Tubac), and sought to entice the settlers to help them, the owners, in making good the recovery of the herd upon its reaching the valley bottom. At first these settlers, remembering the many cautions they received as to their behavior in such cases, refused all participation in the affair; but when the owners of the herd offered as a reward for their assistance one-half of the stock recovered, they abandoned their prudent hesitation, gave way to their rapacity and made ready for the raid which, they might well know, would involve the shedding of blood. The herd was large and the promised remuneration, if the raid were successful, tempted them to their ultimate utter destruction. The original herders of the stolen stock had hovered unseen by the Apaches, upon the latter's tracks.

On account of the exhaustion of the animals, these were driven but slowly, and as soon as they had entered the Turkey Canyon, the owners of the herd were notified and started with the Canoa settlers up the river in order to be ready for the robbers when they should debouch from the canyon. The river here was shallow, running between low, sandy borders and easily fordable; on its eastern side there is a dry river bed descending upon the latter almost perpendicularly, which during the rainy seasons carries the water gathered in the San Cayetano range of mountains into the Santa Cruz. Along the edges of this dry river bed stood a dense growth of elder trees and other bushes, affording a fine ambush. Here the owners of the stolen stock, with their herders and the squatters from the Canoa, pounced upon the stolen herd, surrounded the Apaches, and a short but furious combat ensued, for which the Apaches were not prepared, and in which the firearms of the well-aiming squatters were used with deadly effect. The Indians were defeated and fled, leaving seven dead upon the field, an almost unheard of thing with them, showing that they could barely make good their escape, as they invariably carry off or hide their dead whenever they have any possible opportunity to do so.

The deed was done, the herd recaptured, and the American allies received their reward; but on that day was born a relentless feud of thirty years duration, which had in its train innumerable murders of men, women and children, rape and rapine and the destruction of hundreds of homes established by the hardy pioneers of the West. Cochise might have forgiven the recapture of the herd, but never the killing of his warriors, who had hitherto observed a strict abstinence from all violence against the American population. From this time dates the relentless warfare, if the cowardly way of the Apaches to kill from behind may deserve that name, which retarded for a generation the development of those regions, and which began with the complete destruction of the settlers of the Canoa, their families (to the smallest baby) and their homes by a band led by Cochise in person.

I fail to find in Bancroft's *History of Arizona and New Mexico* the smallest mention of the occurrence here related. Referring to the unsettled state of the country and the frequent depredations of the Apaches, he says on page 502, Vol. XVII: "Hostilities became more frequent and general, and were greatly aggravated by bad management and injustice on the part of the officers, by which Cochise, a prominent chieftain, was made the lifelong foe of the Americans."

LIFE AT CAMP BOWIE

During the short time of our stay at Fort Bowie nothing of interest occurred except a sentry firing at the commanding officer on a dark night. This gentleman, being aware that we were now in the midst of the Indian country, had given strict orders that after nightfall all sentries should give but one challenge, and if not answered fire at once upon the approaching object. This precautionary measure was well taken, as many instances were known of Apaches prowling about at night with a view to ascertaining how the stock of a camp was guarded and perhaps of stealing now and then a stray animal. But Major Brown almost invariably forgot to answer a sentry's challenge when he made the tour of the camp at night to ascertain for himself if due vigilance was observed by the camp-guard. This he did frequently. As he was the tallest man present, he was generally recognized by the sentries even in the dark by his stature, and had thus far escaped being made a target of. But when, on a very dark night, he made his solitary rounds and came suddenly upon the sentry posted at the mule corral, who received no answer to his prompt and loud challenge, he was fired at, the ball passing through the top of his high hat, whereupon he found his voice quickly. I may as well mention here that Captain W. Harvey Brown possessed very few soldierly qualifications and a very indifferent school education; he knew next to nothing of the army regulations; but as the administrator of a recently established colony, he would have been a great success, being a practical farmer, who knew well how to obtain as much work out of men as their physical development would permit.

The New Mexico Volunteers soon entered upon their home march to be mustered out. Our two drummer boys were sent to Fort Goodwin, where the headquarters of the battalion had been established, and our time for the most part was taken up by manual labor in repairing the old buildings of the fort.

Towards the end of May the mail rider brought the news that a recently established new post on the upper San Pedro had sustained a great loss, being attacked by the Apaches, who captured all their horses and cattle and drove them off. This news was confirmed the following day by an express rider, who brought the order for our instant removal to that bereaved camp. We were soon ready and on the march toward our new destination, returning upon the same road upon which we had come as far as the San Pedro crossing, where we turned south and arrived in camp on the evening of the fourth day of our march, June 4, 1866.

The location of the "new camp on the upper San Pedro," as it was officially called at its incipiency, had been selected by Maj. Gen. McDowell himself while on the inspection tour previously mentioned. From a strategic point of view the selection could not have been better, as it stood in a central position where nearly all the Indian trails crossing from mountain range to mountain range met. It stood on an elevated plateau, surrounded at various distances by the mountains most generally used by the Indians of Cochise for the establishment of their "rancherías," whence they pounced upon the unwary travelers, miners, and stockmen. But there existed other conditions which rendered its first garrison at least altogether inefficient for scouting purposes.

This garrison consisted of Company "G," First U. S. Cavalry, which had been reduced by desertions at the Presidio and at Wilmington to about fifty-five enlisted men, from which the necessary mechanics, teamsters, cooks and herders had to be detailed on extra . . . duty, much reducing the effective contingent for military undertakings. The carbines of this garrison were of the old Sharpe's pattern, to a great extent out of order, having been obtained at Wilmington from the California Volunteers returning from Arizona after three years' service, without being subjected to a rigid inspection and without receiving many much-needed repairs, for which the means were not at hand. These arms were to a great extent useless, so that the men detailed for the important duty of guarding the herd had to be furnished carbines carefully selected from the number on hand. Add to this that many of the men had sold their revolvers on the march, and that this company of cavalry arrived to settle upon a new camp without a surgeon, without forage, and without beef cattle (this was supplied later on), and we have the, to say the least, remarkable fact before us that here was a feeble garrison, insufficiently armed, in an open camp surrounded by mountain fastnesses known to be the regular haunts of several bands of the most wily, active, and fiendish Indians that ever existed, meant to do scouting duty and to protect their camp at the same time with an available force of less than forty men.

The robbery of the herd we learned to have occurred as follows: There being no forage on hand, First Lieutenant McDonald, the only commissioned officer present and as such post commander, committed the grave error of sending out to graze the cavalry horses in the number of about ninety . . . together with such mules as were not working with the wagons and with the herd of cattle that had reached the place about the middle of May, numbering one hundred head.

At the time of the attack the herd was grazing about three miles from camp (another imprudence) toward the south, on the eastern border of the upper San Pedro, which was then and still is, called by the Mexicans and the Indians Babocomari Creek. The grass here was very luxurious, and the creek running between low borders offered every facility for crossing and watering the stock.

On the morning of May 29 the Apaches swooped down in three bands from the east, south, and west, surrounded and stampeded the herd with their yells and swinging of blankets and lariats, and killing one herder. Then they headed the frightened animals toward the Huachuca Mountains, and were off like the wind. The whole visible transaction had not occupied more than five minutes. Sergeant Davis, who had been in charge of the herd with the other three uninjured herders, barely escaped being carried along in the stampede, their frightened horses making every effort toward joining the frantic contingent. They ran to camp and reported the disaster, by which Lieutenant McDonald was so overcome as to fall into a trembling fit, rendering futile his efforts toward loading his revolver. He was soon thereafter ordered to Washington to "explain" the catastrophe, unsuccessfully, it soon appeared, as his name disappeared from the roster of U. S. commissioned officers.

There being no horses left wherewith to undertake a successful pursuit of the robbers (which would probably have proven a futile undertaking at best), the garrison was now again deprived of fresh meat and on foot. A remount was, however, soon sent in charge of First Lieutenant and Brevet Major Kinney, who replaced the former commander.

OUR NEW CAMP ON THE UPPER SAN PEDRO RIVER

Upon our arrival at this place in the beginning of June, we found the new camp under canvas, with the exception of an old adobe building, which had been the main feature of a former old Mexican rancho. The walls of this large building surrounded a spacious corral or yard; they were somewhat out of repair, but still showed traces of former watch towers at the corners. The fresh cavalry horses, a fine lot, were nightly driven into the enclosure and fastened to long ropes. Brevet Major Brown, being the ranking officer, assumed command, and soon displayed his particular capacity for getting work out of the men.

The camp was situated upon a plateau bounded, on the east side by a ravine, on the west by a low bottom through which flowed the creek, and on the south by a declivity leading into the bottomlands. The part destined for the parade ground was, to a great extent, not yet cleared from the numerous mesquite bushes standing everywhere. We began to clear the ground, and while pursuing this occupation quite frequently disturbed rattlesnakes, often of a very large size. The great number of snakes encountered in this neighborhood, and even within the cracks and chinks of the old adobe walls, was easily accounted for by the presence of numerous rats, bats, and mice upon the premises. As the summer progressed and the heat increased, large hairy spiders, tarantulas, centipedes, and scorpions put in an appearance, frequently dropping from the roof upon the table where I was writing, having been made quartermaster and commissary sergeant of the post. I have often wondered at the fact that, notwithstanding the continual presence during at least four months of the year, of these venomous reptiles and insects in our very midst, not a single case of poisoning occurred among the men from their bites or stings.

The government, refusing to furnish funds for building purposes (probably because it considered the camp as temporary only), Major Brown induced one of the Mexicans who were employed as herders of the newly-acquired herd of wild Sonora cattle, to teach our men the process of making adobes, and had soon several thousand of these large sun-dried bricks ready for use while the teamsters, with a detail of axemen, brought the required timber for rafters and lintels from the Huachuca Mountains, over a distance of about nine miles, from the vicinity of the present Fort Huachuca.

All this unpaid labor, carried on from day to day, from month to month, by men enlisted for military service, created an almost universal dissatisfaction and desertions became frequent. Sergeant Bundy of the cavalry, while acting as officer of the day, together with three men guarding the herd, deserted together in plain daylight, abandoning their duty in order to go mounted, and made tracks for the Rio Grande, taking with them their horses, arms, and accouterments. Others deserted during the night, singly and in pairs, generally taking the direction of the small Mexican town of Santa Cruz, ten miles south of the boundary, which by going through the Huachuca Pass they could reach on foot in about twelve hours. Among these latter was the ex-drum major, Dewitt, who, however, returned after two days' absence in a pitiable condition, ragged, hungry, thirsty, tanned, and much crestfallen. He had lost his way in the dark and wandered about looking for water, when he happily fell in with the wagons of the grain contractor, which were making for our camp loaded with corn, and took him home. His welcome here was far from cordial. Instead of being court-martialed, however, for deserting in the enemy's country, he was made to submit to a daily performance with an ax for the period of one month, clearing bushes from the still unfinished parade ground. "Oh, what a fall was there, my countrymen!"

Two of the deserters were murdered by Apaches in the Huachuca Pass, where a small scouting party found them a few days after their disappearance, stark naked and mutilated in a manner too shocking to relate. One of these was a shoemaker by trade, named Ross. The sad fate of these two men caused the desertions to come to a dead stop.

Previous to this occurrence, however, Corporal A. Buttner of our company, who had been sent with ten men and thirty days' rations to relieve a detail of the California Volunteers that were guarding the mail station and stock at the San Pedro crossing, soon after his arrival deserted his command, packed his rations upon a donkey, and crossed the boundary into Mexico, where he joined the army of the Liberals fighting the Imperial Mexican troops. I met this man again in 1871 in Tucson, where he related to me all his adventures. After the tragedy of Queretaro, where Maximilian was executed in 1867, he had obtained a three-months' leave of absence, holding at this time the rank of Captain. He had foolishly gone to San Francisco, was recognized, arrested there as a deserter from the U.S. army, and sentenced to imprisonment at Alcatraz Island for a term of three years. Here he managed to obtain a hearing before Major General O. O. Howard, on the latter's inspection tour to Arizona. The result of this interview was that Buttner was released and taken to Arizona by the said general to be used as an interpreter. He obtained a situation at the San Carlos Indian Reservation, whence he drifted back to Tucson later on. He was made chief of police by the newly incorporated city, and as such rendered good services for several years, finally dying of consumption in 1884, after having exposed his life time and again while keeping order in that turbulent frontier town.

Some scouting was done during the summer and fall of 1866 by the cavalry of the camp, whose official name had been changed to Camp Wallen, but with indifferent success. One large scout was organized, consisting of cavalry and infantry, to which three garrisons contributed a contingent; but no results were obtained, except that of reconnoitering and becoming acquainted with the country. Our contingent returned very tired and footsore after three weeks, with the backs of the pack animals in a fearful condition, owing to the absence of experienced packers. The manner of scouting in those days, before Generals Crook and Miles took the matter in hand, was far from effective, on account of the impractical means employed. Some Apaches who gave themselves up later on at Fort Goodwin related that they were following that big scout from day to day at a safe distance, enjoying the scraps of food, etc. scattered in its wake. They hugely enjoyed the bugle calls, large campfires and general hubbub attending that enterprise, and continually expected that a band with a bass drum would turn up somewhere to render the clumsy, big . . . still more conspicuous. I shall treat of the other scouts in a chapter separate, and relate an incident, or rather two incidences, which rendered the day of their occurrence the most unlucky of all the July Fourths I have passed in my life, and as such I shall devote a separate chapter to these.

Three characters entered prominently into my celebration of July 4, 1866. These were "Strawberry," "Blind Tom," and a woman.

The first two of these were horses, and the third a company laundress married to a member of my company whom we will call "Snarley," not because that was his name, for it was not, but because it is characteristic of the fellow's mean disposition and manners. His wife was the only woman our eyes beheld during a period of over one year, with the exception of a young Apache girl supposed to be the wife of our Apache hunter, and the wife of Margildo, our Indian guide, a very dark halfbreed.

Among the remount brought to replace the stolen horses was a very pretty, lively, and graceful animal, which the first sergeant of the cavalry, named David Grew, having the first pick, immediately selected for his mount. This horse became the apple of his eye, his comrade and friend, and was never permitted to be used by anyone else. Now it will be remembered that there were only two commissioned officers in camp, from which circumstances resulted the fact that the junior officer had to perform the duties of adjutant. A. A. Q. M., A. A. C. C. and post treasurer, besides commanding his company, the cavalry, and doing occasional scouting service. He was also the only available officer to perform the functions of officer of the day without ever being relieved therefrom. This state of affairs caused the following order to be issued from headquarters:

New Post on the Upper San Pedro.
Department of Arizona, July 3, 1866.

Post Order No. 26.
On account of the reduced number of commissioned officers present
in this camp, it is ordered:

1. From and after tomorrow the following non-commissioned
officers will be detailed in regular turns to do duty as officer of the
day of this garrison.

Max Lipowitz, first sergeant, Company "E," Third Battalion,
Fourteenth U. S. Infantry; David Grew, first sergeant, Company
"G," First Cavalry; John A. Spring, quartermaster and commissary
sergeant of the post.

2. The officer of the day will report for orders to the commanding officer immediately after the guard mount.

3. The first sergeant of the cavalry company will have a good
horse, saddled and bridled, in readiness for the use of the officer
of the day from guard mount until retreat.

By order of the commanding officer:
Kinney, Adjutant.

The last-mentioned of the three non-commissioned officers was my
own humble self and I had a suspicion — or shall I call it presentiment?—
that I would be the first one detailed for the designated purpose. I knew
that the principal and most important function of the officer of the day
consisted in visiting the herd at least twice during the day, and posting it
so as to preclude the possibility of a sudden surprise by Indians, by placing sentinels selected from the herd detail upon prominent points affording
a good view upon the surrounding country. With the exception of a few
occasions on which I had been lifted up on one of my grandfather's farm
horses during harvest, while I was yet a tender age, I had never been on
horseback. What was I to do? Confess my total ignorance of all horsemanship, and thus be deprived of the great honor of almost "bossing"
the whole camp and wearing a red sash crosswise upon my ambitious
breast for a full twenty-four hours? Rather die! I bethought me of Lipowitz's functions as acting sergeant-major of the post, which would necessarily cause the detail to be made by him, and at once resolved to bribe
him into detailing me as third or last to do the honorable office. If successful I would profit by the delay in obtaining a gentle old horse and practice
riding upon him in an out-of-the-way canyon. In order to accomplish my
purpose, I provided myself with a bottle of Treble-X old bourbon and a
box of decent cigars from the sutler store, and was crossing the parade
ground with these articles toward Lipowitz's quarters, when I met the
adjutant's orderly, who handed me a paper containing this legend:

"Detail for officer of the day for July 4. John A. Spring, Q. M. and
C. S. sergeant."

What now? The next best thing was to visit Grew, who had to furnish the horse, and induce him to select for the purpose the most gentle animal in his charge.

Sergeant Grew was a jolly Irishman, who had seen much service, and who loved liquor. In fact, he boasted sometimes in a jocund manner that he had "made away" in his lifetime with whiskey enough to float a modern-sized squadron of men-of-war. Still, he was never found unfit for duty; he either selected the time for his heavy libations when his services were not urgent, or, if unexpectedly called for, he would sober up in the space of a few minutes, unfortunately a very rare and useful talent. He was nearly always in good humor, and easily incited to merry doings; yet nobody had ever heard issuing from his lips a full-throated breezy laugh, as he rather indulged in a kind of spasmodic chuckle, which finished with an abrupt jerk. He had a very large, wide mouth that in time of hilarity assumed such a broad smile as to make the corners disappear seemingly behind his ears, while his eyes kept winking and a tremendous grin spread over his whole physiognomy.

It would take too much space were I to give the whole conversation that ensued between us two, neither is this necessary. Not having been acquainted with Grew for much more than a month, I did not at first notice that he had imbibed already, probably in anticipation of the "Fourth" on the day following; neither did I observe in the half-darkness of the tent, illumined by a solitary tallow candle, a tumbler, a sugar bowl, and some lemons standing on a cracker box near his bed. The sutler had permission to sell to us three, Lipowitz, Grew, and myself, all the stimulants asked for, and the other men were not much stinted in that regard either.

I placed my bottle and cigars on Grew's homemade table; he carried a corkscrew of course. We began by having a social drink, and then another, upon which I began to develop the purpose of my errand. Foolish pride caused me to hide the fact that I had never been on horseback. I stated that I had never been much of a rider, and had had no horseback exercise for a long time. All this, although strictly true, was nevertheless a prevarication under existing circumstances. Grew took several drinks during these preliminary remarks, and became somewhat elated. Which I now began to notice from the widening of his grins and increasing thickness of his speech. When at last I made my request that he would select for my use on the following day a very steady, gentle horse, he jumped suddenly from his seat and exclaimed!"

"John, old boy, I am your friend; you shall ride Strawberry!"

With this he seized my hand, pressed and shook it till my arm ached to the shoulder.

"Who or what is Strawberry?" I asked, somewhat astonished at the, to me, unknown name, as connected with horsemanship, as well as his sudden excitement and remark.

"Why, don't you know Strawberry, my own horse, the pearl of all the horses, the most gentle, the best —" he began, when I interrupted him with the observation that I had seen the horse, appreciated his beauty, actions, etc., but that I apprehended he would prove too lively to be intrusted to my inexperienced guidance.

Grew filled his glass anew, and saying: "Here is to you and Strawberry," emptied it at one gulp. He then enlarged extensively upon the numerous virtues of his horse, becoming quite sentimental over it. He assured me that a child could ride him, that no other man should ever straddle him, but that I, his comrade and friend, should be welcome to his use, and that he would give orders to that effect at stable call in the morning. Whatever was to happen, I was in for it.

Of course, I proffered profuse thanks, although I had some misgivings as to the outcome from this business until on the following morning Sergeant Henry, the q. m. sergeant of the cavalry company, set my mind at rest by telling me also that the horse was perfectly gentle. Having already received orders from Grew in the premises, he expressed his astonishment at the fact of the latter's permission to have Strawberry ridden by any other man.

The Fourth of July opened, after several days of rain, bright and clear. In the thin, pure air of those regions even the faraway mountains of the Chiricahua Range in the east and the peak of the Picacho, more than 120 miles to the west, could be plainly seen. The rich ozone of the morning atmosphere entering my young lungs filled my whole anatomy with bracing vigor. The guard mount was gone through in the usual manner, and I reported to the commanding officer for orders, not a little proud of the newly-acquired honors.

Oh, that pride should come before a fall!

As expected, these orders were to ride forthwith to the herd, to see that it was not taken farther than one and a half miles from the camp (there was fine grazing everywhere), to post sentries in such locations as would command a good outlook in every direction, and to examine their arms and accouterments as to their efficiency for immediate use. In front of the adobe building I found Strawberry, rightly named, as I now observed, for the color of his hide, ready saddled and bridled, and perfectly groomed, held by Grew himself, and surrounded by several cavalrymen. Being a "dough-boy," I carried the straight sword which in those days formed a part of the armament of the sergeants of the line, a useless weapon which the cavalry irreverently designated as a "cheese-knife," or "toad-sticker."

Grew examined me from head to foot; he objected to my wearing this straight sword tightly strapped to my side, as being inconvenient, and spoiling a man's looks on horseback, and tried to induce me to wear his saber. To this I objected, for good reasons. He remarked, however, that a pair of spurs was indispensible — not for use on the horse, indeed, but for the looks of the thing. Grew being an old regular, with far more military experience than I had, I acquiesced to this proposition. A pair of spurs were brought and strapped onto my infantry brogans, at which Grew threw a glance of unutterable contempt. I mounted very easily, having found time to practice that part of the performance in the early morning. As I was ready to start Grew cautioned me (with a grin, I thought) against turning my heels inward; he also told me that the horse had on only a snaffle bit, so that he might drink at the crossing without removing the bridle. "In case of need," he added, "touch him up lightly with a spur: the lightest touch will be sufficient."

I started across the parade-ground, passing in front of the officers' quarters, towards the crossing at the southwestern corner of the camp. There existed a standing order that no horse should be ridden at a faster gait than a walk within the parade-ground. Of course, all the horses were already accustomed to this, and I reached the crossing without trouble. The preceding rains had caused the creek to overflow its banks for some days, and had washed some ground away from the opposite edge, which was now somewhat steep and slippery. Strawberry stopped in the middle of the creek to drink, and there waited for directions whither to proceed, turning his pretty head toward me, as if he wished to ask. "What now?"

Up to this day I cannot pretend to explain what demon of the infernal regions possessed me and urged me to use the confounded spurs, when probably a little encouragement with the voice or a shake of the bridle rein would have fully answered the purpose. Yet I know I spurred Strawberry, although I cannot say whether I touched him lightly or strongly — probably, after the manner of inexperienced horsemen, it was a spasmodic backward kick of my heels — for the horse made a gigantic leap forward which landed him squarely upon the opposite bank, threw me forward out of the saddle upon the animal's neck, which I hugged with the powerful embrace born of sudden uncontrollable fear of falling. And Strawberry went, oh yes, he was going. Being urged to cross the creek, he understood full well that our destination was the herd, and thither he ran, or, as it seemed to me, he flew. My infantry trousers, not adapted to the saddle, gradually rolled up above the knees, exposing my drawers, the empty stirrups dangled aimlessly about, striking the horse's legs and belly; the tassles of my sash rose and descended in rhythmic motion, and that confounded cheese-knife kept hammering against the horse's breast and forelegs. I had lost my hat at the first jump, and I felt my hair rise "like the quills upon the fretful porcupine." The giant cacti, mesquite, and creosote bushes along the route seemed to fly backward like the telegraph poles observed from a fast-moving express train. All at once Strawberry came to a sudden stop and I fell off, inert, like a sack of flour.

The sergeant of the herd, with two of his men, came running towards me and turned me over and over; they thought that I had been shot or stabbed with a lance by Apaches on my way from camp, or perhaps that I had been trying to run away with the best horse in camp, as they knew that nobody was allowed to ride the horse on which I had come. Finally, not finding any blood either on my person or on Strawberry, who had quietly begun munching the tender grass, they thought I had had a fit of some kind, and threw a hatful of water over my face. They told me afterwards that I looked very weak and pale. Well, knowing how I felt, I readily believed that; not only that, but much more, to which, however, they only gave expression in whispers, as the real cause of my sad plight began to be realized in their minds.

As soon as I had recovered somewhat I began to attend to my duties; I visited all the sentries on the surrounding elevations, on foot, be it understood, and examined their arms, finding the positions which they occupied satisfactory for the purpose intended.

After I had finished this fatiguing tour, I selected from the herd what looked to me to be the oldest and feeblest animal present, and requested one of the men to unsaddle Strawberry and to saddle "this horse," pointing to the object of my selection.

The man looked at me with an expression of astonishment and almost horror. "You cannot ride this horse," said he, "he has a sore back."

"He is also lame in the left hind leg," remarked another.

By this time the sergeant in charge of the herd had come up, and upon being made acquainted with the subject of our conversation, he shook his head ominously and said: "You will never reach camp on that horse; it is nearly blind, or at least has the blind staggers; how he ever got to this camp is a mystery; he certainly did not come with the remount. We call him 'Old Blind Tom'."

But I was obstinate; the horrors of my late ride were too fresh in my memory. "That horse and no other will I ride to camp," said I, and so I did. Although I had reached the herd in something less than ten minutes, my return ride occupied nearly two hours, during which I made the only use I had ever found, so far, of my toad-sticker, by means of which I encouraged Blind Tom's progress by gently sticking the point of it into the skin behind his ears, having found that spurring was with him a waste of time and energy.

As I had expected, I found a considerable number of our cavalrymen standing at the adobe building when I reached it, after delivering by the way my report to the commanding officer. Among them was, of course, friend Grew, who immediately asked for Strawberry, not without some anxiety vibrating in his voice. I answered with a short "Strawberry be—," and retired, locking my door. Giving a temporary pain in my stomach as an excuse, I was allowed to have the afternoon inspection of the herd performed by a deputy. When, towards retreat, the herd returned to camp, my arrival at the herd was minutely related, soon became the talk of the camp, and my existence was henceforth made miserable by frequent underhand illusions to my "Strawberry ride," as the adventure was universally called.

The conclusion of this matter we must delay for a short space, while I relate what befell me during the remainder of the twenty-four hours of my duty as officer of the day, the glory of which had already faded into sad disappointment.

Alas! How true the saying that "misfortunes never come singly!"

ATTACKED BY APACHES

It was nearly midnight when a loud challenge of the sentry in front of the corral, the gate of which I locked every night before retiring, awoke me from my slumbers. Before I had time to dress fully, a loud knocking at the gate called me thither, and upon opening it I found standing outside, with the corporal of the guard, who had run to the spot, an old Frenchman named Magentie, whom I knew very well, as he supplied the camp with vegetables and eggs from time to time, bringing these articles from the already-mentioned Mexican town, Santa Cruz, in a cart. This man, who spoke no English, and therefore conversed with me always in French, stated, while he gesticulated in the manner of his people with his wounded and bleeding hands, that he and two companions had been attacked that afternoon by the Apaches in the Huachuca Pass while traveling towards our camp with a cartload of vegetables and eggs; that his two companions were probably killed, as he had seen them drop, and that he himself had barely escaped by hiding in the bushes and gullies of the locality, with whose surroundings he was familiar; that he had watched the Apaches from his hiding place behind a rock, saw them unhitch and drive off his oxen, and that they seemingly took the direction towards Babocomari, our camp. I sent the man to the doctor's tent with the corporal of the guard, and, holding the matter to be of sufficient importance, reported it to the commanding officer.

A short time after our arrival at the camp, the government had employed as Indian guide or scout the Marigildo mentioned previously as having been a captive with Cochise's band. Major Brown now ordered me to take a detail of ten foot soldiers and to search carefully the creek bottom and surrounding ravines under the guidance of Marigildo.

Now, there existed in the camp one laundress, wife of the man "Snarley" of our company. She was a hard-working woman, who, however, on account of the constant bickerings and naggings of her worthless husband, was not allowed to lead a peaceful life. It was well known that their tent, situated behind the company quarters, on the edge of the plateau, was frequently the scene of marital quarrels that sometimes reached, at least on the part of the man, the fighting stage. The latter was on guard duty on the night of which we write, but had obtained permission to visit his tent about midnight, for the purpose of eating a late supper.

As I was exploring with my patrol, guided by Marigildo, the ravine running below the eastern edge of the camp, and we were approaching the location of the infantry company above us, there rang out through the silence of the night a fearful cry of "Help!" emanating from a woman's throat. I was carrying a revolver in my left hand, while with my sword in the right one I was examining and probing into the brush for possible Apaches. Addressing the men with a hasty "Follow me," I ran up the incline with a few jumps that brought me to the tent-flap of the Snarley family's wall tent, through which I saw the woman standing in partial undress in front of her bed, while her husband, with fury in his eyes, held his bayonet poised over her naked throat and bosom, apparently ready to strike, clutching at the same time with his left hand her hair and bending her head backward. There are moments in this life where all hesitation is out of place and may prove fatal. Without any reflection upon possible consequences, I struck the miscreant a violent blow upon the top of his head with the hilt of my sword; he fell like an ox struck by the butcher's pole-ax. I lifted him up, placed him on the bed and, dispatching one of my men for a doctor, began to apply cold water to the wounded man.

Upon an adobe hearth built into the rear wall of the tent there sizzled some meat in a frying pan full of greasy gravy, and near it stood a coffee pot. As soon as the woman had recovered from the first effects of the sudden catastrophe, she cast a look upon her would-be murderer. When she saw him lying there ghastly pale, or rather gray, speechless and bloody, she was seized by a sudden fury, made a grab for the frying pan and howling at me: "You have murdered my 'Arry," struck me over the head with the redhot cooking utensil, having apparently selected the exact spot where I had struck her 'Arry. The blow was administered with all the force she was capable of in her frenzied condition. The frying pan, having just come from over the fire, was hot, I should say extremely hot, and its contents were boiling. The sizzling grease had spread over my face, nearly blinding me, and then descended in small rivulets down my front, rendering me a most pitiable thing to look at, a none-such, as it were. It was said afterwards that I looked very "comical." I believe it, for I know I felt very "comical." The doctor arriving about that time, I left the wounded man in his care, and hied me homewards, having placed the patrol under charge of the corporal of the guard, while the hospital steward kindly attended to my hurts.

Such was my Fourth of July in the year 1866. He who has lived any length of time among soldiers at an isolated spot where few occurrences of an unusual nature come to divert the minds of the men from the usual everyday life, will readily understand that my miscarried ride on Strawberry formed for some time to come the daily theme of conversation not only, but also, that I was constantly subjected to covert remarks, insinuations and innuendoes referring to that unfortunate circumstance, especially by our cavalry contingent. When I came to reflect impassionately upon the matter I readily arrived at the conclusion that Grew was in no way to blame; that from the point of view of a cavalryman Strawberry was an excellent and gentle horse, and that the untoward outcome of my ride on him was entirely due to my prevarication and awkwardness, or rather inexperience in the saddle, as Grew would never, drunk or sober, have offered me his horse if I had stated my total ignorance of horsemanship. I had therefore sought Grew's presence and we had renewed our friendship in another bottle of Treble-X bourbon. On this occasion he helped me to concoct a scheme by which all further mention of the Strawberry ride should be stopped, the plan being to provide the cavalry company "a good feed," or extra fine dinner, to be given them in the near future.

On the morning following this interview, I attended with Grew the stable call where, as a rule, no commissioned officer was present. With Grew's consent I then and there offered to his assembled men that I would give them the finest dinner then obtainable in Arizona on the following Sunday, having ascertained that the commanding officer would be absent on that day on a visit to Tucson. I promised them the best that the subsistence department could furnish in barrels, bottles, or cans, together with the meat from two fat sheep, etc., all of which would be prepared under the personal supervision of Romanoff, the French "chef de cuisine" of the officers' mess; all this, provided that they would promise then and there that hereafter no more mention of the Strawberry ride should be made, either openly or covertly. They promised this one and all. The dinner was a howling success, and ever after was mentioned when the occasion was referred to as "Blind Tom's Treat," and I soon learned to ride like a cowboy, after which I enjoyed to the full the fine points of our darling Strawberry, whom Grew never refused to lend me.

In the fall of the year, Major Kinney, who had resigned his commission in order to enter civil life as a man of leisure, was relieved by Second Lieutenant Jeremiah Harrington, whom I shall introduce by an anecdote, knowing from experience that one becomes often better acquainted with the characteristics of a person by seeing him introduced in action, as it were, than by a long and too often tedious description. The incident related is somewhat out of the chronological order of this narrative, but treats of a man with whom we were long and pleasantly associated and with whom it is therefore necessary to become acquainted.

Lieutenant Harrington was quite young, lively, and sociable, and, although he was a commissioned officer and the writer only a non-commissioned one under his direct orders — being, in fact, his quarter-master and commissary sergeant — there sprung (sic) up between us an intimate friendship born of similarity of character, temper, rearing, and tendencies, manifested only, of course, in private intercourse, while in the line of duty the decorum of military discipline was always strictly observed.

If Lieutenant Harrington knew how to do one thing better than any other, it was to play the fiddle; excuse me, I must say the violin, for the music which he produced on that melodious instrument precludes the use of the common term "fiddle." He could play every aria of every known opera, and his adagios would stir a man's soul to the very bottom. I am sorry to say that our commanding officer, who possessed neither a poetic soul nor a musical ear, failed to appreciate the innate talent and nice execution of his junior co-officer, and that it therefore frequently came to pass that when my musical friend was pouring forth sweet melodies upon the balmy breezes of the silent, moonlit night, he would be roughly interrupted by the coarse voice of the mighty commander coming from the neighboring tent, requesting the performer to "please stop that noise." At such times Harrington would sadly gather up his beloved instrument and notes and hie himself to my office, where he could indulge in his melodious pastime without fear of interruption, being, moreover, sure of my unqualified admiration, and unrestricted applause, for he certainly played well and with feeling.

Now, it had happened some time previously that the commanding officer — unquestionably with an eye to roasting-ears in the near future — had given permission to a Mexican family, named Mendoza, to plant a patch of corn on the Babocomari Creek, about three-quarters of a mile south of the post, within the military reservation, and to erect for their accommodation a small adobe house, which was built upon a little hill, cut in places by several rather steep and rocky "arroyos," or gulches running from the top of the hill to its foot. The family consisted of Mendoza, a man of mature years, his mother-in-law, rather aged, his wife, and a daughter of from fifteen to sixteen summers, named Trinidad; this latter was unquestionably — when washed — a very pretty girl, with a clear, olive skin and large, black eyes of unsurpassed beauty and fire — in short, a semi-tropic belle. The family was very poor, but, as far as we knew, strictly honest, decent, virtuous.

Lieutenant Harrington and I had visited them several times during our frequent rambles, and had discovered that the girl, Trinidad, was the possessor of a very pleasant musical voice; in fact, she had regaled us with several innocent love ditties which she accompanied with some skill upon a super-annuated guitar. Our conversation had been extremely limited, on account of the difference in our vernacular; but Harrington and I had resolved to precipitate ourselves with might and main into the study of the Spanish language, a rather difficult undertaking in the absence of a competent teacher and the needful books.

There was, however, at our post one Marigildo, a half-breed Mexican, who spoke English somewhat, and after a protracted and diligent search, we succeeded in discovering a few fragments of an *Ollendorf's System* of learning the Spanish language. Marigildo himself could not read at all, but he could to some extent correct our pronunciation when we read Spanish sentences to him. At all events, he undertook the task of being our instructor at odd times, when he was not engaged in his legitimate occupation as Indian guide with scouting parties. It will be readily understood that his method of teaching being rather primitive and spasmodic, so to speak, our progress in that musical language was far from satisfactory or encouraging. I had somewhat the advantage of Lieutenant Harrington, inasmuch as I had studied Latin at college, up to a few years previously.

THE FATEFUL SONG

All at once Lieutenant Harrington conceived what, after some argument and deliberation, we came to consider a brilliant idea. One evening, after making the rounds of the stableyards and having locked the gate, I found my friend, upon entering the office, sitting in an office chair before the fire with his violin across his knees, apparently in a brown study.

After the usual "good evening" there was a silence of some minutes, during which I wondered what the fertile brain of my friend was concocting. Suddenly he broke forth with: "See here, Spring, I have been thinking of giving these Mendoza people a great surprise." (I knew that "these Mendoza people," used thus collectively, meant simply the dark-eyed daughter). "What sort of a vocalist are you? Could you sing a simple easy tune fairly well if I study it with you on my violin for some time?"

I humbly informed him that I had a fairly good voice for eating beef, but as for singing tunes, I apprehended considerable difficulty.

"Bah!" he exclaimed, "anybody can sing with the accompaniment of a violin, which comes nearer than any other instrument to being a perfect imitation of the human voice. Our study of the Spanish language progresses very slowly, and I was just thinking we might do this: We will get Marigildo, who sings quite well, to teach us a simple, easy, short Spanish song; we will study it together, and next Sunday we will give Miss Trini — I mean the Mendoza people — a Spanish concert. Just think of it! What a grand surprise it will be!"

"How about the text, the words, you know?" said I mildly; "We do not know enough Spanish yet for the purpose."

"What of it," said Lieutenant Harrington, "if you can but clearly pronounce the words? A Latin scholar ought to be able to do that. Many birds have learned to pronounce distinctly a number of words, and whole sentences, even. Please do not thwart me in this project. Let us find Marigildo at once."

At that very moment this identical gentleman appeared upon the scene, bent on business with the office. We communicated to him the plan of our surprise party forthwith, and found to our great joy that he entered upon the spirit of the thing with great ardor and gusto. From his extensive repertoire of Spanish love-songs (save the mark!) we selected one which sounded certainly melodious enough and had furthermore the great merit of being easy and short, consisting only of two stanzas of four lines each.

We studied bravely. The Lieutenant fiddled and I sang till I began dreaming of it in my sleep; we practiced during two hours for four consecutive days, never asking, never caring, what we sang, after Marigildo had declared that he did not possess sufficient command of the English language to explain the meaning of the words. It certainly sounded Spanish — that was all we wanted. Marigildo simply called it a love song, and assured us that we would give the Mendoza people a surprise and create a great sensation. He averred this with the most earnest mien and the soberest possible face.

Sunday came, and after the usual morning inspection and parade we retained our parade uniforms. Harrington waxed his pretty blond mustache till it fairly shone; he was, beyond a doubt, a very handsome young officer, with his cream-and-strawberry complexion and lovely eyes of deep forget-me-not blue. As soon as the commanding officer had ridden off with a small escort toward the Huachuca Mountains to look at some ash timber, we set out for the humble dwelling of the Mendozas, I carrying the violin case.

We found the whole family assembled around the chimney-fire, for the most part squatted upon raw-hides. They received us most hospitably, tendering us the only two available seats raised above the earth floor — an old office chair without a back and a home-made three-legged stool. Trinidad looked lovely, being, in honor of the day, freshly washed, combed and gotten up in her best wearing apparel.

After the first salutation the conversation naturally lagged, and Mendoza, to bring some life into the thing, soon requested his daughter to enliven the scene with a song or two. The time-honored instrument was produced, a broken string mended, and considerable time spent in tuning the ancient guitar, during which time we had ample opportunity to admire the exquisitely shaped hands of the dark-eyed daughter of Mexico. She sang two songs, love songs of course — Mexican girls know no others — she sang correctly, even prettily, but like all their illiterate class, like an automaton, without feeling or expression. At the conclusion of her second song, she leaned the instrument against the wall, smilingly acknowledging our compliments expressed in rather questionable Spanish.

The Lieutenant evidently thought this the propitious moment for our performance to begin. He unlocked the violin-case and tenderly lifted from it his beloved instrument, while I emitted the usual preparatory short cough intended to clear one's throat. In a very few words, laboriously acquired from Marigildo for the occasion, we announced our intention of regaling the company with a Spanish song. My friend, having already tuned his instrument at home, now brought it to concert pitch with a few twists of the screws, and began at once a tender introductory adagio, from which, at a given preconcerted passage, he gently floated into the melody of our song, when I at one fell into the tune, taking particular care to pronounce the oft-repeated words with the greatest possible clearness.

Did we create a sensation? Did we give these good people a surprise? Well, rather.

Hardly had I arrived at the end of the first line when I observed that the girl's features assumed an expression of unmistakable alarm, while the eyes of her grandmother began to glisten in fiery anger and Mendoza's hair to assume an erect position. Lieutenant Harrington, who was busy manipulating his bow in the most graceful manner and fingering his strings, evidently failed to notice these alarming signs, he kept on playing and I, somehow, *nolens volens,* kept pace — force of habit, I suppose, caused by the unremitting practice of several days, impelled me to persist.

Reaching about the middle of the second line (the song was set to very slow music), I saw the girl blush a deep crimson and pull her shawl violently over her face, hiding it completely. The old lady approached the fire with the evident intention of seizing a firebrand. Mendoza was reaching out for an ax that stood against the wall in the corner of the mantelpiece, while his wife held out her hands in horror, uttering an exclamation of supreme anger that was beyond my understanding. While these movements were going on we had still continued our performance, although I had begun pulling Harrington somewhat violently by his jacket.

As we were entering upon the third line the climax came; there was no longer any possible doubt as to the hostile intentions of our audience, who now stood before us with weapons clinched (sic) and fury in their eyes.

With the cry of "Murder!" I pulled Lieutenant Harrington by main force from his seat and through the aperture intended for the door, which, fortunately for us, had not been hung yet.

We struck the gulch which led directly from the door down the hill, and began a rapid descent over rocks and crags, between boulders and small bushes — none too soon, for while descending we were made aware of sundry missiles being fired after us. Lieutenant Harrington's fine uniform was badly scorched by a firebrand, my right shoulder was slightly grazed by the ax, while the violin-case came after us in a hop, a skip and a jump from rock to rock, to the great detriment of its mechanical construction. After a steep descent of about fifty yards we came to a large boulder, behind which we came to a stop of common accord, hiding behind it to catch our breath and to await the abatement of our excitement. And here we found the rascal Marigildo, rolling over and over in uncontrollable laughter. He had watched the whole performance through the open doorway from this safe spot, and saw the "grand finale" of his (as he called it) good joke.

Joke, indeed! We felt like murdering him on the spot, and I know we kicked him unmercifully. Further severe bodily chastisement and other unpleasant consequences he escaped only after giving his solemn promise that he would immediately visit the insulted family, give a full explanation of the whole horrible business, and exonerate us from all blame in the matter.

This he did at once and thoroughly. We paid many more pleasant visits to the Mendoza family after the deep feelings of shame had been obliterated.

What was it we sang? I know it now, kind reader. I blush today when I think of it!

OUR BEEF CATTLE

Our camp had no regular slaughterhouse, and the killing of the beef cattle offered many difficulties from the beginning. At first the cattle corral, the enclosure of which was constructed hastily of branches and twigs from the mesquite tree, held in place indifferently, was the scene of some pretty wild and unbusinesslike performances whenever a steer had to be killed to supply the garrison with beef, which occurred about twice or three times a week. Our butcher, a German named Sassle, was detailed on daily duty for this purpose from the cavalry company, and, although in every other respect a good man, soldier, and butcher, he had one peculiarity which often proved detrimental and embarrassing when he was called upon to bring into play the preliminary functions of his calling.

On account of the prevailing heat, which had abolished, together with the continual manual labor, all military exercises except dress parade, the cattle to be slaughtered were dispatched by a bullet very early in the morning, and by 9 a.m. would be in the kettles of the cooks, as we had no way to keep meat fresh and no receptacles in which we might salt it down. Now whenever Sassle undertook to bring down a steer with his carbine he would invariably either fail altogether in hitting it, although he would generally fire from a distance not exceeding fifteen feet, or he would wound it in almost any place except a vital spot, and not infrequently would wound more than one. His (for a soldier) ridiculous performance resulted from the fact that Sassle, at the moment of pulling the trigger, would jerk his head, and with it his shoulder, backwards, and consequently render the most accurate aim futile. Generally a stampede on a small scale would result from such shooting and wounding; the cattle, excited from the shot as well as from the violent motions of the wounded animal, would break through the frail fence and escape at a run; then the herders had to be called, and sometimes a squad of cavalry, and a chase would begin that often ended a dozen or more miles from camp at a late hour, often after a considerable expenditure of ammunition in finishing the wounded steer. When I was appointed commissary sergeant, I regularly shot the cattle myself, and never made a misshot, having been trained to marksmanship in Switzerland from the age of twelve years.

During the month of August we received a herd of Sonora cattle that were quite wild, and could not be approached by a man on foot, (as they were accustomed to see only mounted herders), without becoming restless and frightened at the unusual sight. With them came two Mexicans experienced with the lasso, who were hired by the government and stayed with us until the herd had become accustomed to the new surroundings. For the reason stated, I now selected an old steady horse upon which I could ride around the herd in the open, and instead of shooting the cattle in the crowded corral, I would go to the herd towards evening, when the cattle had eaten their fill, were lazy and quiet.

Acting upon the advice of Marigildo (who was an indifferent marksman himself, and therefore declined the job) I abandoned my former practice of shooting the cattle in the forehead from their front, and as soon as Sassle had pointed out to me the steer he wished killed, I would ride to the rear of the animal, so as to take aim behind the ear, the bullet never failing to penetrate the brain in its forward course and bring the steer down in instant death. Then the herders would drive the herd off and Sassle could begin his work of skinning and cutting up the carcass on the ground, ready to be hauled to camp in a wagon.

But "it is a long lane that has no turning." One very hot afternoon towards the end of September I started out on a steer-killing errand, Sassle riding behind me with his camp-kettle, which he used for carrying water to wash the blood off the meat on the spot, containing his butcher steel and knives. The herd had been slowly driven towards the camp, and was quietly grazing in the river bottom south of the crossing. Sassle pointed out to me a fine young, fat heifer, and I took aim in the manner above related and fired and — missed, at least failed to kill. I could never understand how it occurred, as the animal stood apparently still; perhaps the horse, much worried by flies, made a movement at the moment of my pulling the trigger, or, more probably, the animal lowered her head at the moment of firing. At all events, the ball passed through the skin just behind the horns, very near the vital spot aimed at, but just a little too high, and struck the horn of a full-sized bull standing obliquely in front of the heifer, at its base. The blood spurted out at once in a bright red jet, and as the animal forthwith began shaking his head, ran into his eyes and blinded him.

The fury of a wounded bull is proverbial. This bull did not differ in this regard from the generality of his class. For a moment he stopped where he was, lowered his head, stuck his tail straight up into the air, and tore up the ground with his forefeet, all this to the accompaniment of a noise which was neither a bellow nor a roar, but partook of the nature of both, and soon assumed the sound produced by the deepest bass of a million of humming bumble-bees. Then he started; the herd had been driven off quickly, to be out of danger, and only Sassle and I were left to face the music. He did not turn towards us, however, and I would not have cared much in any event, as we had needle guns by that time. However, I had neither then nor had I had before a good opportunity for a second shot, the shell of the cartridge having given me some trouble at first in its removal, and now the bull was running in a direct line towards the creek near the crossing, where about twenty men were bathing.

The scramble which now ensued beggars description. Some of the bathers sought to reach deep water and submerge themselves; others crossed to the farther side; but by far the majority climbed upon the trees standing on the borders of the creek; from this elevated position they made to one looking on from a distance the impression of a family of chattering, overgrown, nondescript monkeys, breaking off twigs and branches which they threw at the bull as he reached the creek.

All men who have had experience with cattle are unanimous in the assertion that an infuriated cow is much more dangerous and difficult to deal with than a mad bull. They give as a reason that the maddened cow never loses her presence of mind, so to speak, but seeks revenge with deliberation and calculation, while an infuriated bull becomes mad with frenzy and blind with the blood which fury causes to rush to his head and into his eyes. I fully believe this. Furthermore, "my" bull was blinded by the blood streaming unceasingly from his wound over his eyes.

Assailed by the missiles showered at him by the bathers, he suddenly turned to the right and — horror of horrors — made a beeline up the southern declivity of the camp straight towards the officers' quarters. I kept following him with a view of obtaining a finishing shot, and Sassle came on behind with his clattering camp-kettle. The bull reached the high ground between the hospital tent and the officers' tent and I was already hoping that he would run through upon the parade ground, when the hospital steward's little bull terrier jumped at him, and thus turned his mad career towards the left, where stood the first wall tent of the officers' quarters, containing the kitchen. Adjoining it was the dining tent, and next to this was the commanding officer's tent. All these tents were put up with a view to protracted service, surrounded on the sides by timbers resting upon forked poles, upon which were fastened the ropes stretching the tent flies. The tents themselves were fastened to the ground by innumerable ropes held by pegs. This "bungalow" was covered by a roof or "shed" constructed of willow branches supported by timbers resting upon forked poles. The bull rushed headforemost through the tent flaps into the interior of the kitchen tent, whence the clatter of an overturned stove and sundry kitchen utensils thrown about soon announced that he was doing great execution. The noise suddenly changed into that of broken crockeryware, while fearful cries for help issued from the tumbling mass, evidently emanating from the throat of Monsieur Romanoff, the French chef, whom I found half buried in the debris when I appeared upon the scene.

All of this had, of course, taken place with great rapidity. I had dismounted and was looking, with rifle ready cocked, through the torn canvas, and was about ready to shoot at the bull, who was entangled in a mass of canvas and ropes that had been pulled hither and thither in the fracas, when I observed Romanoff in front, directly in the line of fire. He spurted out: "Don't shoot!"

While I was trying to obtain a favorable angle for firing without endangering the life of the cook, the bull suddenly disengaged himself from the tangle of ropes, bursted through the east wall of the tent, and galloped across the parade ground, dragging after him several ropes and tent pins, while from one of his horns dangled a large piece of torn canvas, flapping in the wind. Thence he crossed the eastern ravine and soon disappeared over the high ground in the direction of the Whetstone Mountains. Some cavalry were sent in pursuit, and succeeded in bringing him down seven miles from camp, after an expenditure of thirty-seven cartridges. He had been hit eleven times, but not in any vital spot, and finally succumbed to loss of blood and exhaustion.

UNDER ARREST

In the meantime, the commanding officer, who had been suddenly awakened from a quiet afternoon by the general commotion in his immediate vicinity, had appeared upon the scene and stopped me from following the bull just as I had remounted. With a purple countenance and eyes emitting veritable sparks of fury, he demanded an explanation of the passing events, which he called "this infernal hub-bub." But I could not explain for laughter. I had been seized with an uncontrollable fit of mirth that nearly shook me from my saddle, so that, I believe, if my life had depended upon the uttering of a connected sentence at that moment, I was unable to utter it. All danger to life was now over, and I saw in my mind only the ridiculous aspect of the scenes just witnessed; the frightened bathers, the tumble of the tents and the frantic cook half buried in the debris. I was very young then, full of fun at all times, and the causes of mirth were of so recent occurrence, that I was utterly unable to render a connected account of the dramatic display. An unrestrainable fit of laughter would cut off my speech, of which the only comprehensible utterance was: "The bull — wounded — mistake." This disrespectful behavior on my part incensed Major Brown greatly, the more so as I had omitted to dismount and salute him when he addressed me. Nearly bereft of speech himself by fury, he was just able to articulate the words: "Go to your quarters under arrest!"

My quarters were in the adobe building in a room used as Q. M. and C. S. office, and thither I went to have my laugh out, and then to reflect in a general way upon the vicissitudes of army life in the Far West, and in particular upon the ingratitude shown me for voluntary services rendered to our camp in the way of promoting the expediency of slaughtering cattle.

While I was still ruminating upon my grievances and the problematic outcome of my adventure, Romanoff came in and demanded, in his short, jerky way, five pounds of white sugar for the officers' mess, which I flatly refused, stating that I was under arrest, could therefore issue nothing, and was waiting for somebody to arrive and relieve me of my authority and receive the keys. As we shall have to mention this cook again in the course of our narrative, it is perhaps well to mention here that Monsieur Romanoff was an original of an uncommon sort. He claimed to be a native of Russia, spoke but little English, and that little with a strong French accent; this latter language he spoke with great fluency, purity, and even refined elegance; he was a first-class cook; in his abrupt manners and short, jerky sentences he reminded me forcibly of the insect called tarantula killer, a kind of wasp with quick, seemingly always angry motions, whose whole life seems to be passed in a state of permanent excitement bordering on fury. Romanoff had no patience at any time, and was, or seemed to be, always in a great hurry.

His answer to my announcement of "being laid on the shelf" was simply: *"Il me faut du sucre pour souper."* (I must have sugar for our supper.) He always spoke to me in French. With these words he made his exit, slamming the door behind him. In a very short time the commanding officer's orderly appeared upon the scene with the official message that I was released from arrest, the Major having ascertained that no blame could be attached to me, and that he requested me to resume my duties. With the orderly came Romanoff and received the sugar.

After the French peddler, Magentie, whom we have left wounded under the care of our surgeon in a previous chapter, had recovered, he resolved to abandon, for a time at least, his lucrative trading with the camp, partly because he had lost his oxen and cart, which latter we found burned to cinders, partly because the Apaches made traveling through the surrounding country, and especially through the Huachuca Pass, very unsafe. We received all our forage (corn, either on cobs or shelled) from Mr. Warner, a contractor, living in Santa Cruz. He was an American, about 60 years of age, a mason by trade, and had erected all the buildings constituting Fort Yuma in 1858. Thence he had drifted to Arizona, settled near Calabazas at first, and "when the country broke up" had moved across the boundary to the small Mexican town of Santa Cruz, where he began farming, erected a small flouring mill, raised cattle, and kept a small store. He became engaged in freighting between the port of Guaymas and Herscmillo (sic), now the capital of the Mexican State of Sonora, and thence to Tucson. This latter place was supplied with many goods by that route, the distance being fully one hundred miles shorter than from the harbor of San Pedro, the shipping port of Los Angeles, Cal.

Mr. Warner had married a Mexican widow in Santa Cruz, the mother of as beautiful a sixteen-year-old girl as one might see in a hundred days' travel. Further mention will be made of this family presently.

The corn was freighted to our camp in heavy prairie schooners, pulled each by four yoke of oxen, driven by strong and fearless Texans with enormous whips, called "blacksnakes," which these sturdy drivers handled with great dexterity and, I am sorry to say, accompanied by a great profusion of profanity, especially where the route lay over a steep grade or heavy sand. For greater safety these trains were escorted by several well-armed laborers and house servants of Mr. Warner, and sometimes by himself.

All grain furnished to Camp Wallen in that year, 1866-'67, was contracted for at the rate of six-and-a-half cents in gold coin (greenbacks stood at seventy-five cents per pound). The hay was also provided by a contract then held by Messrs. Capron & Aguivre, who received forty-eight dollars in gold coin per ton of two thousand pounds; this was a very "fat" contract, the grass being abundant all over the region, the only expense being the cutting and hauling over a distance not exceeding three miles. We must, however, take into consideration that some risk was involved in the business, on account of the insecurity of life and property.

THE CENTURY PLANT

When Magentie had recovered from his wounds he accompanied the wagons of Mr. Warner on their return to Santa Cruz, and there formed a small company of Mexicans for the purpose of establishing a distillery of mescal, an establishment called by them *vinatería*. The mescal, a fiery liquor, is distilled from an agave plant, called by the Mexicans *maguey,* as well as by the Indians. To us it is known as the century plant, because it was formerly supposed to bloom only once in a hundred years; while the actual, now well-known fact is that this agave sends forth a tall stem from its center, as soon as it has reached its full growth, which in its wild or uncultivated state it attains in about five or six years. This stem reaches within a few months a hight (sic) of about fifteen feet, and extends then from its top and upper end numerous branches carrying yellowish blossoms, which within a short time become seed capsules containing each several well-separated compartments filled with flat, black seeds, tightly fitting against each other. The plant having now fulfilled its duty demanded by nature, begins to decay, and is soon a mass of rotting leaves, under which innumerable small plants propagated by nature appear on the surface and begin their existence in their turn. The seed capsules having burst open and the seeds distributed by the wind in every direction, the whole country of southern Arizona and Sonora is very prolific in the production of this plant, which is found on all the innumerable knolls and foothills surrounding Camp Wallen.

Magentie established his mescal ranch on the edge of a small mountain creek running between the foothills about six miles northwest of the post. Of course, the distillery was an illicit undertaking, and might have been objected to by our post commander on several lawful grounds; but inasmuch as the article was good and cheap liquor, and the sale of it was limited to the sutler of the camp by fearful threats of punishment, should Magentie or his people even attempt to dispose of it to the soldiers without a written permit, it was tolerated. In those days the United States revenue officer, or marshall, if he existed at all, was located in the then [Territorial] capital of Prescott, about four hundred miles away, and never dreamt of visiting our part of the country.

The liquor called mescal is manufactured in the following manner, first observed by me at Magentie's establishment: The agave plants, upon reaching their full growth, but before the stem starts, are cut off with axes or the long, heavy, Mexican knives called *machetes,* just above the roots; the long thorny leaves, attaining a hight (sic) of about three to four feet in the uncultivated maguey, are then chopped off, leaving a more or less round ball like a cabbage-head. These are left on the spot to be gathered either by a cart or by donkeys and transported to the mescal ranch on the creek. Here there is a large underground oven, in which the heads are well baked. While undergoing this process they become soft and develop a great deal of juice resembling and tasting not unlike molasses. In this state the agave plant forms a good article of diet if eaten in moderation. It can be pressed, dried, and kept for future use, and our men found a great supply of it when they surprised an Apache ranchería later on.

Near the oven there is a cellar-like room, which must have an abso-lutely watertight roof, as the smallest amount of water mingled with mescal either in process of manufacture or in its finished state will turn mescal sour in a very short time. In this room there are rows of rawhides fastened in the form of sacks to cross poles resting upon forked upright sticks.

When the plant is thoroughly baked, in which state it is readily plucked to pieces, it is placed in these rawhide vats; fermentation soon sets in, and after some days it is ready to undergo the process of distilling applied in some form or other in the manufacture of all spiritous liquors by means of a copper snake called by the Mexicans *alambique,* which is the only article of foreign manufacture needed in the production of mescal, all other appliances being handmade from the material on hand. Much care must be taken towards preventing the smoky taste often acquired by the liquor through overhaste. Good mescal is quite colorless and forms a fine, sparkling bead when poured into a tumbler; its taste resembles that of brandy distilled from prunes. Of course, it improves with age.

The mescal ranch of Magentie was very small and primitive in its appointments, yet these answered the purpose. Later on, while traveling in Mexico, I had the opportunity of visiting the manufacturing plants of the celebrated mescal of Tequila, the best, by far, in the market. The process there employed is essentially the same as described, although the appliances were modern and on a much larger scale. The agave is there cultivated in large fields irrigated by immense ditches; its leaves attain a hight (sic) of fifteen feet and more, and the mescal heads are, of course, proportionately large, having to be cut into four or sometimes eight pieces for convenient handling and transport.

A PROJECTED VISIT TO OLD MEXICO

In my position as quartermaster and commissary sergeant of the camp, which was no sinecure by any means, I had to receive and check the grain and hay as fast as these articles were delivered by the contractors, to issue all clothing, rations, forage, horse medicines, etc. Besides, it devolved upon me to "run" the bakery, blacksmith, butcher, and carpenter shops, keep an account of all the material used therein, and to make out all the monthly returns, with their corresponding abstracts and many vouchers. This latter part of my work was more tedious than difficult, because at first we had very few blanks, and these had all to be ruled by hand, in accordance with the forms prescribed by the army regulations. Sometimes I had a clerk, more often none.

Being in almost constant touch with the contractors it will be readily understood that I soon became well acquainted with Mr. Warner, the grain contractor, who repeatedly invited me to visit him at his home in Santa Cruz. I was well aware of two facts: First, that no man in the service of the United States army was allowed to go beyond the boundary line without the written permission (furlough for instance) of the general commanding the Division, in my case that of the Pacific; I also knew that I could not absent myself for any length of time without running the risk that things might get "mixed up" during my absence, because the quartermaster left all the business to me, he being frequently absent with scouting and escorting parties, and had besides the duties of adjutant, company commander, etc., to perform.

However, I had heard so much from the teamsters of the grain wagons and from Marigildo of the beauty and graces of Miss Eulalia, Mr. Warner's step-daughter, that I was very anxious to make her acquaintance. Please to remember that I was only twenty-two years of age at that time, that I was considered goodlooking in those days, and that I had been an ardent admirer of feminine beauty ever since I could remember. Add to this a healthy physique, a superabundance of vitality and a poetic vein, and you will readily understand that the wish to see her began to gain upon me from day to day. There was still another inducement for me to make this visit: Mr. Warner had intimated to me that he had several fine saddle horses at Santa Cruz, from which I could take my pick and accept, as a token of his good will and friendship, the one I might choose. Mr. Mendoza, who had relatives at Santa Cruz, and was very willing to accompany me, also told me of the loveliness of Miss Eulalia, and said that Mr. Warner had among his horses a black gelding that was a "love of a horse." By this time I had not only learned to ride quite well, but had become very fond of horses. The idea, at first entertained, to go with the ox teams for safety, was soon abandoned, as these teams, even without a load, took three days for a trip and could not return with new loads of grain short of about two weeks. After several discussions with our sutler, my friend, Mr. Leslie B. Wooster, and with Mendoza, we resolved to go together, making a night trip for greater safety, provided the commanding officer would give me the required leave.

I doubt very much that Major Brown knew of the aforesaid provision in the army regulations prohibiting any member of the United States army going across the boundary without the specified leave. At all events, he did not mention the circumstances when I applied for his permission to make the trip, and I did not feel compelled to do so on my part. He graciously gave me permission to go and stay away three days, more or less.

The route to Santa Cruz lay for about twelve miles over the foothills extending in a southwesterly direction from the camp to the foot of the Huachuca range of mountains, about where the present Fort Huachuca stands. Here we entered into a long, tortuous canyon called the Huachuca Pass, about twelve miles long, which took us to the farther side of the mountains, where a gentle descent brought us to the ruins of an old adobe building, the remnants of an old Mexican sheep rancho, then generally called San Rafael Ranch. This ruin, rebuilt in modern American style, is now the residence of the cattle king, Mr. Cameron, who acquired and extended by purchase the lands appertaining to the old Spanish land grant, recognized by the United States land courts, known as the "San Rafael de la Zanja" land grant. About 1,000 yards south of this old ruin stood the monument, a pyramid of natural stones with a marked pole protruding from its apex, which marked the boundary line. (This boundary line has been rectified lately, and the former crude monuments replaced by structures of cast iron.) Hence there was all hard, level ground over "mesa" land for about ten miles, at the end of which one descended into the valley of the Santa Cruz River and entered the little town of the same name, our destination.

Wooster, Mendoza and I, all well-mounted and well-armed, had prudently selected the dark hours of night for our trip. Mendoza knew every foot of the road, and, having started from Wallen about 6 p.m., of a lovely September evening, we arrived without accident at the old ranch about midnight. Here we dismounted, partly to rest our horses, to water them later on and partly to sleep a few hours, as we did not wish to enter the town before daylight. We rubbed our horses down, picketed them near by, spread our saddle blankets against a wall of the house, and two of us prepared for sleeping, while Wooster made a little fire inside the walls to cook some coffee. But there was no sleep to be had. We had hardly lain down when we seemed to be alive with vermin, mostly fleas — fleas in squads, platoons, companies, battalions, regiments, brigades, divisions, and whole army corps! That was under our clothing. We were soon made aware, however, that our outer surfaces were not to be neglected; all sorts of bugs began to crawl over us, big bugs, small bugs; Wooster killed within ten minutes two scorpions and a centipede, which, probably, attracted by the heat of the fire, came crawling out from the chinks and crevices of the old cracked walls; soon another army, seemingly allies to the flea forces, came to attack us. Already the skirmishers were coming, and how well they shot! They never made a miss, and each shot was accompanied by a buzzing not unlike that made by a distant shell traversing the air. They were musketos (sic); they understood their business, and they did it like experts.

There being no possibility of escaping our tormentors, we resolved unanimously that it was far better to arrive in Santa Cruz during the night in presentable condition, even though we should awaken the inhabitants from a peaceful slumber, than to arrive in daylight with our physiognomies so punctured as to give us the appearance of runaways from a smallpox hospital or pesthouse.

We saddled up quickly, and after an easy canter of about an hour, arrived at the outskirts of the town, where we awoke an indefinite number of dogs, that gave tongue forthwith.

Mendoza having relatives living near by, branched off towards their lodgings, before we had fairly reached the interior of the village, after indicating to us the direction we were to take in order to reach Mr. Warner's dwelling, where we were to stop, and to meet him, Mendoza, during the day. He added some more or less lucid explanations which we only partly understood, he speaking Spanish only. We had, however, no apprehension as to our ability of (sic) finding Mr. Warner's house, as he was by far the most prominent inhabitant and property holder of Santa Cruz. The town itself was small, although many houses and huts were scattered about on the outskirts. When Wooster and I reached what seemed to be about the middle of the town I approached a house and shouted "Hello!" We dared not dismount, because by this time we were surrounded by a steadily-increasing lot of yelping, snarling curs, the like of which I have never seen anywhere before or since, except in the streets of Constantinople. After repeating my call several times, a door at last was opened and a man stuck out his head cautiously, asking:

"What do you want?"

"I want to go to Mr. Warner's house," I answered in my best Spanish. (I had learned a good deal of this language by this time, but unfortunately not the peculiar expression required in this case.)

"Where did you say?" inquired the man at the door; "to whose house?"

I repeated the name distinctly: "el Señor Warner."

"There is no such person in this town," said the old man, and slammed the door to.

We rode a little farther, restraining with difficulty our horses, made restless by the snarling dogs, and came to the church against which leaned another smaller building that we took to be the priest's or sexton's habitation. After "helloing" without any result for some time, I spurred my horse through the bunch of canines and rode up to the door near enough to reach it with the butt of my revolver, with which I gave several hardy knocks. The door soon opened, showing the features of an old woman, still half asleep, who looked at me as if I were a phantom. Upon my very polite request to be shown the habitation of Mr. Warner, she shook her head and said there was no such person in the whole village.

"See here," said Wooster, who was at no time remarkable for great patience, "Mendoza said it was a very long house, with a large entrance gate in the middle and a corral on either end. Let us look for it ourselves."

And indeed, we soon came upon a building that answered this description. There was the long house with an ample portal in the middle, a cattle corral on its left, and a horse corral on its right. It had now begun to dawn, and between the bars of the gate we saw a boy carrying some sticks toward a rear building. We hailed him and he came to the gate, but to our inquiry for Mr. Warner he looked blank and said he knew no such person.

Wooster was just beginning some remarks with the purport that we had come to a town of lunatics, or idiots, or both, when a wooden shutter near the gate opened in the wall and an intelligent looking young man said: "Good day, gentlemen; are you looking for Don Solomon? Are you from Babocomari; the fort, I mean?"

With a great sigh of relief I answered: "Yes, sir, we are from the fort at Babocomari, and are looking for Mr. Warner."

"That's he, that's Don Solomon," said he; "I will be with you in a minute."

So this was the secret that solved the riddle of our unsuccessful search for Mr. Warner's house. I may as well explain it fully for the benefit of

such of my readers that may visit Mexico. In all Spanish-speaking countries a person is always addressed in conversation and mentioned among
the townspeople by his given or baptismal name, with the prefix Don
for a man, and Doña for a lady. Thus Mr. Solomon Warner was in all
Santa Cruz known only as Don Solomon, the more so as the word "Warner" in Spanish is absolutely unpronounceable, there being no "W" in
the Spanish language, and the short slurred end syllable "er" never occurs.
Whenever a Mexican attempts to say Warner, he will invariably pronounce
unless specialy (sic) drilled, Guarna; my friend Wooster to them was
either Busta or Gusta; the small town of Willcox, on the Southern Pacific
Railway, they spell and write, (sic) is not specially taught otherwise,
Guilcoques; all of which creates much merriment and confusion in the
postoffices of the Southern frontier.

To return to our story. The Mexican appeared quickly at the gate,
which he opened for us. With a whip he soon dispersed the dogs, and we
rode into the yard. He introduced himself as Pedro Urguides, the mayordomo or general overseer of Mr. Warner, and said that my uniform led
him at once to suppose that we were from the fort. Being told that we
had come on a friendly visit, he became at once a fair example of personified hospitality. He clapped his hands violently together, not, as we
at first supposed, as an expression of glad welcome, but as a call for the
aforesaid boy, who came at once to take charge of our horses. Then Pedro
took us to a room with two cots, very simply furnished, but very clean,
brought water, towels, a crystal bottle of sparkling mescal with glasses,
a plate of oranges and a box of cigars. Then he left us with the words:
"Gentlemen, I leave you to your repose; you are very welcome; this
house is yours. I do not like to awake Mr. Warner, as he arrived from
Yenuris only a few hours ago, but you will meet at breakfast, to which
I shall take pleasure in calling you."

Wooster and I, being both tired, did not engage in much conversation. We ate an orange, and took a drink; then we lay down and soon
fell asleep. Once, it seemed to me that I was awakened by Wooster talking. I sat up in bed and said: "Wooster, were you talking to me?"

He made no answer, so I turned over and was about falling asleep
once more when I heard him mutter distinctly: "Eulalia, Eulalia, Eulalia!"

"The devil!" said I to myself, "I begin to see a nigger in the woodpile."

It was about 8 o'clock when a gentle knock at the door caused us
to rise from our beds, and presently the genial features of Mr. Warner
appeared within. He bade us a very hearty welcome in the generous, off-
hand way which endeared him to all that ever met him. We had a hearty
laugh together upon the cold reception we had received from the few
townspeople we had met during the early hours. Mr. Warner was highly

amused at our astonishment we could not help to express that he, the foremost man in the town, was an unknown quantity in it, even in his own house, and we solemnly declared that he should be henceforth Don Solomon to us as well as to Santa Cruz. I never called him by any other name from that day, and when, thirty-three years later, he died in my arms at Tucson, Arizona, in September, 1899, I bade him good-by forever with the words: "Don Solomon, my dear old friend, I thank you for all your kindness, for your friendship through these many years; you are going to enjoy the well-earned, peaceful, eternal rest."

Mendoza joined us at breakfast, and he also laughed heartily at our misadventure, which he, above all men, could have prevented, had he been more thoughtful. The breakfast was served by a middle-aged woman, assisted by a *mozo* (boy of all work), who was no other than the wood carrier whom we had addressed through the gate. Only now he was washed and combed and wore a clean shirt. Mr. Warner said that the women folk would put in an appearance later, after they had "fixed up some," and he gave orders to hitch up his traveling carriage, a vehicle resembling somewhat an army ambulance on the exterior, so that we might take a ride along the river after we had looked the town over. He had business to attend to, which admitted of no delay, but said he would join us later. He put us under the guidance of one Mr. Brown, who, besides Mr. Warner and his clerk, was the only American then living in Santa Cruz, and was a subcontractor. We found Mr. Brown a very clever, jolly fellow of middle age, a frontiersman from top to toe, fond of a good glass, a good story and very fond of the royal game of poker.

We first visited Mr. Warner's small store, which was situated in another block or cluster of houses. His stock of goods was very limited, indeed, consisting mainly of such articles as poor people need for daily use in those countries in isolated places. The store was for the most part kept up as an accommodation for the comparatively many people employed by Mr. Warner, and their families. The clerk was an old-fashioned, quiet German of advanced age, named Henry Dietrich, at home, but known in those parts as "Dutch Henry" by the Americans, and by the Mexicans, of course, as "Don Enrique." We had to take a glass with him as a welcome drink and several more as a sign of good fellowship, and then one more for the Fatherland. He was indeed a very good-natured man, somewhat slow and methodical in all he did, and as a salesman in an American store would probably not have been considered a shining light, but in the sphere in which he moved, he filled the bill completely, and kept the accounts of Mr. Warner as to goods purchased from, amounts paid and balances due to mercantile houses in clear American booking, while he kept at the same time a separate account book for the Mexican people and employees in a peculiar fashion. This latter, although then in use at every small Mexican store and by every one who employed the illiterate class of Mexicans as teamsters, herders or laborers, is now becoming obsolete, and as I hold it to be of some interest I shall here describe it. It combines great simplicity with undeniable clearness, and was therefore just the thing to be used in dealing with people who could neither write nor read, but could readily figure out their accounts with this system and have at all times a clear understanding as to their financial status with their employers.

Whenever a man or woman (the latter as cooks or washerwomen only) entered anyone's employ they received a paper as follows, called a *vale*. Of course, the writing was in Spanish:

Vale of A. B. — Comm'd work Stpt. —, 1866, at —— per diem.

Paid _____

Days _____

Whenever the holder of this paper desired to draw money or goods from the store or from his employer anywhere, he was charged as follows: X for $10, V for $5, O for $1, U for one-half dollar, + for one shilling, and ⊥ for one-half shilling. (The horizontal lines represent the long horizontal line following the word Paid.) Every Saturday night or Sunday morning the holder would bring his paper to the *patrón* (boss), clerk or *mayordomo* and say: *Ráyame* (Mark me the time). Upon this the latter would mark the days and half days by perpendicular lines, crossing the horizontal line for a whole day and stopping at it for a half day. Thereupon the holder would receive his vale back, which he generally carried in a bit of rawhide or buckskin, doubled like a book, or leave with his family if he worked at a distance. The store would keep a page corresponding to each vale in a book, and in this manner both the employer and employee could figure out in a moment, each in his way, how the account stood. (After I left the army I was frequently so situated as to be compelled to use this system, and I found that it was quite practical.)

Very frequently the balance in those days was on the side of the employer, resulting from the fact that many Mexicans were allowed to overdraw their accounts, sometimes to quite a large extent. I have known some working at twenty-five cents a day who were indebted to their employers in sums which they could never, and never expected to pay. Especially was this the case with good house servants, who in course of time came to be considered as members of the family, with good workmen, and with expert horse and cattlemen. The employer had then for his protection the now abolished so-called peon law, which gave him the right to pursue, arrest, and bring to the whipping-post any absconder.

A TYPICAL MEXICAN CITY

After a while we left the store and sauntered through the town, and surely I thought at first that I was back in a small village of Palestine. Very few men were in the street, and all of these wore neither socks nor shoes, but in their stead homemade sandals of rawhide fastened by strings passing inside of the big toe and over the ankle; their whole vestment consisted of a pair of wide, blue or white cotton trousers held in place by a leather string, and a more or less clean calico shirt, a handerchief around the neck and a very broad-rimmed, coarse straw hat. Tied in a corner of the neckerchief they carried a little tobacco and cigaret paper, or rather cornhusks shaped into small oblong pieces; in another corner of the same they carried a flint, a piece of steel and some rotten wood or punk for tinder to strike fire with; few of them had matches.

The women, all of more or less dark-complexion, had fine, dark eyes; they wore a calico skirt of gaudy colors and a white chemise. Their heads were covered by a bluish cotton shawl with fringes, called a "rebozo." This article of dress was allowed to come well over the face, barely allowing the eyes to exercise their function, and falling over their shoulders. Few of them wore stockings or shoes, but nearly all carried upon their heads either a large round vessel of earthenware called an *olla,* which is generally used as a receptacle for water, or else a smaller vessel called a *cajete,* which resembles a kettle with a round bottom, and which they used to cook their beans in and also to carry the meals to their husbands working in the fields. Their walk and erect carriage strike everyone at once as being very graceful.

The houses, all built of adobe, were of one story, and had flat mud roofs, resting upon sticks of the decayed giant cactus, or upon reeds when obtainable. There was not a cooking-stove in the whole town, nor a sewing machine. The poorer people simply cooked their scanty meals in earthen bowls upon a small hearth of adobe or upon the ground between some stones, baking their flat paper bread, called "tortillas," upon a sheet of tin supported over the fire. Their chief article of diet were the red or pink beans of the country and at times a stew of beef or mutton; all their food is well seasoned (much over-seasoned to our taste) with the hot red pepper that everybody cultivates. Spoons we saw in use at a few houses, principally large wooden spoons for kitchen use; but we looked in vain for knives and forks, except such knives as are adapted to general use. Here the tortillas came quite handy; they are really a large, thin, flat cake, which being pliable in every direction is used as a scoop with which the food is taken up and carried to the mouth and is finally eaten after it has rendered the services of a spoon.

There was no cooking-stove at Mr. Warner's either, but a glance into the kitchen allowed me to observe that one whole side was taken up by a hearth of adobes and that besides many earthen vessels there were frying pans, stew-pans, kettles and pots, Dutch ovens, and, in short, a good assortment of the modern appliances.

And this brings me to the dinner and — Miss Eulalia. We had been looked up by Pedro, the *mayordomo,* or house steward, who found us about 2 p.m., and informed us that dinner was ready.

We were received at the door by Mrs. Warner, dressed in heavy silk, and wearing a splendid silk shawl with heavy fringes. These shawls, very much in use then in Mexico, were nearly all cream-colored and carried beautiful hand-made embroideries in silk, worked in large flower patterns in their natural colors. Many of them were heirlooms, and worth a great deal of money for their intrinsic value alone. She introduced us to two ladies of uncertain age, her sisters, and to an aged lady, her mother, and last of all to her daughter, Eulalia, then in her sixteenth year. To say that this girl was beautiful is saying nothing. She was simply divine; of that most beautiful Mexican type which carries with it a perfectly clear light olive complexion, slightly tinged with rose upon the well-rounded cheeks, large, dark, liquid eyes, finely moulded forehead and arched eyebrows, luxurious, dark eyelashes, and hair held together upon the back of her shapely head by a high tortoise-shell comb mounted in gold filigree, and an exquisitely-shaped mouth, whose upper lip formed a perfect Cupid's bow. Her form also was perfect; she was a little over medium hight (sic) and, being the child of sunny clime, all her charms were fully developed. She was dressed in a simple white gown of a clinging material and cut out in front just enough to show her beautiful throat, which looked like chiseled alabaster or, rather, ivory. Over her finely-shaped head she had pinned a Spanish mantilla of white lace, a diaphanous fabric that fell over her shoulders in graceful transparent waves, under which her rosy small ears were perceptible. When she acknowledged our presence with a slight bow and a graceful smile, two rows of perfect pearls appeared between her cherry lips. All the ladies wore, alas, a profusion of jewelry; this is unfortunately the custom of all Spanish-American ladies, even of the refined classes. Mrs. Warner seated us with the request that we might waive all ceremony, as we were friends of her husband and hence of the family, and would kindly excuse all shortcomings.

As to the dishes served, I will only say that they did honor to the best cooking known, in variety as well as in their preparation, and Mr.

Warner uncorked several brands of fine imported Burgundy. But the dinner as a social function would have appeared to any American lady, and especially young lady a very tame and ceremonial affair. According to the Mexican custom of those days (which prevails to a great extent now) the ladies spoke very little during the whole meal, leaving the burden of conversation to us men, who, I regret to say, carried on the conversation in English, against all polite custom and etiquette generally observed on like occasions, although we knew that not one of the ladies spoke or even understood the English language. Miss Eulalia sat opposite to me, and I had, therefore, every opportunity of observing how beautiful her hands were in shape and texture, and could feast my eyes with her graceful ways. She seemed, however, to be exceedingly modest, hardly ever lifting her eyes fully to mine, except when I addressed a few Spanish words to her. Then she would look up for a moment, answer politely, and again let her eyelids hide those magnificent orbs I was so anxious to fathom. The ladies merely nipped at their silver goblets, while Pedro, who acted as butler, kept ours constantly replenished. After the dinner, which lasted about half an hour, we all went together into an adjacent parlor to take our coffee. A harp was standing against the wall, and Miss Eulalia regaled us with a few pieces of music, closing the performance, at the request of her mother, with a mild love song, during the rendition of which she did not at all appear to be at ease. Poor, sweet bird, she had not yet tried her wings! Having lived heretofore in great seclusion, she was not accustomed to sing or play before company, especially male company.

For the better understanding of my readers I wish to mention here that a well-brought-up Mexican girl, whether she had any educational advantages or not, whether she be of rich or poor family, is never allowed to be in company with men without the presence of her mother or other female relative, who act as chaperones. She is taught modesty and reticence at all times; she is not permitted to walk, ride, or drive alone with any young man not her brother, even though she may be engaged to marry him, and the whole family would be thunderstruck with horror, were her lover, aye, even her promised future husband, to attempt to kiss her. Hence a Mexican courtship is generally short, as it is void of those blissful hours so dear to our sweet American girls.

There is never any lack of mothers, married sisters, grandmothers, aunts or other female relatives who will kindly offer, or, rather, intrude their company, when you take your Mexican sweetheart to a ball, a circus, a picnic, a ride-out, or a full fight. They are, like the poor, "always with us." This, in our eyes, singular custom has two good reasons: In the first place, a girl who would be allowed to enjoy any of the enumerated pleasures, though in a perfectly innocent manner, without the escort of an elderly female relative, or who would hold a secret interview with her lover, would, upon these facts becoming known, from that moment lose caste, because she would offend a long-established custom which is frequently more forceful than a written law. In the next place, it must be remembered that a woman's chastity is not protected, as with us. The laws, indeed, exist for the purpose, very similar to ours, but in this particular they are almost a dead letter. Hence an injured girl, who, perhaps by reason of her constant chaperonage and ceaseless surveillance, was too innocent of the threatening danger, would be the easy, unprotected victim of the first unscrupulous man with evil intentions. Therefore, the frequent saying in Mexico: "South of the line (boundary) we must look out for our girls, north of the line for our boys;" meaning by the latter part of this sentence that their youngsters must be very careful how they infringe upon the laws of morality in the United States, where a woman is nobly guarded and protected.

In a future paper I intend to say more about the uncomfortable state, sometimes bordering on frenzy, in which an honorable loving courtship is apt to keep one on account of the strict rules which render an intimate interview, so dear to all lovers (being the very essence of joyful bliss) next to impossible. As I married a Mexican girl of good family myself, I know exactly "how it is myself," the more so she belonged to a family containing more elderly female members than any I have known before or since.

Under these circumstances it will be readily understood that Miss Eulalia could not be approached except in a relative's presence. In fact, I heard later on during the day that on account of her being constantly under her mother's wing, so to speak, she was known in the whole town as *la pollita* (the little chick) and in course of time (of which more hereafter) I was always mentioned as "el Sargento de la pollita" (the Sergeant of the little chick). I soon understood the situation, and saw that Wooster must be already acquainted with this Mexican custom of chaperonage, although he had not mentioned it to me, for reasons easily imagined. However, eyes may speak and so may indirect insinuations, and from various indications I soon perceived that Miss Eulalia was not altogether indifferent to my more than modest advances when during the evening Mrs. Warner gave a small dance in our honor, to which a few señoritas were invited and at which, of course, a large contingent of watchful female relatives attended. When we retired I was as much in love with Miss Eulalia as any young man ever was with a beautiful maiden.

On the following morning we were up quite early, and I heard Mr. Warner's voice in the yard giving orders to keep in certain horses. Soon after he called me and pointing to a bunch of horses in the corral, said: "Here, pick one out; you know I promised to give you one." They were all good saddle horses, but I began looking at once for the black gelding that Mendoza had mentioned to me, and soon found him. He was, indeed, a beautiful animal of middling hight, (sic) young, clean-limbed, with a glossy black coat, long, flowing tail and mane, and perfectly gentle. They called him *Tinto* (the ink or black one). I patted him on the back and stroked his fine neck, whereupon he actually "made up to me" in the manner of affectionate horses, and looked at me with his beautiful clear eyes.

"May I have this one?" I asked Mr. Warner.

"Well," he said, somewhat hesitatingly, as I thought, "yes, I think you may; in fact, yes, you may. We will have an early breakfast, and then you can try him. He is very easy in the saddle; Eulalia rides him often; he is quite gentle. Pedro, saddle up Tinto after breakfast for the Sergeant." Then he went into the house.

"All right, sir," said Pedro, but not cheerfully, as I thought.

In the meantime Mendoza had joined us, and I saw him hold some conversation apart with Pedro, during which they both seemed looking at the horse and at me in turns. Presently Mendoza stepped up to me and said: "You have selected the black horse, I understand, and, of course, I do not blame you; but I just found out that Miss Eulalia has constantly ridden him of late, and has become very fond of him."

I felt very, very sorry, and immediately proceeded towards the house to tell Mr. Warner that I retracted my choice, and under the circumstances I could not think of accepting Tinto, when he, Mr. Warner, and Eulalia and her two aunts came towards me. I began immediately to explain my total ignorance as to the young lady's predilection for the horse, and begged that she would not think for a moment I could be capable of so discourteous an act as to deprive her of her favorite saddle horse. I had, however, hardly finished my somewhat lengthy apology when she smiled sweetly and said: "I am so glad you like my horse; he is so gentle. Please take him; papa wishes it, and I desire it; but treat him well, be good to him, be kind to him; see how well he knows me and how well he repays kindness." She walked towards him and the horse came to meet her and — kissed her, as well and as plainly a horse may be said to perform that act of affection. Happy horse!

I felt like a thief, and began to argue with all the Spanish in my power that the thing could not be thought of, that I could not for a moment entertain the idea of depriving a lady —

But she interrupted me with the question uttered somewhat haughtily, and with her beautiful eyes looking straight at me: "May a gentleman refuse a lady's gift? It is not so with us. You must take him, and sometimes, when you ride him, think of . . . Santa Cruz and . . . us. You see we have so many more horses. Please say no more; take him, accept him from . . . from . . . me."

Don Solomon said nothing; he looked away and smiled; I think he rather liked it. I bowed low and uttered a profusion of thanks. But Eulalia's mother looked at her child, her innocent, modest, reticent child, with a look of such utter astonishment, not to say horror, that I expected her to burst out presently with: "Well, I never!"

The breakfast following this making-over of Tinto into my possession was much less ceremonious, less constrained, and more animated than the dinner had been on the previous day. We were becoming acquainted, and I was especially astonished at the rapidity with which I seemed to develop an easy fluency in this melodious language which from the lips of the beautiful girl sounded like heavenly harmony. I was never known for immoderate bashfulness, and the dawning happiness that I thought I saw looming up in the horizon made me very mirthful.

Wooster, however, was silent. He looked gloomy.

After breakfast I mounted Tinto and rode him for a couple of hours up the valley along the river bordered by splendid cottonwood trees. The horse had a very easy gait, walking or cantering, and I soon discovered that he was an exceptionally fine pacer. I remember today how beautiful everything looked to me that morning; I was brimful of happiness, bursting with the mere joy of living; I seemed to be in love not only with Eulalia, but also with Tinto, with the river, with the sky, with the trees!

When I returned I thanked the young lady once more for her generous present. She answered nothing, but she gave me one look from those wonderful eyes that said more than words could express.

However, I am not writing a sentimental novel, and we will hear nothing more of Eulalia (except in a short incident, presently to be related of Miss Warner) until the last chapter of this true narrative. Of course, I tried, before saying good-by to see her for one moment alone, were it only to press my lips for one short moment upon her beautiful hand. But it was not to be; there were too many female relatives who, each and every one, considered herself a self-appointed guardian of my treasure.

Mr. Warner told me where I was to find my friends, and said he would join us later on. The gay trio, consisting of Wooster, Brown, and Mendoza, I found under a large fig tree full of ripe fruit in a beautiful, shady garden appertaining to a Mr. Fernandez, who kept a small grocery and liquor shop combined at the outskirts of the town. With this gentleman my friends had already become sufficiently acquainted to call him Don Alfonso. It seemed to me upon approaching that the company was some-

what hilarious, the anon gloomy Wooster not excepted. The cause of this
hilarity I soon found to be the contents of a new tin bucket which was
standing at their feet and from which they dipped with large foot tumblers
a very rich-looking, aromatic creamy liquid, apparently to the utter satisfaction of the concrete and abstract being. They offered me some at once.
I tasted and drank, and drank and tasted — was I in my senses or was I
under the spell of a benevolent bacchanalian power? It was eggnog, and
very good eggnog at that. The incongruity of the thing, to find the delicious
American eggnog in the small Mexican town of Santa Cruz incited me to
uncontrollable mirth, and we were soon a merry crowd indeed. At Wallen
we had neither eggs, nor milk, nor nutmeg. Here these articles were to be
had fresh and in plenty, and Don Alfonso kept a very fine article of mescal,
which we all preferred to the brandy he offered at first. I am afraid to say
how much of this delicious drink we imbibed in the next two hours. I know
when we came to settle, the bill was $11, an almost unheard-of-sum in
those surroundings for the articles consumed, be they in ever such quantity.
We were, however, too happy to ask for details or items, but paid. I only
asked our host if these articles were so scarce in Santa Cruz, to which he
replied: "No Señor, but sutlers and quartermaster-sergeants of the U. S. A.
are scarce here." I understood later on that ever since our visit to Santa
Cruz eggnog was called there "Leche de Babocomari" (Babocomari milk).

Soon after 2 p.m. Mr. Warner arrived while we were engaged in the
rendering of the beautiful song: "We won't go home till morning," to
which he listened with apparent great satisfaction while his lively eyes
twinkled, probably in remembrance of his youthful days.

He told us dinner was waiting, and gave us the kindest good-by messages from the ladies, who, he said, had suddenly been called away to
San Lazaro, a farm nine miles distant, where still another sister of Mrs.
Warner had been suddenly taken ill. Thus I would not be able to say
good-by to my angel; Santa Cruz had no more charms for me just then;
but what was that? As we were saddling up in the yard towards evening
preparatory to our return trip, I saw little Carmelita making signs to me
from behind the kitchen door. This little maiden was a much younger
half-sister to Eulalia, about twelve years of age, a lovely, very affectionate
child, who loved her elder sister passionately. I approached her unseen
and whispered: "What is it, my little dove?"

"Only this," she said, handing me a folded paper sealed with a wafer:
"Eulalia said to give you her 'adiós' and this paper, which contains a
pretty Spanish song. You know you asked for one."

I now remembered to have made that request, and thanked the little
child kindly, I stooped to kiss her on the forehead, but she offered me her

sweet little lips; I kissed them. "Once more," she said, "for her." Oh, you chaperones!

I kept that paper very carefully in my inmost pocket until our return to Wallen, upon which we started after very hearty leave-takings from Don Solomon, Mr. Brown, and "Dutch Henry."

We arrived home during the early hours of the morning, meeting with no accidents on the way, and never stopping a single moment at the "flea ranch."

As soon as I had set things to rights and reported my return to the officer of the day, I brought forth the little sealed packet. I have the paper before me now.

A free translation of it would be as follows:

GOOD-BY!
Good-by my dreams
Of happiness;
Of my sweet hope
The flower died.

Or lives it still?
Yes, for the memory
Of glorious joy
Can never fade.

This I believe
And ever shall;
May Heaven grant:
Forget me not.

I abstain from all comment upon these gentle words. My friend, Mr. Harrington, who had also learned considerable Spanish since our serenade episode, and who arrived at the office immediately after breakfast, admired them greatly; in about five minutes he had them by heart, in five minutes more he had brought his violin, and in three minutes by the clock he had composed an "aria" with variations.

I had to give him a detailed account of my trip, and did so cheerfully. Before him I had no secret, could not have had if I wished to, for our erstwhile superficial friendship had become as strongly knit as any brotherly love. He saw into the inmost recess of my heart, he saw I was happy, and it made him happy to see me thus.

But Wooster was my friend also. What about him? We shall see later.

About a month after my visit to Santa Cruz, in the first week of October, 1866, the traveling carriage of Mr. Warner, escorted by half a dozen mounted and well-armed Mexicans, drove into camp in the early morning hours. Among them I recognized at once Pedro Urquides, the *mayordomo* of Don Solomon, and upon my approach to the vehicle I saw this benevolent gentleman himself descending from it.

In the wagon, stretched upon a mattress, lay Mr. Oscar Buckalew (now living at Helvetia, Arizona,) with a leg shattered by a musket ball. He was then the mail rider who carried the United States mail from Calabazas to Tubac and thence to Patagonia, in the range of mountains bearing that name, where the so-called Mowry mines, located by Lt. Sylvester Mowry, had been operated about 1856, before the Apaches began their hostilities; although the country thereabouts was by then pretty well abandoned, a few mail stations were still maintained, and about three or four Americans with some Mexican laborers spasmodically worked these silver mines, generally believed to be quite rich, and turned out a few small silver bricks, or *planchas* from time to time. These small bricks bore the stamp of the mines, and from them the latter had received the Mexican appellation of the "plancha de plata" mine, under which it was quite well known.

The pure metal was extracted from the ore by grinding the rocks in a contrivance called an *arrastra* by means of a horizontal wheel turned by a horse, mule or donkey, while a man continually poured water around the axle of the wheel to soften the rock. The ground ore was then smelted in small crucibles. These mine workers lived in an old adobe house situated near by, to which access was had through a large, heavy gate that admitted a good-sized wagon and team into a spacious corral or yard.

As the mail arrived once a week at about the same hour on regular days, the Apaches knew the time when Mr. Buckalew would pass, and waylaid him in an "arroyo" or dry river bed. Although he received a severe wound, which shattered one kneecap, the mail carrier retained his seat in the saddle and his mule started on a run. Of this the men at the house knew nothing as yet, but Mr. Thomas Yerkes, who was at the gate on the lookout for the mail, thought he heard several shots; from his position, however, he could not see the road, as it made a sharp turn almost directly in front of the house, and thence led towards the left under a bulging rocky bank of considerable length.

The Apaches, knowing, from the thud of the bullet, fired according to their custom from ambush at short range, that they had hit either the man or his animal, attempted to cut them off from the house by taking a short cut over the hill. The shooting had taken place about a half mile distant from the house, and the mail rider arrived at the woodpile, about fifty yards from the gate, at about the same moment that the Indians debouched from over the ridge. No longer able to keep in the saddle Buckalew here fell off, pulled his revolver, and began firing. Yerkes and the blacksmith, Joe Lawson (Dawson?), now aware of the situation, rushed to the wounded man's assistance and succeeded in dragging him inside the gate at the very moment when the Apaches came in sight over the bluff. It was a very narrow escape, indeed.

There being no vehicle of any kind at the mines at the time, Buckalew had to wait two whole days before he could be transported and brought under medical care. Mr. Yerkes made a night trip to Santa Cruz, the nearest place where efficient help could be expected, and fortunately found Mr. Warner at home. This gentleman, ever ready to lend a helping hand to his fellow man, got his ambulance ready, summoned an escort, and thus Mr. Buckalew was brought to Wallen on the fourth day after he received his wound, which upon his arrival was found to be in a very inflamed and dangerous condition. Fortunately we had at Wallen by this time a very skillful surgeon, Maj. Bailey, who performed the amputation of the leg in a highly satisfactory manner and with ultimate good results.

PROVISIONING A SCOUTING PARTY

The commanding officer now thought that a scouting expedition was in order. He sent for Lieutenant Harrington and Marigildo, and consulted with the latter as to the feasibility of following up the Apaches, by taking up their tracks at the Patagonia mines. Marigildo thought well of the project, and said that he could guess very nearly the direction the Indians had taken, in all likelihood, as he had been with them over the same ground quite frequently, while he had been their captive; that probably they might be cut off somewhere at the extreme southern end of the Huachuca Mountains; but that the trailing of them from Patagonia, although more slow, would be more certain, as the rainy season was over and there existed no possibility of their tracks being obliterated, unless they did so themselves, a thing they seldom did, reducing the danger of being caught to almost a minimum by traveling faster than any horse could follow.

The men of the garrison being far from numerous, only twenty-five could be spared. These were, of course, more than sufficient to follow and punish, provided they caught them, a handful of Apaches; but what if they came suddenly upon a war party in the many intricate canyons abounding in the country? As Marigildo very correctly remarked: "When you go out hunting for Apaches you have in your mind's eye what you are going to do, but you can never know what you may be led into or what you are going to find. It is a very uncertain business."

The scouting party was made ready as well and as soon as circumstances would permit, and these circumstances were far from favorable. The rationing of the men for any protracted absence offered several difficulties. We had no hardtack, officially called dry bread. I am afraid to state how many requisitions, representations, and even remonstrances, had been forwarded from our camp with a view of obtaining this ration so eminently fitted for scouting parties; somehow the article was overlooked over and over again. In this emergency I had induced our baker, one Gilbert of Company "G," First U. S. Cavalry, to attempt the production in his bake-oven of something like a cracker that might answer the purpose; but notwithstanding his persistent efforts he had succeeded in turning out only a quantity of very small and very hard round disks that could be loaded into a cannon and used as grapeshot with good effect. They turned so hard within two days that they resisted mastication by the stoutest jaws and teeth, and proved insoluble even in boiling water. Those were not the days of canned meats either, and the only way to provision the scouting party with meat was either to give them pork or bacon, which we did not always have, or to provide the men with as much cooked meat as each man could carry individually. There were neither trained packers nor suitable pack animals at Camp Wallen at any time.

I had seen the scouting rations of the Mexican soldiers at Santa Cruz; they consisted of dried (jerked) beef or other meat, which will keep almost forever, *pinole,* and panocha, and answered the purpose very well, the more so as no cooking was involved and consequently no fires were needed. The dried or jerked beef is simply beef cut in long, narrow strips, rolled in a little salt and pepper, and dried in the sun. We could easily have prepared this scouting ration ourselves, if every available man at the camp had not been from morning till night employed as an adobe maker, an adobe turner, an adobe layer, a plasterer, carpenter, or builder of some sort.

The pinole is simply parched wheat or corn, ground to about the fineness of corn meal. Panocha is the dark brown Mexican sugar in small cakes, which, bitten or crushed into small pieces, is kept in the mouth while one drinks the pinole mixed in some water; this makes a palatable and at the same time nourishing drink. Lieutenant Harrington had made a requisition for these articles, setting forth the necessity, practicability, and urgency of their issue as scouting rations; but fully six months elapsed before the requisition had run through its red-tape course and we were provided with the first two articles, while we used brown sugar to take the place of the Mexican panocha.

At last the Patagonia scouting party was gotten under way, carrying as much cooked meat and soft bread as could be conveniently placed upon the saddles of the men. There was no need of carrying forage, the whole country at that season being in those days an immense region of rich pasture. Lieutenant Harrington was in command and Marigildo guided the party.

They found the tracks of the Apaches at the Patagonia mines without difficulty, and followed them fast enough, because Marigildo, at once divining the general direction the Indians had taken, knew how to lead without losing much time, as he always came upon the tracks again, even though there had been none visible for miles where the route lay over rocky hills. It led across the Santa Cruz-Wallen road, leaving the latter to the left and the former to the right, over the foothills on the south side of the Huachuca Mountains, at the eastern end of which they crossed the San Pedro River and headed towards the Dragoon Mountains; before reaching these, however, the trail led somewhat abruptly in a more easterly direction, and Marigildo then knew and said that the Indians were evidently going towards a place in the Chiricahua Mountains where they formerly always had a ranchería or at least a place of rendezvous for the coming together of smaller roving bands, and he recommended the greatest prudence, as our force was small and hiding places suitable for ambush were abundant.

I will say here and now, that Marigildo was an excellent Indian guide, knew all that country perfectly, even to the most hidden watering places (a very important matter in that dry region), and was an expert trailer of tracks; he also knew the wiles and stratagems of the Apaches, and would never have allowed his party to enter into a cul-de-sac or canyon where the soldiers might have been annihilated from inaccessible places on the surrounding ridges or where their exit might have been cut off, before thoroughly ascertaining from surrounding hights (sic) the security of the undertaking. His eyesight was almost marvelous in that respect. Besides having the responsibility of avoiding all disaster threatening the troops confided to his guidance, he also had a wholesome fear of falling into the hands of the Apaches alive, one or the other of whom, he had no doubt, would recognize him as having been their former captive, a surmise which proved to be entirely correct, as we shall presently see. Of course, if he could prevent it, he would never be taken alive by them, and he strictly adhered to the right rule observed by everyone in those days to always keep one bullet in reserve.

Apaches travel fast, and far, much faster and farther on rocky up-and-down-hill roads or trails than any horse I have even (sic) seen. They attribute this, as I have heard them say, to their abstinence from salt and coffee, and the very sparing use of drinking water.

The sixth day of our scout was just dawning when the party, turning the extreme end of a rocky ridge, suddenly came within sight of a squaw filling a water jar at a spring about two hundred yards within the mouth of the canyon hidden by said ridge. This woman had evidently neglected her duty as sentinel or lookout, without which no Apache camp was ever left. Perhaps, also our men had not been seen, on account of the hazy mist emanating from the canyons at this early morning hour, and as the column traveled in as perfect silence as the nature of the march permitted, had not been heard. However, if the squaw had failed in vigilance, she now made up for it by raising such a hue and cry as would have awakened the dead. She left the water jar behind, and before she could be intercepted, had run farther into the canyon, where we could see a number of huts or shacks, whence aroused by the woman's alarm, about twenty-five Apaches ran out and began climbing up a very steep, rocky hill rising directly from the opposite side of the canyon; when I say "climbing" I really mean that they leaped from boulder to boulder, from rock to rock, like the chamois I had seen in Switzerland. Now and then one would stop and fire at us, but the shots were very few and went wide of the mark.

It was absolutely useless to follow the Apaches mounted; the command dismounted, and we began the ascent on foot, while the usual fourth man stayed behind with the horses, which were left in charge of a sergeant. The Apaches, among whom were a few women and two small children, carried upon the women's backs, would cease running at times, to catch their breath or, which is more probable, to entice us farther up. Well they knew that we could never rival them in climbing the steep declivity, full of sharp-edged boulders and lava rocks plentifully interspersed with "prickly pear" growth. They would hide after each jump behind a rock and make fun of us from a safe place, insulting us by voice and gestures of the most indecent description. I abstain, for obvious reasons, from quoting the words they hurled at us (they would keep too far off to use their bows and arrows or throw stones), for, if the lowest class of Mexicans use in their ordinary conversation many vulgar and obscene expressions, the Apache seems to have selected the quintessence of the most obscene Spanish terms.

Marigildo, who was in the front line of the ascent, side by side with the agile and light foot Lieut. Harrington, received the "principal benefit" of their harangues; some of the Apaches had indeed recognized him; they vilified him to their hearts' content and let him know in unmistakable terms how much they loved him and what they would do to him, if ever they should get possession of his carcass. One of them even had acquired that hideous American expression, unfortunately heard so frequently along the border, which in those days a man (and cowboys even to this day) only used when he was ready to shoot or prepared to be shot at.

None of the soldiers claimed to have hit an Apache, although we kept up a steady enough firing, and it is highly probable that none were wounded, as they kept in perpetual motion, shooting hither and thither almost as fast as lightning flashes. Presently the foremost of them had reached the ridge and disappeared over the brow of the hill, while we were still far from the top. It was evidently useless for men accustomed as we were and shod in heavy boots to attempt to catch up with men endowed with the swiftness of mountain goats; furthermore, Marigildo did not like the looks of things, and turning to Lieutenant Harrington, he said: "These rascals are leading us on, Lieutenant, for a purpose; they are surely up to some deviltry: this place is all made up of little canyons, turning and twisting in all directions; it is useless to follow them, it is foolish; we had better turn back and look out for our horses." This most sensible advice was heeded and the descent began.

We soon found that if we had persisted in our pursuit ten minutes longer the command would have returned to camp on foot, perhaps deploring the death of one or more of its comrades. We had not quite reached the bottom of the hill when we saw a commotion among the horses, and presently saw the sergeant (Jones) in their charge, together with one of his men, firing into a small canyon which debouched directly upon the level place where the horses stood. This accelerated our descent greatly, and we arrived just in time to prevent with a good volley the stampede of the herd. The Apaches, who had disappeared over the brow of the hill, had rapidly descended on the other side, and, turning to the left had entered from behind the canyon at whose mouth the horses stood. Fortunately Sergeant Jones had placed himself upon an elevated spot near by, saw the Indians coming, and immediately guessed their intention. He also perceived that we had turned and were descending towards him; still, he fired, rather to accelerate our steps than with any hope of hitting any Apaches. He never lost his presence of mind for a moment, but shouted to his men: "Take a good grip of the reins, men, and hold on for dear life; I'll stand them off; our men are coming; stand fast!" We arrived upon the spot in double-quick after we were out of the rocks, and the Apaches, seeing the uselessness of their attempt at stampeding, retired.

A sufficient picket was placed to guard against any further surprise or attack from the Indians, and we now began to examine into the contents of the captured temporary rancheria. It consisted of about a dozen huts put together very indifferently with dry sticks of decayed giant cactus, the thorny branches of the candlewood *(Fouquiera spinosa),* some scrub-oak and willow branches, all covered in a slouchy manner with the long, coarse bunch grass called here *sacaton* grass. We found two small hollows excavated from the hillside in which we discovered quite a lot of jerked deer meat, cut in long strips and tied into bundles, several dried but untanned deer and antelope skins, and several nets or bags woven from the fiber of the agave plant, containing roasted agave heads (roasted mescal), dried hard for future use as we dry apples or peaches. The men picked up two old blankets, two lances, four bows, eight arrows, several baskets of very crude make, and the head of a deer with antlers prepared for hunting purposes. All these things had that peculiar, indefinable odor which I can only call the "Apache smell," as it does not compare even approximately with any other odor known. The stores of food were destroyed by fire upon the spot, while the other articles were carried off as trophies of war.

After the return to Wallen, which was effectuated without any occurrence worthy of record, a man brought me a very old and much-used buckskin bag, about the size of a haversack, which he had found in the Apache camp. In it I found several arrowheads, two bow strings, one wristlet of rawhide (worn by the Apaches upon their left wrist as a guard against the stroke of the bow string), several anklets made of a number of bell-shaped tin pieces strung loosely together, a baby rattle made of a small gourd hollowed out and partly filled with pebbles, and several tablets of what appeared to be whitish baked clay. Upon them there were engraved, apparently before baking, as the raised edges of the designs showed, representations of bears, deer, raccoons, trees, acorns, bows, arrows, etc., in varying arrangements.

These Marigildo at once pronounced to be playing cards in general use with the Apaches. He remembered the games played with them very well, and explained me one or two, but I have forgotten them and only remember that these games seemed to me more intricate than one would suppose savage people to indulge in.

The Indians, with the exception of the few squaws, who wore skirts and what seemed to be short chemisettes, were without clothing, wearing only the usual cloth around their loins fastened around the body with a string. I do not think they would wear this, were it not that they carry, either in its base or tied up in a corner, the small trifles of daily use. There were only three firearms among them that we could see, and the small use they make of them was not at all alarming. Probably they had but few cartridges. Some of them had bows and arrows, but made no attempt to use them during the fight, if our laborious uphill pursuit may be called so. Two had lances. As to the head dresses, jingling anklets and other finery so frequently seen in pictures of Apaches, be it understood that they exist indeed, but are only worn at home while indulging in a dancing festival of ceremony, and not infrequently at a tiswin spree, but never by Apaches who are "out for business," when they carry or wear nothing superfluous. Some of them, when out on an expedition, tie a strip of red or white cloth tightly across the forehead, to prevent their long hair from falling over their eyes and obstructing their eyesight.

SNOWBOUND AT CAMP WALLEN

Towards the end of each month I had to prepare the monthly ration for our picket post of ten men who guarded the mail station and stock at the San Pedro Crossing, about thirty-five miles to the north of Camp Wallen, whence Corporal A. Buttner had deserted during the early summer. To these men I generally sent more and more fresh meat as the season advanced, and generally also a live sheep. The rations were taken to their destination on a camp wagon accompanied by an escort of six men under a corporal. When the party that had taken the rations for the month of January, 1867, returned, they could barely reach our camp on account of the snow, which had fallen in unusual quantities during that season. All the surrounding mountains were clad in spotless white from top to bottom, and by the time the wagon returned there were from two to three feet of snow all around us on the immediate tablelands. The pass leading through the Whetstone Mountains to Tucson was blocked with snow, as well as the passage through the long and tortuous Davis Canyon, lying about half-way between Tucson and Wallen. Of this we were informed by our mail rider, who came in with frozen toes, and lost two of them by amputation. He also said that the wagons loaded with commissary stores for our camp had been obliged to turn back to Tucson, as they found the road in the canyon impenetrable, and that they could in all probability not reach us before two weeks, and not then, if more snow were to fall. This would not have mattered so much, as we were still well supplied with articles of food; but the commissary department, as well as the sutler store, had completely exhausted their stock of burning-oil and candles. By January 1, there were just three candles left in the whole camp; the sweet oil issued as horse medicine had been exhausted in the few lamps and lanterns we possessed; on account of the severe season the sheep and horned cattle, deprived by the snow of their usual pasture, had become so poor and feeble that no tallow could be extracted from their carcasses; seventeen head died of sheer exhaustion and exposure. I had begun to use turpentine in my little tin lamp for the time necessary to dress and undress, although it gave but a very unsatisfactory light, smelled bad and flared away rapidly. By 6 p.m. the camp would have been in utter darkness, had it not been for the bright fires shining through the walls of the officers' and first sergeant's tents, in which adobe hearths had been constructed.

When the escort returned from San Pedro they reported that Indians had been seen prowling about that mail station, and had nearly succeeded in driving off the grazing stock. Lieutenant Harrington asked to be sent in that direction with a scouting party, perhaps less with the expectation of finding Indians than with the desire of interrupting the monotony of camp life and to give his surplus vitality an opportunity of expending itself, which he called "to let off the surplus steam." Marigildo gave it as his opinion that perhaps a few Indians from the Arivaipa tribe of Apaches had descended from the mountains, driven by hunger, to see if they could steal an animal or two. That no Indians would be out in such weather, except to still the pangs of hunger. These Indians belonged to a small tribe obeying more or less the orders of a wily murderous chief called Es-ki-men-zin; their numerous acts of murder and robbery were generally confined in those days to the region beginning at San Pedro crossing and extending along the river banks in a north-westerly direction to Camp Grant, a distance of about one hundred twenty miles.

OLD CAMP GRANT

This Camp Grant must not be taken for the present Fort Grant, which is situated in a northeasterly direction from Wallen. The old Camp Grant here spoken of was first established in 1856, under the name of Fort Breckenridge, and garrisoned by a party of the First Dragoons, who came to take military possession of the Territory about the same time as Fort Buchanan was established on the Sonoita Creek. The Mexicans and Indians called the old Camp Grant "Arivaipa," because it was situated at the mouth of a wild, rocky canyon of that name. The garrison buildings had been erected upon the dilapidated walls of the former fort, and stood upon an elevated plateau, on one side of which the San Pedro River passed in close proximity. The Indians of Eskimenzin's band committed many murders and robberies in the surrounding region, some even within gun-shot of the camp and within sight of the garrison. We will see later what an unsavory notoriety this camp acquired, after a "fool" treaty had been made with that chief and it had become a sort of reservation for those Indians, to which they returned with their spoils not only without molestation by our troops but actually under the protection of those who were placed there for the protection of the whites. We shall see that this criminal management was maintained for a long time to the detriment and in many cases to the destruction of the lives of the early settlers, and reached such a degree of depravity that the latter, driven to despair, at last took the matter of their protection in their own hands, from which resulted (in 1871) what is known in the annals of Arizona as the "Camp Grant massacre," which I shall later lay before my readers in its naked truth and every detail.

Marigildo thought that the matter of seeing a few prowling Indians at the San Pedro crossing was not worth a scouting expedition; he pointed out the unfavorable state of the weather and pasture, and repeated his statement referring to the utter improbability of Apaches being on an outing with any serious intention of mischief. Lieutenant Harrington, however, argued that after they would once have descended into the lowlands along the river bottom, the snow fields would be left behind and they would find pasture everywhere. I do not know, but rather incline to the belief that he called his fiddle to his assistance. His tent was just opposite that of the commanding officer, from which it was only about fifteen feet distant and he was fully aware of the fact that his playing had upon the commander's ears about the same effect as a fiery red cloth swung to and fro before a vicious bull produces upon the latter. At all events, he succeeded in obtaining the permission to take twenty men and start upon the coveted expedition, with orders to carry two days' forage and to return within six days.

Of course this scout had no results except that of making the men acquainted with the region traversed by the San Pedro River and the situation of a spring of clear water in the foothills of the Arivaipa Range, a knowledge never to be despised in that country. But they found snow everywhere, and consequently returned, many of them snowblind, with much jaded and worn-out horses by reason of scanty pasture. This expedition was ever after known as the "snow scout," for soldiers will have a nomenclature of their own, be it to designate peculiarities in men, animals, geographical situations or occurrences. They had started on a Monday morning and returned on the following Saturday evening just as darkness was setting in. I saw them descending over the ridge on the top of the rising ground north of the camp, and observed that many of the men wore some sort of bandage over their eyes. I walked across the parade ground towards Marigildo's habitation, which he himself had constructed of adobes with the help of Mendozo, in order to learn the results of the expedition.

Now it happened that sometime previously a member of my company enlisted under the name of Arthur Sulverins, whose real name I knew from his correspondence with his parents at Toulouse, France, to be Arthur de Louville, had been assigned to the quartermaster's office as clerk, he being so deaf that he could not be entrusted with sentry duty in the dark hours of the night. This Frenchman, who was then a full colonel in the French army, proved to be a good copying clerk, writing a fair round hand, and an all around handy man in issuing forage, clothing and rations, in which occupation there was no need of any conversation; he was very useful to me in my position, as I have always enjoyed the privilege of possessing strong lungs. Conversation carried on with Sulverins in an ordinary tone of voice was bare of results, as only a sound approaching the fortissimo of a well-constructed foghorn could make an impression on his eardrums. How he was ever accepted by the examining surgeon into the regular army is one of the mysteries that only the idiosyncracies of the recruiting officer of those days can account for.

While I was conversing with Marigildo, the officers' cook, Romanoff, came to the quartermaster's office, as I ascertained afterwards, with a tin quart cup and demanded in his brisk manner "De l'huile pour le lieutenant." This means simply an intermediate quantity of oil, without specifying the kind of oil; turpentine is called in French *"huile de terebenthine."* The explanation that may have ensued between the two Frenchmen, who were on anything but the best terms, as to the particular oil wanted, has never been fully ascertained, and I doubt very much that there was any. Romanoff said afterwards that he asked simply for "oil, quick," and Lieutenant Harrington did not remember if he specified the kind of oil he sent Romanoff for. I suppose Sulverins thought that inasmuch as it was becoming dark, Lieutenant Harrington wished to fill his lamp, and as he had seen me using turpentine for that purpose, he filled Romanoff's quart cup with that substance.

When a few minutes later I arrived at the door of the office from Marigildo's place, I saw Romanoff running towards me with violent gestures as if he were a living semaphore, coming from the officers' quarters. Before he was within speaking distance he shouted at me: *"Venez vite, le Lieutenant est devenu fou"* (Come quick, the Lieutenant has become demented.) I ran towards Lieutenant Harrington's tent, and looking through the tent flap beheld a scene that struck me dumb. With trousers and drawers, spotted with coagulated blood on the inside, fallen to his ankles and there forming a sort of voluminous hobbles, wildly waving a wet towel and howling like a demented dervish of India, was my friend Harrington hopping and skipping about the tent in miscellaneous short steps or rather jumps. As soon as he perceived me peeping cautiously in he uttered such short jerky sentences, interrupted by polka steps as: "Holy Moses" step to the right oblique — "what is that" — step to the left oblique — "that you sent me?" — forward step — "How it burns!" — side jump — "this is fire!"

The tin quart cup stood half empty on a table. One-half of its contents had been soaked into the towel that Harrington was brandishing like a flag of distress.

The unfortunate man had started on his scouting expedition with ill-fitting trousers. In consequence he had become sadly chafed. He had sent Romanoff, as soon as he had dismounted, to fetch some oil wherewith to wash the raw places, meaning of course, sweet oil. When the cook returned, he had soaked the towel in the contents of the tin cup, a severe cold having obliterated his sense of smell for the time being, and without any preliminary examination of the fluid had applied the "medicine" in unstinted measure where it would do the most good. The effect of this lavish application seemed to have been not only instantaneous but also far reaching.

I went for the doctor, and then retired to my room to reflect upon the vicissitudes of army life in the far West and upon the peculiar effects of turpentine applied to certain parts of our anatomy.

When Lieutenant Harrington had arrived among us, he had at once begun to prepare a terrain upon the eastern plateau above the camp, for cavalry drill. Upright posts had been fixed into the ground with targets for revolver practice, and later these posts had been surmounted with dummy heads of canvas filled with hay, for sword practice from horseback. There were also a few ditches and hurdles, to train the horses in the long and high jumps, in both of which "Strawberry" delighted and excelled. But from the fact that the commanding officer kept nearly all the men constantly occupied with labor of some kind, these drills were generally not well attended, except by such non-commissioned officers as were not on duty for the day as overseers of working squads, and therefore soon abandoned.

As soon as the winter of 1866–67 was well over and the sun began to shine from day to day without intermission, the manufacture of adobes was resumed; by that time our men had acquired the "knack" of it to such an extent that six of them would turn out about four hundred good, serviceable ones in one day's work. These adobes were simply made of clay; spread and packed down into wooden moulds of three partitions each; as soon as the mould was well filled and the overlapping mud detached, the former would be lifted up and shifted to the adjoining space, previously leveled and freed from all projections, as clods, etc., and the process would be repeated. These mud bricks were twenty inches long, eight inches wide and four inches thick, and would weigh, after being thoroughly dried in the sun, about sixty pounds each. After about four to six days, according to the season and weather, they would be hard enough for handling, and would then be set upon edge, in order to allow the air to circulate all around them.

There is never any fog in southern Arizona; with the exception of the rainy season in summer, lasting about six weeks, and the winter rains, occurring at uncertain intervals for about four weeks, and sometimes, as we have seen, interchanged with snow for rain, the air is perfectly dry and pure and the sky is absolutely clear, so that within two or at the utmost three weeks these sun-dried adobes could be safely put into the walls, the mortar employed being the same mud mixed somewhat thinner than the adobe material.

I was kept busy by the commanding officer at making crude drawings of the buildings to be erected, laying out the lines upon the ground for the foundations and marking the places where doors and windows were to be placed, there being no professional builder present. There were two bricklayers, who found no difficulty in erecting perpendicular walls with the uncouth, voluminous bricks. Mendoza undertook to "boss" the erection of the hearths or fireplaces and chimneys as an expert, and I will admit that if our intention had been to build smokehouses his work was deserving of a prize medal, as the future showed. Our camp carpenter was given some assistants to help in preparing the doorsills, lintels, and door and window frames.

With the exception of a few windows, with glass panes placed in the hospital building and the officers' quarters, which were furnished by the depot quartermaster at Tucson, everything in and about the buildings was made and put together by the enlisted men of the garrison, who worked without extra pay. They worked so well and steadily that by September, 1867, the aspect of the camp had completely changed.

SICKNESS IN CAMP

The hospital was, of course, built first. Although the general health of the garrison had been good so far, we experienced during that summer what appeared to be almost an epidemic, as many as fifteen men being seized in one day with chills that shook their whole frame, accompanied in some cases with vomiting and followed in every case by a burning fever and unquenchable thirst. These chills would occur every other day, and after a few days of the sickness the patient's bones would ache so that we called it the breakbone fever. The doctor, I believe, pronounced the disease to be intermittent malarial fever. In most cases it yielded after about one week to a treatment with strong doses of sulphate of quinine, leaving the patient somewhat weak for sometime longer, with a strong desire for something sour.

There existed at the time a patent medicine called cholagogue, or colagog, which was sold at Tucson at $3 per (small) bottle. Our mail rider was allowed to bring a great deal of this medicine with the outlandish name, when our supply of quinine began to run short; it proved to be a very effective medicine. Our surgeon, Dr. Jaquette, pronounced it to be a preparation whose principal ingredient was arsenic.

Although our men worked about eight hours in the burning sun while the thermometer registered from 102° to 110°F in the shade, none were ever overcome by heat, and we had not one case of sunstroke. They perspired freely, but soon became accustomed to the work, which they never interrupted on account of the heat during the hottest hours of the day.

During the summer of 1867 my friend, Leslie B. Wooster, sold out his sutler store to Mr. James Toole, who had received the appointment from Washington, and went into business at Tubac. Mr. Toole had been a lieutenant in the California Volunteers and reached the Territory of Arizona with the so-called California Column in 1862. He built a convenient sutler store, the rear of which was utilized by our officers as a club-room. Later on he became a banker at Tucson.

Of course, when Lieutenant Harrington was not out scouting, his time would hang heavily on his hands. He had hardly any men that he might have drilled, and so he turned his mind to hunting and fishing.

When Lieutenant Harrington went on a hunt for large game he would take me along, even though he had to wait several days until the business of the office would allow my taking a day off. We had at the camp an Apache who was carried on the rolls of civil employes as a herder, but who did nothing except to provide the officers' mess with deer and antelope meat and wild turkeys. We had furnished him with an old horse, upon which he would start out in the morning with his hunting gear and return towards nightfall with a deer, antelope, or several turkeys. I never knew him to return empty handed. The deer he brought back were generally "blacktail" bucks. His manner of hunting these was "stalking." He said that the success in that kind of hunt depended entirely upon the correct manner of approaching the deer herd and imitating exactly the actions and motions of these animals; he was by no means what is generally called a good marksman, and never fired his rifle until he was reasonably certain to hit from a distance not exceeding three hundred yards; but he was a very patient, cautious, tireless, and experienced stalker.

As soon as he would come within sight of a herd of deer in the far distance he would hide in the nearest hollow and make his preparations. He had a dried head of buck, with antlers, which he would wear like a shako by placing it upon his head and fastening it with a chin band, there being about ten inches of the animal's neck left on the deer head. Over his body he wore a shirt of brown muslin, the back of which, as well as the upper part of the sleeves, was smeared over with yellowish clay to give them the appearance of a deer's back and forelegs. He had an old Springfield rifle, which he carried perpendicularly grasped in his right hand forming a support for his right shoulder while the ramrod did the same service upon his left side.

Thus by stooping over he could apparently walk on four legs. His legs were bare and he was careful to present to the hunted deer his front as much as possible. Of course he would pay some attention to the direction of the wind, but he did not consider this as of nearly so much importance as he did the best possible imitation of the hunted animal's actions and motions. He frequently told us that we over-estimated the powers of scenting of the deer; that he had, compelled by the difficulties of the terrain in approaching the deer against the wind, or sometimes on account of sudden changes in the direction of the wind, approached deer to within 150 yards and killed the buck of his selection from among the herd, although the wind blew directly from him towards it; while the latter would at once become suspicious, restless and ultimately be frightened off if the stalker makes by accident (misstep) or carelessness a motion unfamiliar to the deer or its leading buck, even at a long distance. I believe this readily, not only on account of the Apache's invariable success in hunting, but also because Marigildo had seen Apaches stalk and kill deer in the described guise with bow and arrow from a distance not exceeding fifty yards. We had seen our Apache stalk deer and could not refrain from admiring the almost marvelous correctness with which he imitated the deer's actions in every particular, lowering his sham head from time to time as if grazing, then lifting it high up and looking cautiously around for a possible enemy; satisfied that no danger was imminent, lowering his head and bending it backwards, as if scratching himself between the ribs, as it were, and again returning to his diet of grass. His motions when he was ready to shoot were very few and executed very deliberately, altogether without haste. While still "eating grass" he would keep his left foreleg steady (the ramrod), bring his rifle gradually into position, resting it upon the left wrist, never losing the natural stooping position until the very last moment, when he would slowly raise his head, look around in approved deer fashion, take careful aim, and fire. His motions were so true to nature, as we observed him from a distance, that we took him for a stray deer joining the herd.

Lieutenant Harrington and myself, having obtained a second deer head, attempted this stalking experiment, but to no purpose. Long before we arrived to within shooting distance our backs ached so that we could no longer "eat grass," nor overcome the difficulties of the terrain; neither did our patience hold out.

With numerous herds of antelopes, however, we had such good success that before long the excitement of hunting them wore off, as it resembled more a deliberate butchery than the sport of the chase. There was a long, narrow ravine stretching along the foot of the Whetstone Mountains; between it and the mountains there was a plateau upon which the so-called fine antelope grass grew luxuriously. There were nearly always two or three herds of these swift and graceful animals grazing along this spacious mesa land; our herders frequently chased them when the animals of the garrison were pasturing in that neighborhood, and had several times succeeded in capturing and bringing to the camp an antelope kid too weak to follow the chased herd. These are very pretty creatures; spotted all over the back in white, yellow, and red patches; these spots disappear as the animal grows up.

Whenever we were hunting in that region Mr. Harrington would upon coming within sight of our herd make a signal to our herders, some of whom would circle around the nearest herd of antelopes and drive it in the direction of the aforesaid ravine, in which we would lie hidden, after having fastened a handkerchief to a pole or stick which we planted into the ground about one hundred yards from the edge of our hiding place. After the herders had headed the running antelopes towards us they would return to their business, and the antelope would gradually abandon their run, begin to graze, coming nearer and nearer to the ravine. They would soon perceive the rag on the stick fluttering in the wind and, seemingly compelled by resistless curiosity, come within easy shooting distance to ascertain, as it were, the nature of the thing that exercised such a power of attraction upon them. Thus one of them at least, more often two, would fall a prey to our rifles and, although this maneuver was frequently repeated, they never appeared to be aware of the impending danger or to have any remembrance of their comrades' death into which they were enticed in a similar manner. It is best to shoot an antelope or deer in such a manner as to break its shoulder blade, unless one is so sure a shot that he can with absolute certainty of success aim at the upper part of the head. An antelope with a broken shoulder blade can run neither far nor fast, and will fall at the shot; while one shot through the heart will generally give a tremendous jump upwards and not infrequently run a distance of over five hundred yards before it may drop dead, a circumstance which more than once caused us to lose the game, as the animal wounded unto death disappeared among inaccessible mountain crags.

ADVENTURE WITH A CINNAMON BEAR

In the middle of the summer of 1867, I had an exciting adventure with a cinnamon bear, which had a profitable outcome. There were eight men of our garrison in a canyon of the Huachuca Mountains, where they had established a temporary camp while getting out the timber used in our buildings. The commanding officer had suddenly resolved upon a change in the arrangement of the officers' quarters, which would necessitate the cutting of four timbers of unusual length, and I undertook to carry this order to the timber camp. As we had killed a steer that afternoon, and the wagons were not to be sent for the timbers for several days to come, I placed about 25 pounds of the fresh meat in a gunny-sack, which

I fastened upon the saddle, and started towards evening for the wood camp. The road lay straight towards the mountains, but when it reached the foot of them it suddenly made a turn to the left, there being a long, wide ravine with very steep banks between the mountains and the road.

I had just entered upon this turn when I heard a noise to the right above me, and looking up perceived several rocks rolling down the mountain side, which was in places covered with small scrub oaks and creosote bushes. Presently there came into view what at first seemed a large tumbling fur ball rolling down the steep declivity. As it came nearer I made out that it was a bear running obliquely towards me. What astonished me not a little was the fast gait he was able to maintain while descending steep ground covered with loose stones, a feat that no horse, not even the Mexican mustang, can accomplish. He reached the edge of the steep opposite bank of the ravine, and as I had stopped he stopped also, audibly sniffing the air, which probably carried to him the odor of the fresh meat upon my saddle. The ravine was fully thirty yards wide, and across this chasm we surveyed one another. The bear looked sad, as if he thought: "How near and yet how far." I knew very well that he could not cross the ravine, and at first I intended to shoot him with my revolver; upon second thought, knowing the lay of the land perfectly, a better idea occurred to me.

I continued my road and saw the bear turn also, keeping abreast of me on the other side of the impassable barrier. Gradually I rode faster and faster, but Bruin kept step with my canter in a sort of seemingly easy trot which covered the ground in lively fashion. I knew that the ravine itself extended, maintaining the same steep formation, to within about 200 yards of the timber camp, when it gradually widened into a gentle slope easily accessible from either side. Thus we went peaceably along; I could see that the bear was very fat, as his hindquarters fairly shook at every step he made. A ride of about one mile would surely bring me near enough to our men to make my revolver shots heard, which, if fired in rapid succession, would bring some of the men to the spot with their rifles.

Even if the worst came to the worst, I could hardly run any risk, as I could, by unfastening and dropping the meat, detain the bear and readily escape over the comparatively open ground to my left on my good Tinto, who eyed the bear suspiciously, it is true, but still without showing any excitement. When I knew from the surroundings and the aspect of the ravine that we were near enough to the timber camp to be heard, I fired three shots in succession, which had the effect of rousing the camp into prompt armed activity. Presently the corporal in charge appeared upon a little knoll; I pointed out to him the game that was running straight into his campkettle, as it were. The bear was soon dispatched, and furnished several good roasts, for one of which I took half a hindquarter to camp in exchange for the beef I had brought. The bear was not large, probably not over three years old, and could hardly weigh more than 500 pounds "on the hoof"; but its meat was tender and juicy. The skin I have still, and regret to say that it contains more bullet holes than the desirable number, and certainly far more than are generally made in the killing of a cinnamon bear.

The men at the wood camp were really not in any need of fresh meat, as they had killed several wild turkeys that very morning, and had game of some kind at all times. The Huachuca Mountains were then and are to some extent still a very paradise for hunters, although, on account of the numerous cattle herded all over Arizona since the forced pacification of the Apaches, the deer and antelopes have become quite scarce and those remaining are very shy. But it is a fact well known to prospectors, hunters and trappers that a steady diet of game of any kind will soon pall upon the palate and a beef steak or a rasher of bacon is, under those circumstances, a feast.

We also went a-fishing at times in the few deep water holes that the creek afforded. When first the idea seized me to look for fish in our little stream, I discovered to my great dismay that the fish hooks I knew I had packed among my traps had unaccountably disappeared, nor was there a single one to be found in the whole camp. In this emergency Marigildo showed me a cactus growing everywhere in that region which provided a substitute for the missing implement, if not to perfection, at least to some purpose. This cactus, known to botanists as *Echino cactus brevihamatus,* is called by the natives *biznaga,* and by the Americans, barrel cactus and also nigger-head, on account of its shape. It is covered all over by ridges running from top to bottom, from which protrude at distances of about two inches numerous clusters of sharp and tough thorns; from the center of these clusters grow hooks as sharp as a needle and as tough as steel. If these hooks were barbed they would be ideal for fish hooks, as the circular creases around their base seem expressly made for the successful fastening of the fishline. With these hooks I caught many fish, some weighing from one to two pounds, taking care to jerk quick and hard as the bobbin or cork would go under the surface of the water, towards the shore, where the fish, not being retained for lack of a barb, would generally drop off the hook. Of course, some would fall back into the water while in transit through the air, but with a little practice I learned to overcome this difficulty. Unfortunately the fish we caught were more remarkable on account of the prevalance of bones, which seemed to criss-cross their anatomy in every direction, than by reason of any fine flavor. They were of two kinds: one a sort of bastard trout, the other the well-known yellow-bellied sucker. These latter would bite best during a thunderstorm. For the former we used grasshoppers for bait with great success, while the common earthworm seemed best adapted for the catching of suckers.

Referring once more to the above-mentioned cactus, I obtained from Marigildo the information, confirmed by herders, etc., later on, that this plant had saved many a man's life in the desert, provided that the man was acquainted with the peculiarities of the plant. It attains a height of about three feet when full grown, is very juicy, and forms in its center a hollow large enough to contain, according to the size of the plant, from one quart to nearly a gallon of liquid. When one makes and maintains a fire around it, all the juice of the plant gathers into the hollow, where it may be scooped out and drank (sic) by the thirsty, wandering traveler, after cutting the top of the cactus off. A plainsman, be he prospector, herder, or hunter, is never at a loss how to make a fire, though he have neither a dry match nor a flint and tinder; he simply takes a woolen rag or one of his socks, holds it to the mouth of his pistol, and fires into it. The stuff will ignite at once from the powder, and by gathering a few leaves or dry twigs or the cast-off dry clusters of cactus thorns, which are, without any exception, all resinous, a fire is quickly built. The Mexicans gather the young barrel cactus and manufacture its meat or pulp into a candy, which they call "dulce de bisnaga" (Bisnaga candy); it has the appearance of our sugar-preserved citron and tastes not unlike it. The beautiful flowers growing upon the top of this cactus are purple, with yellow markings; the fruit is fig-shaped, lemon-colored, but tough, and although not unpalatable, is not put to any use.

Between Camp Wallen and Camp Crittenden we saw almost on every occasion we had to make the transit between the two places a herd of wild horses, numbering about four hundred head, among which were conspicuous two very large stallions that seemed to be engaged in an everlasting feud. One was coal-black, the other of a spotless, glittering white. Lieutenant Harrington had a powerful field-glass, through which we observed their fierce combats which seemed almost interminable; they kicked and bit one another like animals possessed by the fury of inextinguishable hate, while the herd was quietly grazing near by, apparently taking no interest whatever in the combat or its result. These wild horses were exceedingly shy, and ran off as soon as they would see anything in the shape of man approaching from a far distance. Marigildo and myself, having both long-winded and fleet horses, pursued them several times in their flight, and on two occasions succeeded in capturing a small colt too young to keep up with the herd on the long run. We brought them to camp and reared them with cow's milk, as we did the antelope kids. I do not know what horses they ultimately turned out to be, as they were not yet full-grown when we abandoned Camp Wallen. Their appearance then did not justify any hopes towards their becoming more than ordinary, common-size mustangs.

CAMELS OF ARIZONA DESERT

At one time while Lieutenant Harrington had gone with me upon that road to look for a rattlesnake in a prairie-dog village, we naturally looked in the direction where we were accustomed to see the wild horses. We could not see any, but near the place where they frequently grazed we saw two animals that presented a strange appearance. We could readily see, even from a far distance, that they were neither horses nor cattle, nor yet deer nor antelope; bears never descended so far upon the plain, at least not in daylight. Presently Harrington adjusted his eyeglass and took a long, steady look; he shook his head, wiped the glasses and looked again, breathing hard. All at once he bursted (sic) out with: "Well, I'll be forever damaged, if these are not camels, regular Egyptian dromedaries; look!"

Well, I looked at him first and I looked at him hard, but could discover nothing unusual in his features except the most unbounded astonishment. Then I directed the glass towards the object of our curiosity. Sure enough, there were two camels looking as natural as the one that had carried me to the pyramid of Cheops in Egypt. We could hardly believe our senses, but the fact was there, indisputable, undeniable. We rode towards there but found them so shy that they scampered off before we were within five hundred yards of them, and they ran like the wind toward the sandy desert lying south of the Santa Rita Mountains.

We forgot all about the rattlesnake whose skin we wanted for a belt, and made haste to camp. Here nobody seemed willing to believe us until Marigildo, hearing of the matter, not only confirmed our statement, but said in addition that he had seen the whole herd of forty camels when they were brought to Arizona from Yuma in 1858. The Government, believing that they would make good pack animals in a country where water was so scarce, had imported this herd of camels and sent it to Arizona under charge of an Arabian, or Turk, or Greek, whom everybody called "Greek Charley." I met this man during the following year (1868) at Tucson. Referring to his charge, he said that the enterprise proved a complete failure, on account of the nature of the ground. The roads in Arizona, he averred, were very hard, while the feet of the camels, accustomed to the yielding sands of the desert, were very tender, and a trip of one hundred twenty miles, say, from Wallen to Fort Bowie, rendered them unfit for travel for the next two weeks to come. To use them as pack animals with a scouting party was out of the question altogether, not only because they would refuse to make a step upon rocky ground, but also on account of the antipathy towards them of the horses. They were therefore put up at auction and ten of them disposed of to a mining company that wished to use them as carriers of ore, an altogether vain undertaking upon mountain paths. For the reasons already mentioned and the additional circumstances that these animals could not find their accustomed feed (which consists in young branches or sprouts of trees, meal and dates and not in grass or hay, as was erroneously supposed) their utility was found to be non-existing, and they were allowed to take to the desert and their liberty. I think the last of them were seen on the Maricopa Desert about 1872.

The road from Wallen to Camp Crittenden, which latter was in 1867 garrisoned like the former by one company of the First U. S. Cavalry and one company of the Thirty-Second U. S. Infantry (formerly the Third Battalion, Fourteenth Inf.), led through several "villages" of prairie dogs, which live in excavations surmounted by small tumuli full of holes that are used for ingress and exit by these pretty, graceful ground squirrels, called by the zoologists, *Cynomys Ludovicianas.* The little animal bears a great likeness to the marmot of the Swiss Alps. It generally sits upon its haunches at the entrance of its lair, fixing its little lively eyes upon the passerby, emitting at short intervals whistling or grating sounds not unlike those produced by a swinging door whose hinges need oiling. Keeping time with this music, it moves its bushy tail hither and thither in jerky motions. Upon near approach this little animal disappears into its cavern, not by crawling, but it seems to jump first upwards, to turn a somersault and thus enters into the ground with the same short, jerky action with which it does everything. A few seconds afterwards the pretty little head will appear at the opening again, peep out and examine its surroundings.

Their habitations, excavated by themselves, are shared with a small bluish-gray ground owl (*Speotyto hypogaea*), which lives with them in perfect harmony. Some people assert that these underground lodgings are also occupied as common property by the rattlesnake, found everywhere in Arizona before the development of the cattle industry; but this I am not prepared to assert, as I have never seen a rattlesnake either come out or enter one of these squirrel holes, while I have seen the owls do this frequently. But this I do know, that I have frequently seen rattlesnakes lying quietly in the sun among these tumuli while squirrels and owls were playing all around them, and whenever I wished to procure one of these uncanny reptiles for an experiment, or for stuffing or for a belt made of its skin, I would find one or more without fail upon or about the numerous hills forming a village of prairie dogs. It is not impossible that the rattlesnake may have a cave and corresponding hole for his use in one and the same hill with the birds and quadrupeds, but I should not think it likely, on account of the utterly vivacious nature of the prairie squirrel, which is a *perpetum mobile,* and the phlegmatic temper of the snake, to which all motion not connected with self-defense or maintenance, seems a superfluous exertion.

GILA MONSTER OF THE ARIZONA DESERT

Before closing this chapter I will say something of the Gila monster, its appearance, habits and venom, about which so many erroneous ideas exist to this day. In Noah Webster's Dictionary you may still read: "Gila monster, the only lizard with poisonous fangs"; while, as a matter of fact, this lizard has no fangs at all, venomous or otherwise. It is a few years since some medical gentlemen of Philadelphia have established the fact beyond a doubt that the venom of the Gila monster is contained in its spittle (saliva), and causes death by producing a sort of rabies or hydrophobia when it enters into the wound produced by the very sharp teeth of the lizard. After much tedious research, a German zoologist has also discovered very lately that the Gila monster has in its lower jaw only a few small receptacles where venomous matter is secreted and thence probably enters into the saliva of the infuriated animal.

The name Gila monster has been given to the lizard in the United States because it is found upon the sandy bottoms and adjoining table lands of the Gila Valley more often than anywhere else, and on account of its "uncanny" appearance. It is not found in the United States anywhere except in the southern portion of the Territory of Arizona, whence it extends its habitat into the adjoining Mexican State of Sonora. The scientists have named it *Heloderma suspectum,* and the illiterate Mexicans call it "escupion" (the spitter), derived in ungrammatical manner from the Spanish verb "escupir" — to spit. It appears on the surface of the ground only during the hot season (May to September), hibernating underground during the remaining months.

My first introduction to the lizard occurred as follows: A short time after our arrival at Wallen, our mail rider, returning from Tucson, related that he had suddenly come upon a peculiar animal, about three feet in length, which was crossing the road directly in front of him, near the Whetstone Mountains; that his horse shied so violently as to nearly throw him from the saddle, that the "thing" looked very much like a young crocodile or cayman (the mail rider was a native of Louisiana), and had quickly run to cover, hiding in a pile of stones near by; that the horse had been so much frightened that he, the rider, had to dismount, and could quiet the nervous animal only with great difficulty.

I translated, as best I could, the mail rider's report to our Mexican herders, and they declared immediately that the animal must be an "escupion," although they said it could never have been of the size described, as one exceeding two feet in length had never been seen. They forthwith cited cases that had come to their knowledge (from hearsay), of people dying overnight, or within a week, or a month, after being bitten by this lizard, and I became so interested in the matter that I offered them two dollars for a dead, but outwardly uninjured, *Heloderma,* and four dollars for a live one. A very few days afterwards they brought to the Quartermaster's office a live Gila monster, which they had caught with a hair-rope sling. It hung by the neck fastened to the middle of a long dry cactus stick held by them at either end. When I stepped out and was approaching the reptile they both exclaimed at once, "Por Dios, Señor, ciudado!" (For God's sake, sir, take care).

I had them carry the lizard into an empty corn room with a dirt floor, into which we drove a picket pin having at its top a movable ring. After several manipulations with two pairs of blacksmith's tongs, we succeeded in fastening the little animal, measuring about twenty inches, to the ring on the picket pin, giving it about two feet of rope from neck to pin. The Mexicans were terribly unnerved by this operation, especially when the lizard, having become greatly excited, began to spit freely; so I paid them, gave them a nerve restorer, and let them go.

The somewhat lengthy operation of securing the "natural curiosity" had made the *Heloderma* furious. It presently began to snarl and spit like a mad cat; it also straightened out its forelegs and assumed a more erect position, showing by that time quite a threatening attitude. When I tendered it the corner of a woolen blanket it bit into it with such fury and retained its hold with such tenacity that we had to make use of an iron poker to release the blanket for (sic) its jaws. We brought a cat and placed it on the ground before the spitting lizard, but not within its reach; pussy showed immediately the greatest fear and horror and ran out, the room having no door. Then we brought a rat catcher, known to the whole camp as the bravest little dog. Its owner encouraged it to tackle the reptile. The dog seemed at first completely dumfounded by the singular and strange appearance of the lizard; then he approached cautiously nearer and nearer, began to growl, bark and snap, scratched the floor, dancing and whining with eagerness to attack; but when the *Heloderma* suddenly rushed at him as far as the rope would permit, the dog turned tail and ran out. From these and later experiments we established two facts: First, that the *Heloderma* never lets go voluntarily its hold upon whatever its teeth have seized; and, second, that every animal brought into its immediate vicinity shows signs of fear or horror or detestation, or all together, at the first aspect of the Gila monster, with only the exception of the rattlesnake, which will live with the lizard in the same box in perfect peace and harmony. Both are of a very phlegmatic temper, slow of motion, of about the same color, and both seem to say to you: "Please leave me alone; I wish to go through life undisturbed."

I set before my prisoner some chopped raw meat and hard-boiled eggs, and left him alone. On the following morning he had departed, without, apparently, having touched the food. As the rope was neither gnawed or bitten through, he must have managed to slip the sling over his head with his dainty little hands, which are not unlike those of a human being in shape.

Since then I have captured or bought at least a hundred of these lizards at different times for various purposes. I was not a little astonished to find during my first dissection of a *Heloderma* that it has neither fangs nor venom glands in its upper jaw, where these dangerous implements of self-defense exist in the venomous snakes, although the shape of the head, triangular, flat and wide across the base of the jaws, is alike in both. The *Heloderma* has an upper and lower roof of very sharp, slightly-curved teeth, and its tongue, which protrudes in an excited state from a tube, is black, flat and formed like that of most snakes. Unlike the latter, however, it cannot swallow any article of food thicker than about an ordinary lead pencil, because its jaws are hinged and will not admit of the elastic extension of the food canals of snakes. Its interior anatomy is altogether that of a lizard, with a lizard's ovary, etc. Its eggs, which it lays in the month of July or August, to the number of four, in a slightly-excavated sandy hollow, measure about 1 x ¾ inches (diameter); they are yellowish-gray, and as tough as rubber balls.

The skin of the *Heloderma* is of very peculiar formation. It has no scales, like the snakes, but appears to wear a garment made by sewing closely together a number of glass beads strung upon strings of threads, the whole forming an arrangement of irregular designs in straw, yellow and opaque black. On the back the skin is as thin as paper, on the belly as thick as ordinary cardboard.

The young when they slip out of the egg stretch out at once to a length of about two inches; they can easily be handled, and look very pretty as they assume, after about two days, a pale rose color; in about a week the dark pattern begins to show in blue-black.

At one time I thought that the *Heloderma* had partly an amphibious nature, although it is always found upon dry, sandy or rocky ground. I had a large fine live specimen brought to me by a boy, who carried it in a gunnysack. As I wished to stuff it, I tried to kill it without any injury to its skin. I placed it, therefore, in a full water butt, anchoring it to the bottom with a heavy rock. When I fished it out after two hours, expecting it to be as dead as the proverbial door nail, I found, to my astonishment, that it was not only very much alive, but very angry as well. My Mexican brother-in-law, who happened to arrive about that time, killed it by administering what seemed a very light blow with a poker at the base of the skull, where the vertebrae join the brain.

I have several times cooked the body of the *Heloderma,* giving the meat and broth to stray dogs and cats. These would devour the unusual diet with great relish, and without showing any ill effects.

The Gila monster lives upon worms, bugs, larvae, etc. In captivity it is best fed with raw eggs offered with the shell broken.

In these days, whenever any person is bitten by a *Heloderma,* he or she is at once sent to the nearest Pasteur Institute. So far all persons who had recourse to the treatment there obtained have overcome all evil consequences of the wound.

LT. HARRINGTON ORDERED EAST

During the fall of 1867, Lieutenant Harrington was ordered on detached service to the East, and was replaced by Lieutenant W. H. Winters, First U.S. Cavalry. When the latter arrived, Lieutenant Harrington brought him to the quartermaster's office, where the invoices and receipts for the turning over of the quartermaster and commissary of subsistence property were ready for signature. Lieutenant Winters asked me if all the property for which he was to receipt was actually on hand, and upon my giving an affirmative answer (which I could honestly do), he signed the receipts and requested me to stay in office under him. I promised to do this until First Sergeant Lipowitz, whose term of enlistment would expire at the end of two months, should be discharged, when Colonel Brown (by that time his brevet as major had become that of lieutenant-colonel) would undoubtedly wish me to return to the company as its first sergeant, as I was the ranking sergeant of the company.

Lieutenant Harrington's leave-taking from me was very cordial, affectionate in fact; he presented me with a fine Colt's revolver on his departure. I regretted very much to see him leave, as he had been to me more a friend than a superior officer, or had at least made me feel thus. I soon found, however, that Lieutenant Winters was a fine officer and perfect gentleman also. Physically he was a model of a man in stature, bearing, and features, which latter would frequently assume the kindliness of sweet expression of a person who loves his fellow man. He was also a fine soldier, well versed in all the military duties, and had the polite manner and refined speech of our modern graduate of West Point.

I felt at ease with him at once; the more so as I perceived that he treated me like one of whom he had heard good reports, and whom he could trust implicitly.

One of his first orders in the line of commissary of subsistence duties was to have me prepare scouting rations, put up ready for immediate use. We had by this time received dried meat and a good supply of the above-mentioned *pinole,* prepared by contract in the adjoining Mexican state of Sonora. He had me prepare forty small canvas sacks or pouches, which were filled with ten pounds of *pinole* and brown sugar mixed. These when filled looked like a large sausage and could be strapped upon the saddle, while the eighty small bundles containing four pounds of dried meat each, could be accommodated in the saddle-bags, where each man also placed a small ready-made bag containing one-half pound of ground coffee for emergencies. These rations were supposed to be sufficient for forty men for ten days; a scouting party could be thus equipped, ready to take the field within about one hour. As we had no pack animals or experienced packers, a protracted expedition was out of the question with our garrison.

It was not long before these scouting rations were put to the use intended. In the first days of November a wounded Mexican came into camp and reported that about in the middle of the Huachuca Pass, about nineteen miles distant from Wallen, he and his party had been attacked by Apaches, his three companions had been killed, and the oxen driven off. They were taking a cart load of oranges to Camp Crittenden. The attack had been made at daybreak, and his escape was due only to the heavy mist arising from the mountain canyons after the heavy rains of the previous day and night. The rainy winter season had set in early. As soon as he had ascertained that the Apaches had gone, he had left his hiding place and struck out for our camp, where he arrived between 9 and 10 o'clock in the morning.

SCOUT TO RETRIBUTION CANYON

By 11 a.m., "boots and saddles" was sounded, the rations having been quickly distributed, and Lieutenant Winters was off with thirty men, Marigildo guiding the party. The wounded man had described the spot of the attack very minutely. It was soon found. The bodies of the three men, all Mexicans, horribly mutilated, were allowed to lie where they were, as a burying detail was to follow us; we covered them with some brush.

Marigildo soon found the tracks of the Indians upon the wet ground; they showed the Indian party to consist of eight or nine men, one of whom must be the owner of feet of an enormous size. As usual, all these tracks were slightly bent inward, a peculiarity of many Indians; they do not take long, striding steps, but travel with a sort of steady trot that covers a great deal of ground — I should say about five miles an hour. From them we could see that they were driving the two oxen before them, having taken a southerly direction after leaving the pass at its western outlet and skirting the whole length of the Huachuca range, at the utmost end of which they crossed the San Pedro River. Here we found part of the remains of a slaughtered ox and the ashes of a very small campfire, and as night was setting in we camped and had a pinole supper with jerked beef. No fire was allowed to be lighted.

On the following morning, as soon as it was light enough to follow the tracks, we broke camp and resumed our march, after a breakfast which was, like all the following meals, partaken of during this scout, an exact counterpart of the previous supper, until we had accomplished our task. The tracks now led in a straight line, over hills and through canyons, many of which we had to cross by ascending and descending from steep, rocky sides, often being obliged to dismount and lead our horses, towards the western end of the Chiricahua Mountains, over the partly sandy, partly rocky plateau that separates the Huachuca from the Chiricahua Range. We soon came upon the other ox, which had been abandoned by the Indians, as it could not keep up with them.

About noon we came to a small spring emanating from a fissure in the rocks of a deep canyon. Here we made a short halt to mix a pinole drink, and resumed our march, but soon found that we had to make a detour of about six miles, as the farther side of the canyon was so steep and rocky that our horses could not be made to climb to the top of the ridge. However, Marigildo soon found the tracks on the opposite side, after we had turned the canyon, and away we went. Heavy clouds now began to gather in our front, and towards evening we could plainly see that rain was falling in the Chiricahua Range. Our horses began to show signs of exhaustion, for they had traveled over difficult ground almost unceasingly ever since we had left the Huachuca Pass, and we were all glad to take a rest when night set in. We had by that time reached a small grassy knoll, where some slight pasture could be obtained. The Chiricahua Mountains were still about twenty-five miles away, but as yet we were upon the tracks of the murderers. During the night we saw many lightning flashes in the sky over the Chiricahuas and heard loud peals of thunder at intervals. Marigildo was beginning to fear that the rains, which in the mountains of Arizona frequently come down in torrents, would wash away the tracks, and we started at the peep of day, covering as much ground as the state of our horses and the difficulties of the terrain would admit of. The tracks never deviated from the direction taken at the San Pedro camp; it was a beeline easily enough followed by an Apache on foot,* but offering many obstacles to mounted men, as well as to men unused to climbing steep ridges with heavy boots on their feet.

Towards nightfall we came into the numerous rocky foothills of the Chiricahua Range, and here we found that the Apaches had separated into two parties of about equal numbers, one maintaining the original direction, while the other struck out more towards the east. We followed the former for about a mile farther, when night overtook us and forced us to make camp. The horses were picketed under a strong guard, relieved every hour on account of the fatigue of the men, and allowed to crop the scanty grass. The clouds that had been gathering during the whole day formed a very dark canopy over us, and towards midnight a steady rain began to fall, which at intervals assumed the proportions of torrents of rain, compelling us to seek higher ground, as the small canyons all about us almost suddenly assumed the aspect of mountain streams. Of course, no fire was allowed, and we passed a very uncomfortable, chilly night. Towards morning the sky began to clear up somewhat, but, as Marigildo expected, every vestige of the Indian tracks had been washed away. However, as he knew the lay of the land and the probable direction the few Indians we were pursuing would take, he proposed to guide us by intuition, as it were.

After a short consultation with Lieutenant Winters, he led the silent column farther into the foothills, until at last we could see through the dissolving mist the mouths of several large canyons leading directly into the mountains. Marigildo struck out for the one lying directly before us, knowing it to be leading to a high plateau hidden from the valley side by precipitous rocks, where Cochise's bands had in former years frequently rendezvoused after a marauding expedition. He was riding about fifty yards ahead of the column, and had just ascended a small knoll on foot, when all at once he stopped, stepped back, and held up his hand as a sign for us to stop. Then he descended somewhat from his high position and made signs to Lieutenant Winters to join him. They both crawled together to the top of the little hill, where they lay down flat and looked towards the mountains, using Winters' field-glass. They saw a feeble column of smoke ascending from a grassy plateau in front of the large canyon's mouth upon slightly rising ground. Marigildo said it would be useless

---

*Apaches have been known to travel from sixty to seventy miles on foot in twenty-four hours, over all kinds of ground, without water. They have been known to keep this up for several consecutive days. They themselves attribute their endurance to their total abstinence from salt and coffee and great moderation observed at all times in the use of drinking water. To this must, of course, be added their manner of life from their early youth.

to approach them from where we were, as they would be sure to see us from afar and could easily reach the, to us, inaccessibly high rocky mountain ridges from which they were only about five hundred yards distant. He therefore proposed to lead us into another parallel canyon, in which we could ascend to the high ground unseen and from which we could debouch in such a manner as to cut off the Indians' retreat to higher ground by a swift dash. He explained the situation fully, and Lieutenant Winters gave corresponding orders to the men. We turned towards the mountains, riding as noiselessly as possible, although we were still very far out of hearing distance.

ATTACK ON INDIAN CAMPS

After about an hour, during which Marigildo had frequently ascended available high ground in order to learn the exact situation of the Indians, who he now ascertained were three, sitting around a small fire in the open, we began the ascent, which we found gradual and easy. Marigildo and Lieutenant Winters once more took an observation with the utmost caution, and found that by making a sudden rush we could easily intercept the Apaches from reaching the mountains.

We rushed over the ridge at a run, Winters, Sergeant John, Marigildo and our citizen blacksmith, Wm. McFallen, in the lead, they having the swiftest horses. When within about two hundred yards, about twenty of us stopped and fired a volley, as previously agreed, upon the fast-fleeing Indians, while the foremost rider circled somwhat to the right-oblique, to be out of the firing line. One of the Indians dropped at our fire, while the other two kept up their run, but were soon cut off from further flight and dispatched pretty well up towards the mountains.

Near the place where the wounded Indian fell there was a large fissure in the ground; into this he crawled, and seeking cover behind a large rock he began to shoot arrows with great swiftness at our men to such good purpose that he slightly wounded a man and two horses. These men had dismounted to take better aim, while the riders were still up towards the mountain, with the exception of Marigildo, who had descended and now appeared in the rear of the wounded Apache unseen by him. When Marigildo grasped the situation he made a sign to the advancing column to withhold their fire; like a monkey he swiftly crawled down over the edge of the fissure, held his revolver against the head of the Apache, and dispatched him. We found upon examination that he had his thighbone broken at the first fire; it was generally conceded that the ball came from the carbine of Daniel Rooney.

Thus ended the scouting expedition known in the official report as the one that killed three Apaches in Retribution Canyon.

During the much-needed rest that was now indulged in, and during which some coffee was enjoyed, Marigildo managed to slip away and obtain, unperceived, the scalps of the three dead Indians, without the knowledge of Lieutenant Winters. He did this in order to produce ocular proof of the Indians' death, with which he could claim the reward promised him by Mr. Conrad Aguirre, our hay contractor, who had offered Marigildo a reward of $100 in cash for each Indian killed by a scouting party under his guidance.

Among the Indians killed was the one with the enormous feet. All three were naked, but wore a loincloth. They had one rifle (an old Springfield) two bows, two quivers of raw hide, about twenty arrows and two lances. As they had only one large knife, a Mexican "machete," I suppose that the other party had carried off the few trifles which were taken from the murdered Mexicans. I was surprised to note that, although they were well and strongly built men as to bones, their biceps were very small, almost flabby, and that, contrary to all reasonable expectations, their legs from the knees down were quite thin, showing barely a trace of calf.

Shortly after this scout Lieutenant Winters was sent out to command a large escort accompanying the surveying party which mapped out the railway projected to run along the San Pedro River by Tres Alamos.

On December 1, Sergeant Lipowitz was discharged, and I returned to duty with my company as its first sergeant. Almost simultaneously there arrived at the camp Lieutenant Gallagher, Thirty-Third U. S. Infantry, he being the first and only subaltern officer serving with our company during my three years' service.

A few weeks before the departure of First Sergeant Max Lipowitz we had received about a dozen copies of *Upton's Infantry Tactics,* with orders to drill the men accordingly. Colonel Brown turned them over to Lipowitz, who began at once not only a thorough study of the new system by himself, but also assembled the sergeants and corporals of the company in his room of evenings, in order to teach them, by means of matches and beans, the company evolutions, their respective positions, and, in short, all the intricacies of the new drill. At these theoretical teachings I was present as often as my time allowed, as well as at the daily drill, which was now resumed, as the buildings were all finished. Lieutenant Gallagher also interested himself in the matter, and acquired a full knowledge of the company drill as taught by the new tactics.

About December 1 our company received a contingent of forty recruits, composed of much better material then the original. We now had two hours' drill every day, Upton's tactics in the morning and bayonet exercise in the afternoon. I can conscientiously say that we had a very well-drilled company from that time forward, with one exception, however, which was brought about by the rapacity of our old peddler, Magentie, who broke his promise of abstaining from selling liquor to the garrison, and thus caused the "biggest drunk" I ever saw, and which it fell to my lot to subdue.

The commanding officer had gone out hunting; Lieutenant Winter was still away escorting the railroad people; Lieutenant Gallagher had gone toward the Huachuca Mountains to look for some wood suitable to make furniture, as he had brought his family with him, and First Sergeant Grew, who was acting sergeant-major, was left in charge of the camp. About 3 o'clock p.m. he came to my room and said: "Spring, I am going out riding for a couple of hours; take charge of the camp."

He had not been gone half an hour before "coming events cast their shadows before," and their shadows were cast in rapid succession, promptly revealing awful realities. My first duty sergeant, William Burns, came to inform me that several of our men were staggering about. Upon my going into the company quarters I saw, to my astonishment and mortification, that the men were well provided with mescal, which they drank from canteens and tin cups. Still, as yet none had become boisterous. Upon my going to notify the sergeant left in charge of Grew's company of the existing circumstances, I met several staggering cavalrymen. We soon ascertained that their company was also well supplied with the fiery liquor. I immediately doubled the guard and told the sergeant in charge to watch the door of my room, which he could easily see from the guardhouse, for a signal, upon seeing which he should come on a run with all the men not on sentry duty.

I held a short consultation with Burns and Sergeant Henry of the cavalry the result of which was that I had "assembly" sounded three times in quick succession. This brought all the sober men and all others that could still "navigate" to roll call in front of their quarters; while Sergeants Burns and Henry, with several corporals and a few stout men, each armed with a good club from the woodpiles, entered the quarters and poured out all the liquor they could find, knocking down without ceremony any and all men who offered resistance. Then I signaled the guard, who came on the run; they led, dragged, and carried the drunken men to the guardhouse, around which they were securely tied with ropes fastened to the projecting rafters. Of course, there were a few "scraps," but, still, the impending pandemonium was nipped in the bud.

Toward 5 o'clock the commanding officer returned. As he came over the northern ridge, about the first objects he must have seen were the forty delinquents adorning the walls of the guardhouse. His orderly presently hunted about for whomsoever might be in command; but before he reached me I had already approached the commanding officer and begun to explain the situation.

Immediately ten men were ordered to mount and search the neighborhood carefully for the source whence so much liquor flowed. They were not long in discovering Magentie with a cart hitched to two oxen, although he and his vehicle were pretty well hidden in the undergrowth along the edge of the creek about a mile downwards. Upon the cart there were two barrels that would contain about thirty gallons each; one was empty, the other nearly full. A number of men in different stages of intoxication were lying about and a few were picked up on the way. Magentie was made to drive his cart to camp where it stopped in front of the guardhouse while its owner was led before the commander. As any intelligible conversation between the two was out of the question, I was sent for to interpret.

Colonel Brown was in a state bordering upon fury; Magentie was a sample of personified humility and utter dejection. The conversation was as short as the "corpus delicti" in the shape of two barrels was bulky. The remaining mescal was ordered to be locked up in the commissary storehouse; the oxen were put into the cattle corral, and Magentie was led to the guardhouse, where he had to carry a pretty heavy log in front of the building all night, with one hour's intermission in every three.

The following morning Magentie was again ordered before the high tribunal, and I was requested to tell him that as a matter of fact his mescal, oxen, and cart could be lawfully confiscated then and there and sent, together with his person and necessary witnesses, to the nearest United States Marshal; that, for various reasons, principally on account of he (Magentie) having a large family, the commanding officer would abstain from the said legal proceedings, but sentence him to imprisonment in the guardhouse for the term of one week, during which he would have to police the camp thoroughly, using his cart and oxen in the removal of all brush, papers, sticks, and other impurities; that upon the expiration of said week, he (Magentie) should take himself, his oxen, and cart, without the liquor, beyond the limits of the military reservation, and never set foot upon it again, under penalty of being shot forthwith.

This sentence was executed to the great relief of Magentie, who hardly expected to escape the loss of his property.

REMOVAL TO TUCSON

Nothing worthy of mention occurred till the beginning of March, when our whole garrison was ordered to Tucson. Here we found a camp already established under tents, over which a long "ramada," or brush shed, had been erected. The camp was officially known as Camp Lowell, changed to Fort Lowell afterward, and moved about seven miles north-ward on the borders of the "Rillito" Creek. The brush shed was simply a roof composed of rafters covered with several layers of branches, the whole resting upon long, upright forked poles. The camp was situated about a quarter of a mile to the north of the town. Being open to the wind on all sides, it was in a very undesirable location, on account of the frequent heavy sandstorms prevalent there during the spring months. Of course, our men, especially those who had been at Wallen from its incipiency, and had contributed with their hard labor to build compara-tively comfortable quarters, were not satisfied with the change, although the social pleasures that the town offered consoled them somewhat for the fatigue endured in former days.

The heat under those tents, although somewhat reduced by the brush roof, together with the fine dust penetrating everywhere, began to be insufferable towards the month of June, when the thermometer fre-quently registered 110°F in the shade, and even rose to 114° during the two months following. The water supply at Tucson, obtained from wells permeated with alkali, was also a cause of great dissatisfaction, being incomparably inferior to the clear running water we had enjoyed at Wallen for bathing, as well as drinking. As a set-off, however, to these discomforts, we enjoyed the luxury of unlimited fresh vegetables, as we had acquired for the sum of $400 from our company fund the ownership of a large vegetable garden below the town, which was already planted to vegetables of all kinds, and melons, and was easily irrigated from the waters of the Santa Cruz River.

ON FURLOUGH TO SANTA CRUZ

On the fifteenth of June I was pleasantly surprised by a visit from Mr. Warner, whom I had not seen for some time, and who had come to Tucson on business with the disbursing quartermaster, and also to have two of his freight wagons repaired at the blacksmith shop. He said all at home were well, the numerous aunts included, and insisted upon my accompanying him on his return to Santa Cruz, where the whole popula-tion would celebrate, as usual, the twenty-fourth day of that month, it being San Juan's Day (St. John's), with horse and foot races, etc., and that I, being a "Juan" myself, would be especially feasted at home as well as in the town at large. Of course, I desired nothing better than to accept his invitation and enjoy his liberal hospitality in that town that had become endeared to me for obvious reasons.

But how was I to overcome the difficulty of obtaining a furlough at such short notice, when it involved the crossing of the boundary line, and had to be approved by division headquarters? However, I resolved to make every effort. Colonel Brown was ready and willing to help me away, probably because I had insisted that the officer's mess should pay a small amount into the company fund for the vegetables which they consumed with great lavishness from the company garden. However, he said, that we were too near to regimental and department headquarters (they were at Tucson) to attempt any secret circumvention of the difficulties which related to the proper issue of the furlough, and which I had explained to him. He said he would see the adjutant about the matter that same afternoon, and on the following morning I should take the morning report to the adjutant's office myself and interview the adjutant in person. I did so. I found this gentleman (Lieutenant Ripley) to be a fine officer, quite young, yet pleasant and affable. I explained to him my friendly relations with Mr. Warner and his family, and even threw out a hint about the magnet that drew me towards Santa Cruz with irresistible attraction. He smiled a sweet smile, as if he knew "how it was himself," and bade me wait till he could have a few words with the department commander, General Crittenden, who was also then in command of the regiment, in the adjoining room. He returned in a few minutes and said: "We can arrange the matter. Make your application for a furlough, giving as your destination Tubac, which is on this side of the boundary. This furlough the General will approve at once, and it need not go to division headquarters. Then provide at Tubac, through which you have to pass on your way to Santa Cruz, an address or person to whom we can send word, if the emergencies of the service (not likely to occur) should demand your presence. Have this person at Tubac understand that if we call, he must at once send an Indian runner to Santa Cruz to inform you of the fact, and then you return without delay. Thus for us you will officially be at Tubac, and you will understand that neither the General nor I know of anything else. I wish you success and happiness."

What an easy solution of an apparently difficult problem! I tendered Lieutenant Ripley my most sincere thanks, and ran to attend to the furlough, which I dated June 20, as that was the day fixed by Mr. Warner for our departure.

Putting all company matters in good shape, I turned the company over to Sergeant Burns on the morning of that day, and by 1 p.m. we were underway for Santa Cruz. Mr. Warner, Pedro, the majordomo; two house servants, and myself, all well armed, rode in the former's traveling carriage drawn by two horses. We were followed by the two repaired wagons drawn by four mules each, the drivers riding on the near wheelers, while on each wagon rode a well-armed house servant. The rear was brought up by Captain Catterson, who accompanied us on his way to the Patagonian mines. He was a very jovial companion, known to be a brave frontiersman. While in camp he entertained us with stories of frontier life, daring exploits, and hairbreadth escapes, little dreaming that on the very next New Year's Day he would fall a bloody and mutilated victim to a party of Apaches in the Sonoita Valley, where I helped to bury his mangled remains.

At nightfall we stopped at a place called Sahuarito (little giant cactus), for an isolated plant of that kind growing near the place, which was an eating and watering station kept by one Benedict, about twenty-five miles south of Tucson, and one mile west of the Santa Cruz River. This man was wounded by Apaches a few days later while irrigating his cornfield, but managed to reach the house.

On the following day we made an early start, passed by the Canoa about noon, and reached Tubac about dark. Here I found my friend Wooster in his store, and told him that I had given his name to Lieutenant Ripley for the purpose of having me called at Santa Cruz, should the emergency arise, and he promised that in that case he would immediately send me word by a Papago Indian. He also provided that the matter should be attended to in case of the message from Tucson arriving during his absence. I will say right here that, although we might be considered as rivals for the hand of Eulalia, and in fact were so, our friendship never suffered in the least from that fact. When we parted at Tubac he took me by the hand and said: "I wish you luck, old boy; I am out of it." (He and his wife were killed by Apaches in June, 1871, at the Paloparado, near Tubac, at the house which he and I built together in 1869).

As the road so far and even to Calabazas, Huevabi, and the so-called Stone House situated about twelve miles south of Calabazas, led through a comparatively well-populated region, and was therefore not considered very dangerous, we traveled still by day, arriving at the Stone House early in the afternoon, with the intention of proceeding on our way hence at nightfall. (This Stone House had been built by an old man named Pennington, who had been one of the first settlers. One by one the male members of the numerous family had succumbed to the murderous Apaches, from whom a married daughter had an almost miraculous escape. The old man himself and his only remaining, youngest son, Green, were killed by the Indians in the Sonoita in the summer of 1869).

ATTACKED BY APACHES

We started from the Stone House about dark in the same order of march as heretofore observed. From the Stone House to Santa Cruz the distance is about forty miles, for the most part over good, hard road, over mesa land, but interrupted now and then by stretches of heavy sand, where the road approached the river bed to the latter's edge; there were also several dry river beds to cross, where the waters descended from the mountains lying to the west during the rainy seasons. We had traveled about ten miles, when we came to one of these dry beds which we had to cross. It was very sandy, rocky in parts, and about fifty yards wide. The moon had risen early, being nearly full, so that in its clear light everything could easily be seen to quite a distance. The drivers of the wagons had dismounted from their saddle mules and were walking by the side of their teams. There were many large rocks or boulders on either side of the road, some forming groups, others scattered about here and there; many elder trees and considerable lower growth stood in and along the river bed.

We were about half across the heavy sand bed, when suddenly, without any other noise and without our mules or horses giving any previous indication of scenting Apaches (which these animals generally did), we received a volley of bullets and arrows from the righthand side of the road. The horses of our vehicle shied, but Pedro was out of the carriage and at their heads in a second and held them fast. We could see no enemy, but fired immediately several volleys in the direction of a bush situated somewhat above the road level, where we saw a light cloud of smoke. Presently we heard what seemed to be the thuds of jumping feet in rapid succession; then all was still, and we began to examine what damage had been done.

Not a single man was hurt; but one mule had been pierced by an arrow, through the neck, apparently not much to its discomfort, while another was struck by a bullet in the kneecap of a foreleg, which disabled the animal beyond all possible recovery. The shots from firearms could not have been more than four. We afterwards discovered a bullet in the rear part of the ambulance in which we were riding. From the depth to which the iron arrowheads had penetrated the boards forming the wagon beds we could judge of the astonishing effectiveness of that weapon.

Three of us cautiously approached the bush whence to all appearance the Apache volley had been delivered. We found that it grew out of a fissure in a large boulder well covered with wild grapevines and other climbing and creeping plants. Behind it there was a sort of platform formed by a large flat rock, that afforded standing room for at least twenty persons. From this ambush the Indians must have fired, jumping immediately afterwards to the sandy level below and scampering away as soon as they observed the indifferent results of their attack.

The Indians probably numbered about twelve. Against all previous experiences, their shooting had been very poor, probably on account of the uncertain light of the moon, to which they are little accustomed, and which renders them fidgety; probably also by reason of the distance (about forty yards) from which they delivered their fire, their usual manner of waylaying and attacking travelers being to hide very close to the road and to fire into their backs as they pass from a few yards or feet distant. If, however, the main object of their attack was (and I think this most likely) to obtain mule meat, they had succeeded in their undertaking, as we had to abandon the mule with the broken leg.

Captain Catterson seemed more than willing, according to the tendencies acquired in frontier life, to follow and punish the Apaches, but soon refrained from all warlike enterprise upon the dry remark of Don Solomon that "we were not hunting Apaches." We shot the crippled mule through the brain and proceeded on our way, arriving at Santa Cruz without any further accidents during the forenoon of the following day.

My reception at the house was most cordial. When Eulalia gave me her beautiful hand she blushed a rosy red, which circumstance is generally, I believe, accepted to be a good omen. Doña María, her mother, bade me welcome in the accustomed Mexican manner, which is a slight embrace, allowed to married women only. Still, it seemed to me then and later on during my visit that she did not feel quite at ease. Of course, this I rather felt than saw.

Eulalia had developed into still greater beauty and wore suspended on a small gold chain a little locket I had sent her by Mendoza. Ostensibly, of course, I sent it to little Carmelita, her half-sister, but I saw that it had reached its destination, and the wearer of it now either could not or would not hide the pleasure she experienced at our meeting. The aunts were there, of course. Yes, they were all there, and seemed to resume their watchfulness from the very moment I entered the house.

The spacious mansion of Don Solomon, and especially the very roomy kitchen, was full of women preparing all sorts of good things for the coming festivity. Turkeys and chickens were slaughtered and plucked, red pepper was being ground upon two metates at once; dried maize leaves were soaked, stretched, and dried to envelop the toothsome *tamale;* cornmeal cakes were patted flat and fried to assume the beautifully sprinkled appearance of *enchiladas,* while a professional baker busied himself in the manufacture of *biscochuelos* and other sweetmeats. Two large ollas containing the refreshing "tez-win" were conspicuous in a shady corner of the porch.

In another room several lavanderas and planchadoras (washer and ironing women) occupied themselves with the cleaning and general getting-up of male and female attire and finery.

In the large corral behind the house, horses were groomed, saddles and bridles were mended and polished. I became aware that if Santa Cruz was a sleepy town the whole year through, at least on San Juan's Day it was going to be very much awake. Not to be behindhand in the omnipresent preparations, Don Solomon, Mr. Brown (the subcontractor before mentioned), and myself went to the storeroom to look over the stock of bottled wine, from which we selected a goodly portion for future use.

Very early on the following morning one became aware that something unusual was going forward. All Mexicans generally begin to feast the *vespera* (the night preceding) of the feast day proper, and don their best apparel for that purpose. This differs from the workday clothing only by its freshly-laundered appearance, and in some instances by finer material. It consists in a white shirt, a pair of wide pocketless cotton or linen trousers, held up by a cotton or silk sash in brilliant magenta red, and if the state of the finances permit it, of shoes and a richly silver-embroidered hat. During the night preceding the feast days one or more dances are generally started in the house blessed with the presence of young ladies, who invite their friends. The mothers of the young ladies thus attending or their mothers or the aunts, etc., need no invitation; they are there sure, never fear! All this refers to the poorest class of people, the laborers, etc., who make a night of it, and sometimes drink too much, beginning with tez-win and ending with mescal or *aguardiente de cana* (sugar cane brandy), which tastes not unlike New England rum.

Thus it happens that on the morning of a feast day or of a Sunday in out-of-the-way country villages one or more groups of more or less "elevated" men are seen and generally heard on the street corners, singing love ditties and carrying a bottle or two, which passes at intervals from mouth to mouth. If left to themselves they are perfectly harmless, and the terrible stories of Mexicans all carrying knives and making use thereof at the least provocation, are simply "bosh."

I visited my old friend, Don Alfonso, the dispenser of the eggnog spoken of upon a former occasion, during the forenoon. He received me with open arms, which he gently closed upon my back, and forthwith proceeded to concoct the now-famous Babocomari drink. He was dressed with extreme neatness.

If we except the groups of overnight feasters mentioned above, it is a rare sight indeed to see a Mexican on foot on a twenty-fourth of June, as even the last and lowest laborer on a ranch will easily obtain a mount for that day's celebration from his employer, and even frequently buy off his indebtedness to the latter by winning a horse race upon an apparently valueless mustang picked from the owner's herd at random. This they call *perdonar la deuda* (to forgive or cancel the debt). Formerly, when the peon law was still in existence, instances of such canceling of an indebtedness were not at all rare. After the noon dinner everybody will be on horseback, men taking their wives, brothers their sisters, and their lady cousins upon the saddle before them. A girl who either does not care for her reputation or has none to lose will ride with her "fellow" in the same manner.

One of the main features of a San Juan's day was then, and is to some extent now, what they call *la carrera del gallo* (the run for the rooster). In order to enact this barbarous game they select a bit of straight road, upon which they bury a rooster up to his neck in the sand. Then they draw lots for first, second, third, etc., run or start. The order of riding being established, the first man starts, his task being to bend down while on a full run, grasp the head of the rooster, and pull it out of the sand. This is not so very easy as it would at first appear, as the rooster, by ducking and side jerks, tries to evade the grasping hand. But at last a long, slim cowboy succeeds; he pulls the bird up, and swinging it in triumph around his own head by the neck, he darts off. This is the signal for all the riders to start on a wild chase, to reach the carrier of the bird and to pull it away from him. If one obtains it, another rider will pursue him with the same object in view, and presently there is nothing left visible of the poor bird, which has literally been pulled to pieces alive, but a few feathers. It is a disgusting sight to humane people. I hold Mexicans to be cruel to all animals, even to their horses, that are their best friends.

Their horse races also contain a feature that is very objectionable, and, in my opinion, precludes all fairness in the sport. As they care less for a very fast horse on a short run than for a long-winded horse that will come out winner after a long run, their race tracks, which are simply the highways of the country, often extend over several miles. At different stations of the stretch to be run over some of the friends of the rider, or perhaps the owner of the running horse, will post himself as "whipper-in." Whenever the horse of their selection passes by, they will join the run, urging the horse with whip and voice to its utmost efforts, often barring the passage to the contending riders.

(Be it understood that I speak here of races among country people in country towns or upon large stock-ranches.)

The best sport of the day by far was a three-mile-and-return foot race, in which the runners kicked a ball before them. With it they must return, as its loss precludes their winning the race. This ball they are not allowed to touch with their hands under any circumstances; hence they must be careful not to kick it into inaccessible places. The *jueces* (judges) of the race accompany the runners on horseback and see fair play. The six miles made on the day I speak of were covered in fifty-five minutes by the winner, our majordomo, Pedro, who was prouder than a peacock and received a pretty mustang as a prize from Don Solomon. Such little traits of attention and liberality attach Mexican servants to their masters immeasurably.

Of course, being in the swim, I swam with the stream; that is, I bet right and left, with Doña Maria, with Eulalia — aye, even with the aunts and — equally of course, lost about every bet.

The festivities of the day, during which the kitchen of Doña Maria and the cellar of Don Solomon and his stables furnished the best in the land in eatables, drinkables, and horseflesh, ended with a dance, or rather two dances, one being held at Mr. Warner's mansion by a select company and the other, more promiscuous-like, in the garden of Don Alfonso by everybody and his sister. The Mexican women dance prettily and gracefully, even those from the illiterate part of the population; but on account of the everpresent contingent of elderly females as chaperones and the super-modest training of the girls, these dances are of the tamest.

Don Solomon, Mr. Brown, the German clerk, Henry, and your humble narrator concluded the day's festivities with a moderate "quantum suff." of Babocomari milk in the garden of Mr. Fernandez, who had acquired by that time a decided taste for that superior refreshment.

A RIVAL FOR THE HAND OF EULALIA

On the twenty-ninth of June we celebrated the Feast Day of San Pedro and San Pablo (St. Peter and St. Paul) in about the same manner as the preceding one, but somewhat more mildly. There were stationed at that time at Santa Cruz a part company of Mexican cavalry under the command of Lieutenant Reyes, a very gentlemanly but far from good-looking young man. He and I became great friends, and during the whole of that day put his splendid horse Juarez at my disposal. This animal was high-spirited, but gentle, and playful withal, with ease and grace in every motion; it would readily dance of its own accord as soon as it heard music, were it only from a harp or guitar. His master, the Lieutenant, also learned to drink eggnog, which he pronounced *un refresco divino* (a heavenly refreshment); but I could readily see that there was something, or rather somebody else, about that he thought at least as "heavenly." I could not help but see that Mr. Reyes felt entirely at home in the mansion and with the womenfolk of all ages of Don Solomon, and I might have become jealous if his almost repulsive features had allowed such a sentiment to grow within me.

I will not attempt to describe my feelings of impatience at not being able to have a single intimate interview with my beloved, although we both tried every means within our reach to have a secret meeting. We spoke together with our eyes, which implement has been known from time immemorial to be capable of great though unspoken eloquence. We wrote one another a few small notes daily, which reached their destination through the hands of little Carmelita, our sweet messenger of love, who was too young to be submitted to the ceaseless watch that overshadowed her sister. In these missives we had agreed to marry as soon as possible after my leaving the service. Once, indeed, and once only, I managed to kiss the sweet lips of my beautiful treasure through the barred window of her room, after nightfall, and that hasty kiss has remained in my memory forever. I could not obliterate the heavenly remembrance from my mind even when I heard that the adored of my soul had —

But wait!

On the day following St. Peter's Feast, Mr. Warner drove me out to the old Spanish mission of San Lazaro in his ambulance. He must have known that I was wishing for a private conversation with him. We were alone in the vehicle, and I, being aware of the friendly disposition he entertained towards me, frankly broached the subject nearest to my heart. Don Solomon heard me out patiently while I tried to explain my devouring passion, as well as my prospects for the future. I had saved a considerable sum of money, the amount of which I mentioned to him, with which I intended to start a mercantile establishment after my discharge and to engage in contracting also for government supplies. I divulged to him without reserve how I stood with Eulalia, begging him to forgive little Carmelita the kind help she had given us in our mutual correspondence for love of her sister.

He nodded his head from time to time in what I thought a fatherly way. When I had finished he said: "My dear boy, that is all very well as far as it goes, and I wish you all manner of luck. As far as I am concerned, you are welcome to marry Eulalia on the very day you have your discharge in your pocket, and I shall be glad to help you to a good solid start in your commercial undertakings; but — and here is a great but — I am not the father of Eulalia, as you know. You know by this time enough of the customs of this country to be aware that in a case of this kind the matter rests almost entirely with the mother of the girl. I incline to the belief that she will insist upon a marriage with a Mexican."

"But what if Eulalia herself wishes" — I began.

"The girl herself has no will of her own, and will submit to her mother's choice," he interrupted. "You may make sure of that; provided, of course, they (meaning the whole female contingent at the house) will not try to force upon her a husband that would be distasteful to her. If we were in the United States you might run away with her, if you cannot obtain her in the legally acknowledged fashion, but under the circumstances in which we live and from the people among whom we live you can no more abduct her than you can fetch the moon down to earth. My advice to you is to 'get around' Doña Maria, Eulalia's mother. You have acquired the Spanish gift of the gab to a surprising degree."

During the few days more I remained at Santa Cruz I tried to follow his precept, but with very indifferent success. Eulalia's mother was uniformly polite to me at all times; so she was to all the guests of the house; but I did not seem to catch on to the requisite manuver (sic) of "getting around" her for the purpose intended, and finally departed at the expiration of my furlough with happy memories indeed and my breast pocket full of lovely notes from my adored one, but with hopes of the realization of my happiness indefinitely postponed.

IN HOSPITAL AT TUCSON

I arrived at Tucson safely, having traveled one hundred twenty miles without accident by night upon a good horse.

In the beginning of August I became ill. I had to be taken to the hospital at Tucson, in which I remained under the treatment of Dr. Smart, surgeon, U.S.A., until the day of my discharge. My sickness was a very severe one; I lost forty pounds in weight during that one and a half months and left the hospital in a very weak and emaciated state. In those days I think the only remedies employed in the cure of dysentery were castor oil and laudanum. Of this latter ingredient I had been administered very large doses at frequent intervals, so that when the malady was at last checked the desire for that opiate had been created and remained.

Surgeon Smart knew that very well, and spoke like a father to me upon the subject. He said: "Now, young man, the disease is checked. I was obliged to give you this medicine frequently and in large doses, because the disease proved very obstinate, unusually so in one so young and strong. You will find that it has created an appetite for narcotics that you will probably desire to satisfy in any way possible. If you do you will become an opium eater and destroy any and every happiness that is yet in store for you. I do not believe in the so-called process of 'tapering off.' Break off at once and forever. I say all this for your own good, partly because it is my duty as a surgeon and partly because I love you well. We all like you very much. Therefore, be a man! In order to facilitate the success of your resolution I will put you in a room by yourself, where you can burn a light all night and read the interesting books I am going to send you. The steward will give you a spoonful of brandy from time to time to subdue the nervousness from which you will suffer. But do not try to obtain the drug, no matter what you may suffer from the lack of it. In a few days you will, with the help of good diet, have overcome the craving for opium."

Notwithstanding the sufferings created by intense nervousness and an unsatisfied craving for the narcotic, I withstood all temptation and feel grateful to that kind doctor to this day.

But not to him alone. Many indeed are those, officers and enlisted men, whose names are engraved in my memory in deep lines of affection and gratitude for the forbearance and kindness they have shown me, thus contributing towards making my three years' service "With the Regulars in Arizona" a period of almost unalloyed happiness.

My comrades who left Tucson a few days previous to my discharge for their muster-out at Wilmington (Drum Barracks), Cal., came one and all to the hospital to say good-by.

On Sept. 16 I started on the buckboard of the mail rider, my friend and comrade, William Burns, to Camp Wallen, where my friend, Leslie B. Wooster, had the hay contract for that year, in which I was financially interested.

*   *   *   *

I never married Eulalia. A short time after my last visit to Santa Cruz Mr. Warner was stricken down with a severe attack of pneumonia and was taken to the hospital at Camp Crittenden. A few months after his recovery he was attacked and seriously wounded by Apaches on the road from Santa Cruz to Magdalena, Sonora, and was taken to Tucson for surgical treatment, which was protracted for a long period, the wound being very complicated. He ultimately recovered, but with the loss of all power and motion in his right arm. During his extended absences from home Lieutenant Reyes sought and obtained the hand of Miss Eulalia in marriage from her mother.

In 1885 I was employed by the Mexican government to establish public schools in the State of Sonora. While performing this service at the town of Magdalena I was suddenly accosted on the street by Pedro Urquides, the former majordomo of Mr. Warner, then occupying the same position with Lieutenant Reyes, who had quit the army and was farming an extensive hacienda upon the lands of San Lazaro. Pedro said that he had brought his poor master to the town in which we were that he (Mr. Reyes) might be examined by a skillful Spanish surgeon who was there looking at some hot springs; that Mr. Reyes was evidently a very sick man, although nobody could discover the source of his malady, which manifested itself principally through insomnia, melancholy, and loss of appetite. I went with Pedro to visit the patient, and found an aged-looking, broken-down man, with glassy eyes, sunken cheeks, wrinkled skin, sad, listless, and totally indifferent to his surroundings. Pedro had cautioned me not to mention his wife Eulalia.

"Don Juan," he had said to me; "it was an unhappy marriage, an ill-sorted union. Soon after the first child was born Doña Eulalia took to drinking mescal — soon to excess (his voice began to tremble here); then she — oh Don Juan, how can I tell you? — then — she went to the bad — in another way — and — "

Here Pedro broke down and wept. I wept with him out of pity for the sweet, broken flower, the love of my early youth.

Pedro took Mr. Reyes home after the doctor declared that he could do nothing for the patient, as the disease was caused by mental disorder.

Next week's mail brought me a postal card from Pedro. It read:

"Lieutenant Reyes shot himself through the heart this morning.

"Yours,

"Pedro Urquides."

PART II

Troublous Days in Arizona

John Spring sketched this scene in the Arivaca region of Southern Arizona, the site of Frank Oury's assassination.

Troublous Days in Arizona

FROM SOLDIER TO PIONEER

IT WAS September, 1868 when John Spring left the military hospital in Tucson with an honorable discharge in his pocket. During those last weeks of his enlistment he had been beset with a siege of dysentery, an ailment then common in southern Arizona. Now he was well enough to join his friend, Leslie B. Wooster, with whom he had a government contract to deliver hay from the Babocomari Valley to feed the horses at Camp Wallen.

A new day had dawned for Spring. Four years of army life were behind him as he stepped out of the hospital at Alameda and Court streets. From there, in all probability, he made his way to Main Street to secure transportation with the mail rider to Camp Wallen on his way to the hay camp. Clearly visible were the Sierra Tucsons (Tucson Mountains) which stretched their jagged tops across the western sky. The clanging of anvils could be heard in blacksmith shops as shoes of tempered steel were shaped to fit the hooves of horses and mules which pulled wagon trains and buckboards over old Spanish roads and trails. These were the wagons, coming and going, which brought merchandise to the stores of Tucson, and equipment to the farms of the valley and to the mines of the nearby mountains. Wines from San Francisco and cigars from Havana were luxuries enjoyed by those who prospered in this booming town. Not all the trains, however, survived the long and painfully slow journey to the Old Pueblo, for not infrequently Apaches would swoop down from the mountains to kill and rob or take captive some poor souls unfortunate enough to be spared.

Curiously enough, these Apaches were indirectly responsible for the prosperity of the region. Because of them, soldiers and military establishments were needed to guard the early settlements. The chief supply depot was in Tucson. Soldiers were stationed at Camp Lowell, at what is now Scott and Broadway to "guard the stores of the depot quartermaster and to escort his trains to the various posts of southern Arizona." Business was good and government contracts were lucrative sources of income for Solomon Warner, Tully & Ochoa, William B. Hooper & Company, Hinds & Hooker, Goldberg & Company, and many others. This land, old as the conquistadores but now a new and thriving frontier, attracted also such men as the Zeckendorfs, the Drachmans, and the Hughes, and Steinfeld, Mansfield, and Safford.

From a population of six hundred in 1866, as noted by Bishop Salpointe, Tucson increased in numbers to 3,224 as reported in the census of 1870. The census is good reading for there we find blacksmiths, silversmiths, carriage makers, wagon masters, saloon keepers, lawyers, gamblers, and soldiers. Listed are the names of such soldiers as Patrick Callahan and John Devine from Ireland and Julius Bechtold from Germany as well as the names of men from the Atlantic seaboard and the middle-west. Among the professional gamblers enumerated were Daniel McCarthy, an Irish immigrant, and easterners such as Edwin C. Haines and John B. Hart.

Blue uniforms were commonly seen in the drinking and gambling places of the day. Well known were the Palace and the Congress Hall saloons where the Fifth Territorial Legislature supposedly first met when it moved down from Prescott. Frequented also were the establishments of Foster and Hand and the Wheat Saloon, the latter run by Augustus Brichta, best known as the first public school teacher in Tucson. It was Brichta who advertised in the *Weekly Arizonian* in 1869 that "the undersigned having leased the above saloon is prepared to furnish his friends and the public with a general assortment of wines, liquors, and cigars."

Advertisements were an index to the times. Sweeney and Etchel advertised their blacksmith and wagon shop on Pearl Street by stating that "wagons are made and repaired at this establishment and everything in the blacksmith line done with promptness and dispatch." Tully & Ochoa, in addition to furnishing supplies to military posts by government contract, and operating wagon trains, ran a general store located "on Main Street, Tucson, A. T." as stated in their advertisement in the *Weekly Arizonian* of Sunday, January 24, 1869. They gave "general notice to their friends and the public generally that they have received direct from the East a full and complete stock of DRY GOODS, GROCERIES, HARDWARE &c and are prepared to sell at as reasonable terms as any merchant in the Territory." Goodwin and Sanders, dealers in general merchandise, announced in the January first issue that they have "this day on hand and are constantly receiving a large stock of goods expressly selected for this market Dry Goods and Clothing, Hats and Caps, Boots and Shoes, Military Furnishings, goods of all descriptions, Staples and Fancy Goods, Belts, Pistols, powder, percussion caps &c, &c, which they will sell cheap for cash."

Belts, pistols, powder, and percussion caps were needed for protection from the undesirable elements of the town and from the Apaches who were a constant threat to travellers and to the inhabitants of the smaller communities. Spring wrote in his *Troublous Days* "that quite frequently its [Tucson's] population awoke to find a dead man in the street, sometimes killed over-night while seeking his habitation in the then unlighted streets, sometimes also, and this quite frequently, killed in a brawl over cards or women in a barroom or dancehouse, when his body would be simply dragged some distance away and abandoned." Then he added, "As everybody kept firearms in their houses, house-breaking was very rare."

Courage was a commonplace quality possessed by the pioneers living in the valleys and villages of southern Arizona. Counting all who had suffered death at the hands of the Apaches, Spring wrote "My own data gives the number of murdered men, women, and children during those years of 1869, 1870, and 1871 as 227." Among the numbered dead were Leslie B. Wooster and his common-law wife, Trinidad Aguirre, killed in a raid on their farm home in the Valley of Tubac. The position Spring took in *Troublous Days in Arizona* in defense of the Camp Grant Massacre was undoubtedly influenced by the death of his best friend and by that of many others whom he knew personally. It is to the pen of John Spring that we owe much of our knowledge of the Camp Grant incident. William S. Oury and Jesus M. Elías were the leaders in the reprisal against the government-fed Indians of the camp who in spite of their daily ration of beef sallied forth to plunder and kill. Oury some years later was asked by the Arizona Pioneers' Historical Society to read a paper describing the massacre at one of its meetings. There is little doubt that Oury had asked Spring to write it for him, for it is unmistakably written in Spring's style and words. It was not unusual for Spring to record occurrences of special interest for other citizens.

The feeling against the Apaches was shared by most in those early years. The *Weekly Arizonian* of January 24, 1869, editorialized, "I shall first speak of the Apache who roams with freedom through his apparently inaccessible mountain retreats without any pretense to civilization. This latter Apache has for years carried on a system of warfare with greater or less success as the mutilated remains and whitened bones of our valuable citizens, picked up from time to time in various parts of the Territory provide an awful but incontestable proof."

Again on April 16, 1870, a news item appeared in the *Weekly Arizonian* concerning an individual who had been killed by the Apaches. "The head was severed from the body and laid at its side, the hands likewise were cut off and carried off."

In spite of their courage and steadfastness of purpose, the citizens of Tubac and surrounding vicinity felt the necessity in 1869 of requesting help from the military. Among the thirty-five signers of a petition addressed to the Commanding General of the Southern Military District of Arizona were the names of Spring and Wooster, then partners in a general store on Main Street in Tubac. The petition on file at the Arizona Pioneers' Historical Society reads as follows:

> Petition to the Gen'l Cmdg.
>   So. Dist. Arizona
>   Tucson, A. T.
> General:
>   Your petitioners the citizens of Tubac and vicinity would respectfully represent that they are subject to frequent raids of the Apache Indians, their depredations have extended to this town murdering our citizens, stealing stock and spreading terror wherever they have been.
>   This section of the country visited by the Apache represent (*sic*) one of the finest sections of agricultural land in the territory. A very large portion of the grain consumed by the troops has been raised on the banks of the Santa Cruz and Lonoita (*sic*) [Probably Sonoita].
>   We are under the firm conviction that unless military aid can be rendered this part of the country will eventually have to be abandoned.
>   This being the main thoroughfare to Sonora, it gives the Govt. annually a large revenue, and the richly loaded trains from that State offers to the savage a rich harvest.
>   Your petitioners would earnestly request that at least one company of Troops be stationed in this vicinity.
>
> (Signed by thirty-five citizens)

John Spring's Arizona included the town of Florence where, as indicated earlier in the introduction, he was engaged for a period of time in the brewery business. Life along the Gila River in the proximity of Florence was rough and ready and fraught with danger for prospectors in search of minerals. Less than a year after Spring decided to return to Tucson to accept a teaching position, D. C. Thompson, a member of the Board of Trustees of Florence School District No. 2, then in Pima County, wrote a letter on December 9, 1872, to L. C. Hughes, *ex officio* superintendent of schools. After dealing with certain business matters concerning the school census, he wrote of life along the Gila as a copper prospector:

> Also We have been verry buissy here at different times in Regard to Shooting and Killing men & etc. They are making verry good Shots now on the Gila they shoot them Now rite between the two eyes — dead Shots, and dead center — Hell of a country — I am almost completely desgusted with the Country and if I could Wind

up, my buiseness Without loosing So much I would leave it for a
while anyway. The Country is good Enoughf but Some of the people
Lord bless them — What will become of them is more then I
can tell. . . .

Camp Wallen, Tubac, Tucson and Florence, all were part of the
Arizona of which Spring wrote. At different times he mentioned a scrapbook in which he recorded the happenings of the time. Nowhere today
is the scrapbook to be found, but undoubtedly it was from these original
accounts that he later wrote most of the material found in this volume.
As to why the second part, *Troublous Days in Arizona,* ends so abruptly,
one can only speculate. Perhaps it was because his health was such that
he could not continue.

As a writer, John Spring was an important contributor to our present
knowledge of early Arizona. He deserves recognition both as a foremost
citizen of the frontier and a sensitive lay historian. For although he was
in a sense encapsulated by his own times, his humanity and his gift of
articulation enabled him to communicate with men and women of the
future as well.   —A. M. G.

To a person sitting of a cold night in a comfortable armchair before
a lighted backlog in a luxuriously furnished room, the news brought from
day to day of reverses of the English army in the Transvaal were matters
of great astonishment and called forth his or her severe criticism of
English strategy.

How many of these critics have looked back to the months from
June to August 1886, during which period we had in a corner of our
vast dominion about five thousand regulars in the field under General
Miles, for the purpose of capturing the wily Apache chief, Geronimo,
and his band, who had for many years rendered life and property insecure
in Southern Arizona? With these troops there was an efficient signal corps
manipulating the heliograph, which in the thin pure air of the Arizona
highlands was necessarily of great service. In addition to these regular
troops, General Miles had employed a goodly number of the best Apache
scouts from San Carlos, while about one thousand Mexican soldiers, under
General Carbo, were strung along from east to west, south of the frontier,
in order to intercept the warriors of Geronimo, should they attempt to
enter the mountain fastnesses of the Sierra Madre where General Crook
a few years previous had met with untold fatigue difficulties, etc., and —
well, let us call it "very indifferent success."

After Lieutenant Gatewood had persuaded Geronimo, who saw himself surrounded on all sides, to surrender, the fighting force of his band

[Geronimo's] consisted of less than twenty able bodied men or warriors.

For the better understanding of my readers how it was possible that a few bands of Apaches were able to keep a territory equal in area to one-half of France, as the latter was before the cession of Alsace and Lorraine, in almost constant fear and trembling by countless murders, robberies, and destruction of property for a period exceeding thirty years, I shall begin this serial with a description of these Indians not taken from books, but given as a result of my own observations during the many years I have had more or less "intimate" relations with them, suffering personally from their depredations in various ways.

THE APACHE INDIAN IN WAR AND PEACE

Mr. Bancroft, in his work treating of "The Wild Indian Tribes of America," includes the Navajos, Comanches, and almost all the other tribes that have been conquered and more or less civilized during the last forty years in Arizona, Texas, and New Mexico, in the nation of the Apaches. I would therefore remark beforehand, that my sketches refer only to the tribe of the real Apaches, in whose immediate surroundings I lived almost continuously from 1866 to 1893. This tribe consists of several sub-tribes, called respectively Chiricahuas, Coyoteros, Mescaleros, Tontos, and Mohaves.† Insignificant differences in dialect excepted, all these subdivisions speak nearly the same language and have ceased years ago to acknowledge an hereditary chief. Even when they roamed at large and committed their sanguinary depredations, they would elect from their midst for a war chief a man who was known to the tribe for his bravery and sagacity to lead them for the time being; him they would implicitly obey while he was in power, but as soon as he was outdone in warlike actions by another, he would have to cede his authority to the more worthy rival. It is thus seen that the political condition of the Apache tribes was entirely of a democratic nature, a condition of things which undoubtedly impeded frequently possible peace negotiations on account of the frequent changes in leadership and incident dissensions in the tribes. When, however, a chieftain excelled in warlike qualifications and led his warriors again and again in their bloody work of murder and robbery with successful results, he would remain for years the acknowledged and undisputed ruler of his tribe. This was the case with Cochise, who remained undisturbed in dictatorship of the Chiricahua tribe, the wildest and most

---

†There are, of course, more sub-tribes of the Apache than John Spring realized. His report on Bancroft's broad interpretation of Apache, however, is essentially correct, although ethnologists now regard Apaches and Navajos both as Southern Athabaskans, and Comanches as members of the Shoshonean family.

bloodthirsty of them all, from 1856 to 1874, in which latter year all the
conquered Indians of southern Arizona were gathered upon the Indian
reservation of San Carlos, the tribe of Cochise alone excepted. During
the negotiations which had this result, his crafty diplomacy came into play,
for he knew how to concoct and advance so many plausible reasons to
demonstrate why his tribe should have a reservation apart and why this
reservation should be situated in or near the rocky fastnesses of the Chiricahua range of mountains, and made so many promises of future good
behavior, that he was accorded the privilege he sought.

These mountains are of such a nature as to afford almost everywhere
a natural and in some places impregnable fortification; in such places
Cochise would establish his rancherias (temporary camps or dwelling
places where the squaws, children, and old men find a safe retreat) when
he desired to rest awhile from his nomadic life and depredatory excursions.
From these mountain fastnesses he undertook his innumerable death-
dealing and plundering expeditions till death overcame him, in 1878.
His son, Natchez, and later on Geronimo and other chiefs, followed in the
dead man's footsteps and led the tribe with equal daring in all atrocious
deviltries until, in 1883, the government lost its ill-applied patience and
forbearance and sent General Crook to either subjugate or annihilate the
Chiricahua tribe. In view of the fact that the Mexican states of Chihuahua
and Sonora, which adjoin the territory of the United States on its southern
frontier, had suffered at least equally as much from the frequent depredations of these Indians, a treaty was entered into between the two republics
granting each other the right to cross the boundary line with armed forces
in pursuit of hostile Indians. By virtue of this treaty General Crook crossed
the Mexican frontier with his troops, and penetrated, under dreadful hardships and difficulties, into the very heart of the Sierra Madre range in the
Mexican state of Sonora, where he came up with the Indians, took some
prisoners (old men called "hostages") and received from the chiefs their
solemn promise that they would surrender themselves within a given time
at the reservation of San Carlos. After a considerable lapse of overtime
they did so, marking, however, their route hither with numerous bloody
deeds and acts of robbery.

But let us return to the time when the Apaches were still in their
wild state, following almost untrammeled and unchecked their murderous
career. Arizona is a country where every highway, every path, every hamlet and nearly every rancho could tell, had they the gift of speech, of
devilish deeds, of crafty ambuscade, murdered settlers and travellers,
unfortunate captives tortured to death in the most cruel manner and then
mutilated in a disgusting fashion. I have statistic proof that in the then very

sparsely settled territory (about 20,000 souls in 1886, exclusive of Indians), between the years 1854 and 1875, more than nine hundred persons met their death at the hands of the Apaches. My own memoranda for the years 1867–1871, during which period I took part in several expeditions against the Apaches, show that within a circle of about one hundred miles' diameter, with the center at Tubac, in the Santa Cruz Valley, many fell victims to these Indians, for the most part Chiricahuas, who, at that time, had comparatively few firearms. Especially severe was the loss of life of settlers and travelers in the Santa Cruz valley and near the present site of the city of Nogales and about the Sonoita Creek and the pass of the same name, leading from Heubaba to Fort Crittenden.

That the powerful government of the United States allowed such a state of affairs to exist had several reasons; one was, I believe, of a purely political nature, which I shall here ignore. Another was undoubtedly to be found in what we sufferers considered the mistaken philanthropy of some eastern enthusiasts, who did not understand the character of the Apache Indian, and who ignored the sufferings of our white people, whom they looked upon (from a long distance) as a wild sort of unruly cowboys to whom they ascribed in their ignorance the role of "agents provacateurs." The main obstacle, however, to the suppression of the wild marauders, consisted unquestionably in the great difficulties which opposed themselves in the Territory of Arizona and surrounding countries to a successful expedition against the fleet and crafty wolves of the mountains and desert plains. Arizona has an area of 113,010 square miles. With the exception of a comparatively very small portion in the southwest, where the peaceable Pimas, Maricopas, Yumas and Papagos, since centuries the sworn enemies of the Apaches, live upon their scanty crops, the whole country was open to the savages. It consists to a great extent of sandy plateaus or highlands, generally called *mesas,* intersected by innumerable gulches and large and small canyons, of long chains of craggy mountains with many inaccessible cliffs, and of some valleys through which flow the few rivers, nearly dry during the summer, that now feed the irrigating canals and minor ditches. With the exception of these streams, water was exceedingly scarce during the dry season. As a rule the Apaches would establish their rancherias in a hollow between two mountain cliffs, near a spring or small stream, known to them only. From the heights above, they would have a good lookout upon the plains in every direction. From afar they would espy the tired, thirsty caravan of travelers, pursuing their weary way upon the sandy road, the grazing herd of draft animals in camp and the primitive Mexican oxcarts, laden with grain or flour, panochas (unrefined Mexican sugar in cakes) and oranges. Quickly they would descend, and, from a well-selected ambuscade, attack their victims; a flutter of arrows, a few thrusts from lances and perhaps a few shots from an old carbine or musket, and all was over. The knife did the rest.

It is almost incredible with what innate talent for the assimilation of colors these savages are gifted. With the help of an old blanket, some bunches of cut grass, some clay smeared upon their bodies, thorny leaves and leafy branches, they will imitate to perfection the appearance of natural rocks, bushes, cacti, or other objects suitable to their purposes. When they have decided upon an attack, agreed upon the time and place, they will proceed to the rendezvous, in small parties of four or five, make their dispositions and wait for their prey in absolute immobility and with great perseverance. They will generally allow their victims to pass by them a few steps and then, with a sudden jump and fearful yells, fall upon them from behind. Rare indeed are the instances when a man escaped their murderous aim; as a rule all grown male persons are killed on the spot, while women and children are carried off into captivity; when, however, they have reason to fear speedy pursuit, or when the captured women prove unruly and "show fight" the Apaches will not hesitate in lancing to the last survivor. If they feel themselves secure and the attacked party is but small and defenseless, they will carry also men off alive as prisoners. Woe to them! They are destined to such torture as only a Torquemada could invent, and the executioners of the middle ages could apply.

A favorite manner of putting their male prisoners to death consists in suspending them by their feet from the branch of a tree and maintaining a low fire under their heads. We found once two soldiers in the San Simon Valley, near Fort Bowie, who had gone astray from their comrades while hunting, hanging thus dead; their noses, ears and other parts had been cut off. A scalped victim of Apache Indians I have never seen or heard of.

Our Indian guide, Marigildo, who had been in early youth a prisoner in the hands of the Chiricahuas under Cochise, for the period of seven years, related that these Apaches, whenever they had the opportunity of carrying off adult male prisoners as far as the ranchería, would turn them over, bound fast, to their squaws to be dealt with according to the latters' fancy; that these squaws would generally take great delight in whipping their helpless victims with the exceedingly thorny branches of the silvery cactus, called by the Mexicans *cholla,* and then torture them slowly to death by inserting heated pointed sticks into all parts of their bodies — a process which at times lasted for several days. Four cases have come to my personal knowledge where male prisoners have come out alive from the hands of the Apaches. The first case was that of an old settler in the Santa Cruz Valley, who being shot through his hips with an arrow, began to howl and dance and perform other strange antics which led the Apaches into the belief that he was demented. This saved his life, as the Apaches, like most Indians, abstain from willfully hurting an insane person. There was nothing to prevent them from either killing or carrying off this man, but seeing his strange, to them inexplicable, performance, they allowed him to walk off. Another male prisoner, whom we knew as Colonel Smith, was given his freedom after suffering castration at the hands of his captors. (The case of the escape of the other two prisoners, which forms quite a dramatic episode, will be related in a chapter apart.) Of the force, quickness, and accuracy with which the Apache manages his bow and arrow, as well as of the manufacture and appearance of these weapons, I have given a description in "With the Regulars in Arizona," and will therefore not repeat it here. The same remark applies to their food, manner of hunting, etc.

SUPERSTITIONS OF THE INDIANS

It is at all times very difficult to penetrate into the soul life of an Indian tribe or individual; with the Apaches this task seems hopeless. One instance, however, came under my observance, which leads me to believe that the Apaches are in a manner spiritualists. We had in the guardhouse at Fort Goodwin a small number of Chiricahuas whom we had captured redhanded while completely intoxicated. They were veritable hyenas of the desert. After capturing two carts loaded with mescal (a fiery liquor distilled from the agave) and killing the drivers, they drove the oxen into a secure place, and killing one, began to feast upon the meat roasted on the coals of a small fire, devouring like the inveterate gluttons that they are, paunch, intestines, etc. Unfortunately for them, they could not resist the temptation of indulging freely in the fiery stimulant exuding from between the staves and bungholes of the liquor barrels. They became so intoxicated that they failed to use their customary precaution against attack, some of our soldiers, out on a scouting expedition, had their attention attracted by the smoke of the fire; they hurried towards the spot, found and captured the drunken savages without firing a shot, and took them to the fort, where they were confined in the guardhouse. During the night two of them asked to be taken to the rear; four men of the guard were sent with them; after a few moments some shots were heard and the returning guard reported that the prisoners had attempted to escape, and were fired at in consequence. The would-be fugitives were brought in dead and laid in the corner of the guardroom. Their comrades contemplated them in stoic silence. On the following day they were buried, and we then had the opportunity of observing that during the captivity of the band the survivors were most careful not to approach the corner where their dead comrades had lain. They would look at the spot with awe in their faces, and edge away from it as far as space would allow, giving one the impression that they saw phantoms there. All Apaches have a superstitious fear of darkness, and some indefinable feeling of dread (?), respect (?), awe (?) for the dead. A combat with Apaches is possible only in case of coming upon them unawares, and even then, they will fight only when in greatly superior numbers, or when every chance of escape is cut off from them. On level ground they will soon outrun the best infantry; on a steep incline they will leave a good horse far behind, and on steep rocky hills I verily believe they will even outclimb a goat.

Of San Carlos Reservation I shall say nothing. Sanguine people like to believe that the Apaches will there be made self-supporting and civilized. Let us hope so, but still — we had better feed them yet awhile. Tie your camel up first and then pray to Allah that you may find it safe in the morning!

Every Apache has, like nearly all Indians, a so-called good medicine or talisman, which he carries with him generally in a small buckskin bag; it consists generally in a few bear's claws, a braid of horsehair, a colored rag, a dry snakeskin, a small sculptured stick, the tail of some animal, or a combination of several of these things. For the celebration of certain feasts they put on their finery; helmets of buckskin beautifully and taste-fully adorned with turkey feathers, red and striped cloth and blankets, anklets and wristlets with rattling and jingling metal bells, and moccasins and leggings with more or less elaborate beadwork. Their dances, accompanied by the monotonous music of a reed flute, a crude fiddle and drum, and several rattles consisting of hollowed gourds partly filled with pebbles, appear to us, together with their equally monotonous and plaintive chant, very clumsy and devoid of all elastic or graceful motion; in fact, they merely consist of continuous circling round of six or eight men (squaws take no active part), who, with bodies bent forward, clap their hands together and then slap in turn their thighs and protruding hips, keeping time with the music as well as they may and chanting about the following meaningless words which they repeat over and over again in a sad minor key: "Hoyah, hoyah, hoyah, hah, hayah, hoh, hoo, hoo, hoyah, hah, hayah hoo," the "h" at the beginning of each syllable being strongly aspirated.

A very important occurrence appears to be for them the period when a girl attains to her womanhood. For this occasion all the members of the family are invited to a grand feast which consists mainly of eating, drinking, dancing, various ceremonies, and giving the girl in question a new name, of which more anon. The female Apaches are, as a rule, virtuous, both before and after marriage. Adultery committed by the wife is immediately, upon its discovery, punished by the husband by the cutting off the guilty one's nose, and her eviction from the premises. A real marriage ceremony does not exist; the candidate for conjugal bliss simply bargains for the object of his affections with her parents, and, the conditions of the trade being fulfilled, takes her to his wigwam; a girl is, however, never forced into marriage against her inclination. In the case of proven infidelity the husband demands and obtains from the parents of the erring one, the return of his purchase value, which generally consists in horses or horned cattle. When such a separation takes place the mother keeps the female children and smallest male ones, over which latter, however, the father never loses all control. The birth of a child gives very little trouble to the mother; still, large families are rare. At forty years, the Apache woman, mature at twelve, is old, wrinkled and hideous. Very soon after birth the child is strapped upon a board at whose head a sort of protector against the sun is fixed, consisting of basketwork, in which latter the Apache squaws must be said to excel, manufacturing mats, watertight jars, baskets, etc., of pleasing forms, symmetrically and tastefully adorned with colored figures. The coloring matter they extract from different barks, roots and berries; they also employ the cochineal, which they find here plentifully on the nopal cactus (prickly pear plant; botanically *Opuntia*) and with which, simply pressing the nests of the little insects between their fingers and mixing the juice with some alcohol fluid, they produce a beautiful, indelible purple color.

The birth of a boy, especially if he is the firstborn, is made the occasion of a feast, which is celebrated with great rejoicings; but the name given to the suckling baby is not permanent. As indicated above, another is substituted upon the child's attaining his or her puberty, when another more elaborate family feast takes place. The boys learn from their earliest youth that they are born to rule all womenkind (the men do this quite frequently and with a heavy hand); and they are taught from a tender age the use of arms and the tricks of the chase and are very seldom punished.

In case of sickness or wounds the Apache generally make use of such herbs and roots as are recommended and gathered by their old women; the bite of a rattlesnake they treat, it is said, quite frequently with success, by the application of poultices made from a kind of *Euphorbia,* a small creeping plant here called *Golondrina,* which is beaten into a pulpy mass and applied upon the wound. In desperate cases of disease, however, they will call in a medicine man, whose treatment is generally pretty severe upon the patient. For stomach ache and colic I have seen massage with fists and knees applied upon the lower part of the torso, as well as an application of red hot coals. Their dead they burn in the presence of all the deceased's relatives and friends, who maintain during the ceremony a complete silence. (I have never seen a sober male Apache either laugh or cry; i.e. shed tears.) As a sign of mourning they cut off from the manes and tails of the departed man's horses a few strands of hair, which are kept as a momento by the members of the family.

The following anecdote which is said to be well authenticated would go far to show that our troops during at least some of their earlier expeditions undertaken against the hostile Apaches failed to impress these wild rovers with any great amount of respect or fear; when General Sherman, in 1882, visited the reservation at San Carlos he was repeatedly importuned by some Indians with a request for cartridges, alleged to be for hunting purposes. "Cartridges," finally said the impatient general, "I suppose you want them to kill my soldiers with?" "Oh, no," answered the unsophisticated redskin, "cartridges for cowboys; for your soldiers club good enough, Great Father."

In a former chapter I have stated that while yet in the army a sincere and lasting friendship had sprung up between Leslie B. Wooster and myself, a friendship which ended only with his tragic death at our ranch in the Santa Cruz Valley in the fall of 1870, at the hands of part of Cochise's or else Ez-ki-men-zin's band. Of this wily chief I shall speak more at length in another chapter.

OUR HAY CAMP

On September 15, 1868, having been discharged from the army on the previous day, I left the military hospital, at Tucson, A. T., in order to join my friend Wooster, who was at that time cutting and delivering hay at Fort Wallen, (which was still garrisoned by one company of infantry), under government contract in which I was financially interested. The grass along the Babocomari Valley was quite abundant and could easily have been cut with a so-called buckeye cutter, but I doubt that such an agricultural machine existed in those days within several hundred miles of our hay camp, situated about two miles below the Flagstaff, upon the borders of the upper San Pedro, called by the natives Babocomari Creek. Neither were men very plentiful who could handle a scythe with any skill or load up a wagon with hay properly.

Wooster was, I verily believe, a born farmer, and could perform or very quickly learn to do everything appertaining to agricultural pursuits. After several vain efforts on my behalf to make myself useful in every branch of the hay department, I finally came to the conclusion that all I was fit for upon the premises was to cook the meals for the men — in a sort of a way. I remember distinctly that the first loaf of bread I attempted to bake in a Dutch oven turned out to be a very black, flat cylinder, which upon being broken, disclosed under a heavy, hard crust a mass of perfectly raw dough. The first beans I put to boil in a camp kettle, together with a big "chunk" of very salt pork developed a very remarkable talent of becoming harder and harder the more I fired under them.

I will spare my readers of several other feats in the culinary line and will only say that I learned in the course of time, after spoiling a good lot of valuable provisions and burning my arms and hands wherever there was a possibility of doing so.

The tents of the hay cutters had unfortunately been pitched too near the creek, which carried at that time considerable water. The men began very soon to suffer with chills, fever, and ague to such a degree as to render several of them unfit for work. What was to be done? The quartermaster demanded hay, and it was, besides, to our interest to deliver the quantity contracted for us as quickly as possible, for fear that the winter rains, which put in their appearance quite early in those higher altitudes, might interfere with our work. One Saturday evening, therefore, Wooster said that on the following morning he would go over to see one Samuel Wise, the hay contractor for Camp Crittenden, who, it was said, was well ahead with his delivery of hay, in order to learn if we could borrow from him the services of a few hay cutters. Wooster knew that Wise's hay camp was near a place called the *cienega* (meaning a swampy spot of ground); he therefore struck out on Saturday morning, accompanied by our Mexican teamster, Ramón Moraga, towards the pass leading through the Whetstone Mountains, telling me before leaving that he would return if possible that same night, or at all events on Monday morning. He was mounted on our only horse, a coal black, rather old, but still serviceable horse. Ramón rode one of the wheel mules of our hay teams. Monday morning and Monday night passed and Wooster did not return. As I knew him to be perfectly reliable in all things, I could not help but think that he had met with some accident, and went to the commanding officer of the fort (Brevet Major Downey, Thirty-second U. S. Infantry) to see if I might procure a mount and perhaps a small escort in order to start on a search for my friend and partner. Of course, the first idea in those days when thinking of an accident was Apaches. Major Downey was willing enough to give me all the assistance he could, but he was powerless; the entire garrison consisted of about fifty men of infantry; neither of the two commissioned officers had a horse, and the only animals at the place were the draft mules of the camp wagons. I felt very uncomfortable, to be sure, but as I was utterly helpless in the matter I had to resign myself.

AN APACHE RAID

During the afternoon of Tuesday, the mail rider from Tucson arrived. He came by way of Fort Crittenden, and reported that on Sunday afternoon the Indians had attacked old Mr. Pennington's ox teams, which were hauling the hay from Wise's camp to the fort; that they had killed a teamster and driven off a number of oxen in the direction of the Dragoon Mountains. Now, if Wooster was on his return trip on Sunday afternoon from Wise's camp, as he intended, those Indians must have seen him on that open, undulating plain extending from the Whetstone Mountains to the Cienega. There was no longer any doubt in my mind that my friend and our teamster, Ramón, had fallen into the hands of the Apaches with the inevitable result. I made up my mind to start out that night, come what may, to go to Crittenden and obtain there a cavalry escort, and to find and bury my lost brother. As to ever seeing him again alive, that hope had vanished from my breast. From Major Downey I obtained an old wagon saddle, which I placed upon a former wheel mule of our hay teams, and proceeded to the Sutler store to get some crackers and tobacco. The sutler, a young man named Royal B. Barnes, must have been moved by my apparent misery. He said: "I will be _____ if I let you go on this trip alone; you will get lost; I will saddle up and go with you." I need not say how grateful I felt at this offer, although it was really no more than one would and could naturally expect under like circumstances in those days of dangerous frontier life. While he was making ready I observed that the sky became dark. Ominous black clouds were gathering over the top of the Huachuca range; the atmosphere felt heavy and oppressive, and it became soon evident that a thunderstorm was approaching.

When Barnes led his saddle horse out from under the shed, he also observed the darkening of the sky, and I noticed that he began to waver, even before he said: "Had we not better wait till morning?" "No," I answered. "I have waited already too long; besides it is much safer to travel at night."

After some hesitation on his part we mounted and started, taking the road which leads along the creek in the narrow valley towards the north. Our conversation was very limited, being chiefly confined to suggestions as to what other contingencies besides Apaches could possibly have detained Wooster. As far as I was concerned I could not muster the slightest feeling of hope; all efforts towards evading the thought of my friend's horrible fate were in vain; in my imagination I saw his mangled body lying beside that of Ramón upon the sandy plain. Of one thing I was sure, he could never have been taken alive. Very soon the clouds began to thicken and to travel gradually towards us; now and then a sudden flash of lightning would dart across the horizon, and heavy raindrops began to fall. Soon after, the lightning became more frequent and more vivid, and was followed by tremendous thunderclaps, which made the animals very nervous. Soon a heavy rain began to pour down. Within five minutes we were wet to the skin. My companion, as we were about emerging from the lower upon higher ground, recollected all at once that he had completely forgotten a certain business transaction which was pending with some parties from Santa Cruz, and that these parties were to arrive at Wallen on the morrow for that purpose. As the thunderstorm and rain increased from minute to minute, that business at Wallen seemed to become more and more urgent. Six miles north of Wallen there stood and stands today (I saw it two weeks ago) a solitary cottonwood tree. Here the road to Crittenden turns off to the left, and after traversing the valley ascends the foothills which form a large plateau of mesa. Just as we were reaching the top, while the rain was now pouring down in torrents, a terrific streak of lightning followed by a deafening thunder clap, passed almost, as it seemed to us, directly before our faces. Our animals stood still, trembling in every limb, and my mule could not be induced to take another step forward. This brought the climax to that urgent business at Wallen. Barnes declared positively that he must be there without fail or suffer heavy pecuniary loss; he proposed we should turn back. But to this I would not listen for a moment. I had certainly no claim on him or his companionship, unless it were that of a fellow feeling towards a man in great mental distress and bodily danger. Anyhow, I remember distinctly that I used no inducements whatever to make him stay by me, however much I desired it, but only requested him to exchange animals with me, seeing that the mule appeared very willing to back, but not forward, and that I had at least twenty-four miles before me before reaching Camp Crittenden, while a little over an hour would take him home. He consented to my proposition, and after giving me some directions about my route and remarking that I would probably be guided on the morrow by some crows and carrion buzzards in my search for my dear friend, we parted. Cheerful parting words these were?

The tempest now was at its height. The horse, however, had become calm and trudged along at an easy trot for about half a mile, when his movements became wavering and hesitating. All at once he came to a dead stop. He had evidently lost the road, which, leading here over very hard gravelly ground, was not distinctly marked, not being traveled over with frequency; besides the heavy rain had surely obliterated all tracks and traces of travel. I dismounted and knelt down, lighting with difficulty the few dry matches I carried in a tin match box. While doing this I had thrown the bridle rein over my left elbow. All at once another fearful thunderbolt struck in my immediate vicinity. The horse made a tremendous jump, broke loose and started on a run somewhere; I lost sight of him almost immediately in the inky darkness. His sudden jerk had caused me to drop the match box . . . Of course, the most sensible thing I could have done under the circumstances would have been to sit down right there and wait for daylight, or at least for the clearing up of the sky. But I did not do this sensible thing; I was too restless to sit or stand still! I commenced to grope about in the dark, and walking slowly on, taking care to maintain the direction of the Santa Rita Mountains, whose lofty peaks I could plainly see at short intervals, standing out boldly in the lightning-illuminated sky. I knew that Fort Crittenden was situated at or near the foot of these peaks. After awhile the thunderstorm began to abate, the torrents of rain diminished into a light, steady drizzle, the streaks of lightning became fewer and fewer, and at last ceased altogether; by this I lost the only guide for my bearings, for around me was the blackest darkness and the deepest silence. But hark! here comes a sound wafted over the mesa by a rising wind coming through the Huachuca Pass. A howl, then another, then several more, and directly an infernal concert breaks loose, emanating from the throats of at least a hundred howling, hungry coyotes, striking upon my nerves, already overwrought to a high degree of tension. Had they scented or perhaps already found and devoured my wandering horse? Would they dare to attack me, encouraged by numbers and the all-pervading darkness? As I carried a good new Colt revolver, carefully loaded before starting, I had but little fear of their attack, knowing their cowardly nature; but, still, made for every object whose density of darker darkness in the obscurity indicated a solid body, be it a tree, or rock or a bush, in order to keep, at all events, my back covered. The howling seemed to increase every minute, and I am afraid to tell the number at which I estimated those packs of prairie wolves. While I thus wandered, stepping slowly with extended arms, I came suddenly to a steep descent, lost my footing and partly rolled and partly slid down a steep incline to the great detriment of the rear part of my trousers. The declivity I traversed in this manner, fortunately, not steep enough to cause a direct fall, must have been fully one hundred yards. I landed safely at the bottom of a gulch, out of which I crawled with ease. Upon reaching level ground I discovered one of the oak trees that grow in great profusion in that region, and, oh, wonder and joy! under this tree stood my horse. The sky by this time having become somewhat lighter, I mounted and urged the horse on with my spurs, giving him his own choice as to the direction to be pursued. He turned slightly to the left and almost immediately began to canter without hesitation upon what I soon discovered to be a highway or wagon road. This road, known as the lower road, leads directly to Fort Crittenden, but on account of being very sandy and rocky is not used as frequently as the higher or mesa road. How and why the animal descended on his own accord from the higher road has been a mystery to me ever since.

How long this gallop lasted I fail to remember. I was suddenly brought to a stand by a sonorous voice of somebody calling out in the darkness: "Halt! who comes there " This challenge, which in wartime has frequently an ominous sound and import, sounded like sweet music to my ears, for it could only proceed from a sentry of the garrison at Fort Crittenden. The corporal of the guard promptly appeared and guided me, at my request, to the tent of Lieutenant J. W. Hopkins, First U. S. Cavalry. By him I was received most hospitably and made as comfortable as my mental distress would permit me to be. I told him the tale of my friend Wooster's more than probable murder, and he promised me all the assistance I should require in the execution of my sad task. Being completely exhausted, I soon fell asleep.

Early on the following morning I went to the sutler store, where I mentioned the object of my errand. Here I learned to my inexpressible joy that Leslie B. Wooster, my already lamented partner and friend, was alive and well; that he had been detained at Wise's hay camp on account of the latter's absence in Tucson, which precluded the transaction with the needed haycutters; that Wooster had been at the sutler store on the previous evening and had stated that he would return to Wallen on the very day of my arrival at Crittenden.

I therefore returned to Wallen also, later in the day, accompanied by a small escort kindly furnished me by Captain Moulton, First U. S. Cavalry, commanding Camp Crittenden.

At the very moment that I was approaching the adobe barracks of Camp Wallen upon the Crittenden road, I saw across the creek my friend Leslie B. Wooster and party descending the hill on the Whetstone road; the last rays of the setting sun shone brightly upon his handsome face as he took off his hat and waved to me a friendly welcome.

What a beautiful sunset that was!

From parties worthy of belief I received the information that the urgent business Mr. Barnes had at Wallen on that day with some parties from Santa Cruz did not come off then or ever.

In the month of November, 1868, when we had the management of our hay contract well in hand and had already delivered about fifty tons, we were notified by the A. Q. M. of the fort that orders had been received from Washington to abandon the latter for good and all, and that our contract was canceled from that day. This caused us great consternation, as we naturally foresaw inevitable financial loss in the sudden disposal of draft animals, hay wagons, implements, etc., which we had purchased at a rather high price. However, our contract, like all others entered into with the government in those days, contained the proviso that the latter reserved to itself the privilege of canceling the contract at any time. Wooster had a small store at Tubac at the time, to which one Captain John Owen, a mustered-out California Volunteer officer, was attending in his absence, his former partner in the business, one Joseph Carroll, having been killed a short time previously in the Sonoita Pass by Apaches. This Captain Owen had been elected a member of the Lower House in the Territorial Legislature, which was to meet at Tucson, then the capital of Arizona, early in December.

We packed up all our belongings and started for Tucson, in order to dispose of our animals, wagons, scythes, and camp equipage. This was my first visit to the town as a citizen, and I soon discovered that it was one thing to be fed and clothed by Uncle Sam and quite another to provide for your maintenance with your own purse. By this time a hotel had been established in the place, which charged one dollar for a plain —very plain—meal; board by the week was rated at eighteen dollars; by the month at seventy-two dollars. A room furnished with a cot, two blankets, a pillow stuffed with hay, a chair and a tin basin was reckoned at a dollar a day, or rather a night, as you were supposed to "clear out" by 8 o'clock on the following morning. A decent pair of trousers could be had for fourteen dollars; a pair of overalls for four dollars; an indifferent pair of boots (hardly anybody except the U. S. Infantry wore shoes there and then) for fifteen dollars. The price of everything else was in proportion with the contents of the purses carried by two suddenly suspended hay contractors, who were hardly able to realize about one-half of the money outlay caused by the preparations incident to an incipient contract.

We acquired by trade a rather old buggy with a team of fairly good horses and kept one wagon with six mules. As I had a considerable amount of money still left from my savings in the army, we loaded up the wagon with groceries and some dry goods in order to replenish the stock of the store at Tubac. Towards the end of November we started for the latter place. Arriving at the Canoa towards evening of the second day, Wooster kept straight on alone in the buggy towards Tubac as soon as night fell, while I remained in camp at the Canoa, on the western border of the Santa Cruz River. With me were Hamlin, the teamster, and the man-of-all-work, Ramón Moraga.

Here a singular thing happened which religious people would attribute to a kind Providence, superstitious people to God-knows-what, and the matter-of-fact Western or frontier people of those days simply to "a streak of bull-headed luck."

As we were sitting around the camp fire eating supper there appeared suddenly in our midst a very lean dog, probably attracted by the odor of our sizzling bacon. Notwithstanding his starved and neglected condition, I perceived at once that he was a thoroughbred hunting dog, either setter or pointer. I have forgotten which. We fed him liberally; he showed his gratitude in the well-known ways which every intelligent dog knows so well how to employ, and when we lay down to rest for the night he coddled up against me like a child to its mother.

Of course, in those days at least one man in a camp was always told off to keep watch while the others slept. The mules were securely tied to the wagon wheels. Ramón took first watch and woke me up about 10 o'clock. He reported everything quiet. I sat up and lighted my pipe. Without being called, the dog sat upon his haunches between my knees. From time to time he would look at me with almost human eyes, with such a pleading expression that I expected him momentarily to address me with some such words as: "Will you please keep me with you always?"

Towards 11 o'clock the half-moon rose and gradually diffused a gentle light upon the sandy bottom of the river bed, along the middle of which a narrow silvery ribbon of water flowed. Scattered along the edges of the river there stood some tall cottonwood trees, in that season bereft of foliage, while the numerous elder trees growing partly in groups, partly in solitary state, for the most part had still retained their leaves and cast weird shadows over the vast sandy waste. These trees were interspersed with considerable undergrowth that impeded one's viewing the surroundings to any distance.

Towards midnight the dog began to show signs of restlessness. Now and then he would take an occasional run to the very edge of the water, sniff the ground, shake his head, then pointing with his nose into the air would sniff again and finally return to me and resume his sitting posture between my knees, no longer looking at me, however, but keeping his head turned toward the stream.

About 1 o'clock I awoke Hamlin. He was a short, fat man, and to this I attributed the difficulty I experienced in getting him fully awake. I did not then know, or even expect, that he had a bottle of whiskey under his saddle which served as his pillow, and that about one-half of the liquid was still on hand. After much rubbing of eyes and stretching of legs and arms he reported himself ready to take the watch, and I lay down with the dog by my side. I suppose I slept at times, but was awakened frequently by the restlessness of the dog, who would take a run towards the river at intervals. That he did not go there to drink I had seen, and furthermore knew that a bucket full of water was standing within easy reach.

At last he seemed to have overcome whatever had caused his strange behavior; he lay down quietly by me and I fell sound asleep.

I had slept probably an hour and a half when I suddenly awakened from two simultaneous causes: One was the jumping up of the dog and his pulling violently at my overcoat (whereupon he ran towards the river, barking furiously), and the other was the stamping and rearing of the mules which kicked and struggled to free themselves from their halters. I was up in an instant with gun in hand, and so was Ramón. Looking in the direction of the dog, we just perceived several Indians disappearing behind the undergrowth in the river bed. We fired almost simultaneously over the dog's head at the fleet-footed rascals, probably without any better result than that to show that "we were awake and ready." Then we called the dog back and gave our attention to the mules. After considerable trouble in untangling their fastenings and quieting them with our voices and gently patting and stroking them with our hands, we investigated the status of our night watch.

Hamlin was fast asleep, as fast as the proverbial log, or faster. His bottle, now empty and exposed to view, lay by his side. As daylight was now beginning to peep at us over the peaks of the Santa Rita Mountains, Ramón began preparing the breakfast, while I undertook to interview Hamlin.

Did I wake him up gently? No, kind reader, I did not. In fact, so far from gentle was my manner in "stirring him up," that he showed great resentment at it. A few words of explanation, however, settled all controversy, and when I ordered him to feed the mules he did so quite meekly. I may as well mention here that upon our arrival at Tubac I had a final explanation with him and have not seen him since that day. According to the unwritten code of frontier life in a country swarming with hostile Apaches, he had committed the same crime as the soldier falling asleep while on sentry before the enemy, the end of which according to the written code of every well-regulated army means a firing squad, a coffin, and a hole in the ground, all preceded by the playing of Plegel's hymn by the band.

When daylight appeared we examined the tracks of the Indians. This was an easy task in the wet clay and sand surrounding the shallow river, easily fordable by simple wading. To our horror we discovered that the foremost of them had reached within less than forty yards of us. Had it not been for the dog's watchfulness a very few minutes would have sealed our fate, and this tale would never have been told. That dog enjoyed a most luxurious breakfast on that morning — and oh! how I hugged him!

And now I must confess a most grievous misdemeanor on my part, for which I have not forgiven myself to this day, notwithstanding the many moral and mental kicks I have administered to myself since the occurrence, which was as follows:

The roads being dry we started during the early morning hours on the lower or valley road, which leads to Tubac, for the most part along the river bottom. All along this route there are many mesquite trees, among which innumerable wild doves flew hither and thither. In order to guard against any surprise from the Apaches, as well as to provide some fresh meat for the camp kettle, I took my shotgun and walked among these mesquite trees on either side of the road a short distance ahead of the wagon, bagging a few birds now and then, but always taking care to have one barrel ready for emergencies. Breech-loading shotguns had not come into use yet, at least not there. While thus hunting and watching, our faithful dog, who was a good retriever, would frequently get between my legs when he was bringing in the fallen birds. I was just walking towards the foot of a rather tall tree, in whose branches I had seen several dozen doves settle, in order to approach within shooting distance. In order to do this I had to describe a continual zigzag, so as to evade the numberless tall tufts of bunch grass growing everywhere. Just as I was taking a side step the dog got between my legs and caused me to stumble and fall, with the result that the gun went off into space — I mean the ammunition, of course. This so exasperated me that I administered a severe kick upon the dog's lean flank. He gave one howl and started off into the underbrush, where he was soon lost to view. No amount of searching and calling (his name I had not yet hit upon, and the metal plate probably bearing his or his owner's name, had become detached from his collar in his wanderings) brought him back. Like a phantom of night he had come; like a ghost fleeing from the light of day, he had disappeared!

I learned later on at Tubac that about a month previously a party of officers from some fort had been hunting in the Santa Rita Mountains, and that they were accompanied by numerous dogs.

TUBAC IN 1868

Arrived at Tubac, we placed our merchandise in the store; of the mules we disposed one by one, to occasional buyers, and the wagon we sold to one Thomas Yerkes, who also had a small store at Tubac, a steam flouring mill, and did considerable freighting, besides being the local U. S. postmaster. Captain Owen departed the next day upon his legislative duties, and I took charge of the store (Wooster's), where I had much leisure time on my hands, which I dedicated principally to the serious study of the Spanish language, occasionally hunting ducks along the Santa

Cruz River, while Wooster was generally out looking for hay, wood, and grain contracts and doing general trading.

Inasmuch as the population of Tubac at that time did not exceed three hundred souls, two-thirds of whom were living in great poverty, it appears to me necessary to explain here why four stores existed in that small adobe town; for, besides ours, there was the store of the above-mentioned Thomas Yerkes, also that of one Major Richardson, at one time holding the position of harbor warden at San Francisco. Behind us was the store of Goldtree & Tapie. Opposite to our store there also lived one Henry Glassman, honorably discharged from the California Volunteer Cavalry that up to the winter of 1865–'66 garrisoned the military post of Calabazas on the Santa Cruz River, about twelve miles south of Tubac. He kept a barroom, did some butchering, and traded principally in flour and beans, of which two articles he generally kept a good stock on hand.

Now, along the Santa Cruz River there existed about twenty farms, principally cultivated by hardy American frontiersmen, who with the help of Mexican laborers produced grain, worth then from six to seven cents gold coin per pound. The storekeepers advanced to these farmers the necessary provisions for putting in their crops, cultivating — i.e., irrigating — and harvesting it. A liberal profit was made on all merchandise thus advanced, and, besides, the recipient of the advanced goods would give a note of hand, payable at harvest time, bearing interest at the rate of two per cent per month till paid. Such Mexican farmers as were known to be industrious and trustworthy, and cultivated small fields on their own accounts were also given credit under like conditions. At harvest time the storekeepers, who generally managed to obtain a contract for grain to be delivered at Tucson, Fort Crittenden, Fort Walker, Fort Calabazas, or Fort Bowie or Fort Lowell, or at least a sub-contract, received the grain at the previously stipulated price from the farmers, and a good profit would have been made all around as a rule, if the military posts had been stable and if the Apaches had not cut a figure, a very great figure, in the carrying out of the conditions established between traders and farmers.

This narration will show how great and detrimental that figure was a little later on.

Our store at Tubac was situated upon a small elevation from which two declivities gently descended to the south and west. In front of us, just across the street was the house of Mr. Henry Glassman, mentioned in the last chapter. He was a German, well advanced in years, I think at that time about fifty-eight. As honest as the day was long, he was of a congenial disposition withal, and generous and liberal in a high degree. Notwithstanding the unsettled state of the country and the everpresent danger from Indians, he had, like many others, resolved to stay in Arizona, even after the garrison of Calabazas, from which the major part of Tubac had derived their living, had been abandoned. He owned a pretty good adobe home, where he dwelled alone, dispensing liquors to farmers, laborers and waysiders; from time to time he would kill a yearling, a calf, a kid or sheep, occasionally a hog, and sell the meat to the inhabitants of the town, the ranchmen and few outlying miners, salting down or turning into sausage whatever he could not dispose of in a fresh state.

He had a herd of about two hundred sheep, over which his intelligent dog, Stubbs, the product of an indefinable pedigree, watched all alone along the river bottom, bringing them home exactly at sunset of each day.

When I became first acquainted with old Henry, as we used to call him, all his affection was concentrated upon the aforesaid dog and a white horse that he had bought at an auction of "inspection condemned stock." He had taken great pains to obliterate, nearly successfully, the telltale brand, I. C. In his opinion these two animals had never been surpassed by any other of their kind in sagacity, endurance, beauty (the dog was the ugliest I ever saw) and all-round usefulness. This the population of the whole valley was perfectly aware of, and loud praises of the two quadrupeds by occasional visiting farmers and miners were the legitimately recognized means of obtaining free drinks at Henry's bar.

In the first days of December, however, I began to observe a new manifestation in old Henry's general bearing towards me which led me to believe that he had transferred or was transferring a part of his affection, heretofore entirely absorbed by his two pets, upon humble me. His "friendly move" was due to Henry's discovery of the fact that I was applying myself steadily to the study of Spanish. He soon became very friendly, not to say confiding, at first, but evidently ready to make advances towards intimacy, a circumstance which, taking into consideration the great difference in our ages and the short period of our acquaintance, led me to some speculative reflections.

After he had made sure that I had mastered the Spanish language sufficiently to speak and write it understandingly, and, in his opinion at least, as made up from the information furnished by Mexican neighbors, quite fluently, the explanation for the peculiar sudden friendship came all at once, when upon a Saturday evening, we being alone, several drinks loosened his tongue and he confessed to me that he was in love — oh! so much in love! — with a Mexican widow, with whom he was unable to converse on account of the disparity of language.

He then and there solicited my services in the matter of making advances and proposing matrimony in the old, recognized only proper Mexican style, as laid down and practiced from times immemorial according to the unwritten law of Mexican courtship. His *sine qua non* proceeding consisted in sending to the object of his affection a nice, clean letter of proposal couched in the best style of the language of the hidalgos.

I saw that Henry was in earnest — very much in earnest, and therefore placed myself at his disposal forthwith. We hied ourselves to my sanctum adjoining the store, where I discovered, after some rummaging in my trunk, some of the flowery stationery upon which I was then still in the habit of indulging in fine language, sent, whenever opportunity offered, to Miss Eulalia at Santa Cruz. I now learned from old Henry that the much-beloved and coveted widow was one Mrs. Raney, the relict of a member of the California Volunteers, who lived at Tubac at the time, in rather reduced circumstances, with two small children, a girl of about ten and a boy of about six years of age. I hope [?] it is useless to go into details as to the elaborate composition of that letter, which contained a bona fide offer of marriage. Suffice it to say that I did my best in grammar, syntax and fine writing, and sent old Henry away with the missive confided to a highly ornamented envelope.

He was very happy, for "he had it bad."

Already on the following evening my now fast friend returned to me with an answer. He made me lock the store door, and seating himself by my side on my bed, he pulled forth the fateful letter with trembling hands from his breast pocket. A hurried perusal convinced me that he had not knocked at that door in vain, and I said to him at once: "You are all right, old boy; listen!"

And he listened — with ears, eyes and mouth, while I translated to him slowly and distinctly the legend of happiness in store.

The lady's answer, which, numerous orthographical errors excepted, was couched in fair enough Spanish, was to the purport that Mr. Glassman's proposal of marriage was looked upon favorably; that his affection was returned, but that there existed a serious impediment to the marriage, inasmuch as legal proof of her husband's death was not in her possession, and that rumors were afloat that he had been seen alive a short time previously in the city of Hermosillo, Sonora, Mexico; that under these circumstances no priest would perform the holy rite of matrimony and that of course he, Mr. Glassman, would not expect her to receive further advances until such time as the aforesaid legal proof had been obtained, when nothing would oppose itself to the performance of the marital ceremony by the holy Roman Apostolic Church, the only manner in which she would ever consent to be married.

Old Henry was very, very happy, because he knew that said Raney, a blacksmith by trade, had actually died in said city and was buried there. He took my hand, in which I was still holding the letter, in both of his, which were fairly shaking with emotion, and implored me to write at once to one Mr. Garrison, who kept a hotel at Hermosillo, and whose uncle of the same name was U. S. consul at Guaymas. He knew, he said, that from these two the much-desired document proving legally the demise of the lady's first husband could surely be obtained.

I wrote that letter forthwith and then another to the widow, expressing infinite happiness, bliss, etc., and informing her of the steps that were being taken toward the consummation of said happiness and bliss. Thereupon we adjourned to old Henry's place, where a bottle of good champagne did honor to the occasion.

On the following day, about noon, old Henry called me over to his place and exhibited to me with great pride and circumstance a large platter upon which rested a finely roasted kid, flanked by several nondescript delicacies, the whole arrangement being ostentatiously decorated with impossible paper roses. These substantial proofs of his deep love he dispatched, together with a bottle of his best sweet wine, to his dulcinea. The whole offering was neatly adjusted in a covered basket much larger than the youthful grinning carrier. From that day on, Mr. Glassman was only seen attired in a black suit (pattern of about 1845) of which the principal feature was a very long frock coat with a very broad and high collar, over which stood out a tremendous shirt collar of spotless white, whose upper corners seriously impeded the free use of the wearer's eyesight. Inasmuch as I tied the cravat myself every morning, I know whereof I speak when I say that his throat protector went around old Henry's neck four times and left ample ends wherewith to tie a voluminous knot under the chin.

The American consul, old Mr. Garrison, happening to be on a visit with his nephew at Hermosillo when our letter arrived there, the desired certificate of demise arrived much sooner than expected, and preparations for the wedding and ensuing housekeeping were well underway when — something happened.

While all this courting had been going on, there had arrived at Tubac during the third week of December a Tyrolese named Flora, with a letter of introduction to me from a friend at Tucson. In this letter Mr. Flora was highly recommended as a first-class manufacturer and concocter of liquors, wines, and cider. As Wooster and I kept no barroom, I took Mr. Flora across the street to old Henry, introduced them to one another, and explained to the latter the accomplishments for which the former was held famous. Henry had at the time quite a stock of liquors on hand, but, being in too happy a frame of mind to disappoint anybody, he bespoke the services of Mr. Flora for the manufacture of two barrels of cider from dried apples and brown sugar. Two whisky barrels were thoroughly cleansed; the large kettle in which hogs were usually scalded and lard was tried out, was scoured, and with this the cider factory was established. After the newly made cider had been filtered into the barrels by means of a sieve and funnel, the barrels were stood up on end against the rear wall of Henry's bar room, alongside of the shelves behind the bar, which contained the liquor bottles, glasses, tumblers, and other paraphernalia of the retail liquor trade. Along the side walls of the bar room, upon which hung several large strings of red peppers, were piled up about three thousand pounds of flour in one hundred and fifty-pound sacks, and about forty sacks of beans. The front of the barroom, facing upon the street, had one door and two windows.

Neither Henry Glassman nor the writer had the least idea of the manufacture of cider or its treatment in its different stages of becoming the saleable article. A few days before the time when the cider in the barrels ought to have shown signs of fermentation or becoming "fizzy" (I do not remember exactly what Mr. Flora called it), this gentleman received a message from the sutler at Fort Crittenden, requesting his services as cider maker and general liquor doctor. Before Flora left for the fort he gave old Henry a paper containing a prescription, with the injunction to send for that stuff to the drug store at Tucson, in case the cider should "not get steam up" within a given time, and to pour some of the powder into each barrel through the faucet hole. Two days, or at most, three days, after said operation the cider would be ready either for sale over the bar or for bottling. The last words I heard Flora say, as he started, were "That stuff will do the business, sure."

Well, there seemed to be no fermentation or "steam-up" forthcoming, and Glassman gave the mail rider two dollars and the prescription for "the stuff," which was brought just one day after the death certificate from Hermosillo had arrived. It was a white powder in a package, weighing about two pounds. Glassman came over to the store, showed it to me, and asked my opinion as to the quantity required for each barrel. I thought it best to begin with a small quantity, which could be increased as things either did or did not develop. Old Henry's mind was not very much given to the matter, because he had sent "the document" to the widow on the previous evening and he knew that the priest had already cognizance of it. He was therefore anxiously and momentarily expecting an important message from his lady love, and was very impatient as to all other matters. He said: "I am going over and I am going to put one-half of this powder in each barrel and shut them down tight to keep the steam in." He departed. It was not till later that I learned from him that, after putting in "the stuff" he had carefully knocked the bungs tight, also the faucet holes and finally plugged the vent holes.

He had been gone about ten or fifteen minutes when he returned, crossing the street in great strides. As he entered my door I could see "great expectations" fairly oozing out from his animated features. He handed me a letter with a trembling hand, while he could hardly articulate the words: "From her — boy just brought — read — quick!"

I opened the missive and read, while Henry steadied himself with his arm around my shoulder, as follows:

"Thanking you sincerely for the trouble you have taken in procuring the legal proof of my former husband's death, I now beg to state that, there being no other impediments to our matrimonial union, I — "

Here we were startled by such a tremendous sound of an explosion in the near neighborhood that I dropped the letter and ran to the door, followed by old Henry. At the moment we reached it another similar thunderclap made the very air tremble. Across the street we could see things tumble about in a dense cloud of dust. Henry, starting on a run across the street, exclaimed:

"Dat ish mine cider — poot de py widow ish mine!"

Both of these assertions were true enough, but the marriage was considerably delayed on account of the havoc created by the explosion. When we reached Glassman's premises we found the front door and windows blown out into the middle of the street. They had evidently acted as a safety valve, as in their absence the roof would surely have come off. In the inside we found a chaos of flour and bean sacks promiscuously tumbled about, partly bursted and intermingled with strings of pepper pods, barrel staves and innumerable fragments of broken glassware. There was not a whole bottle or tumbler in the place; the walls and ceilings were dripping with the cider, that had suddenly got "steam on."

Fortunately by far the greater part of Henry's stock of liquors and groceries were stored in a small cellar under the kitchen, and had thus escaped the general destruction.

I will here mention that old Henry married his widow, and lived happily with her for many years; but his marriage did not take place till sometime in January of the following year; before that time events of a far more serious nature took place, which I proceed to relate.

By Christmas time the damages caused by the explosion were so far remedied that Henry Glassman could and did prepare a farewell bachelor banquet in the shape of a Christmas dinner, to which he invited all his intimate friends in the town, to the number of about ten. For the occasion he hired a poor German traveler, whom some ill wind had blown into our wild country, to render services as waiter. This man he dressed up with some of Glassman's decent clothing (said traveler having arrived in rags), in order that he might present a respectable appearance while performing the functions of a Ganymede at the festive board. Inasmuch as Henry stood full six feet in his stockings and the improvised waiter barely five, the latter's appearance, with turned-up trousers and sleeves, footgear equally out of proportion, and wearing a spotless white vest with a deep hollow under its front, and one of Henry's famous gigantic shirt collars framing a diminutive face, was certainly striking, the more so as the poor wanderer was blind of one eye, had a harelip, and, in the hurry of shaving for the occasion, had managed to inflict upon some of his features several gashes deep enough to keep bleeding during the whole dinner. (I am pretty certain that some of us had a taste of the man's blood in the gravy.) But, then, as the French say: "À la guèrre comine [?] a la guèrre!" a free translation of which, applicable to this case, would be about: "Don't quarrel with your victuals in time of war."

Mr. Glassman was, of course, dressed in full regimentals — i.e. in his black suit with aforesaid choker and cravat, which he had not discarded for a single day since the incipiency of his new-found happiness. Previously to sitting down to the table old Henry had acted in person as *chef de cuisine,* assisted by a Mexican herder, the corners of whose "serape" (a gaily colored blanket thrown over the shoulders in cold weather) would persist in introducing themselves into the pots and pans. Our host was by no means a poor cook, and the roasted kid which formed the *pièce de resistance* of the dinner was toothsome indeed. By common consent, although not audibly expressed, it was, in honor of the day, invariably referred to as "the fowl," "the turkey," or "the bird." Besides it there were many other dishes, all well prepared indeed; we could not help but compliment our host, and that very justly, upon the variety of the good things set forth and the fertility of his resources in obtaining them at that period and in that place.

Neither did the liquid refreshments leave anything to desire in quality or quantity. (I shuddered involuntarily on the following day when I contemplated the array of empty bottles in Henry's backyard.) In accordance with the custom of the times, we all imbibed a liberal cocktail before dinner. With the entree which followed a succulent oxtail soup, and consisted of codfish balls, we drank white wine — actually imported Rhine wine, in long, slender tapering bottles. The pseudo turkey and accessories we washed down with imported French claret of the brand Chateau Lafitte. And this in Tubac in 1868! These wines, as well as the champagne which was uncorked as the dessert was served, were undoubtedly smuggled in by somebody by way of Guaymas, where a great many European goods were landed monthly. They tasted none the worse for that.

The banquet lasted from 1 to 3 o'clock, and was enlivened by speeches, stories and song. By that time everyone present knew of old Henry's engagement to the Widow Raney, and he received the liberally offered congratulations with — for an oldish man — exquisite, graceful smiles.

Among the invited guests were Mr. Joseph Goldtree and his partner, one E. Tapie. The latter had been a soldier in the French army before Sebastopol during the Crimean War; later he had belonged to Bazaine's army of invasion in Mexico; had been discharged at Guaymas and made his way inland till he reached Tubac, where he had entered into partnership with Mr. Goldtree in the composite business of trading, farming and contracting. This Frenchman, who was then about forty-five years of age, was the gayest of the gay at Henry's banquet, enlivening the fleeting hours with many songs, principally of a military character. He had a very sweet baritone voice, well modulated, and sang with fine expression. I remember distinctly to this day the following lines sung by him with true French vivacity and military élan.

"Je danserai, tu danseras,
Foie de Français, papa Nicholas!"

(I shall dance, thou wilt dance,
As sure as I'm a Frenchman, old Nicholas.)

And the lines —

"Entendez-vous? c'est le tambour qui roule,
C'est un canon qui fait trembler le sol;
C'est un boulet, c'est un fort qui s' ecroule,
Ta fin est là, pauvre Sebastopol!"

(Do you hear? It is the roll of the drum,
It is a cannon, shaking up the earth;
It is a shot, it is a fort that totters,
Thy end has come, oh, poor Sebastopol!)

Of course, we all joined in when he sang the inevitable Marseillaise Hymn, at least as far as the air of the song was concerned. The greater part of the company present, not knowing the words, sang la – la – la, if singing it could be called. I am afraid that toward the end of the "seance" there was more noise than melody noticeable in our combined efforts. Hilarity had reached a very high degree, if I may use this mild expression.

Before, however, this status was reached, Mr. Tapie sang a very sweet song which I have never heard before or since, although I have traveled extensively in nearly all French-speaking countries and visited among that class of people who would be apt to know and sing that kind of songs. I remember but one stanza of the song, but these six lines have remained engraved upon my mind and memory with indelible ink, so to speak.

What is it, what can it be, that brings these lines so vividly before my mind's eyes, or rather ears, from time to time, so plainly and distinctly? Is it the sweet melody to which the beautiful text is set? Is it the pathetic expression with which Mr. Tapie rendered it? Or is it perhaps the sad fate which befell the sweet singer only five short days later? I cannot tell, but still I hear his gentle voice and see his small, aristocratic hand with which he beat the measure as he sang:

> "Beaux seducteurs au doux language,
> Qui semez l'or à volante:
> Des jeunes filles du village
> Respectez l' humble pauvreté!
> Laissez les enfants à leurs mères,
> Laissez les roses au rosier —
> Laissez, laissez les enfants a leurs mères;
> Laissez, laissez les roses au rosier."

> (Gay seducers with smooth language,
> Who throw gold to right and left:
> Respect the humble poverty
> Of the innocent country girls.
> Leave the daughters to their mothers,
> Leave the roses on the rosebush!
> Leave, oh, leave the daughters to their mothers;
> Leave, oh, leave the roses on the rosebush!)

Before we retired to rest our heavy heads for awhile, it was mutually agreed, in order to give the festivity a worthy close, that we should all form a committee of invitation toward nightfall, in order to visit the female part of the population and try to induce as many ladies as possible to join us in an informal, impromptu dance to be held that night at 8 o'clock in old Henry's spacious front room, which the latter promised to hold in readiness for the purpose, while Mr. Sabino Otero took unto himself the task of providing the necessary dance music, consisting of harp and fiddle. We succeeded in obtaining the gracious attendance of about ten ladies of different ages and enjoyed ourselves greatly, dancing into the small hours of the next day.

Inasmuch as I shall soon, in the course of my narrative, reach an episode where a Mexican *baile* of much larger proportions will be described, I shall here omit all descriptive details of that night's terpsichorean performance.

MY PARTNER SECURES A CONTRACT

My partner, Wooster, had not been at the banquet, owing to his absence in the Sonoita Valley where he had succeeded in obtaining a subcontract for the delivery of ash timber and charcoal to Fort Crittenden. He returned to Tubac on December 27, and we went at once into a consultation as to ways and means toward fulfilling said contract. Woodcutters he had already hired, also an experienced coal burner, while passing through Calabazas, but we were altogether bare of means of transportation. We decided to close up the store for a few days, the small amount of local trade having of late become insignificant, and to make a trip to Santa Cruz, where we were reasonably certain of obtaining at least one wagon, probably more, and the requisite number of draft animals, either as a loan, or by way of hire, from Mr. Warner.

This proposition suited me to a "T," as I had not seen Miss Eulalia for a long time — not since my furlough trip in June — and was more than anxious to look once more into her beautiful eyes. Wooster, having taken upon himself a wife, was now out of the race; but that Mexican *caballero,* the aforementioned lieutenant of cavalry, seemed to make good progress in his courting of my sweetheart, in which, if the reports that reached me from time to time were true, he had the full support of Doña Maria, the girl's mother.

On the twenty-eighth, in the morning, as we were ready to start, there entered into town a cavalcade of United States Cavalry, consisting of one corporal and six privates, from Fort Crittenden. They rode directly up to our store, where I was greasing the axles of our buggy, and stated that the object of their visit was to employ a woman as laundress for the fort from among the Mexican women of the town. Incidentally we learned from them that on the previous day Mr. Warner had been brought, accompanied by his wife and escorted by several men from Santa Cruz, to Fort Crittenden in a very precarious condition, caused by an attack of acute pneumonia, and was then under treatment at the hospital of that place. This information of necessity changed our route from a direct one to Santa Cruz, to the roundabout one by way of Crittenden. Goldtree and Tapie, who had a contract to deliver corn at Crittenden from their farm on Sonoita Creek, hearing of our intended trip, also made ready to join us, in order to visit their "rancho," there to meet their wagonmaster in charge of the teams hauling the grain to the fort. During the day a Mexican woman was found, willing to undertake the profitable duties as laundress at the fort, and the start was set for the following morning at 8 o'clock.

Tubac has an altitude of about two thousand feet above sea level,† and the morning was, for Arizona at least, very cold. Everybody rendezvoused on time in front of our store, and we started south along the road leading up the Santa Cruz Valley, crossing the San Cayetano Creek and leaving the old ruins of the Tumacacori mission on our right across the river. Three cavalrymen were in the lead of the party; then followed Wooster and myself, with the women in the buggy; next came Goldtree and Tapie in their buggy, and the remaining cavalrymen formed the rear guard. In this manner, every one of us being well armed, we could have traveled in perfect safety all over Arizona, but as the trite saying is: "There is many a slip between the cup and the lip."

A FATEFUL PARTING

As we were approaching Calabazas we met a party of about ten Mexicans, who were driving before them perhaps forty donkeys laden with crates full of oranges and panochas, bundles of sugarcane and jars of sugar-preserved cactus fruit from that peculiar large prickly pear plant called by the Indians and Mexicans *pitahaya*.†† They were coming from Crittenden, where they had disposed of part of their wares, and were taking the remainder to the market at Tucson. These men Mr. Goldtree questioned as to the whereabouts of his teams, as they must have passed his grain farm on their way, and was by them informed that the wagons of Goldtree and Tapie were undergoing repairs at the blacksmith shop of the fort and would not start to load up at the ranch until the following day or perhaps not till one day later. This conversation had stopped our progress and Goldtree called out to Wooster and me from his buggy behind us: "See here, Tapie and I are going to stop at Calabazas over night. There is no use in our going to the ranch till tomorrow or next day. It is very lonesome and uncomfortable there. Blanchard here at Calabazas has a good warm house and a good cook. We have no business up there till our wagons reach the place. You have heard what these Mexicans said."

It was in vain that Wooster and I tried to persuade Goldtree and Tapie to keep along with us and the military escort, that rendered our trip safe. We tried to show them that they had far better come along with us to the fort under a safe escort, there await the completion of the repairs

---

†In a day of less accurate data recording, John Spring here failed to make even an "educated guess." Tubac, higher considerably than Tucson above sea level, has a recorded altitude of 3,250 feet.

††In southern Arizona and northwestern Sonora, this term usually applies to the organ pipe cactus, but several other varieties are called *pitahaya* elsewhere in Mexico.

on their wagons, and thence return to the ranch with the teams, accompanied by the wagonmaster, four teamsters and their cook, all well armed. They remained obstinate. When we reached the river crossing, they branched off to the right and drove to Blanchard's stone house at Calabazas, where we will leave them for the present. Goldtree said afterward that we had hardly driven out of sight when a certain presentiment seemed to overcome him, and he proposed to turn back and follow us, but that Tapie would not listen to the proposition.

Wooster and I branched off from the valley road at Huebabe†, about four miles south of Calabazas, where turning to the left upon the Crittenden road, we soon entered into the Sonoita Pass. We reached Crittenden about 2 p.m. While the escort with the laundress went straight to headquarters to report their arrival, we put up at the Sutler store and then proceeded to the hospital. We found Mr. Warner in a very serious condition, but still able and willing to listen to our request for wagons and animals, which he readily granted. He made me write the requisite order to his majordomo, our old friend Pedro, which he signed. We resolved, being now alone and about to travel over a road oftener than not infested by roving bands of Apaches, to start at nightfall for Santa Cruz by the road leading over the Patagonia Pass. I gave the horses a good rubbing down and a liberal feed, while Wooster replenished the lunch basket at the sutler store.

A SNOWSTORM IN THE MOUNTAINS

We started a little before dark, passed by the *Casa Blanca** (white house) about 6 o'clock and about two miles farther on we turned westward, crossed the Sonoita Valley, entered among the foothills, and soon reached the long, in some places very steep ascent leading into the Patagonia range of mountains. Although by this time the sky was overcast with dense clouds, the cold became more and more biting, and toward 9 or 10 o'clock it began to snow. At first only tiny, downy feathers fell, and we had no apprehension of any serious consequences. Higher and higher we climbed along the rocky road; soon the snowflakes became of a much larger size, and by midnight the downpouring snow seemed to form one vast sheet, impeding our eyesight. The cold was now piercing our gloves and heavy clothing, and penetrated unmercifully to our legs whenever our

---

†On maps of 1869, the place name closest to Huebabe (a) appears to be Huebarri, a gold mine four miles south of Calabazas. Ten miles to the north are the Huebavi mountains. The illiterate rural people of the time could easily have confused Spring with regard to the name.

*This farmhouse, although situated only about four miles from Fort Crittenden, was, during 1869-1871, attacked four times, to my certain knowledge, by Apaches, who drove off the stock and twice killed a man walking behind the plow.

buffalo robe was shifted from its position upon our knees by the frequent jolts of the buggy. The road could no longer be seen but as long as we were ascending among the rocky cuts in the cliffs, it was hardly possible to lose it, [it] being reduced to a narrow defile by the surrounding cliffs. Our greatest fear was being frozen stiff upon our seats. I remember that Wooster, becoming impatient at the slow progress of our team, made a vicious stroke towards the leader with his slender blacksnake whip; the stroke fell short, passed over the horse's back in a half-circle and the hard buckskin knot at the end of the whip hit me fully and fairly upon the center of my nearly-frozen nose-tip. I thought I saw more and more vivid stars than had ever been discovered up to that time, or, for that matter, would ever be discovered to the end of time, and the fire that shot through my nose and thence through my whole system, was about the hottest thing I have any remembrance of.

Soon we were surrounded by what seemed a vast, limitless tablecloth, because we had reached the fairly level top of the divide and could have seen our surroundings to quite a distance in every direction, had our eyesight not been impeded by the dense snowflakes that kept descending upon us. The horses were now evidently willing to assume a faster gait of their own volition, but their wavering, hesitating manner soon showed us that they were no longer upon the traveled road, which upon the level ground was no longer clearly defined. Still, Wooster urged them on with voice and whip, being afraid of being snowed in if we remained standing in any one place.

All of a sudden there was a fall. Down we went, almost perpendicularly down, horses, buggy and all, about ten feet. At first we were so astonished that neither of us spoke. I told Wooster to keep his seat and hold fast to the reins, while I jumped out to the horses' heads to quiet their frantic flounderings. I had the animals soon quieted into immobility, but they trembled all over at the unusual experience. Then I began to investigate the situation.

The buggy rested easily upon about two feet of snow intermingled with the end branches of some small trees whose short trunks emanated from the sides of the very narrow gulch into which we had dropped. Evidently these branches must have formed a sort of network upon which the accumulated snow rested, thus forming a pitfall for us. I waded all around the buggy and horses in order to ascertain if we had sustained any damage. The horses were unhurt, and on or about the buggy there was not a thing broken. The harness also had escaped all injury, there being not even a buckle strained; only the two off-ends of the traces had become unfastened by reason of their sudden shortening. However we were imprisoned, as it were, in a narrow fissure or gully with sides almost as perpendicular as walls, and we had to find an exit somehow. To which side to turn, in order to seek egress was a puzzle indeed. Fortunately we hit upon the side which afforded outlet. With considerable trouble we lifted the buggy up bodily and swung it around little by little, gradually turning the horses's heads and buggy pole in the same direction. We cleared as much snow away in front as we could, and then attempted to drive out of the pit. But the horses would not budge; neither coaxing nor whipping would make them advance a single step. In this stress I bethought me of the brandy bottle, as both Wooster and I always partook very sparingly of liquor while traveling in an Apache region. I cut several slices of bread from a loaf, saturated them well with brandy, and offered them to the horses. They munched and swallowed them readily and at once became amenable. Within half an hour we were out of the gulch and once more upon solid ground, which gently slanted downwards toward the southwest. This direction we ascertained at once, because during the episode of our fall and ensuing labor of liberation it had ceased to snow, and by the feeble light of the waning moon's sickle we distinctly recognized the Huachuca Range of Mountains toward the east. Hence, knowing the relative situation of Santa Cruz, the Patagonia and Huachuca ranges, we knew more or less where we were, and shaped our course accordingly, avoiding carefully all uneven places. Toward about 3 a.m. we saw a feeble light ahead of us, and knowing full well that no Apaches could possibly be out under the existing stress of weather drove directly toward it. Less than two hours brought us to the campfire of Pierson's wagon train loaded with flour from the Terrenate Mills to be delivered at Crittenden. Their camp was at the old San Rafael sheep ranch, which we knew perfectly, and having now once more reached a well-known traveled road upon level ground, we proceeded rapidly toward the town of Santa Cruz, ten miles away, and reached there about daylight, December 30.

We drove directly to the house of Don Solomon, where we were received by the faithful *mayordomo* with open arms, and made comfortable, as well as our horses.

We went to bed at once and slept far into the afternoon. While we were dressing for dinner (we had brought our Sunday suits with us in order to do honor to the ladies of the house), Pedro made me a sign from the backyard to join him. He was chuckling all over. "Don Juan," he said, "don't you think for a moment that you are going to have it all your own way with sweet Miss Eulalia, because her mother is away with Mr. Warner at Crittenden; a special courier has arrived from there while you were asleep with the ominous message to the aunts: 'Don Juan is coming, with Wooster; watch him and Eulalia.' But you can trust me as far as I can be of service, and, of course, you can always rely on little Carmelita."

Well, from the first I had not entertained great hopes of more than perhaps one or two short intimate interviews with my much-guarded sweetheart; but the fact of the three aunts being present at the same time, and the further fact that they had been specially cautioned as to my coming, together with the circumstance that in all probability that Mexican officer by this time considered himself as good as engaged to Miss Eulalia— all these unfortunate circumstances formed a powerful combination disastrous to any love-making on my part.

As usual, the aunts, whom I would rather have located somewhere about Halifax, were profuse in their courtesy; they one and all gave me that gentle slight embrace of welcome customary in that land of most beautiful women and sweet oranges. They could afford that manner of salutation, being well advanced in years. Miss Eulalia gave me her beautiful hand, but that sweet little devil of a Carmelita just jumped upon my neck and kissed and hugged me tight. This latter performance afforded her the opportunity of whispering in my ears: "She loves you still."

Taking into consideration my somewhat fiery nature and great propensity toward demonstrative love-making, this message, while Eulalia was herself so near — and yet so far — was rather cold comfort; but still a comfort. The combination of aunts prepared for our reception a really splendid dinner, which, however, lost much of its gusto, as far as I was concerned, from the fact that the two eldest aunts had seated me between them and placed my adored one on the same side of the table farther down, with Wooster, who, being now married, was considered safe, opposite to her, in such a manner that I could obtain a sideglance at Miss Eulalia only from a distance and by craning my neck either back or forward to an uncomfortable extent. Opposite to us, i.e., the aunts and myself, sat old Henry (Mr. Warner's clerk, mentioned in "With the Regulars in Arizona"), and Brown, the freighter, with Carmelita between the two.

The subjects of conversation with those women whose misfortune, not fault, consisted in almost absolute illiteracy, were of necessity very limited, being reduced to the latest killing of several Mexicans at Los Nogales,* and the scouting expedition of the "lieutenant of the family," ensuing therefrom. The monotony of the entertainment was somewhat relieved by the arrival of two very pretty young ladies whom I had met before, and who announced with great glee that the family of one Commandante Comaduran had resolved to give a ball on New Year's Day at

---

Los Nogales means the walnut trees. There was a group of, I think, about eleven of these trees standing on the edge of the Sonora road, about one mile south of the present town of Nogales, which owes its name to said group of trees. Many murders were committed there by Apaches upon traveling Mexicans, the nature of the ground being very favorable for attack from ambush.

their residence, and requested the presence of the company there assembled at that festive occasion at 8 p.m., January 1, 1869. This announcement brought some life even into the over-steady aunts, who declared with great formality that they accepted the invitation of the Comaduran family, and would feel themselves honored, etc. etc.

All the women present soon rose and retired, probably in order to attend to matters of dress and other arrangements. No one made mention of Mr. Warner's serious condition in the hospital at Crittenden. Toward evening Miss Eulalia played a few pieces on the harp in the general reception room, where refreshments were served, pending a rather late supper, after which I found time and opportunity of inditing a rather long, loving missive to my beloved one. I confided my letter to Carmelita, who assured me on the following morning that it had reached its destination.

By this time I had become sufficiently aware that a young girl of marriageable age in that country had absolutely no will of her own, except perhaps in the matter of her thoughts. Her actions were completely under the control of whatever elderly female relatives might be present upon the premises. Knowing this, I approached the trio of aunts in Eulalia's presence with the humble request of being allowed the privilege of escorting Miss Eulalia to the ball. At first the trio remained mute and stared at me about as stolidly as if I had proposed to marry her out-of-hand or to drink the then much swollen river dry. After awhile the eldest found her voice, and begged me to explain what I meant by the expression "escort." Upon my giving the definition of this word and its meaning as applied to the act under discussion, the three aunts raised their hands simultaneously and exclaimed unisono: "Impossible."

Further explanation developed the fact that under no circumstance would a young girl of respectable family be allowed to visit anywhere, for any purpose, under the escort of a man not a near relative; that even were she engaged to marry a young man, one or more chaperons would invariably accompany her to a ball, a show, or in short, anywheresoever; that the aunts would themselves take Eulalia to the ball where, of course, I would have the opportunity of dancing with her once or twice. They did not say outright that they expected me to dance with them also, but the hints thrown out toward that blissful undertaking were unmistakable.

The house of the Comadurans where the dance was to be given contained a very spacious reception room, and that was its only redeeming feature as a ballroom. For illumination, there stood upon a small table in a corner a very peculiar lamp, peculiar in shape and construction, and even more so through its astonishing capacity of producing smoke and sending forth an indescribable odor of rancid oil of a kind heretofore unknown to me. About a dozen tin holders, held each in position against the bare whitewashed walls, contained home-made tallow candles that required frequent renewing, the candle wicks being altogether out of proportion to the slender tallow sticks which were constantly dripping and thus consumed very rapidly. The floor was bare of boards, but being well beaten down and made hard, answered well enough, provided it was sprinkled at frequent intervals. By far the best part of the festive occurrence was the orchestra or dance music, which consisted of two female harpists, one male guitarist, and one male bass viol. Mexicans are born musicians like the gypsies of Hungary. Two small rooms, one on either side of the hallway, were used as receptacles of surplus clothing for the respective sexes; that appropriated to the men also contained a large table supplied with the everpresent mescal, imported French brandy, and very good cigars. Our friend Fernandez was on hand there also with a bucket of milk, several dozen fresh eggs, a plentiful supply of sugar and ground nutmeg, with which materials he proceeded early in the evening to concoct the royal drink of eggnog, which had been introduced by us, as previously related. The refreshments for the ladies were gotten up in a adjoining kitchen, and were served during the pauses between dances in the ballroom, while the men helped themselves ad libitum in their sanctum.

Well, the ladies began to arrive. I do not think that I overestimated the number of chaperons if I reckon them at about three times the number of the young ladies, married and unmarried, who were supposed to represent the real dancing contingent. But, then, many of these chaperons came here with "malice intent," i.e., with their minds firmly made up to be asked to dance, to indulge in the terpsichorean exercise and to be more or less lenient toward possible adorers of their charges, in proportion to the attention and courtesy extended to them, the elderly contingent, by the youthful swains.

The dances in vogue in the United States at that time were all indulged in except the there unknown "Lancers." The valse (waltz), when danced at all, was gone through to a very slow measure; still slower was the "danza" performed, a sort of waltz with very slow and short steps. The Mexican ladies are very graceful dancers, and rather glide than step along, so much so that a glass full to the brim placed upon a lady's head would hardly spill a drop of its liquid while the bearer would complete a turn around the room. The song "La Paloma," now so well and favorably known all over the United States, had not then been either written or composed as dance music. It is now a favorite "danza" in every Mexican ballroom.

I saw there for the first time a very good performance of the real "fandango," danced by one of the Comaduran ladies and a gentleman employed in the *aduana* (customs house service). They faced each other on the floor, which was given up to them alone for the purpose. The raison d'être of this dance is the imitation of two lovers who seek now to approach, now to evade one another. The movements of the feet and arms and the undulations of the torso are made to imitate loving adorance, bashful or teasing evasion or retreat, tender longing, or temporary disdain, etc. At the conclusion the maiden surrenders herself to the swain, who takes her gently round the waist, and dancing, leads her to her seat.

Dancing aside, a ball of that kind is in our estimation about the "flattest" amusement one may indulge in. The female part of the company present invariably sat on one side of the room, the males on the other. Conversation between the sexes is thus rendered impossible. The highly unsuccessful process of flirting with the eyes and fans only, soon palls upon one. I managed to dance twice with my adored Eulalia, no less than six times was I induced to dance with the omnipresent aunts. Even while dancing with her I was prohibited from whispering into her pink shell ear those sweet nothings an ardent lover will indulge in; she herself begged me to desist, because, as she said, such a proceeding would be observed by all, and would cause her speedy removal from the ballroom by her relatives.

As the dancing became more animated in course of time, a new feature peculiar to Mexican entertainments of that kind was introduced. From time to time a young lady or gentleman would rise from his or her seat, walk toward and stop in front of one of the opposite sex, and break upon his or her head an eggshell filled with innumerable small pieces of colored paper, gold and silver tinsel. A shower of these tiny little squares and triangles would fall upon the victim's shoulders, the removal of which was interdicted by usage. This multi-colored rain was generally begun by the ladies, as a gentlemen was not supposed to perform the operation upon a lady, until she herself by her own act upon him had thus given him permission. I was given to understand that a lady by this act desired to show a gentleman her particular liking for him. If that was so, I certainly was a very much liked youngster, inasmuch as it took me nearly an hour on the following morning, before I succeeded in freeing my hair, somewhat overgreased for the occasion, from the innumerable particles with which I had been distinguished as a well-liked person.

About midnight, when the festivity was at its hight [sic.] a sudden commotion became noticeable in the backyard adjoining the ballroom. Soon I distinguished several voices, some calling loudly for "Don Juan," others for "Wooster." Stepping out I ran full tilt upon Pedro, the major-domo, who was greatly excited, and immediately burst forth with: "Mr.

Goldtree and party were murdered by Apaches this morning in the Sonoita Valley!"

Mr. Goldtree being well and favorably known by many persons present upon the floor of the ballroom, this sudden news of his violent death cast a cloud of gloom upon the erstwhile gay assemblage. The news was brought direct from Crittenden by a messenger dispatched to Wooster and myself at the request of Mr. Warner. We knew, therefore, at once that it could not have been one of those idle rumors so frequently started under the circumstances in which we then lived.

The following day was almost completely taken up by the preparations for our start with two wagons and twelve draft animals which Pedro made ready, according to Mr. Warner's order, to accompany us into the Sonoita Valley, where Wooster was to cut the timber and burn the charcoal.

Through the kind intervention and skillful management of Carmelita, I was enabled to enjoy a short but tender interview with Miss Eulalia, who did not, at the time, seem to favor the suit of the Mexican *teniente* overmuch, but expressed to me her fear that irresistible influence would be brought to bear against her by her mother and the whole elderly contingent of female relatives towards making her marry that gentleman.

Pedro found two reliable teamsters, whom we hired, for the wagons, and after affectionate farewell all around we started towards nightfall, the two wagons in the lead, Wooster and I in the buggy, bringing up the rear, which was in those days considered the post of danger.

From Santa Cruz to Huebabe the road is for the most part upon hard ground, leading along the western border of the Santa Cruz River, only crossed now and then by the sandy river beds of creeks, frequently called "dry washes," through which the accumulated waters from the surrounding mountains flow down to the river in the rainy season. As the wagons carried no load to speak of, we traveled very fast, and reached Huebabe in the early morning hours. We stopped to cook breakfast at the house of a Mexican farmer, situated at the angle made by the valley and Sonoita roads, and learned from him that Mr. Goldtree had not been killed, but had managed to escape through the bushes surrounding the Sonoita Creek; but that Tapie and Captain Catterson were both murdered and had been hastily buried where found.

The road from here to Tubac was considered "comparatively" safe as the valley bottom was occupied by farmers' dwellings at intervals of one to two miles all along the road. Therefore, after a few hours' rest, Wooster and I, with one of the wagons, continued our route in order to load up at Tubac the provisions and tools Wooster would need for the woodcutters. The other wagon with the teamster from Santa Cruz was

184 / *John Spring's Arizona*

left here, and the latter was instructed to find and gather the men previously hired. We met the greater part of them, however, as we passed by Calabazas, where the news of the killing had not yet reached. We hurried on to Tubac, and Wooster set to work at once making everything ready to begin his contract work; he left that same evening for the Sonoita.

At Tubac no one had as yet heard of Tapie's death, and I undertook the sad duty of informing his wife of her husband's sad end. I did so gradually.

On the following day, Mr. Goldtree, who had directed his steps towards Fort Crittenden during his flight, arrived at Tubac. He came directly to the store and related to me the following story:

"As you know, we left you and Wooster on the 29th upon arriving at Calabazas. Here we were hospitably received by Blanchard, Scott, and others, with whom we stayed until January 1, in the morning. Having then received notice that our wagons would be at the ranch towards noon, in order to load up we started early for the Sonoita, accompanied by Capt. Catterson who had business at the Fort. He rode a very good horse, and kept behind our buggy, within sight, all along the road. It was a very cold morning, and we all took a drink before starting. Tapie, according to his habit, as you know, had a bottle or two of French claret along, of which he imbibed freely from time to time, while he would, every little while, sing a stanza or two of his French war songs.

"We had gone about thirteen or fourteen miles when we came to that part of the road where there is a stretch of very heavy sand. The immediate edges of the road are overgrown with thick undergrowth, so dense that a solid wall could not afford a better hiding place. A short distance to the left runs the Sonoita Creek; on the righthand side of the road, beginning immediately behind the bushes, rises a rather steep, rocky hill. We had traveled about one hundred yards in this sandy bottom, the nature of which compelled our team to proceed very slowly and laboriously, the buggy being well loaded with blankets, provisions, etc., when all at once there were several shots accompanied by fierce yells, and the buggy stopped. I was driving at the time. A burning sensation in my right wrist led me to the belief that I was wounded; at the same time my hat was carried off. You know in an occurrence of this kind things happen much faster than you can relate them. I jumped out of the buggy, grabbed a package of carbine cartridges (Sharp's) and not seeing the carbine, ran up towards the hill, whither Tapie had already preceded me. He had the carbine. When I had approached him to within about twenty-five yards (we were both running uphill at the same time), I threw the package of ammunition towards him and sang out: "Shoot, shoot for your life!" He was evidently not hurt in any way at that time, but kept fumbling with the carbine, which must have been out of working order; for he seemed cool enough and would surely have fired his weapon if this had been possible. I had commenced firing with my pistol as soon as I had thrown the cartridges to Tapie, by which time some of the Apaches had started to follow us uphill. I know I wounded the foremost in a leg, and this made them more cautious until they discovered that Tapie's carbine would not shoot. Then they became bolder. They were very sparing of their ammunition, and in fact I could see only two firearms among them. As they advanced they hollowed [sic.] at us several epithets of a nasty nature, in Spanish, followed by the declaration: "You are our meat." All at once Tapie gave a piercing shriek, jumped into the air, and fell. He was very near me at the time. I bent over him and heard him distinctly but feebly utter the words: 'Joe, don't leave me; stay by me, I am badly hurt.' Then he gave a last gasp, a shiver went through his frame, and I saw he was dead.

"I picked up the carbine and discovered at once that it would not work; the hammer would not lift. Still, I made the Indians believe, by holding my pistol alongside of it, that I was firing from the longer weapon; this made the Apaches, great cowards at all times, still more cautious, and permitted me to direct my retreat towards a rocky gulch that descended from the hillside towards the creek. Running from rock to rock I managed to escape unhurt and to disappear into the dense undergrowth. Never in my life did I feel as thirsty as I did then. I drank deep of the ice-cold water of the creek, and then, making my way cautiously through the bushes, returned to the place of the attack, when I peeped through between the foliage upon the enemy.

"While there had been only seven or eight following us up the hill, there were now eighteen, from which I surmised that they had divided up into two parties, one of which probably made away with Capt. Catterson, whose horse, still saddled and bridled, stood alongside of our two animals. When the attack was made he was riding a few yards behind the buggy, but probably turned round at the first fire, and made the sad mistake of running back, about the worst thing to do in an attack by Indians . . . [those] who know [are aware that] human nature tends towards fleeing backwards from the enemy in front. The Indians had unharnessed the horses, and were cutting the harness into such strips as seemed to suit their purposes best. They had unstrapped our bundle containing four pairs of heavy California mission blankets, and were cutting them into single blankets. I saw one take a bottle of claret from the lunch basket, break its neck, and pour the contents of it into a tin cup; but he had hardly taken two swallows when he spit the wine out, making a remarkably ridiculous grimace.

"When they had distributed among them, not without some quarreling, everything they held worth carrying off, they separated into two parties, one taking the direction towards the Santa Cruz Valley, the other eastwards towards the Dragoon Mountains. I did not notice that any of them obeyed the directions of a leader or chief, neither did I notice any one of them giving orders; they seemed to do everything by common consent or mutual agreement; one party took our team, the other the saddle horse. The buggy they left standing in the road.

"Notwithstanding the very cold weather, none of the Indians wore any clothing to speak of; several of them had upon their shoulders pieces of old army blankets, two had Mexican serapes and one, the cape of an army overcoat. All of them were bareheaded, while a few had tied around their foreheads a strip of some cloth, which kept the profuse long hair away from their eyes. Bows and arrows were in everyone's hands; but of firearms I saw only a rifle and two pistols. One had a lance.

"After their departure I waited about half an hour, drank some more water, and picked up a few biscuits that lay scattered around the buggy. Then I made a beeline towards our ranch, where I found our wagons just arrived. With the wagonmaster and two teamsters I returned to the scene of the attack. We found that Tapie's body was still lying where he fell; there were about a half a dozen arrows sticking out of it, a favorite way with the Apaches of leaving a *momento mori*. Otherwise he had but the one bullet wound that penetrated the heart and caused his immediate death. We buried him preliminarily upon the spot, and then began the search for the body of Captain Catterson. This was an easy task, as we had only to follow the backward tracks of his horse from the spot where the attack was made. We found his body about one hundred yards to the rear of the buggy and a few yards to the left of the road. His spine was broken by a bullet, and four arrows stuck out from his back. In his breast and throat there were a few deep gashes, evidently made by a lance. We buried him temporarily where we found him. I met Wooster and party today as I was coming through the Sonoita; they were preparing a deep grave for the two bodies."

Thus ran the story of Mr. Goldtree, who was still very much unnerved. He had picked up his hat, that had been shot off at the first fire; it showed two holes made by the arrows that carried it off. The back of his coat showed two more arrow holes, and his wrist, which had held the reins, was badly powder-burned, showing that the Indians fired their first volley almost within arm's reach. The exceedingly poor marksmanship displayed on this occasion can only be accounted for by the circumstance that the Indian's aim was disturbed by the very dense bushes in which they were hidden, and from which they fired.

MURDER AT NOGALES

After Wooster had fulfilled the obligations of his contract in the Sonoita, which kept him occupied during all of January and part of February, 1869, he returned to Tubac, after having delivered the borrowed or hired animals and wagons to Mr. Warner, who had recovered in the meantime from his sickness and was again residing at Santa Cruz. Our stock of merchandise in the store, the greater part of which had been trusted out on crops that were yet to grow, was at a very low ebb. News of Apache depredations, quite frequently accompanied by murder, were reaching us almost daily from the surrounding country.

In the month of February, all Tubac was stirred up one morning early by a Mexican, who came riding furiously into town upon a saddle dripping with blood, and begged assistance from whomsoever he met, in burying a party of his countrymen that had fallen victims to the wily Apaches at Los Nogales (the walnut trees). Alexander McKay, just returned from the Legislature, of which he was a member, Ramón Romano, one Jose Ortiz, and the writer saddled up forthwith. Old Henry Glassman was very willing to accompany us, but, as he was then in his honeymoon, other influences were brought to bear upon him. A sharp ride of about two hours, towards the close of which we rode through the present site of the town of Nogales, brought us to the scene of Apache atrocity.

The road from Sonora here made a sharp turn around a projecting rock bulging out from a rocky hill on the right side of the road. All along the left side of the road there was, hidden from it by a dense growth of bunch grass (*sacaton*), a natural ditch made in course of time by the water running down from the road during the rainy season. This ditch or natural culvert was about three feet deep, and afforded a fine hiding place for Indians lying in ambush, as it was dry during at least ten months in the year. Here there was a group of, I think, seven walnut trees, from which the present town of Nogales received its name, and here we found eleven victims of the Apaches, all, with one exception only, killed by arrows and lances shot and thrust into the traveler's backs as soon as they had rounded the projecting rock. A woman that accompanied the party was carried off; the only other survivor, who guided us to the place, had a bullet hole between the shoulders. He owed his escape to the running away of his horse, which had become frantic at the yells of the Apaches. All the others, among whom there were two boys, aged fifteen and seventeen, respectively, lay there stark and dead, scattered about like so many rocks promiscuously thrown about by an explosion. All over the place there lay scattered the contents of their four carts constructed according to the then prevailing awkward Mexican style.

The survivor told us that they had at least eight rifles among them, but they had unfortunately been placed upon the carts first and the flour sacks upon them. Well, the Apaches found them all, inasmuch as they had seemingly enjoyed the fun of scattering every pound of flour broadcast, after ripping the sacks. All the space around the carts was dotted with white where it was not discolored with the sickly, gory spots made by the victims' lifeblood.

We gathered the bodies and buried them in a common grave, enveloped in the serapes and blankets, under the walnut trees.

FARMING IN ARIZONA IN 1869

When Wooster returned from the Sonoita, we had one more consultation as to our further *modus vivendi.* We had scarcely any more goods for sale, and, if we had had them, there was scarcely anybody who would buy them; the store had therefore become a sinecure, as far as business was concerned. Under these circumstances that resourceful man developed the following plan: He proposed that I should remain at the store and transact such business as still remained: that he would break ground and bring under cultivation a level piece of land, containing about one hundred acres, situated about one mile below the *Palo Parado* (upright pole). This was a farm principally cultivated by one Sabino Otero and some Mexican renters. All these men lived in houses made of upright mesquite poles, the interstices being plastered over with mud or clay. The roofs were flat, and consisted simply of a thick layer of earth supported by the long wands of the *Fouquieria splendens,* or candlewood of the botanists, called by the natives "ocotillo." This settlement was situated seven miles above Tubac, upon the western border of the Santa Cruz River, from which the cultivated lands were irrigated by ditches.

As I said before, Wooster and I were fast friends. When he developed his plan for farming to me, I could see that he hesitated somewhat whenever his calculations reached the point that needed the explanation of the "wherewith." As I still had some cash left from my economics in the army, I freely offered to put it into the agricultural venture, because, although we might easily find ways and means to obtain animals and implements and had a good lot of provisions left, nothing but hard cash would procure the labor necessary for the digging of the irrigating ditch, which would in all probability be about a mile long and cost several hundred dollars. As for the management of a farm, big or small, I had full confidence in Wooster, as he would always carry out whatever he undertook. Mr. Alex McKay kindly undertook (on credit) to survey the ditch part of the enterprise with an instrument of his own manufacture, and carried it out in a very satisfactory manner.

Wooster, with Ramón, our man-of-all-work, started one fine morning in March to the ground selected for a dwelling and began to cut mesquite poles in the adjoining woods and had before long a *palo parado* house constructed in the approved style of the region, into which Wooster moved with his wife and household goods about April 10, while I remained for the time being at Tubac, boarding wherever I might and sleeping in the small room attached to the store.

The numerous freight trains, consisting of immense red wagons pulled by twelve-mule-teams, and the still more numerous, clumsy, and screeching ox carts, brought to Tucson, by way of Tubac, nearly all the merchandise then sold in that fast-growing town, and a great deal of Sonora produce, such as flour, *panochas,* jerked beef, sugar cane in season, chickens and eggs. Not only was the distance traveled from Guaymas to Tucson about one hundred miles shorter than from Los Angeles, but the rate on freight in itself was much cheaper. These trains were quite frequently accompanied by men who came north of the frontier to seek work as teamsters, laborers, hostlers, etc., and by women who found employment readily as cooks and later on as women-of-all-work. The wages for farm laborers in the state of Sonora was at that time six dollars per month, work being performed from sunrise to sunset. In addition to this monthly stipend, which the wage earner generally spent for provisions and clothing at his employer's store, he was given a ration of twenty pounds of corn, four pounds of beans, and a half-pound of salt each week. As soon as he had crossed "the line," he could readily find work from Calabazas on to Tucson and beyond, at the rate of one dollar per diem, and when he worked by the tarea (daily task) would often earn two dollars per diem, if he was the right kind of man to do it.

These tasks consisted of a certain amount of work which was assigned to a laborer according to a system established in Mexico many years previous. Sometimes it would mean the digging of a certain number of steps along a ditch of given depth; sometimes it was the cutting for a certain number of pounds of hay (with a sharp hoe); in cutting grain with a sickle, a certain area was stepped off for a day's task; the husking of corn was measured by the *fanega,* as also was the shelling of it; a *fanega* of shelled corn weighing about 190 pounds. I have known several young active Mexicans, and principally Yaquis, who earned in Arizona a small capital within one year, which enabled them to start a small grocery store on either side of the line, by performing a double task each day.

The wages of women in Mexico are still lower, although the greater part of them enjoyed the privilege of eating at the house of their employer. A good cook would earn four dollars per month, which was then the price of a very indifferent pair of women's shoes. An ordinary cook would earn about three dollars, and the breadmaker (tortillera) received from two dollars to two fifty according to the size of the family for whom a greater or lesser quantity of the large, flat, round disks of their bread (*tortillas*) had to be prepared.

MY MEXICAN SWEETHEART

These conditions then prevailing in Sonora brought about the steady influx of laboring men and women, who, for the sake of safety, traveled with the trains of wagons and ox carts coming into Arizona. Now it happened that during the period while Wooster was already housekeeping upon our incipient ranch and I was boarding "at large," as it were, there arrived a small contingent of young Mexican women with one of these wagon trains, which stopped over night at Tubac. Major Richardson, being at the time without a cook, and hearing of the arrival of the young women, called on me and requested my services as interpreter in the hiring of one of them to take charge of his simple household. The wagons were encamped in the town itself — in fact upon the large open space lying between his store and Wooster's property. We had no difficulty in procuring the desired help in the person of a very pretty, lively, dark-eyed damsel, who, supported by the testimony of her companions and the teamsters, declared herself able and willing to perform the duties mentioned by us. She was about twenty years of age, unusually well spoken, and very graceful. The major readily paid the five dollars demanded by the wagonmaster for her transportation and board while with the train. She placed her bundle containing all her possessions upon her head and walked with us to the major's dwelling, where I explained to her the work that was expected of her. She understood everything quite readily, and had a fire burning in the kitchen and water boiling within a few minutes.

I do not remember at this present writing how it all came about, that on that very day I became a boarder at the major's; at least, I cannot recollect what arrangements were made to that end; I know I paid the sum of forty dollars for one month's board in advance, because my notebook kept in those days (which I have before me) tells me so, and I know that I never omitted being present at a meal. Ynacia, abbreviated into "Nache," was the name of the semi-tropic beauty, for a beauty she was. I soon fell into the habit when addressing her of using the diminutive "Nachita," which in the Spanish language carries along with it a meaning of endearment. She was far, far above the average of the Mexican women in her walk of life. In the first place she was always neat and clean as to her person and her belongings; she was nicely combed from early morning when she served her breakfast. One Mr. Riordan, a grain contractor, who frequently passed through Tubac and ate several meals with us, used to say of her: "She is the best groomed filly in the whole stud," meaning the whole female population of his acquaintance. He was a "horsy" man and used "horsy" language. Nache's voice was music when she spoke, her songs were sweetness itself; her very walk was a poem. We were not long in discovering that she could read and write her language very well indeed, and before a week was over she had become my pupil in English and I hers in Spanish. The major favored these mutual lessons greatly, because he was anxious that the girl should learn English, and I, having plenty of leisure time, was never backward in teaching.

If my readers will kindly take into consideration my youth and Nachita's youth and her bewitching personality added to my fast-developing knowledge of her language and our frequent intercourse, they will readily understand that before very long we became, at first intimate friends, and soon thereafter passionate lovers. Mexican etiquette, indeed, forbade our being together by ourselves, and our lessons were given in the major's store, seldom frequented by customers, and in his presence. Of course, there were moments when his temporary absence would permit a tender glance, an endearing word and a sweet caress; but otherwise Nache strictly observed, menial though she was, the modesty and reserve practiced in a well-regulated family.

I boarded with the major until Nache left for Tucson, where an incipient consumption compelled her to seek medical treatment. This was, however, of no avail; the complaint rapidly developed into acute phthisis of a malignant character, and early in the following year the sweet girl died.

APACHE ATROCITIES

Although the Indians kept the farmers, travelers, and teamsters continually on the lookout in our surroundings, the Santa Cruz Valley during the year 1869 had comparatively few murders to record. In the Sonoita Valley, E. G. and G. Pennington (father and son) were killed in May while plowing in their field, and all the horses, mules and other movable property belonging to the farm was taken. These two were the last remaining members of the family, all others having previously succumbed to the wily Apaches. A little later Benjamin Aikin and a Mexican were murdered while harvesting their crop in Sonoita Creek. Thomas Vondag was killed while standing in the door of his house. Six United States soldiers were attacked by sixty Indians, and one of them was killed, while they were gathering wood, within eight miles of Fort Crittenden.

In connection with the above-mentioned Pennington family I must here record the capture and marvelous escape of a daughter of old man Pennington, the father mentioned above, with whom I became acquainted in the spring of 1869 at Tubac. This woman* lived with the family at a place called Sopori Ranch, situated on Sopori Creek. This ranch is reached by leaving the Santa Cruz Valley road at the Canoa and traveling about eighteen miles southwest on the road leading to the old town of Arivaca. After the Indian outbreak in the fifties, her husband, one Page, an immigrant from Texas, having invested his all in that region, made a trip into the Santa Rita Mountains with some wagons, in order to procure some pine timber growing there about half way up the mountain. He was accompanied by four men, his wife and a young girl of about fourteen.**

In this timber camp the Apaches suddenly pounced upon the party, killed some of the men and carried off Mrs. Page and the girl. In their flight they reached the edge of a precipice, along which they traveled for several hundred yards. Mrs. Page had not ceased to defend herself against the Apaches with teeth and nails; the Indians, thinking themselves pursued (which in fact they were), and exasperated by the woman's outcries and her violent defense, at last threw her upon the ground, lanced her several times in the upper part of her body, and threw her over the edge of the precipice into the chasm below.

At the bottom of the cliff there was a small creek whose borders were densely overgrown by elder trees and bushes of various kinds. This foliage broke the woman's fall, which was at least fifty feet. When Mrs. Page recovered from her fainting condition, brought about by the cruel treatment she had undergone, she refreshed herself with the water of the creek, and ate and gathered some elderberries. She was, however, too weak to walk. On her hands and knees she began to crawl towards her home, guided by the sight of the Baboquivari Peak near Arivaca which lay directly before her towards the west. She came to water again on the second day while crossing the Santa Cruz River. Her strength she was able to maintain by eating cactus fruit and the pods of the mesquite tree. Completely exhausted, she reached her home on the evening of the third day in a most pitiable state, from which she gradually recovered, however, and today, notwithstanding her advanced age (nearly seventy), she is hale and hearty.

---

*She is now married to W. G. Scott, a justice of the peace at Tucson, Arizona, where they reside.

**The writer knew her very well in after years. She had been obtained from the Apaches in exchange, and in 1868 married Charles Shibell, now recorder of Pima County, Arizona.

FROM FARM TO COURTHOUSE

After this digression I return to Wooster and our agricultural enterprise. The irrigating ditch was completed and nearly fifty acres of the virgin soil had been irrigated preparatory to being plowed. I arrived with the remnants of all the merchandise the store had contained. Wooster had constructed a fairly spacious *palo parado* house for himself and wife, and an addition consisting of leafy branches resting upon horizontal poles was used as a kitchen. A similar construction had been prepared for my dwelling. It was exceedingly airy; in fact, the four sides were nothing but a light framework of candlewood wands, to which some foliage was attached by means of strings; so that during the whole time of my stay there, an Apache or anyone else could have stuck me with a lance during any hour of the night.

Wooster and Ramón were plowing all day in the field with a twenty-four-inch plow. Soon after my arrival Wooster's wife was taken sick, and I took upon myself the culinary department, learning to plow in the intervals between meals and dishwashing. We plowed with oxen. Wooster had his three yoke of oxen pretty well broken in at my arrival, and needed no assistance in his work; while I had to learn the business, assisted by Ramón, who guided the oxen with a sharp-pointed stick. It was virgin land and overgrown with innumerable tufts of bunch grass, there called *sacaton*. This vegetable product has deep roots of a consistency tough as wood, and it was no unusual sight to see my plow point stuck fast at the bottom of one of these roots, while the plow handles, with me dangling between them high in the air, stood at a considerable elevation. Then Ramón would back the oxen, the effect of which action was to suddenly release the plow and dump me upon the ground.

There was absolutely nothing during those days to prevent the Indians from shooting or stabbing us in the back, behind the plow, from sticking me like a pig in my bed, or from murdering the solitary woman in her bed. But none of all this happened — then!

At the beginning of July, I was summoned by the sheriff of Pima County to appear at the courthouse at Tucson as a member of the grand jury, my first experience in that line.

The most interesting case that was brought before our august body was the alleged poisoning of eight girls who were engaged as dancing girls in a dance house by a malevolent barkeeper named "handsome Charley." These dance houses furnished a free hall and free music, and free female partners. However, after each dance, the man was requested to treat his girl to something, and himself also; this double treat involved an expense of fifty cents per couple about every eight or ten minutes.

The testimony as to the perpetrator of the crime, however, was rather meager and contradictory. Among the witnesses summoned before us were two commissioned army officers, who had danced on the night in question in that unsavory resort. It was very evident that they were far from relishing their position as witnesses. We found a true bill against said "handsome Charley," but the subsequent trial jury failed to agree upon a verdict in his case.

TUCSON POLICE COURT

While in Tucson I found time to visit the police court, held by a justice of the peace, on several occasions. I went there partly because any court of justice in those days was a "new venture" in Arizona, and partly because I had been informed that the Tucson judge was absolutely *sui generis,* a composite of severity, humor, nonsense, and some law. I was myself very much astonished that an invariable rule in that court in any civil case seemed to be that the party best supplied with this world's goods, and hence best able to pay, would be made to pay the costs, no matter what the other part of the decision was. Right or wrong, the fortunate possessor of funds had to "shell out."

The town was at that time very badly governed; outlaws abounded, and did about as they pleased, until the merchants and men of property determined to bring about a reform. They decided to elect a judge who would deal severely with the scalawags who were running the town and corrupting the courts. So they chose the above-mentioned man, named Charley Meyer, to be judge. He was a very good druggist, but knew nothing about law. But he was perfectly honest, and that was the principal qualification the citizens desired. Accordingly Charley set up a law dispensary and dealt out justice and medicines with equal grace. In his court could be seen a library of calfbound books, consisting chiefly of the *Materia Medica* and "Somebody" on Fractural Bones. He engaged as an officer of the court, who was afraid of nothing and nobody — one "Jimmy" Douglass, who carried in his leg a bullet that he had picked up at Gettysburg, and who walked with some difficulty and with a peculiar limp.

The first thing that Charley did was to establish a chaingang, and sentence to various terms in its service every offender that was brought before him. The "shyster" lawyers that had run the town before Charley's incumbency protested against this as a violation of the Constitution of the United States; but they protested, if not in silence, at least in vain. In fact, to protest was useless. The process of the judge was rather summary, but the result was very gratifying to the good citizens of Tucson. The wild, rough characters who had ruled the town, were now engaged in cleaning its streets, and that it had not known since its foundation. But if the business men were pleased, the lawyers were proportionately disgusted. The court refused to recognize them, and their business was gone.

One day, however, one of them plucked up courage enough to go before the court in behalf of his client and demand a trial by jury. The court was about to sentence the prisoner to a term on the chaingang, when the lawyer interposed a demurrer. "My client," he said, "objects to being tried by this court, on the ground of prejudice, and demands to be tried by jury."

"By a shury?" said Charley. "Wat is dot shury?"

"He demands," said the lawyer, "to be tried by his peers."

"Oh, he does, does he?" said Charley. "Vell, I sendence him to two weeks in the shaingang, and I sendence you to one veek. Now how you like dot trial by shury?"

And into the chaingang they both went, and served out their terms.

One day a man named Wolf was brought before the court for cheating some Indians out of three dollars. He was shrewd, and he knew all the tricks of the law. "Charley" felt that in this case the *Materia Medica* was not sufficient authority, and so he adjourned the court to get an opportunity to consult some books on the law, or to obtain advice from somebody with a knowledge of it. As he declared the case postponed and the court adjourned, however, he turned to the prisoner and said: "Volf, it is the unanimous opinion of dis community dot you are a tief, and dis court coincides fully in dot opinion."

Wolf lost color, and raising his fist, said: "Judge, I don't let anyone speak to me that way."

"Dis court fines you ten dollars for raising your fist against it," said Charley, "and you stands committed to the shaingang until it is paid."

Wolf knew that there was no recourse (there being no higher court at that time), and he reluctantly paid the ten dollars. The judge gravely took it, and, after dividing five between himself and his constable, Jimmy Douglass, gave the other five to the Indians. And to this day, in the annals of that Indian tribe, Charley Meyer is the most righteous judge that ever held court.

The Quartz Rock Saloon was then the most unsavory place in Tucson. It was a gambling hell, the resort of all the worst toughs and criminals in the place. One night Charley heard a knocking at the door of his house. He had been warned that he would be assassinated if he remained in town and continued to preside over the court, so he was a little cautious whom he admitted to his residence. He went to the front door and opened only the little lookout with which all the doors of Tucson houses were provided.

"Who's dere?" he said.

"A friend," was the reply.

"Vat you vant?" said the judge cautiously.

"I want to give myself up," said the stranger. "I just killed a man down at the Quartz Rock Saloon."

"You killed a man?" queried the Judge.

"Yes, I killed him. He called me a liar, and, you know, Judge, there are things a gentleman can't stand; so I out with my gun and killed him. And now I want to give myself up."

"You say you killed him at the Quartz Rock Saloon?" said the Judge. "Den, my friend you go back dere and kill anoder one!" and he turned back and went to bed. In the morning the body of the dead man was found in the street, and the murderer had escaped.

When I arrived at Tucson after years of absence, in October, 1902, I found the same Charley Meyer still dispensing justice. Of course, as *tempora mutantur* his administration of justice differs materially from that practiced in 1869.

After finishing my duties as a member of the grand jury, I remained in Tucson about two weeks longer, awaiting a settlement by the quartermaster of the army depot vouchers for hay delivered at Wallen in October, of the previous year. During this period I became acquainted with Alexander Levin, who in 1870 became my brother-in-law by marriage, I marrying his wife's sister. He had established a small brewery, with which was connected a bar and lunchroom, situated at the foot or western end of what is now known as Pennington street. This establishment did a flourishing business.

I also became acquainted with one Colonel Levy P. Ruggles, whose residence was at Florence, on the southern border of the Gila River, and about one mile distant from it toward the Casa Grande ruins. This man claimed, as first settler of that region, the usual one hundred sixty acres as a homestead, embracing the then incipient settlement of Florence. He described the land taken up by him as first class for agricultural purposes, and the facilities for irrigation all along the valley as unsurpassed, and offered to give me a good town lot free of charge if I could make up my mind to erect a brewery upon it. Just then, however, I considered myself bound to my friend and partner, L. B. Wooster, and returned to our ranch at the *Palo Parado* where I found that Wooster had in the meantime plowed and planted to corn and beans about fifty acres of our land, and had begun the manufacture of adobes with four Mexicans, whom he had hired for the purpose, with a view of erecting an adobe building and corral upon the site immediately adjoining the *palo parado* dwelling upon the north side. His wife, partly on account of the constantly threatening danger from roving Apaches, partly on account of her precarious health, had temporarily moved to the town of Tubac, and I resumed the culinary duties of the establishment, which also involved the procuring of fresh meat with my shotgun and the gathering of dry wood from the adjoining mesquite groves.

Once a week I would ride to Tubac for the mail, and the purchase of such articles at Mr. Yerkes's store as were needed in the household. On these occasions I would also call for the mail for such farmers as lived along my route, and even those who lived as far south as Calabazas, and had given instructions to the Postmaster to that effect.

One day in August I brought to the ranch several letters destined for neighbors to the south of us, and on the following day I made ready to start upon their delivery. About a mile south of us there lived upon a farm (quite substantial under the circumstances) the brothers Chambers. Their place was called the Bosque Ranch (*bosque* – a grove of trees), from the fact that near their dwelling was a grove of cottonwood trees.

About one and a half miles farther south there was another ranch called the *Agua Fria* (cold water) ranch. Upon this there lived at the time the same Captain Owen who had been a member of the legislature, as before stated. For him I had a letter, as well as several for one Long, J. B. Blanchard and George Saunders, at Calabazas. At this place there was a blacksmith shop. When I was ready to mount, Wooster, who desired to break some ground for a vegetable garden, asked me to take a plow point along and have it sharpened at the shop at Calabazas. I tied it fast upon the rear part of my saddle, and started upon our black horse, which, although of considerable age, was still quite serviceable.

AMBUSHED BY APACHES

Between the Bosque and Agua Fria ranches, about half way, there was at the time a long, narrow slough containing water pretty nearly the whole year through. It was overgrown with canebrake, in which innumerable blackbirds nested in season and found feed at all times, apparently. My route lay along the eastern edge of this slough, and made a sudden bend along about the middle of the slough, on account of the protruding point of a ridge descending from the lefthand side of the road, lined here by foothills.

I traveled along without any thought of danger, when my attention was suddenly called, upon a very large flock of noisy blackbirds arising from the slough and flying hastily away from the road toward the west. I think my first surmise was that somebody, unseen by me, was hunting in the canebrake. At all events, I was put on the alert by the circumstance, and caused my horse to travel at a faster gait. The moment I had turned the protruding corner of the descending ridge, the frantic yells of about a dozen Apaches in my rear startled me, as well as the horse, and I felt a burning sensation along that part of the body which sat upon the saddle. The whirr of several arrows passed by my ears, and I heard the report of a pistol or rifle.

Well was it for me that I had become a good rider by that time, for the horse gave a jump of at least 10 feet, that came very near unseating me, and then ran faster than I ever saw that horse run, straight along the road to the Agua Fria Ranch, where I had to use all my strength to bring him to a stop.

Investigation here showed that the one bullet fired at me had struck the plow point upon my saddle, had thence glanced off, passed between my legs, making a shallow furrow on the inside of my left thigh, and finally lodged in the base of the horn on my Mexican saddle. I cannot understand to this day how it came about that these Apaches, who numbered at least twelve, as their tracks subsequently showed, displayed such poor marksmanship, for even my horse was untouched. The only explanation seems to me that they were in a great hurry, and felt themselves unsafe, as a mounted party of six prospectors going to the Huachuca Mountains was only a short distance behind me. This I did not know at the time of the attack.

When I arrived at Calabazas and related my adventure, Mr. H. C. Long told me the following occurrence which had happened to him only a few days previous:

"I am cultivating a patch of garden truck about half a mile below here. About a week ago my shotgun got out of order, and I started for Tubac on foot to have it fixed by George Toddenworth, who, as you know, is quite an expert in firearms. I took the path leading by my vegetable garden to the main road. At the junction I met two miners from the Cerro Colorado, who were looking for me, having heard that I had onions, etc., for sale. I turned back with them and filled them two sacks with garden stuff, principally green peas, which it took a long time to pick. When they left me I found it was too late to go to Tubac and have my gun mended that same day. I took the lock off, hid the gun among the pea plants, and returned home. On the following day I started early toward Tubac. Just as I reached my patch I heard some shouting in the direction of the foothills toward the east, and presently saw a number of Apaches driving toward me some oxen which I readily recognized as the property of Colonel Lewis, the grain contractor of the Fort (Crittenden). Two of the Apaches were mounted, the others, about eight, were on foot. In order to reach the foothills on the west side of the river they had to pass very near me, say, about fifty yards distant. I grasped the situation at once, and made ready for them with my shotgun, whose lock was in my pocket.

"At first they seemed inclined to attack me at once. They came straight at me, but when I went down on one knee and rested my left elbow on it to take deliberate aim, they swerved off. I lowered my gun and laughed at them. They seemed to be ashamed, stopped a few moments, shot two arrows at me that fell short, and once more proceeded directly toward me, brandishing a lance or two. I resumed my deliberate aim upon the foremost, acting as best I knew how to make them believe that I was reserving my fire for a dead sure shot, and once more they swerved off, this time for good. I honestly believe that if my gun had been in working order and I had been possessed of, say, three cartridges, I could easily have recaptured the oxen and put the cowardly rascals to flight."

It will readily be understood that neither the food obtainable under the circumstances, nor the preparation of it at my inexperienced hands were such as to agree with a debilitated stomach resulting from the long illness from which I had been so recently and for such a long time prostrated.

I became more and more debilitated till at last I was really only a shadow of my former self. Added to this sad physical condition came the financial discouragement caused by the new aspect of things brought about by the arrival of new mercantile firms at Tucson who offered to take contracts at prices heretofore unheard of. Up to this time the contracts for grain furnished the military posts fetched from five to seven cents gold coin per pound; for beans, twelve cents. The contracts given out during that summer were taken at 2.6 cents for corn and four cents for beans, and our crop was at least forty miles from the nearest market, that is, provided we succeeded in obtaining delivery at Fort Crittenden. To Tucson our produce would have to be freighted on teams a distance of fifty-seven miles. Nearer market there was none. This, together with my debilitated condition, induced me to abandon farming, although I deeply and sincerely regretted to leave Wooster. This good man, who had seen my physique dwindling away from day to day, knew full well that it was "high time" for me to seek medical treatment at Tucson; I know he regretted my departure; he felt and expressed his earnest regrets in not being able to reimburse me for the money I had put into the business from time to time, and promised that he would do so as soon as circumstances would allow him; and I will say right here that he made me payments on account from time to time in an entirely satisfactory manner until — well, until the Apaches struck a final balance between us in March, 1871.

200 / John Spring's Arizona

Arrived at Tucson, I placed myself under the treatment of one Doctor Phelps.

As soon as I began to regain strength, I entered the employ of the above-named brewer, Levin, who had taken into partnership the afore-mentioned J. Goldtree. The two together now had enlarged the business of brewing and added to it that of wholesale liquor dealers. With them I learned not only the process of brewing beer (on a very small scale, of course), but also the manner of preparing malt by soaking, sprouting, drying, and roasting barley. The grinding or rather crushing by hand of the whole malt between two metal cylinders is the hardest work by far I have ever performed or seen performed.

A REIGN OF LAW AND ORDER

About the twentieth of July, 1869, there arrived at Tucson the newly-appointed governor of the Territory, A. P. K. Safford, and with him a new era — a period of comparative order and progress began. A few citizens met him at the Point-of-Mountain, a way station eighteen miles out of Tucson; more, when he reached the so-called nine-mile waterhole on the river. When he approached the town it seemed as though the whole population had turned out to welcome him. Governor Safford did not lose any time, but at once began to look into the conditions of Territorial affairs, which presented a more or less chaotic state.

There was but one federal Territorial officer in the Territory; namely, Judge Tuner, located at Prescott. One of the associate judges, Backus by name, had immortalized his judicial career by deciding the acts of the two legislatures held so far illegal and the laws of no force. This decision had created a condition that practically left the Territory without a government, except in name. The regular term for holding the Territorial Legislature had passed; hence, there was no appropriation for carrying on the government. The several boards of supervisors (county commissioners) had ordered tax levied in some counties according to the acts of one legislature, and in others according to the acts of another legislature, accordingly as they approved or disapproved of Judge Backus's decision; and in order that the money should not become a disturbing element, it was generally diverted into the county fund. The Territory was indebted in the sum of $26,000, and there were no funds to meet obligations. Not only was there hardly a foot of ground in the Territory safe from the depredations of Apaches, but Mexican outlaws also were almost weekly murdering and pillaging along and near "the line."

The Governor saw at once that he could not await the slow process of the courts to definitely determine the value of Backus's decision, and with county officers everywhere playing a lone hand, he found it was essential that he should have more power to put the wheels of government in motion and keep them in place until the legislature could be convened. He drafted two bills, which he took to Washington, where he had them introduced in Congress and passed. One legalized all the acts of the legislatures, and the other provided for the election and session of an immediate legislature; and gave the Governor power to remove and appoint, as he deemed proper, any county or precinct officer in the Territory for the period of two years. This was a very arbitrary act, and could only be excused by the extraordinary condition of the affairs in the Territory. Mr. Safford appreciated that it was a power which, if judiciously used by him, would be of great service to the people, but, if arbitrarily, selfishly and unjustly exercised, would work great injustice to the people and render him forever infamous. He used the power so mildly that but very few people, indeed, had any knowledge that he ever had such power; these were principally a few officers who had to be informed by the Governor himself as they were not disposed to obey the law. Very soon all cooperated in enforcing it, so that he was never compelled to remove a single officer by virtue of the arbitrary power bestowed upon him.

Until the first legislature met he ordered the legitimate expenses to be without any appropriation having been made, from the funds in the hands of the counties. Afterward he referred the whole matter to the legislature, and informed it that upon the same grounds which a man has a right to defend his own life, he had sustained the life of the Territory without the shadow of Territorial law; that if a single dollar had been misappropriated, they should hold him to the strictest account. No word of criticism or complaint was ever made that an unnecessary dollar had been expended by him during that period.

Right here, I think, is the place for me to mention two interviews Governor Safford had at Washington, which I heard related by himself. They go far to explain the so-called "Camp Grant massacre," which I shall describe in a later chapter, and which, in the opinion of every right-minded man, was forced upon the population of Arizona by the authorities at Washington themselves, who turned a deaf ear to all representations and entreaties of our long-suffering settlers. Governor Safford, in an address to the Society of Arizona Pioneers, delivered at Tucson, on Aug. 7, 1888, said: "In 1870 I met Gen. George Stoneman in Washington. It was generally understood that he was about to be appointed to command the Department of Arizona. I urged upon him in case he was sent there, the necessity of an active and vigorous campaign. I told him of the fame I believed to be in store for any officer who would succeed in conquering a foe who had held his own against the governments of Spain, Mexico, and for twelve years against the United States. After listening attentively to me, he replied that he did not consider there was any credit to be gained fighting Indians, and that the great mistake our government had made consisted in taking away from the Indians such a desert and worthless country as Arizona and New Mexico. I saw at a glance that if Stoneman was forced upon us we could expect but little relief and no sympathy. I went to General Sherman and suggested that perhaps a younger and more ambitious man might be sent in his place, but in effect was informed that the military authorities at Washington were capable of managing their own affairs."

MY SHORT EXPERIENCE AS A BARKEEPER

All this time I had been working at the brewery of Levin & Goldtree, who had also rented and kept a barroom uptown, which was attended to by a young German. In the month of September this man, having inherited a small fortune in Germany, quit his employment, and my employers requested me to take charge of the establishment until such time as they could find a regular or "professional" barkeeper. This task was not at all to my taste, although, I am sorry to say, I drank liquor enough in those days, probably for the reason that everybody else did. But it was one thing to go before a bar and order drinks, and quite another to stand behind the bar and hand out liquors to — well, let us call them Tom, Dick and Harry.

I had been "running" the place about three days when one afternoon, while I was putting everything in order for the evening customers, a fine old gentleman came in, sat down at a table, and ordered a glass of whisky. He engaged me in a friendly conversation, during which the fact developed that he was Major Duffield, inspector of United States mails for the Territory of Arizona, recently appointed as such. The three doors of the barroom were wide open; presently a man passed by the front door. Like a rock shot from a catapult, the old major darted through the open door and in about two seconds I saw him engaged in a lively scrimmage of "fisticuffs" with the man who had just passed, upon the sidewalk. This one, after about two or three minutes lightning-like give-and-take, ran off into a by-street, picked up a rock, threw it toward his antagonist, who, for some reason or other, seemed unable to follow him and then he disappeared.

The Major came limping back into the barroom and sank upon a chair, apparently suffering great pain. The rock had missed him, but it soon developed that upon going out he had made a misstep and broken an ankle. In this condition he had done the boxing. I summoned assistance; for a wonder, a constable had seen the battle from afar, and upon approaching had heard some of the conversation carried on in a loud and violent manner by the combatants.

As the Major, whom the excitement of the battle had upheld thus far, now collapsed and was almost fainting, he was carried to his room; the constable knew both parties to the fight, and took my name as a witness.

From the crowd that had been attracted by the occurrence, I now learned that the cause of the quarrel was of several weeks' standing, and resulted from the fact that the man assaulted, whose name was Fred Maish, had been employed by Maj. Duffield to plaster and kalsomine several rooms. This work, in the opinion of the latter, was imperfectly done, not fulfilling the conditions of the contract entered into between them, and he refused to make the payment persistently demanded by Maish. I also learned that Major Duffield bore the reputation of being a very brave man; that in the draft riot at New York in 1863 he had seized a Negro by his feet, and planting his back against the closed portal of a public building reached by a broad stairway, had swung that Negro around his head like a war club and thus cleared the way for about a dozen negroes whom the infuriated mob was about to hang upon some lampposts. Also, that he carried upon his person constantly anywhere from four to six revolvers and a bowie knife, and would sooner "fight than eat."

I am thus particular in describing this man, whom every one at first acquaintance would have taken to be a cultivated and mild-mannered gentleman "of the old school," because we shall see further on, in due chronological order, what an amount of trouble he gave to the court at his trial; for in consequence of the testimony given by the constable and subsequent events the judge of the police court held that the occurrence related to him made the case so serious that it had to be brought before the grand jury at its next session. Duffield and Maish, it seems, had arranged to fight a regular duel with firearms, a proceeding which, according to the statutes of the Territory (called the Howell Code), took the case beyond the jurisdiction of a justice of the peace. The memorable trial which resulted during the following year lives still in the memory of old timers as an "event." In the meantime the would-be duelists were put under bonds to keep the peace, and were, besides, held under bonds to appear before the district court at its next session.

There had also arrived in the town about the same time a trio of toughs, called the "Kelsey boys," said to be brothers. I only knew two of them, the younger ones. The elder of these appeared a quiet enough man; he was a faro dealer, and kept sober at all times. The younger one was a hard drinker, an all-around gambler, tough, and bully. He would probably not have been tolerated in the town long, i.e., alive, had it not been for the generally known fact that his two elder brothers would protect him to the utmost and make every quarrel their own in which he might become complicated, whether it were just or unjust, and no matter how provoked.

Now, a few days after the above-described fight, there presented himself at my bar the youngest Kelsey, a heavyset man of about thirty years of age, with a bloated face and a malignant smile, and demanded a stiff cocktail. It being early morning, there was nobody stirring yet anywhere; I interrupted my occupation (I was sweeping out the place at the time) and mixed his drink, which he imbibed at one swallow, immediately demanding another. I complied and said: "Four bits, please."

He reached behind his right hip, pulled out a big Colt's revolver (it looked very big to me), cocked it, and laid it before him on the counter within easy reach of his hand, but out of my reach. I felt no desire to reach out for it, anyway, under the circumstances. "You — Dutchy," he said, "you see this?"

I saw. He grabbed the weapon and retreated backwards toward a door, through which he disappeared.

When I reported the case to my employers they simply said I must not let him have any more liquor on credit.

Mr. Kelsey must have thought he had me badly scared. At all events, he returned early on the following morning. I had consulted overnight with an experienced old German named Cam Wise. This man had been in the Territory since 1854, and he gave me the following advice: "When you see that a scrimmage is unavoidable, see that you get in the first lick, and be sure to get it in good." When, therefore, the Kelsey boy made his demand for a cocktail, I put my hand under the counter as if reaching for a tumbler; in reality I took a good grip on that heavy piece of wood called a bung-starter, and asked my customer for payment in advance. He flared up in anger, and made a motion toward his right hip. This in the ethics of that time and place under like circumstances was a sufficient provocation for using a club not only, but a pistol if desired. That bung-starter came out from under the counter and descended upon the head of the tough with the rapidity of lightning, and all the force I was capable of. Kelsey dropped, and I ran out, making a beeline to the office of Charley Meyer, the justice of the peace. To him I related the circumstance and paid a fine of five dollars — which operation, he said, would settle the matter. It did. When I returned to the barroom the man had gone; there remained only a spot of coagulated blood where his head came in contact with the floor. Then I shut up shop, took and delivered the keys of the place to the owners, to whom I declared that keeping bar in Tucson, or, in fact, in any other place, did not suit my complexion and inclination.

Although no legal proceedings were taken against me for my self-administration of justice, I was told by several persons that I had better be on the lookout for trouble with either the Kelsey boys themselves or others of their "gang," and when I heard that the situation of sutler's clerk at Crittenden had become vacant, and was urged by two officers of that fort, temporarily at Tucson, to apply for the place, I readily accompanied them thither and obtained the situation.

The sutler store at Crittenden was then in the hands of three partners, one of whom, Mr. Sidney R. De Long, acted as manager. It was a well-appointed store that carried a far better assortment of goods and sold them at far more reasonable prices to soldiers, as well as civilians, than any sutler store I have ever seen, taking, of course, into consideration the rate of prices then charged in the Territory by the stores in settlements and towns. It is true that my hours of work were very long, extending frequently far into the night when the officers indulged in a game of cards in the rear room set apart for their use. But the kind, considerate, genteel, and liberal treatment I received at the hands of my immediate employer, as well as his refined manner and conversation, fully compensated me for all extra work, and I was very happy and content during the short stay I enjoyed in his company and under his orders.

Not long after my arrival at Crittenden, I enjoyed a meeting with Wooster, who had a sub-contract for the delivery of hay at the fort. He visited the store frequently in order to purchase provisions, his hay camp being in the Sonoita Valley, distance about six miles from the fort. During one of his visits he complained to me about one of his men. In order to make quick progress in the delivery of the hay, which he had begun rather late in the season, he had procured a "Buckeye" hay cutter and two strong mules. He had also hired a stout young Irishman as driver of this machine at extravagant wages, owing to the urgency of the occasion. Although it had been understood that his man's wages should not be demanded or paid until the delivery of the whole amount of hay contracted for should have been effectuated, this Irishman, who was of a surly temper at all times, constantly demanded his wages, frequently in terms that Wooster designated as "nasty." He had even used threatening language, and at times it would appear as if he were not altogether in his right mind, all of which kept Wooster in an uncomfortable state of mind. He had not the necessary cash to pay the man off, neither could he very well dispense with his services.

Thus matters stood when I unexpectedly lost my situation. The principal partner in the sutler store had sold out and notified Mr. De Long by mail that he would arrive in a few days, together with the new partner, to see his interests turned over; also, that the new man, one Woods, would take active part in the management of the store. This rendered my services as clerk superfluous. I am proud to this day when I think of the evidently sincere and fatherly regret Mr. De Long kindly expressed toward me upon our parting when the two gentlemen arrived from Tucson and the turnover was made.

As I was well acquainted with them, we had a social sitting together after dinner, enjoying a glass of wine and a cigar.

But I was very restless.

It seemed to me that an invisible but powerful mental force pulled me toward Wooster's hay camp. I felt, I may say I know, that he was in imminent danger of his life, although this danger did not take any tangible shape in my mind's eye. At last the feeling became so strong, urgent, and irresistible that I could sit still no longer. Mr. De Long kindly loaned me a horse and saddle, and I started for Wooster's camp. The nearer I approached it the more the sensation increased that I was needed there. I rode at a furious gait. I could see from afar that the mule team hitched onto the mowing machine was standing in the valley bottom all alone, while three men were cutting hay with scythes about one hundred yards from it, and two others were loading a wagon. About fifty yards farther brought me around a turn in the road to a place whence I could see the small adobe house that Wooster used as a temporary dwelling and store house. It stood with its front toward the road, and I saw with astonishment that a man, unknown to me, was piling brush and mesquite wood against its one closed door. Wooster was nowhere to be seen. The man at the door never turned around, although he must by this time have distinctly heard the hoofbeats of my horse. One man, Ramón Moranga, who appeared from behind the house, saw me at once, and ran toward me. In a few hasty words he explained to me the situation. The driver of the mower had become crazy; at dinner he had quarreled with Wooster; still, he had gone to his work. About 2 o'clock, while Ramón was sharpening scythes on the grindstone, he suddenly returned. Finding Wooster mending his sandals and leggings in the house, he suddenly pulled his revolver, shut the door upon Wooster, and dared him to show his nose outside, unless he handed out the amount due the assailant. There was no other opening in the walls of the little house. Ramón had no arms, except a knife. The other man had a full-loaded revolver. After some delay the crazy man obtained from the tool box near the outside of the door two spikes and a hatchet, with which he nailed the door fast to its frame. Then he had gone for some dry brush, which he dragged to the door, and now he was piling wood upon it in order to set the house afire or else suffocate his prisoner.

What was to be done? Ramón and I had quickly hidden in a hollow near the road. Men think fast in such moments. I gave Ramón the lariat which I found strapped on my saddle. I knew I could rely on him. I told him to run quickly around the house and gain the flat roof of it somehow, after having made a sling with a sliding knot at the end of his lariat in the manner of cowboys lassoing a steed. I would come suddenly to the front of the house and engage the attention of the crazy man, as soon as I should see Ramón crawling on the roof. The latter would then profit by the opportunity of the assailant's turning his back, and throw the lariat over his shoulders. The men in the hayfield were too far away to summon them to our assistance. Ramón understood my plan perfectly, and saying so, ran to the house by making a detour through the bushes. I saw him pick up a few rocks by the way and place them inside of his shirt. I waited. In a remarkably short time, although then it seemed long enough to me, I saw Ramón's head emerge from the rear edge of the roof, presently his body appeared, and he made me a sign with his hand that he was ready. The smoke was already curling up from the fire which the lunatic had lighted against the door. He had his back turned to me, and seemed completely absorbed in his occupation of arranging sticks of mesquite wood in the most suitable manner. So earnestly was he engaged in this murderous task that he had observed nothing of what had passed between Ramón and myself. I pulled out my revolver and cocked it, holding it, however, against my side with arm extended downward, so that he could not see it when I sidled up toward him upon the rising ground on whose top the horse stood. I rode up at a slow gait to within a few yards of him and said in voice I tried to make as natural as my emotion permitted: "Well, well, are you trying to smoke out bats, or mice, or what?"

At these words he whirled around quickly and seized his pistol, that lay nearby on the ground. As he rose he looked into the mouth of my cocked revolver. Before he could raise his weapon Ramón's sling dropped over his shoulders and was tightened with such a pull as to throw him to his knees. In another second I was off my horse, and between the two we had him tied hard and fast. Then we released Wooster, who was not a little astonished to see me on the premises.

"How did you happen to be here?" he said.

"I think you called me," was my answer.

"That could hardly be, at such a distance," said my friend, "but I surely wished you here with all my might."

"You thought of me while you were in this fix?"

"I thought of nothing else from the beginning, which was at dinner," said Wooster.

For this reason and on account of two other experiences of a similar nature I underwent later on, I believe that the theory of telepathy is founded upon truth.

The crazy driver of the Buckeye haycutter was sent to Tucson and Wooster undertook to drive the machine in order to fill his contract, which lacked only about fifty tons toward its completion. He learned this work, like everything else connected with farm work, within a very short time, and the last ton of hay was delivered by December 1, 1869. I had stayed with him all this time, making myself as useful as lay within my power, and after everything was settled connected with the contract returned with him to the ranch at the *Palo Parado,* where I found that he had already erected a good house of adobes, of which the sleeping room was completely finished and comfortably furnished. The kitchen had as yet only a temporary roof, because the walls had not yet been brought to the contemplated hight, [sic.] owing to the cold weather, which did not admit of the manufacture of adobes. The house constructed of upright poles, Wooster's previous dwelling, now did duty as a stable, and in it I slept, together with "Jim," a very funny, good-natured Englishman whom we had picked up at Crittenden, and who willingly did the "chores" without any more compensation than the wherewith to keep the wolf from the door.

The whole month of December was principally taken up by hunting. Wooster had harvested a very good crop of corn and beans, but refused to sell at the low prices mentioned heretofore as offered by the contractors. He said that he would retail the beans little by little, and as to the corn he would keep it to fatten hogs, a lot of which animals he proposed to bring up from Sonora as soon as the weather would permit him to build an adobe wall around a corral or yard behind the house.

The hunting was easy sport. Not only could small flocks of geese and ducks be met with all along the Santa Cruz River at almost any time, but these birds would also gather in the cornfields scattered along the borders of the river. Furthermore, we discovered one afternoon that there existed a regular gathering-place of geese and ducks by following several flocks whose flight tended to one spot, whither they came toward dusk from every direction. This spot proved to be a small lake about two acres in extent about one mile west of the river and about two miles north of Calabazas. When we reached it there were at least two hundred birds on the surface of the pond, which was surrounded on our side by a dense growth of elders and bushes of different kinds. As we had approached very cautiously, the birds were not disturbed in the least. In a country where and at a time when people were more often hunted than hunting, game of every kind was not nearly as shy as in later years.

We took a good survey of the numerous game before us. We each had a double-barreled shotgun loaded with duckshot. Wooster bent towards me and whispered into my ear: "Be ready; I shall let go one barrel into the midst of them, and as they rise, fire into the right center and I shall fire into the left." So said, so done. I am afraid to state the result of these four shots, inasmuch as hunting and fishing stories are generally taken *cum grano salis*. However, if the kind reader who has had any experience in duck shooting will take into consideration that the first shot went into the center of at least two hundred birds swimming closely together, that the three following shots were delivered to right and left upon the rising birds, and that all the shots were given at the fine scattering distance of from fifty to sixty yards, he will not be much surprised if I tell him that forty-one birds remained upon the water after our volleys, some stone dead, the others in the different stages of helplessness incident to their hurts.

I hear all my readers who are sportsmen cry out: "Shame! that was not hunting; it was slaughter!" I agree with them perfectly, but wish them to remember that we were not there "for our health," as the phrase goes nowadays. We were at least sixty miles from the nearest meat market, and we distributed our game liberally among the farmers of the valley.

Well, we had swimming upon the pond, as before stated, a goodly number of geese and mallard ducks, and, as we discovered later, a few canvasbacks and several that we did not know the name of. The next question was to fetch them to shore. I could swim like a duck; Wooster had never acquired that art. Both of us were afraid of the nature of the pond's bottom, which might prove, as likely as not, to be of a marshy, muddy, insecure consistency like the ponds near Tubac, where, during the previous winter, I had nearly caused the death of a Papago Indian whom I had induced to enter a pond for the purpose of fetching out two ducks I had shot. The Indian had become gradually engulfed like a man in quicksand, and only the fortunate circumstance of my finding nearby an abandoned wagon tongue, by means of which I was enabled to pull him out, had saved him from the horrible fate of being swallowed up alive in a bottomless pit.

We finally came to the conclusion that we had best send for help. I stayed at the pond, upon whose edge I built a fire to keep warm and also to keep off the prowling coyotes that would not fail, and did not fail, to put in their appearance. Wooster went to the ranch and came back about 9 o'clock accompanied by Jim, who carried a sharp ax. They also brought a goodly number of blankets. There were many dry tree trunks lying about, and within half an hour Jim had constructed a small raft, which he paddled out into the pond, gathering up the dead and wounded birds. He had a peculiar way of killing the latter. He would grasp the bill of the bird in his left hand, placing the forefinger under the throat, thus raising the neck, while with the right hand he would hold the bird somewhat low. This made the neck of the bird stand out in a convex line, through which he gave one good bite that cut or broke the connection of the backbone with the brain. The bird thus treated would give a convulsive shiver and remain motionless in death.

After gathering all the birds, Jim proceeded to build a small hut with our assistance, in which we passed the night comfortably enough. We heard many birds settle upon the pond during the night and at daybreak we repeated the manuever of the day before gathering in many more ducks and a few geese.

Upon the approach of Christmas we passed two days and nights at the pond, returning to the ranch with over one hundred birds. We distributed about one-fourth of these among friends and neighbors, and concluded to take the remainder to Tucson, where we could dispose of them for cash for Christmas dinners. Very few turkeys, if any, had then reached Arizona. The number we intended to take to market, however, was greatly reduced by the coyotes, who carried off at least twenty of them during the night before our start for Tucson, although these birds hung at least ten feet from the ground, upon a rope stretched between two poles. A coyote can either jump to a hight [sic.] of nine feet; he can climb up a pole, or he forms a ladder or staircase by using the backs of his family connections. I had about the same experience with these animals later on in Sonora, of which hereafter.

At all events, we arrived at Tucson with fewer birds than at first intended. They were very welcome, however, as few people in those days indulged in hunting.

QUARTERMASTER'S CLERK

On Jan. 3, 1870, Wooster returned to the ranch alone; I had accepted a position of second clerk in the quartermaster's department at Tucson, then in charge of Captain Gilbert C. Smith (I think, of the Ninth Infantry). He was depot quartermaster, and his brother, Delos, was first clerk. The situation was good enough as far as the emoluments went; the treatment of Captain Smith with his employes was of the best, but the amount of work demanded of one was an absurdity, taking into consideration the fact that all writing at that time had to be done by hand. Typewriting machines had either not been invented in those days, or, if so, had not reached Arizona.

One example will suffice to elucidate what an impossible amount of work was demanded of me. A short time before I was employed by the quartermaster, a wagon train had left Tucson toward California with an escort, it is true, but as the "outfit" was traveling west, where no danger from Apaches was apprehended, the escort, with the officer in charge, of course, riding in an ambulance, anywhere from three hundred to six hundred yards distant from the property under his charge. The wagons were attacked by the Apaches between Point of Mountain and the well-known peak called Picacho, and about twenty mules were cut from the traces and driven off. Nobody was killed, but somebody was responsible for the property, and a Board of Survey was called to hear testimony and remove that responsibility from that somebody. I do not remember the contents of the forty pages of legal cap which contained the proceedings of that Board of Survey, because I did not write them myself. When I was ordered to furnish four copies of the voluminous document by the following morning, I simply went to my old Company "E" of the Eighty-second Infantry, that happened to be stationed at Fort Lowell (then Tucson), and hired the company clerk and several others to accomplish the task. I delivered the four copies on the next day at the time appointed. I think I may here remark that in my varied experience with army papers of those days, it seemed to me that our glorious government could cover more paper with useless writing than anybody else. Otherwise, my position was pleasant enough, and I remember with pleasure some conversations I had with Brigadier General Devin, who was then commanding the Department of Arizona. He was rather deaf, and at times somewhat blunt, especially when he had to deal with Mexican employes who did not understand English. He would often call me to interpret for him, and as soon as he understood the matter in hand, would give quick and correct decisions in every instance.

I think it was in the month of February when Captain Gilbert C. Smith was relieved from his duties as assistant quartermaster by Colonel Lee. This man brought with him a chief clerk, whose name I have forgotten, and a storekeeper, Captain Meredith. Both of these gentlemen were pleasant, good business men, and made the turning over of the quartermaster commissary of subsistence property an easy and comfortable task. Colonel Lee I never could like. He may have been a No. 1 in every respect in a military point of view, and as a member of the First Families of Virginia; but he had such overbearing and supercilious manners that I did not care to stay in the office, and tendered my resignation as clerk about February 15. At his request I remained till the month was up.

Before the month of February closed, Mr. J. W. Hopkins, formerly mentioned as a lieutenant of the First U.S. Cavalry, who had by that time retired from the army and was seeking an investment of his small capital, came to see me at the quartermaster's office, and stated that he wished to buy a half interest in the Park Brewery at Tucson; that he would like to make the arrangements as soon as possible as he desired to make a trip to Milwaukee, and wished to leave me as his agent with full power of attorney to represent his interests in the brewery.

On March 1, I entered upon these new duties, and before Mr. Hopkins went East, he and I made a trip to Hermosillo and Guaymas, principally with the object of buying bottles for the brewery, for which we had to pay from sixty to ninety cents a dozen in Tucson, while we were informed that in the above-named places we could obtain several thousand dozen at twenty cents per dozen. We found this information correct, and purchased about six hundred dozen which I packed into the crates that had brought crockery by steamer from European ports. From Tucson to Hermosillo we traveled with our own team, reaching the latter place on the evening of the fifth day, after covering a distance of three hundred miles. Here we stayed about one week, and then took stage for Guaymas in company with the surveyors, two Mexicans and two Americans who had just finished the staking off of the railroad now running between the two places. The distance by stage road was said to be one hundred miles, and the vehicle used was an old Concord coach, to which were hitched six small mules, the four smallest in the lead in one front line, the two largest ones being the wheelers. There were two drivers on the box. One held the reins and a pretty long whip; the other was provided with a small box, replenished from time to time, which contained small stones. These he would throw with very accurate aim at that particular beast which would seem to neglect its duty.

There were four relays on the road, about twenty miles apart from each other. The animals were at no time trotting; over heavy road, rocky or sandy stretches they were allowed to walk, also over a steep ascent; at all other times they were kept going at a gallop, and quite frequently at a run, especially on a smooth downgrade. The last ten miles before reaching Guaymas, which are over hard, smooth ground on a steady, gradual descent from whose top the ocean can be seen and felt, were covered in a half hour. The stage had started from Hermosillo at 3 a.m. and reached Guaymas at 6 p.m. The stoppages at the relay stations lasted from twenty to thirty minutes.

I was not a little astonished to see a rider in the usual dress of a *vaquero* (herder) who had started with the stage on horseback, although not connected in any manner with it, arrive simultaneously with us at the hotel, still riding the same horse. This animal seemed to be a common mustang. As I did not remember to have noticed this rider at any time along our route, I was led to the belief that he must have known and used several short cuts on the way.

THE MEXICAN STATE OF SONORA

Right here I might enter into a description of many things unusual to our manner of thinking and living that I observed in the state of Sonora, its institutions, schools, commerce, and especially the home life in a family. But as I visited Mexico at different times since, I hold it best to reserve these observations and embody them in the near future in a separate chapter, entitled "What I saw in Mexico." We have a great plenty of picture books giving an abundance of views of Mexico's finest scenery, public buildings, etc., with good descriptions thereof. But I have yet to find a true analysis of Mexican home life among the upper ten, the middle class, and the poor laborers, at that time called *peons* and subjected to laws which held them in a mild degree of slavery. This "long-felt want," if such it is, I shall try to supply. It can only be done correctly by a person who lived among every degree of their population and was admitted into the intimacy of the family circle, knowing their language in every phase and entering into their mode of life with unbiased opinions of them. We Americans have at all times treated the Mexicans unfairly; we have entered their country bearing upon our breast a vast shield bearing upon it in staringly large letters the legend, *Civis sum Americanos*, very much in the manner of the old Greeks and Romans who considered anyone not a Greek or Roman citizen a barbarian, and hardly worth while speaking to.

Many, very many, illiterate Americans have entered Mexico with the maxim that the Mexicans must speak English, because they, the Americans, could not speak Spanish, thus ignoring the golden rule that "when you are in Rome, you must do as the Romans do." Very many have tried to sell goods in Mexico through the agency of a drummer who could not speak five Spanish words correctly, and failing in their enterprise, abandoned their efforts and left the country in disgust, styling it as a "land of greasers." They never enjoyed the exquisite politeness and liberal hospitality extended to every foreigner, rich or poor, by the Mexican people of every station, simply because they did not know how to approach the people whose trade they sought, and, in many cases, believed in such a manner and showed so plainly their superciliousness, that they were naturally given the cold shoulder. This is the principal reason why we Americanos are to-day, notwithstanding the friendly diplomatic relations existing between the two governments, the least-loved (not to say the best-hated) nation in Mexico.

Before leaving for Guaymas I had become engaged to marry the youngest sister of Mr. Levin's wife, who was Mr. Hopkins's partner. When we arrived from Mexico we found that Mr. Levin had during our absence leased a large house, which he had fitted up as a hotel with bar and restaurant attached, so that the whole business of Levin & Hopkins, embracing the brewery and the establishment just mentioned, together with the wholesale liquor business, kept me very busy. But only for a short time. On June 22, 1870, I married the young lady spoken of, who was of a respectable, if poor, family from Hermosillo, Sonora. There were not at the time more than three American ladies in Tucson.

As soon as the summer months were well begun, all business seemed to become "slack." Tucson has at all times passed through dull seasons which put in their appearance at certain periods, but the season of 1870 during the last six months of the year was particularly so. The Apaches were probably the main factor in this condition of things, as they made freighting and travel altogether problematic during that time. Not only did Cochise's small bands terrorize the whole country south of Tucson, but we were now also subjected to frequent murderous expeditions from Indians supposed to be under government supervision at Fort Grant, northeast of Tucson and distant from the latter about sixty miles. This fort was situated on the San Pedro River, and the officer in command was one Whitman, who also acted as Indian agent. How he fulfilled his duties we shall see anon.

Soon after my marriage I made a trip with Peter Will to the Gila River, where we visited Adamsville and Florence. We decided to locate at the latter place.

During the month of August I brought my wife to Florence, and started housekeeping in an adobe house rented for the purpose.

PIMA INDIAN TRADITIONS

We had frequent occasion to hire Pima Indians as laborers during the building process. Many of them spoke Spanish to some extent, and by questioning them at odd times I learned some very strange things, among which was their story of a deluge, their traditions referring to a Montezuma, and [to] the ruins of Casa Grande, standing on the sandy desert about four miles southwest of Florence. I had visited these ruins several times and dug out from the debris covering the first-story floors a stone hatchet. The whole region about the ruins I found covered with broken pottery bearing designs of different patterns.

The main road from Florence to Tucson made a long detour leading first through Adamsville, in a westerly direction, to the California road, where it made a sharp turn to the south. In order to avoid this elbow or angle, Mr. Collingwood and several other citizens of Florence who had frequent occasion to visit Tucson (then the county-seat) began digging a well in the desert, which lay on a direct line between Florence and the Picacho, on the old stage road to Tucson. If water had been found this would have shortened the distance to the latter place by at least nine miles. When the well-diggers had arrived at a depth of about ninety or one hundred feet, the windlass began to fetch up small shells, pieces of bone rings, arrow heads and small pieces of slate with inscriptions on their surface, as if made with a stylus, not unlike the Egyptian hieroglyphics.

This, together with the occasional statements made by the Pima Indians, raised my curiosity and desire for scientific research in a high degree, and I began to devise ways and means toward obtaining fuller and more connected information as to the early history of the Pima tribe.

Little did I dream that I had the best and fullest source of reliable information ready at hand, till I became acquainted with Captain F. E. Grossman, U. S. A., who was Indian agent at the Pima Indian reservation at Sacaton. I met him first at the Sacaton mail station, then kept by Mr. Peter Forbach and one McFarland, as good a man and blacksmith as ever lived. His tragic death, a few months later, will be recorded in a subsequent chapter.

By this time we had got the brewery in working order, and I took a five-gallon keg of our product to said station, which was situated about two hundred yards outside of the limits of the reservation, into which no kind of liquors, distilled or fermented, were allowed to enter. Captain Grossman happened to be at the station on business with the blacksmith, and from him I learned that he had made diligent research into the history and traditions of the Pima Indians by means of interpreters, and that he had prepared a written account of said research as well as of the habits of life of the Indians in his charge in war and peace. He invited me to visit him at the agency, where he would place his notes at my disposal. I need not say that I gladly availed myself of this invitation and at my earliest opportunity, and will submit in my next paper the result in Captain Grossman's complete ethnological sketch of a tribe of Indians who have been at all times at peace with the whites and frequently their faithful allies against their common enemy, the Apaches.

The Pima Indians have but vague ideas of the doings of their forefathers, and whatever accounts may have been handed down to them have been so changed in the transmission that they cannot be deemed reliable now. Their account of the creation of the world is confused, different parties giving different details thereof. The story most generally accepted among them is that the first of all created beings was a spider, which spun a large web, out of which, in process of time, the world was formed. They believe that the Supreme Being or Creator took a nerve out of his neck and thereof made a man and a woman.

According to their traditions, the first human being lived near the Salt River, in Arizona Territory, near the McDowell Mountain. These people multiplied rapidly, and soon populated the valleys of the Salt and Gila Rivers.

There appears to be a strong probability that the Pima and Papago

Indians, who speak the same language, and to all intents belong to the same nation, are the descendants of the earliest occupants of this section of the country. Still, the accounts of the two above-named tribes differ materially in many essential points of their early history. Both tribes seem to have heard of a great flood, and each has its own method of explaining how their forefathers were saved from this deluge.

TRADITIONS OF THE FLOOD

The Pimas relate that the coming of the flood was well known to the eagles; for these birds, soaring among the clouds, saw the gathering of the storm. One of the eagles, well disposed towards the Pimas, appeared to the principal prophet of the tribe, and warned him of the approaching disaster, advising him to prepare for it. At the same time a cunning wolf (coyote) conveyed the same caution to another prophet. The former and his followers paid no attention to the counsels of the eagle; while the other prophet, knowing the wolf to be a sagacious animal, at once prepared a boat or raft for himself, and made provisions to take with him all kinds of animals then known. The Papagos claim to be the descendants of the more cautious one; the Pimas of the one who refused to be guided by the eagle. This bird appeared for the second time and repeated his caution, but the Pimas scorned his advice.

At last the eagle came for the third time, violently flapped his wings at the door of the hut of the principal prophet, and with a shrill cry announced to him and his people that the flood was at hand, and then flew screaming away. Suddenly the winds arose and the rains descended in torrents; thunder and lightning were terrific, and darkness covered the world. Everything on earth was destroyed by the flood, and all the Pimas perished except one Chief, named So-ho, a good and brave Indian, who was saved by a special interposition in his favor by the Great Spirit.

The prophet who listened to and profited by the caution of the wolf, entered his boat, which safely rode through the storm and landed, when the flood subsided, upon the mountain of Santa Rosa. The wolf also escaped by crawling into a large hollow cane, the ends of which he closed with some resinous substance.

The Papagos of today believe that the prophet who saved himself by means of the boat was their forefather, and yearly visit the mountain and village of Santa Rosa, in Arizona Territory, in commemoration of the fortunate escape of the founder of their race. It is also said that a Papago will not kill a coyote.

The Pimas claim to be the direct descendants of the Chief So-ho, above mentioned. The children of So-ho reinhabited the Gila River Valley, and soon the people became numerous.

One of the direct descendants of So-ho, King Si-va-no, erected the Casas Grandes (large houses) near the Gila River. Here he governed a large empire, before — long before — the Spaniards were known. King Si-va-no was very rich and powerful, and had many wives, who were known for their personal beauty and their great skill in making pottery ware and ki-hos (baskets which the women carry upon their heads and backs).*

The subjects of King Si-va-no lived in a large city near the Casas Grandes, and cultivated the soil for many miles around. (This soil is now almost all sand, and produces the largest giant cactus plants in all Arizona.) They dug immense canals, which carried the water of the Gila River to their fields, and also produced abundant crops. Their women were virtuous and industrious; they spun the native cotton into garments, made beautiful baskets of the bark of trees, and were particularly skilled in the manfacture of earthenware.

Remains of the old canals can be seen to this day, and pieces of neatly-painted potteryware are scattered for miles upon the site of the old city. There are several ruins of ancient buildings here, the best preserved one of which is said to have been the residence of King Si-va-no. This house has been at least four stories high, for even now three stories remain in good preservation, and a portion of the fourth can be seen. The house was built square; each story contains five rooms, one in the center, and a room on each of the outer sides of the inner room which is partitioned off into three smaller ones. This house has been built solidly of clay and cement of some kind; not of adobes, but by successive thick layers of mortar which bound together the cubes of wet earth solidly packed into boxes with slides, which could be removed. (This is called in Mexico the "cajon" [box] process.) The walls were then plastered so well that most of the plastering remains to this day, although it must have been exposed to the weather for many years. The roof and the different ceilings have long since fallen, and only short pieces of timber remain in the walls to indicate the place where the rafters were inserted. These rafters are of pine wood, and since there is no kind of pine growing now within less than 50 miles of the Casas Grandes, this house must either have been built at a time when pine timber could be procured near the building site, or else the builders must have had facilities to transport heavy logs over long distances. It is certain that the house was built before the Pimas knew the use of iron, for many stone hatchets have been found in the

---

*From this word was derived the name of the small mining town Qui-jo-toa (literally basket town), west of the Papago country. It flourished towards the end of the 80's, but is now abandoned.)

ruins, and the ends of the lintels over doors and windows show by their hacked appearance that only blunt tools were used. It also appears that the builders were without trowels, for the marks of the fingers of the workmen or women are plainly visible both in the plastering and on the walls where the former has fallen off. The rooms were about six feet in hight [sic], the doors are very narrow and only four feet high; round holes, about eight inches in diameter are used for windows. Only one entrance from the outside was left by the builders, and some of the outer rooms even had no communication with the rooms in the center. There are no stairs, and it is believed that the Pimas entered the house from above by means of ladders, as the Zuni Indians still do. The walls are perfectly true and all angles square.

The empire of King Si-va-no became so populous after a while that some of its inhabitants found it necessary to emigrate. One of the sons of the King, with numerous followers, went, therefore, to the Salt River Valley, and there established a new empire, which in course of time became very prosperous. Indeed, the inhabitants became so wealthy that they wore jewelry and precious stones upon their persons, and finally erected a beautiful throne for the use of their monarch. This throne was manufactured entirely of large blue stones (probably silver or copper ore).

In course of time a woman ascended this throne. She was very beautiful, and many of the warriors adored her, but she refused all offers of marriage, and seemed to be fond of no one except a pet eagle which lived in her house. The rejected suitors, jealous of the eagle, determined to kill him, but he, a wise bird, discovered their intentions, said farewell to his mistress, and flew away towards the rising sun, threatening destruction to those who had contemplated taking his life.

At the death of the Queen, who had married after the departure of the eagle, the government of the nation fell to her son, who was but a child in years, weak and incapable.

During the reign of this boy the eagle returned, conducting the Spaniards to his former home. These came, well armed and some mounted on horses, which before this time had been unknown to the Pimas.

The Spaniards approached in three strong columns; one marched down the Gila River, one came from the north, and the third from the south. These armies of strange white men terrified the Pimas, who, without competent leaders and good arms, were soon defeated. The enemy devastated the whole country, killed most of the inhabitants, and leveled their fine buildings to the ground. The throne of the King was broken into small pieces, and the birds of the air came and swallowed the small blue stones, which, afterward, they spit out wherever they happened to be. This, say the Pimas, accounts for the fact that these blue stones are found but rarely and in very different localities now. Stones of this kind are highly prized by the Pimas, and worn as charms.

A few of the Pimas escaped the general massacre, and hid themselves in the neighboring mountains, whence they returned to the valley after the departure of the Spaniards. They found all their wealth destroyed, their towns in ruins, their fields devastated, their friends and relatives slain or carried off by the enemy, and the survivors were in despair. Some few, hoping to be able to liberate those of their kindred who had been captured, followed the white man toward the south and finally settled in Sonora, where their descendants live to this day. The others remained in the Salt River Valley, increased in numbers, and again tilled the soil. But the Apaches, always bitter enemies of the Pimas, took advantage of the situation, and encroached upon their fields to such an extent that the Pimas finally returned to the Gila River Valley, where they still live. They never re-erected the stately mansions of their forefathers, but, humbled by defeat, were content to live in the lowly huts which are occupied by the Pimas of the present day. Their women were virtuous and strong, and in the lapse of time numerous children were born; the tribe increased in numbers, and, not many years after their defeat by the Spaniards, the Pimas were strong enough to cope with the Apaches, against whom they have carried on a bitter warfare ever since.

At one time they were very poor indeed. Owing to the poverty of the tribe, their leaders never returned to the luxurious style of living of their former kings. They were simply called "chiefs," but the supreme control of the tribe was still in the hands of the old royal family, and descended from father to son. These head-chiefs were brave warriors, and under their leadership the Pimas achieved many victories. At one time the Comanche Indians came from the east, but the Pimas repulsed them after a bloody battle which was fought near the mail station of the Butterfield coach line, called Sacaton.

At last the reign descended to Shon-tarl-Kor-li (old soldier), the last, in a direct line, of the old royal house. He was a bold warrior, and highly esteemed by the whole tribe. During his reign the Maricopa Indians, imposed upon and persecuted by the Yumas and Mohaves, came to the country of the Pimas in two different parties, one from the southwest and the other from the northwest. The newcomers asked for a home and protection, promising to aid the Pimas in their scouts against the Apaches. Their request was granted, and when the Yumas, who had given pursuit to the Maricopas, appeared near the country of the Pimas, the latter turned out in force, and, united with the Maricopas, defeated the Yumas in a battle fought near the present Maricopa Wells.

Since then the Yumas have not dared to molest the Maricopas. The latter remained with the Pimas, were permitted to cultivate a small portion of their land, and have been ever since on friendly terms with them. The Maricopas of today have two villages on the reservation, and number about 300. The Pimas have intermarried with the Maricopas; still, the latter preserve their own language, which is that of the Yumas, Cocopas and Mohaves.

At last Shon-tarl-Kor-li, the Chief, was fatally wounded by the Apaches, receiving a musket-ball in his forehead. Upon his death-bed this old Chief, who had no sons to succeed him recommended that Stjo-e-teck-e-mus, one of the sub-chiefs who was a renowned warrior, should be elected Head-Chief. This was done, and the latter reigned for years, respected and beloved by all his tribe. Young Antonio Azul,* or A-va-at-ka-jo (the man who lifts his leg), as he was called by the Pimas, accompanied his father, the Chief, on all his scouts when he became old enough to bear arms, and at one time went with him to Sonora and visited some of the Mexican towns. Stjo-e-teck-e-mus led the Pimas many times against the Apaches, was repeatedly wounded, but finally died in consequence of sickness. Upon his death Antonio Azul assumed the position of his father, but dissension arose in the tribe. Many claimed that Antonio had no title to the supreme command; that his father had been chosen Chief on account of his boldness, bravery and wisdom; that these virtues did not necessarily descend from father to son, and that the choice of a new Chief ought to be left to the warriors of the tribe. Some asserted that a distant relative of the Chief proper was among the tribe, who, having the royal blood in his veins, ought to govern.

Arispa, a petty chief, well known for his bravery in the field, and withal a crafty and unscrupulous man, took advantage of the general confusion, and, with the intention of usurping Antonio's place, accused the latter of witchcraft. Antonio was tried and declared not guilty, and since then had been generally recognized as Head-Chief. Still, the followers of Arispa, who are the worst Indians on the reservation, refuse to be guided by Antonio, and the latter evidently believes his position to be insecure, and therefore temporizes with the bad men of the tribe rather than run the risk of a revolution and possible loss of his rank by compelling them to behave themselves. Of course, the Indians know him thoroughly, and take advantage of his weakness.

Since Antonio Azul became the Head-Chief of the tribe the overland road from Texas to California, which passes through the Pima land, has

---

*By this name he was generally known among the Americans and Mexicans during the writer's stay in the Pima country, 1870-1871.

been established, and in consequence thereof these Indians have been thrown in contact with the Americans. In 1859 a reservation, containing 100 square miles, was set aside for them by act of Congress, and upon and near it they have resided ever since. In 1862 the smallpox raged among them to an alarming extent, and many, particularly children, died of the disease.

It is a lamentable fact that the Pimas have retrograded since the advent of the white man among them, both morally and physically. In 1855, when Butterfield's mail-coaches first passed through their land, the Pimas were a healthy race, the men brave and honest, the women chaste. Today foul diseases prevail to an alarming extent, many of the women are public prostitutes, and all will pilfer whenever opportunity offers.

The Pimas believe in the existence of the Supreme Being or Creator, whom they call "Prophet of the Earth," and also in an evil spirit "Che-a-vurl." They believe that, generally, their spirits will pass to another world when they die, and that there they will meet those who have gone before them. They say that whenever anyone dies an owl (the screech owl) carries the soul of the departed away, and hence they fear owls which they never kill), and they consider the hooting of this bird a sure omen that someone is about to die. They give a confused account of some priests (par-le), who, they state, visited their country years ago, and attempted to convert them to Christianity.

These priests were French (from the Jesuit college at Queretaro, Mexico (then called New Spain), and to this day the Pimas call the French "par-le-sick"; plural "pa-par-le-sick." It does not appear that these missionaries met with success. The Pimas have no fear of worship whatever, and have neither idols nor images. They know that the Mexicans baptize their children, and they sometimes initiate this ceremony. This baptism is applied, however, only as a charm, and in cases of extreme sickness of the child. When the ceremonies and charms of the native physicians (ma-ke) fail to produce a cure, then the sick infant is taken to some American or Mexican, and even Papago, when the latter is known to have embraced the Christian faith. Generally, Mexican women perform the ceremony. If the child recovers, it receives a Spanish name by which it is known ever after, but these names are so much changed in pronunciation that strangers would hardly recognize them. Pedro, for instance, becomes Pi-va-lo; Emanuel, Ma-norl; Cristobal, Kis-to; Ignacio, I-nas; Maria, Mar-le, etc.

It is certain that their religion does not teach them morality, nor does it point out a certain mode of conduct. Each Pima, if he troubles himself about his religion at all, construes it to suit himself, and all care little or nothing for the life hereafter; for their creed neither promises rewards in the future of a life well spent, nor does it threaten punishment after death to those who in this life act evil. They have no priest to counsel them, and the influence of their chiefs is sufficient to restrain those who are evilly disposed. The whole nation lives but for today, never thinks of the wants of the future, and is guided solely by desires and passions.

These Indians believe in witches and ghosts, and their doctors or medicinemen (ma-ke) claim to know how to find and destroy witches. Almost anything is believed to be a witch. Usually it is a small piece of wood, to which is tied a small piece of red flannel, cloth or calico by means of a horse-hair. Should one of these be found in or near one of the Pima huts, the inhabitants thereof would at once abandon it and move elsewhere. They believe that all sickness, death and misfortune are caused by witches. If, therefore, a Pima is taken sick, or loses his horse or cow, he sends for one of the medicine men, whose duty it becomes to find and destroy the evil spirit who has caused the mischief.

The medicine-man on these occasions masks his face and disguises himself as much as possible. He then swiftly runs around the spot supposed to be infested, widening his circles as he runs, until, at last, he professes to have found the outer limits of the space of ground supposed to be under the influence of the witch. Then he and his assistants, the latter also masked, drive painted stakes into the ground all about the bewitched spot. These sticks, painted with certain colors found in the mountains, are said to possess the power of preventing the escape of the witch. Now begins the search for the latter; everything is looked into, huts are examined, fences removed, bushes cut down, until, at last, the medicine-man professes to find the witch, which usually is the above-described stick, horse-hair and red cloth. Of course, this so-called witch has been hidden previously to the search by some of the assistants of the ma-ke. It is burned at once and the unitiated fondly believe that, for a time at least, they will be free from the evil influences of the witch thus destroyed. Of course this mode of treatment seldom produces a cure of sick people; but the Pimas know nothing whatever of medicines; their medicine-men never administer anything internally, and the above ceremony is the principal attempt made to cure the sick.

Sometimes, for instance in case of pains in the chest or stomach, they scarify the patients with sharp stones or place burning coals upon the skin, and in rare instances the patient is placed upon the ground, his head to the west, and then the medicine-man gently passes a brush, made of eagle feathers, from his head to his feet; after which he runs several paces, shakes the brush violently, and then returns to the patient to repeat, again and again, the same maneuver. They believe that by this operation the sickness is drawn first into the brush and thence shaken to the winds, and bystanders keep a respectable distance, for fear of inhaling the disease when it is shaken from the brush. Some doctors pretend to destroy sickness by shooting painted arrows from painted bows at imaginary evil spirits supposed to be hovering in the vicinity of the patient.

The Pimas know many herbs, which they use as food at times when wheat is scarce, but they have no knowledge of medical properties of herbs or minerals with the only exception of a small weed called *colondrina* by the Mexicans, which, applied as a poultice, is a certain remedy, it is said, for the bite of a rattlesnake.

This weed belongs to the family of the *Euphorbiaceae*; like most of them it contains a milky juice. It is a creeper, with pretty small white blossoms and spotted leaves.

It is generally believed that all efforts to Christianize the Pimas would fail, not because any of them would oppose such attempts but because they all would be entirely indifferent to the new teachings.

BURIAL OF THE DEAD

The Pimas tied the bodies of their dead with ropes, passing the latter around the neck and under the knees, and then drawing them tight until the body is doubled up and forced into a sitting position. They dig the grave from four to five feet deep, perfectly round (about two feet in diameter), and then hollow out to one side of the bottom of this grave a sort of vault large enough to contain the body. Here the body is deposited, the grave is filled up loosely with the ground, and poles, trees, or pieces of timber are placed upon the grave to protect the remains from the coyotes. Burials usually take place at night, without much ceremony. The mourners chant during the burial, but signs of inward grief are rare. The bodies of their dead are buried, if possible, immediately after death has taken place, and the graves are generally prepared before the patients die. Sometimes sick persons, for whom the graves had already been dug, recover; in such cases the graves are left open until the persons for whom they were intended die. Open graves of this kind can be seen in several of their burying-grounds. Places of burial are selected some distance from the village, and, if possible, in a grove of mesquite bushes. Immediately after the remains have been buried the house and personal effects of the deceased are burned, and his horses and cattle killed, the meat being cooked as a respect for the mourners. The nearest relatives of the deceased, as a sign of their sorrow, remain within these villages for weeks, and sometimes months; the men cut off their long hair, while the women cut their hair quite short.

The Pima men wear their hair very long; many have hair thirty-two inches long, and often braid it in strands; only the front hair is cut straight across, so as to let it reach the eyes. The women, who also cut their front hair like the men, part their hair in the middle and wear it usually long enough to let it reach a little below the shoulders. The hair is their only head covering. The men are proud of their long hair, braid it and comb it with care; and to give it a glossy appearance, frequently plaster it over with a mixture of black clay and mesquite gum. This preparation is left on the hair for several days, and is then washed out, when it leaves the hair not only black and glossy, but also free from vermin.

The custom of destroying all the property of the husband when he dies impoverishes the widow and children and prevents increase of stock. The women of the tribe, well aware that they will be poor should their husbands die, and that then they will have to provide for their children by their own exertions, do not care to have many children; and infanticide both before and after birth, prevails to a very great extent. This is not considered a crime, and old women of the tribe practice it. A widow may marry again after a year's mourning for her first husband; but having children, no man will take her for a wife and thus burden himself with her children. Widows generally cultivate a small piece of ground, and their male friends or relatives generally plow the ground for them.

MARRIAGES

Marriages among the Pimas are entered into without ceremony, and are never considered as binding. The lover selects a friend, who goes with him to the hut of the girl's parents and asks the father to give his daughter to his friend. If the parents are satisfied and the girl makes no objection, the latter at once accompanies her husband to his hut and remains with him as long as both feel satisfied with the compact. If, however, the girl refuses, the lover retires at once, and all negotiations are at an end. Presents are seldom given, unless a very old man desires a young bride. Wives frequently leave their husbands and the latter their wives. This act of leaving is all that is necessary to separate them forever, and either party is at liberty to marry someone else; only at the second marriage the assistance of a friend is dispensed with. Instances of fidelity and strong affection are known, but many of the wives do not hesitate to surrender their charms to men other than their husbands, which, though possibly disagreeable to the husband, is not considered a crime by the tribe. Only the worst of the women of the tribe cohabit with the whites, but it is undeniable that the number of such women is increasing from year to year. Although this has caused a great deal of disease in the tribe, and disease is rapidly spreading, not one of the chiefs or old men of the nation appears to have thought it necessary to raise a warning voice or propose punishment to the offenders; prostitutes are looked upon as inevitable, and are by no means treated with contempt or scorn by the Pimas. Modesty is unknown both to men and women. Their conversation, even in presence of children, is extremely vulgar, and many of the names of both men and women are indecent and offensive.

Generally several married couples, with their children, live in one hut, and many of the men who can support more than one wife, practice polygamy. The wife is the slave of the husband. She carries wood and water, spins and weaves, has the sole care of the children, and does all the work in the field except plowing, sowing, and perhaps irrigating. It is the Pima woman that, with patient, hard labor, winnows the chaff from the wheat and then carries the latter upon her head to the store of the trader, where her husband — who had preceded her on horseback — sells it, spending perhaps all the money received for it in the purchase of articles intended only for his use. Pima women rarely ride on horseback. The husband always travels mounted, while the wife trudges along on foot, carrying her child or a heavily laden *ki-ho* on her head and back.

WEAPONS AND WARFARE

The only weapons used by the Pimas before the introduction of firearms were the bow and arrow and the warclub. For defensive purposes they carried a round shield, about two feet in diameter, made of rawhide, which, when thoroughly dry, becomes so hard that an arrow, even if sent by a powerful enemy at a short distance, cannot penetrate it. These weapons are still (1870–1871) used by them to a great extent, and, like all Indians, they are good marksmen with the bow, shooting birds on the wing, rabbits on the run, and fishes while swimming in the shallow waters of the Gila River.

For hunting fish and small game they use arrows without hard points, but the arrows used in battle have sharp, two-edged points made of flint, glass, or iron. When going on a scout against the Apache Indians, their bitter foes, the Pimas frequently dip the points of their arrows into putrid meat, and it is said that a wound caused by such an arrow will never heal, but keep on festering, finally producing death.

The warclub is made out of mesquite wood, which is hard and heavy. It is about sixteen inches long, half being handle, and the other half the club proper. With it they strike the enemy on the head. This weapon is even now very much used, for the Pimas rarely attack their enemies in open daylight. They usually surround the Apache ranchería at night, some warriors placing themselves near the doors of all huts; then the terrible war-cry is sounded, and when the surprised Apaches crawl through the lower doors of their huts, the warclubs of the Pimas descend upon their heads with a crashing force.

The Pimas never scalp their dead enemies; in fact, no Pima will even touch an Apache further than is necessary to kill him. Even the act of killing an Apache by means of an arrow is believed to make the Pima unclean whose bow discharged the fatal arrow. The reason of this is that they firmly believe that all Apaches are possessed of the evil spirit, and that all who kill them become unclean and remain so until again cleansed by peculiar process of purification.

The Pima warrior who has killed an Apache separates himself as soon as practicable from all his companions (who are not even permitted to speak to him), and returns to the vicinity of his home. Here he hides himself, in the bushes near the riverbank, where he remains secluded for sixteen days, conversing with no one, and seeing, through the whole period of the cleansing process, only an old woman of his tribe who has been appointed to carry food to him, but who never speaks.

During the twenty-four hours immediately following the killing, the Pima neither eats nor drinks; after this he partakes of food and water sparingly, but for the whole sixteen days he cannot eat meat of any kind nor salt, nor must he drink anything but river water.

For the first four days he frequently bathes himself in the river; during the second four days he plasters his hair with a mixture of mesquite gum and black clay, which composition is allowed to dry and become hard upon his head, and is washed out during the night of the eighth day. On the ninth morning he again besmears his head with black clay without the gum; on the evening of the twelfth day he washes his hair, combs it, braids it in long strands, and ties the ends with a red ribbon or a shawl; and then for four days more frequently washes his whole body in the Gila River.

On the evening of the sixteenth day he returns to his village, is met by one of the old men of his tribe, who, after the warrior has placed himself at full length upon the ground, being down, passes some of the saliva in his mouth into that of the warrior, and blows his breath into the nostrils of the latter. The warrior then rises, and now, and not until now, is he again considered clean; his friends approach him and joyfully congratulate him on his victory.

The Apache Indians, the most savage on the continent, ever since 1858 have murdered hundreds of whites and half-breeds, and have thus obtained a large supply of firearms and ammunition. In order to cope with them successfully, the Pimas have purchased many guns and pistols, and are now tolerably well armed with improved weapons. No restriction has ever been placed on the sale of arms and ammunition to these people.

The Pimas never capture Apache men. These are killed on the field, but women and girls and half-grown boys are brought back to the reservation at times, though frequently all the inhabitants of the Apache village are killed.

Apache prisoners are rarely treated in a cruel manner. For the first week or two they are compelled to go from village to village and are exhibited with pride and made to join the war-dance. Often, too, the peculiar war-whoop of the Apaches is sounded by some old Pima squaw as a taunt to the prisoners, but after the lapse of a few weeks they are treated kindly, share food and clothing with their captors, and generally become contented, learn the Pima language, and remain upon the reservation. Instances have occurred where Apache prisoners have attempted to escape, but they have invariably been overtaken and killed as soon as recaptured. Quite a number of captured Apache children are sold by the Pimas to whites and Mexicans. These children, if properly trained, are said to become very docile and make good house servants.

In rare instances will a Pima ever marry an Apache woman, even after she has resided for two or three years on the reservation; but generally full-grown Apache women become public prostitutes, and their owners appropriate the money received by these women from degraded white men.

PIMA INDUSTRY AND FOOD

The men do not labor except so far as is necessary to enable them to raise a crop. Each village elects two or three old men who decide everything pertaining to the digging of irrigation ditches (Mexican *acequias*) and making dams, and who also regulate the time during which each landowner may use the water of the acequia from which smaller ditches carry the water to the respective fields. In order to force the water of the Gila River into their acequias, the Pimas dam the river at convenient spots by means of poles tied together with bark and rawhide and stakes driven into the bed of the river. Small crevices are filled with bundles of willow-branches, reeds, and a weed called *galuna*. These frail structures rarely stand longer than a year, and are often entirely carried away when the river rises suddenly, which occurs in the spring of the year, if much snow has fallen during the winter upon the mountains whence the stream issues, and also sometimes during the summer after heavy showers. Their *acequias* are often ten feet deep at the dam and average from four to six feet in width, and are continued for miles, until finally the water therein is brought on a level with the ground to be cultivated, when the water is led off by means of smaller ditches all through their fields. Having no instruments for surveying or striking levels, they still display considerable ingenuity in the selection of proper places for the "heads of ditches."

The Pimas and Maricopas have a reservation containing one hundred square miles and extending along the Gila River for a distance of nearly twenty-five miles; only a comparatively small part of this area, however, is available for agricultural purposes, for a portion of the soil on the reservation is strongly impregnated with alkali; some spots are marshy, and all the land beyond the immediate river bottomland so high above the level of the river that irrigation becomes impracticable, considering the limited means for making *acequias* at the disposal of the Pimas.

The Indians do not cultivate all the land that might be tilled, for their fields do not average more than from ten to fifteen acres to the family; nevertheless, they are dissatisfied with the size of their reservation, asserting that their forefathers had always been in possession of a much larger portion of the Gila Valley, and since the valley above the reservation has been settled up by Americans and Mexicans, the Indians have frequently encroached upon the fields of the latter, whom they consider in the light of intruders, and it is apprehended that sooner or later serious difficulties will arise.

Captain Grossman foresaw what was bound to happen and what has happened ever since his leaving the agency. The Indians had a reservation of land. Any man was allowed to take, or at least not prohibited from taking, the water from the Gila River for irrigation, with complete disregard to the situation of the "dam" or "head of water" of the Pimas. The water was "headed-off" by anybody who, if he thought he could do it without prosecution, simply did so. I visited the Gila River country again in the eighties and found the same conditions prevailing. The Indians were simply robbed of the only means by which they could procure a crop.

The Pima men plow the land with oxen and a crooked stick, as is done by the Mexicans; they sow the seed and cut the grain (the latter with short sickles). Horses, mules, or oxen thrash the grain by stamping. The women winnow the grain, when thrashed, by pitching it into the air by basketfuls, when the wind carries off the chaff; they convert the wheat into flour, grinding it by hand on their *metates*, a large flat stone upon which the wheat is placed, after having been slightly parched over the fire. It is then ground into coarse flour by rubbing and crushing with another smaller stone. The principal crop is wheat, of which they sell, when the season is favorable, 1,500,000 pounds per annum. They also raise corn, barley, pumpkins, squashes, melons, onions, and a small supply of very inferior short cotton.

The diet of the Pimas is very simple; animal food is used only on occasions of ceremony, although they possess large numbers of beef-cattle and chickens. They do not use the cow's milk, manufacture neither butter nor cheese, and do not eat the eggs of their hens. Very few will eat pork. But whenever they kill a cow, steer or calf, they eat every part of it that can possibly be masticated, intestines included. Should the animal die, no matter of what disease, they eat its meat without apparent ill effects upon their health. At times they hunt the rabbit, which is about the only game (quadruped) in their country. Fish, during the months of April and May, are also extensively eaten.

Wheat, corn, beans, and, above all, pumpkin and mesquite-beans are their principal food. The latter grow wild in abundance, and millions of pounds are gathered annually by the women of the tribe.

Although my partner in the brewery business, Mr. Peter Will, was a very good brewer and produced a very fair article of beer, our efforts were financially far from successful. The influx of population into the Gila Valley, anxiously expected by all and predicted by many, failed to materialize, so that we found it frequently difficult to dispose of a single brew of sixty gallons a week. I had therefore much leisure time on my hands, and made frequent excursions into the surrounding regions. Being in the country of the Pimas and Maricopas, whither no Apache dared to penetrate, traveling was perfectly safe, so that I often pursued my exploration entirely alone. Sometimes I would engage a Pima Indian as guide over the tortuous mountain trails.

One of the most prominent landmarks near Florence is located between two and three miles northwest of the town, on the opposite side of the Gila River. It is now generally known as "Poston Butte," from its association with a scheme of Hon. Chas. D. Poston (this remarkable, somewhat erratic man, died about a year ago in a lone cabin near Phoenix, Arizona, at the age of eighty-two, alone, and in utter poverty), a former delegate to Congress from Arizona, who conceived the idea of erecting upon its summit [the butte's] a magnificent temple dedicated to the worship of the sun. While he was holding the office of Register of the United States Land Office, at Florence, he conceived the idea of obtaining from some of the wealthy Parsees of India, whom he had met in his extensive travels through China and Hindustan during his earlier years, a donation to build a temple on the summit of the little hill northwest of Florence, which has an elevation of about six hundred feet. At that time the Colonel had sold some stock in the Arivaca land grant, and possessed the means to take the initiatory steps toward building the temple. He caused a survey of a road to be made from the base to the summit of the hill, and built a good buggy road at considerable expense.

For a long time Colonel Poston devoted his leisure hours to the study of hydraulics, and contemplated putting in a hydraulic ram somewhere on the riverbank that would force the water to the summit of the hill, for the uses of the worshipers at the temple.

He argued and contended that the religious belief of the Pima Indians was similar to that to that of the Parsees of India, and that they were descendants of the sun-worshiping Aztecs, and [that] if he could establish that fact to the satisfaction of his Parsee friends in Bombay, they would willingly donate a hundred thousand dollars for the purpose of building a temple to be dedicated to the fireworshipers of the Gila Indian reservation.

However, no donation ever came, and after Colonel Poston had expended about $1,000 (some say from $2,000 to $3,000) on his pet scheme, it gradually faded from his memory, and in after years, when the people of Florence spoke of it as "Poston's folly," he did not have much to say.

A great many people climb up on the butte even to this day. When I reached its summit in 1870, I enjoyed the splendid view of the valley and surrounding country. The butte itself rises abruptly from a broad expanse of somewhat sandy prairie land strewn with prehistoric remains, and is the closest of the various peaks adjacent. It is nearly black in color, a huge mass of limestone and lava. Romantic cliffs and almost inaccessible caves and nooks abound on its rough exterior. Here the various birds of prey find a safe retreat and security for their young. In the caverns rattlesnakes and other smaller reptiles in great numbers find a home.

A person is at once struck with the adaptability of the vast monument for a lookout or signal post during hostilities of savage tribes. Situated in the center of a once prosperous community of people — a people whose habitations were all built with a view to defense — we would at once expect to find that some advantage had been taken of the opportunity offered by nature.

I ascended with difficulty the terraces of hard, forbidding rock (Poston's road had not yet been built). In such an ascent one must be very careful to avoid rattlesnakes. It often happens, not only on this mountain, but on hundreds of others in Arizona, that the explorer must walk on the edge of some cliff or narrow ledge, must sometimes stoop down and creep, on account of overhanging boulders, where but an outward movement would precipitate him upon the jagged rocks below. While thus imprisoned, a mountain wall on one hand, a dizzy depth of the other, a narrow ledge on which to creep — one must pass undaunted myriads of crevasses and openings, any one of which may contain rattlesnakes of the most venomous kind — and the explorer entirely at their mercy. The writer has been attacked by rattlesnakes in similar positions, but has escaped by a hair's breadth from the double danger.

When I say "attacked" by rattlesnakes, I mean to imply that there exists a kind of rattlesnake in that region which, unlike the common *Crotalus,* will not go out of your way, but curl up right before you, elevate his head with about a foot of its neck, and hiss and strike at you, compelling you to either walk around it or kill it. This species is entirely black, although the diamond-shaped pattern upon its back is distinguishable, being somewhat paler black than the body itself. This kind of rattlesnake is not sluggish like the one with the yellow-diamond markings; it is more slender in body and very quick in its motions. The same black rattler is often met with in the canyons of the Arivaipa (old Camp Grant, at first called Fort Breckinridge) region.

After a few falls and bruises from rolling stones, a few scares from frightened hawks and owls that frantically escaped from their holes, and a few painful stings from the barbs of the ever-present cacti, I considered myself lucky at having gained the summit without serious accident. The beautiful vista that met my eye and the exhilarating effect of the fresh breezes at once banished all memories of the fatigues of the ascent. When I had gazed to my heart's content at the scene before and around me — the verdant, winding valley of the Gila River, the distant town of Florence clothed in a beautiful green, the far away hazy mountains of grotesque shapes and forms that bound the horizon on the north — I turned to examine my immediate surroundings.

A circular, almost level, depression on the summit, of perhaps twenty feet in circumference, is strewn with ashes and charred remains of ancient camp — or signal — fires. Evidently the use of the site was long in the past that of a lookout or signal hill to which, perhaps for thousands of years, the tribes in the valley below have been wont to look for the daily signal "All is well" or "Danger ahead."

The once smooth face of the cliff has been damaged and disintegrated by the ravages of time. But we can still see the public records of the prehistoric race, in a few spots, written in an unknown language. Even these reminders will ere long vanish, while yet no tongue has been able to explain their meaning. Near the summit, on the face of a much-broken cliff, appear the figures shown in the cut. Originally these were united, but crevasses have separated them and broken off portions.

In the fall of 1870, a deputy sheriff arrived in Florence from Tucson, the county seat of Pima County, with a summons for me to appear as a

232 / John Spring's Arizona

witness in the case of Major Duffield, mentioned in a previous chapter, whom the Commonwealth of Arizona accused of disturbing the peace of the community with weapons — i.e., firearms, "then and there being loaded, as aforesaid, with powder and ball, as aforesaid" — as the ancient form of the indictment read, as drawn up by the district attorney in pursuance to a "true bill" found against said Duffield by the grand jury.

I arrived in Tucson too late for the trial, however, being detained en route by a "silvery yucca," a cactus growing over-plentifully in southern Arizona. I spoke above of the "barbs" of the cacti encountered upon Poston's Butte, and I did so advisedly, for although many species of the *Cactaceae* produce straight, smooth thorns or prickles there are some which carry at their points an exceedingly fine barb that will lift up a person's skin, when being pulled out, fully a half inch before they "let go." Now it happened that on the day following the deputy sheriff's visit, I hired a horse to make the trip to Tucson in obedience to the court's summons, with the intention of making a short cut across the desert by the new road we of Florence had partly established, and upon which we had begun the digging of a well about thirty miles south of the town, as related in a former chapter.

I started about dark, and soon after my start the rain began to pour down. The road had not as yet been traveled over much, and was therefore not very distinct. I knew that after about five or six hours' riding I would arrive at the camp of the well-diggers, where I intended to stop till early morning, when a sharp ride of six hours' duration would bring me to Tucson in time for the session of the court, set for 10 o'clock. I perceived that the road I was on was very hard and led more and more to the left into some foothills, while in the distance straight ahead I could plainly perceive a high, dark, jagged line. Then it occurred to me that somewhere and somehow I, or rather my horse, had branched off upon the road leading to old Fort Grant, and that I was making a beeline for the mountains surrounding that military camp. I had no sooner made this discovery when I came to a branch road leading still farther to the left, which shone out quite white and plain even in the dark. As soon as I realized that I was really lost I resolved, remembering former occurrences of a like nature, to stay where I was and wait for daylight, when I could probably get my bearings from the "lay" of the surrounding country. I led my horse to a small palo verde tree, tied him to it, and unsaddled. Near by there was another tree that looked very inviting, on account of its overhanging branches. Thither I carried my saddle blanket and spread it under those inviting branches, holding it by two corners some distance from the tree and shaking it open towards the latter's trunk. Then I brought my saddle and placed it at the outer edge of the blanket, for a pillow, not wishing to have it too near the tree trunk, for fear of ants.

Then I lay me down. But only for a second. Immediately I made a masterful jump, as if bitten by a million trantulas. For you must know that this silvery cactus carries at the ends of its innumerable branches equally innumerable clusters of the finest needle-like prickles, from a half-inch to one and a half inches long. These clusters of bristles the cactus sheds during the winter months, before clothing itself anew with another edition in the spring time, when the new and fresh needles glisten with a silvery sheen, which circumstance gave this Yucca its adjective. It had been my ill-luck to stumble upon a tree of mature age, upon whose many shedded crops of clusters I had prepared or attempted to prepare my bed.

As I had lain down carelessly and heavily without the least suspicion of lurking danger, I had received the full benefit of the penetration and adhesiveness of several thousand sharp needles, which even penetrated the light saddle blanket and any summer clothing. (They can penetrate shoe leather.) I will not attempt to describe my sufferings during that night and the next day when I began my return walk to Florence. I say walk, because to ride was out of the question. I could not have sat on a feather pillow. When I reached the town I was completely exhausted and in a high fever. Still, these thousands of needles had to come out, had to be picked out one by one, each single operation lifting the skin nearly an inch high.

Although I had missed the court proceedings in the case of the Territory vs. Duffield during that session, I came in later on when the "grand dramatic finale" of the case passed upon the boards (so to speak) of the First Judicial District of Arizona. But of this later.

A MYSTERIOUS AFFAIR

About this time the mysterious disappearance of a man well known and universally liked by all the Americans in the valley created a great sensation, caused the violent death of several men, and came near producing a race war between the American and Mexican inhabitants of the valley. I have mentioned the mail station at Sacaton kept almost on the immediate border of the Pima reservation, then in charge of Captain Grossman, U.S.A., by Messrs. Peter Forbach and Wm. McFarland. The latter was the blacksmith of the place, a whole-souled, congenial man about forty years of age. One Saturday afternoon in the fall of 1870, this man went to Adamsville on his saddle mule and purchased several articles of female wearing apparel at the store of the Brothers Bichard. About 4 o'clock p.m. he mounted his mule and set out on his return trip, taking the regular much-traveled road leading by Blackwater and a small station called Montezuma to Sacaton. Near Blackwater there lived on the high bank of the Gila River a Mexican farmer, married, and having quite a large family of children, named Gandara. This man had two full-grown, pretty daughters, one of whom was said to be McFarland's sweetheart. He himself told me a short time before the occurrence now to be related that he intended to marry the oldest daughter of Gandara, but that there was "something in the way." Probably the articles of wearing apparel were destined for that young lady and perhaps she received them, because when McFarland's mule returned home to Sacaton on that Saturday evening about dark without its rider, these articles were not on the saddle, where McFarland had fastened them before his departure from Adamsville in presence of several persons. At all events, McFarland was not seen alive by anybody except two Pima bucks and a squaw after he left the store of the Bichard Brothers. Neither was his body ever found. Several clots of blood upon the saddle pointed towards his probable assassination. But although the best trailers of the Pima and Maricopa tribes were employed to track the supposed murderers and nearly everybody "took a hand" in trying to solve the mystery of McFarland's death, it has remained a mystery to this day. Gandara and his whole family positively denied having seen him on that day, but the fact of the female wearing apparel having disappeared from the saddle kept rankling in the minds of McFarland's more intimate friends, and on the third day after his disappearance they formed a "committee of inquiry." About six of them armed themselves with "full batteries" and proceeded in a body on horseback to Gandara's ranch with the intention, as they said, to get to the bottom of the mystery. When they arrived at the latter's place, one of the posse quickly got to the bottom of the mystery of the future life, for Gandara had heard of their coming and had barricaded his strong adobe building in good shape. He was requested to come out and answer questions. As he refused to do so and on his part uttered the reasonable request to be let alone, the posse fired into the door and windows. This called upon them Gandara's fire, which reached the center of a young fellow's heart and stretched him out cold. Then the remaining five Americans set the roof of the house on fire. The women and children were allowed to pass out unharmed, but Gandara was pierced by five bullets the moment he tried to run out from the burning and smoking building.

On the following day hostilities were resumed without any particular reason or tendency, except to kill a "few Greasers." Two of them, known to be Gandara's friends, were hunted down till they found refuge in a small adobe house in the town of Adamsville. A ten-pound keg of powder was procured, let down through the chimney, and ignited. The explosion killed one of the Mexicans and threw down the wall on the chimney side;

through this opening, favored by the powder smoke, the other one made good his escape.

Thereupon we held a short meeting, the result of which was that we advised the hotheaded firebrands to desist from further violence. We intimated to them that if they persisted in their wanton criminal murder and destruction we, the cooler-headed and order-loving inhabitants of the valley, would "take a hand in the game." This phrase meant a good deal in those days and under those circumstances. They knew it, and dispersed. Four of them have since died a violent death; two over a game of cards ending with a game of pistols and two were hanged for stage robbery accompanied by murder.

The snow was yet lying upon the mountain peaks of even southern Arizona in the spring of 1871 when the hostiles descended from their mountain fastnesses in which they usually made their winter quarters, and began a bloody raid through the Sonoita and Santa Cruz valleys. Personally I was safe from them, living in the country of the Pimas; but I had good and staunch friends in the dangerous regions.

A TELEPATHIC WARNING

The morning of March 21, I was planting some seeds in a small garden behind the brewery at Florence, with a view of raising some vegetables for home consumption. While thus occupied a feeling of restlessness or rather apprehension for impending danger gradually came over me and soon took possession of my mind to such a degree that I abandoned my work, went into the brewery and engaged my partner, Will, in conversation. Mentioning to him this feeling of mental and hence at least partly physical depression, he suggested that I was suffering from indigestion. That was downright ridiculous, as in those days I was not aware that I had a stomach at all except after protracted fasting.

"You do not understand, good Peter," I said to him. "What I feel is mental, a certain anxiety of mind, a fear of impending danger, a sense that I am wanted somewhere to avoid a disaster, a — "

"I see," said he, "a person sometimes is overcome that way. We call it at home a *Vorabnung* (presentiment), and sometimes I have heard it said it is the forerunner of an actual catastrophe. Well, you had better go and see if anything is wrong with your wife, although we left her quite well this morning after breakfast."

I followed his advice, and walked the two blocks to the lodgings where I had installed my wife some months previously. She was then expecting in the near future that happy event which makes a young father act temporarily like an insane man laboring under the delusion that never before was such a baby born nor ever will [be] again.

I found my wife quite well and cheerful — in fact, she was singing a lullaby in anticipation of said happy event, while her deft fingers were busily plying the needle upon some snow white material cut into sundry diminutive patterns.

She was somewhat astonished at my visit at this unusual hour, and I explained to her my really inexplicable uneasiness and anxiety. She knew the story of my telepathic warning at Crittenden, and although she certainly could not understand the ethics of the mysticism, she was far too sensible to ridicule the matter or doubt its possibility. After some reflection she said: "You know, my dear, you have not heard any news for a long time from your dear good friend Wooster upon the Palo Parado Ranch, nor from or of your many other friends and pioneer comrades all along the Santa Cruz River. There was a man here yesterday from Calabazas, and he told Don Manuel (our landlord) that the Apaches up that way had already put in an appearance in the valley, and bloody doings might be expected almost any day. Perhaps your friend Wooster is in danger at this moment, thinking of you, and wishing your presence with all his mind power."

My sweet little, untaught, almost illiterate, wife had guessed right. I knew then that Wooster's life was in danger, that is I felt it with such absolute certainty that when towards noon my feeling of unrest subsided, I was morally certain that Wooster was dead — for in his isolated situation, if he was attacked at all, there was no help. I knew the Apaches, I knew their ways, and from that moment on I gave up all hope of ever seeing Wooster again.

About a week after these occurrences there came to Florence Mr. Hiram Stevens of Tucson, and my old friend J. W. Hopkins, late first lieutenant, First Cavalry. The latter had retired from the army, and was then farming at the Agua Fria Ranch, in the Santa Cruz Valley, as before related. The two had come to Florence to seek some farming lands upon which they might pursue their agricultural enterprises in peace and quiet, protected by the Pimas and Maricopas. Mr. Hopkins looked me up at once at the brewery, and shaking hands with me (mine was trembling) he said: "Dear boy, are you prepared to bear sad news?" "I am," was my answer; "you have come to tell me that Wooster, my friend and brother is no more."

"And his wife also," continued he; "they are buried together under the tall cottonwood tree that stands in the middle of the corral. It happened thus: On the twenty-first of this month, about 8 o'clock in the morning (the identical hour and date of my presentiment experienced about one hundred forty miles distant) Wooster was feeding his hogs in the corral. Since you left there he had built an adobe wall inclosing a space of about forty by thirty feet. As he was unable to obtain a decent price for the corn you and he planted together, owing to the low contract rates, he bought about fifty hogs and was turning them into bacon and ham while his wife tried out the lard for the Tucson market. The wall surrounding the corral was only about five feet high, and over the wall he must have received the first shot, which struck him in the thigh. The bloody tracks leading from the corn pile into the house led to the surmise that he went into the latter in order to procure a rifle or carbine, both of which were standing in a corner of the room adjoining the kitchen. He must have taken the carbine and hurried with it to the window opening upon the corral, when a bullet struck him in the right eye and penetrated the brain, causing him to drop dead. The carbine was missing, but the rifle was found standing in its accustomed corner. As soon as the Indians saw Wooster drop, and had made sure of his death, they penetrated into the house through the same window, as their moccasin tracks upon the window sill proved, and dragged forth his wife Trinidad. They partly dragged and partly carried her about a half mile from the house in the direction of the neighboring San Cayetan Mountains. She must have fought them tooth and nail, as her condition showed when her body was found. This and the further fact that her brother, who was plowing in a field about five hundred yards from the house, had heard the shots and was running to the rescue, induced the Indians to abandon the idea of taking her captive. They killed her with lances at the beginning of a steep path over the foothills, and made good their escape. They drove off all the animals except the hogs, which were nearly all roasted by the fire the Indians started in the corral by igniting the haystack and a big pile of corn fodder."

Thus ended my brave, good, and true friend. Since my departure from the ranch he had from time to time made me such remittances as his limited income permitted in payment of my outlays for the establishent of the ranch, surveying and making the irrigating ditch and the purchase of stock. Had his life not been cut short when it was he would undoubtedly have liquidated the whole debt with the proceeds of the ham, bacon and lard enterprise, for he was a perfectly honest and exceedingly industrious man.

The Indians had indeed begun a bloody raid. On March 18 they killed William Cook of Lieutenant Ross's company, at Hughes's Ranch, in the Sonoita. We have seen how three days later L. B. Wooster and wife succumbed to their bullets and lances. The same band* swept down on

---

*It was later ascertained that it was reinforced by Indians from Es-ki-men-zin's band, supposed to be under friendly agency control at old Fort Grant.

the San Pedro settlements, killing Alexander McKenzie, H. C. Long, Walter and Owry Chapin on April 18, 1871. On May 6 of the same year Lieutenant H. B. Cushing, Third U.S. Cavalry, citizen Wm. H. Simpson and Private Gurn, Third U.S. Cavalry, were killed in an ambuscade in the Whetstone Mountains; on May 23 two Mexicans were killed on the upper Santa Cruz River, near the Mexican boundary. On May 21 J. P. Planchard and George Saunders were killed near Calabazas. June 17 Chas. McKinney was killed by the Es-ki-men-sin gang; on July 17 a son of Peter Kitchen, aged eleven years, was killed at the Potrero, four miles west of Calabazas; W. H. Harris was killed July 18 near Cienega, about fifteen miles distant from Fort Crittenden.

But why make a long, detailed enumeration? I have before me a list of the number of people killed in the years 1856 to 1862, made according to a record kept by Hermann Ehrenberg, a civil and mining engineer, which enumerates 425 persons, being at that period about one-half of the American population. My own data give the number of murdered men, women and children during the years 1869, 1870 and 1871 at two hundred twenty-three.

Although I was, during the period of the above detailed murders, safe from Indian attacks, I had other troubles. As already stated, our business proved to be a far from remunerative undertaking.

Therefore, when, towards the middle of March, a communication of the recently established school board at Tucson reached me containing the inquiry if I were willing and ready to become the teacher of the first public school in that town, which now had become an incorporated city, I answered in the affirmative. My new duties were to begin on April 1. Before leaving Florence I paid a visit to Ruggles. In order to guard my partner, Will, against loss and litigation, I offered to give to him (Will) and Ruggles jointly a quit claim deed to everything absolutely that belonged to the brewery — the lot which we never really owned, the buildings, barrels, hoops, bungs, bung-holes, etc., provided that he gave Will a deed to one-half of the lot and acknowledged him, said Will, as full partner and owner of one-half of all real estate, utensils, material, etc.

In this manner I stepped out of the brewery business, very much poorer in pocket than I had entered it, but a great deal richer in experience.

I arrived in Tucson March 27, 1871. After passing an examination as to my qualifications before Mr. Sidney R. DeLong (At this present writing president of the Historical Society of Arizona Pioneers) I was duly appointed teacher of the public school of that "ancient and honorable pueblo." The board of trustees consisted of Messrs. W. F. Scott, Sam Hughes (both living to-day) and W. C. Davis. Mr. Scott conducted me

SAN XAVIER.

By Pioneer John A. Spring.
June 12 1885

An example of John Spring's art is this cover illustration for a paper he wrote and read before the Arizona Pioneers' Historical Society in 1885.

to an oblong adobe building situated on the northwest corner of Meyer and McCormick streets, then the property of one Mariano Molina. This building contained the one long room intended for and furnished as the contemplated school room. There were two long rows of homemade desks, forming each one piece, together with its respective bench. Between the rows a space of about six feet was left unoccupied throughout the whole length, in order to allow passageway to and from the seats and the one blackboard which, being constructed of masonry with a cement finish painted over in dull black oil paint, was firmly imbedded in the south wall. One of the desks being reversed so as to face the two rows formed by the pupils' seats, was made to serve as the teacher's desk. The best feature of these desks, which were calculated to seat, each, three large, or four middle-sized boys, or from five to six "toddlers," was their absolute solidity. However, if we take into consideration that the recently established school laws admitted boys from the age of six to 21 years, and that boys varying in size anywhere from three to nearly six feet did frequent the school, you will readily admit that the uniform size of the combination desks and benches was rather an inconvenience, as well as their manifest propensity for shedding splinters; the more so as many of the boys were poorly clad and quite often put in an appearance with bare ankles and feet. Two doors placed about the middle of the east and west walls respectively were the means of ingress and egress. Two brooms and a sprinkling pot finished the inventory of the furniture, and by these means the floor was kept in proper condition by two boys who were detailed for that purpose every day. The floor consisted of that useful material known as mother earth, and had acquired a good, hard, solid top finish by previous pounding.

When I look to-day upon the first-class appointments of our educational establishments, at our modern school buildings, their furniture, appliances and conveniences which surround us everywhere, Arizona not excepted, and then look backwards over a space of only thirty-two years, seeing again in my mind's eye that dirt floor, those two rows of uncouth, unpainted, and unvarnished desks and the many bare feet of the youngsters dangling from the benches, then am I forcibly reminded that verily "The mighty oaks from the little acorns grow."

Mr. Scott delivered to me a number of school books with the injunction to sell them to the pupils at the original wholesale cost, of which he gave me a price-list, and to supply them free of cost to children of indigent parents. Of all these transactions I was required to make a monthly statement to the board of trustees.

Being thus fully equipped, we lost no time in opening the school,

and within one week of my arrival, all parents and guardians of boys†
having been duly notified, the school doors were thrown open for their
admission. This was on the second Monday of April, 1871.

A TUCSON SCHOOL IN 1871††

On the first day nearly one hundred boys were enrolled, and on the
closing of the lists on the third day the names enrolled numbered one
hundred thirty-eight.

Of all these boys, of whom a few showed already a forthcoming
beard, while others could barely manage to climb upon the benches, not
one could express himself intelligently in the English language, although
many of them possessed quite a variegated vocabulary of bad English
words; about five or six understood sufficient English to know what to do
when asked to perform a common household duty, as, for instance, to
sweep the floor, to fetch water, etc., and could, perhaps in "a sort of way"
make themselves understood in that language, when speaking of the most
common things of everyday life. About twenty boys, ranging in age from
thirteen to sixteen years, were in attendance, who had been to school in
Mexico or had received private lessons in Spanish; some of these possessed sufficient knowledge in arithmetic to make a long division. Of
fractions, none knew anything.

No little difficulty was encountered in trying to ascertain the correct
age of these boys as their names were entered upon the school lists; for
although they almost invariably knew where they were born, they had a
very limited knowledge as to when. It soon became evident that the most
familiar landmark (if I may use the expression in this connection) in
their parents' memory for the reckoning of time was "el tempo del colera"
in Sonora. From that terrible period (1852), when the population of
Sonora was reduced about one-half by the cholera, they seemed to reckon
their births and deaths, speaking of it as a historian would of the French
Revolution or any other conspicuous historical event.

Another period which seemed to form the basis of their later reckon-
ings was "the revolution of Pesquecira." This was an exceedingly uncertain event to reckon by, unless someone could give the information which

---

†A school for girls was established a few months later under the tuition of Mrs.
L. C. Hughes, whose husband, later, under Mr. Cleveland's administration, was
appointed Governor of Arizona.

††This date is apparently in error. Spring, himself, stated in a letter to the board of
trustees, dated November 25, 1872, that "on the first of March last I was engaged
by the then existing Board of Trustees as teacher of the District School No. 1 . . ."
The Arizona Citizen of June 1, 1872 stated that "the first three months had closed
on the 21st ultimo."

of the twenty-three revolutions was meant that took place during the governorship of Ygnacio Pesquecira, which lasted eighteen years.

I am afraid of occupying too much space and exhausting the patience of those of my readers who are not specially interested in educational matters if I enter into details describing the manner in which I classified and taught this perfect chaos of boys, whose minds, intellects, former training, or, for the greater part, absence of all training, offered about as great a variety of intellectual qualifications as their complexion did of colors.

To attempt to speak English to them all at once, and English only, as proposed and urged by a member of the school trustees, and to teach them arithmetic and geography in English before they could understand a single word of that language, would have been a futile undertaking involving an absolute loss of much valuable time. I therefore explained everything in Spanish, the boys' mother tongue, so that every sentence that was translated or read or spoken in English was immediately conveyed to their intellect in a comprehensible manner. The school was taught from 9 a.m. to 12 m., and from 1 to 4 p.m., the little toddlers being let out at 3 p.m. These hours were found to suit the parents best, as many of them required the services of their children for running errands, etc., before the morning and evening meals.

Upon opening school in the morning an hour was devoted to penmanship. The older boys liked the pretty American copy books very much, and made every effort towards keeping them neat and clean. The smaller boys would copy the letters and figures, which I put in large size on the blackboard, upon their slates and became proficient in a remarkably short time, their greatest incentive being to arrive at the pen-and-ink stage and to possess a copy book. Governor Safford had kindly presented to the school two dozen of Ollendorf's Spanish-English systems for the use of the boys who could read Spanish fluently and write without difficulty. To these boys I would, after they had written a page in their copy books, read and thoroughly explain a lesson in Ollendorf and show them how to translate the Spanish exercises properly into English. These they would immediately proceed to do while I left them, in order to go from desk to desk looking at the writing of the others and correcting the ill-shaped letters, after which they all had a lesson in the first reader. The Ollendorf class soon became very proficient and fairly doted on the little stories in Appleton's First and Second Readers, but I found it absolutely necessary to translate and explain to them everything they read, as otherwise they would take no interest in a story. The afternoon was generally devoted to figures, and twice a week I gave all the boys a drawing lesson, which all of them considered a perfect treat.

My readers will easily understand that having to teach such a large number of boys (the average daily attendance was ninety-eight) of all ages, the greater part of whom had never learned to submit their "sweet will" to any school discipline and to little of it at home, and being in one room, it was absolutely necessary that the most rigid discipline should be enforced from the beginning. To "spare the rod" under those circumstances would not only have "spoiled the child," but probably something else more nearly connected with the teacher. This, however, offered no difficulty as far as the parents were concerned, of whom a great many seemed to measure the teacher's capacity by his ability to administer severe corporal punishment. It was an almost everyday occurrence to have the father or guardian of a pupil call at the school with a new switch (ash preferred), which he would recommend highly for the correction of unruly youth, sometimes specifying the delinquent's misdeeds, sometimes urging the frequent application of the switch on general principles. Many a time I was urgently requested to flog a boy to the blood because he had started from home at 7 a.m. to buy some coffee for breakfast and had not returned till nightfall, and then put in an appearance without coffee and without cash, his crime being further aggravated by his having played truant from school. At first this playing "hookey" was much in vogue; but as soon as the boys understood that I invariably informed their parents, whenever practicable, of their absence from school, the attendance became much more regular.

At first it was somewhat difficult to make the boys understand that they must arrive punctually at the hours established and must put in their appearance washed, combed, and brushed. This last was the hardest struggle, but fairly good results were attained after a few weeks, when a few unwashed boys had been taken to the well in the schoolyard and there submitted to rather copious ablutions under my personal supervision and with my personal assistance.

INDIAN POLICY OF GEN. STONEMAN

In the meantime the condition of affairs with regard to Indian atrocities grew worse and worse; a committee of our citizens was appointed to meet General Stoneman, commanding the Department of Arizona, on the Gila River, to explain to him the death and destruction that was being dealt out on every hand, and to plead with him for assistance. They received no words of sympathy nor any hope of relief.

The Legislature of 1870–71 had met and prepared a pamphlet showing the slaughter of men, women, and children that was going on; but no relief came. Finally a resolution was drafted and submitted to Governor Safford before introduction, alleging inefficiency of Stoneman and asking for his removal. Governor Safford advised against its introduction. He told the members of the Legislature that every word of the resolution was true, but that in a few days they would return to private life, and the fight would be alone on his hands, and to give Stoneman public notice of what they intended to do would place him in a position to muster all his forces towards preventing his removal, and that the small patronage and influence of a Territorial Governor would not be equal to the influence of a Department commander, assured of office for life. The Legislature adjourned Jan. 31, 1871. The Governor started for Washington, and met Stoneman at San Diego. The latter at once proceeded to show the Governor the difficulties of the position. He pulled from his pockets Eastern papers denouncing him for a very sanguinary proclamation he had issued sometime before.

"Now," said he, "you can see I am between two fires. If I pursue a relentless war against the Apaches, as indicated in this, my proclamation, then the peace party will attack me."

The Governor replied that his proclamation had not placed a soldier in the field nor had it killed an Indian. The General replied that the proclamation was "intended for the Arizona market." Whatever that might imply has never been very clear to the writer nor, I think, to Governor Safford, from whose lips I quote the conversation. From that moment the Governor made up his mind that a man who would trifle with the lives and property of the people he was sent to defend, should not hold the place if he could prevent it. He went to Washington, where he had already once before interviewed General Sherman, from which interview he was satisfied that if Stoneman was to be removed, the President would have to do it. He went, therefore, to President Grant, in company with Delegate McCormick, from Arizona, and Senator Stewart, and asked the removal of General Stoneman and the appointment of General Crook in his place.

The President listened attentively, and replied that he believed all the statements made by Arizona's Governor, and also that General Crook was the best Indian fighter in the Army, but said that it would require the cutting of a great deal of red tape to send Crook, as he was only a lieutenant-colonel, and pretty well down on the list at that. The President was told that the frontier expected from him protection, and that if it became necessary to cut red tape, they believed he would not hesitate to do it. After a moment's though he said: "I believe I can send him on his brevet rank of Major-General." He called the Secretary of War, and in a moment the Governor's proposition was agreed upon and Stoneman's head rolled into the basket.

Before it was known in Arizona that General Stoneman had been removed, the people had lost all hope of relief, and had determined that self-preservation was the first law of nature. To make matters more intolerable, the hostiles, or some of them, had come to old Camp Grant, and professing peace, were put under charge of Lieutenant Whitman, who fed and protected them. It was soon demonstrated beyond all question of doubt that these Indians were carrying on a more destructive warfare than ever before, upon the sure plan of protection for their own lives and their stolen property by the troops of the United States. People were murdered in cold blood, while traveling, while pursuing their agricultural pursuits, while herding their cattle; the stolen property taken from them was traced to and found upon Whitman's reservation. He himself turned a deaf ear to every complaint, and defended his own position by claiming to the deluded peace party in the East that he alone was defending the innocent Indians against the brutal frontiersmen, who would be satisfied with nothing but the extermination of the Indians.

Under this state of affairs the citizens saw no relief, except to take the matter in their own hands, and the "Camp Grant massacre" was the result of the Government's neglect and the long and patient suffering of a body of pioneers who tried to bring civilization into a heretofore wild country.

To give a mere recital of the act of killing a few, more or less, of bloodthirsty savages, without the details of the causes and provocations which drew a long-suffering and patient people to the adoption of remedial measures so apparently cruel in their results, would be a great wrong and injustice to those of our friends and neighbors who in various ways gave sanction and aid to the undertaking, and would fall far short of the object and aim of the writer to give fair and impartial history.

In the year 1870, in accordance with the peace policy which had been decided upon by the government, the Pinal and Yavapai bands of Apache Indians were collected together and placed upon a reservation around old Camp Grant, at the junction of the San Pedro and Aravaipa Creeks, about fifty-five miles from Tucson, under the supervision of military stationed at that post. One or two agents for them had been taken from civil life, but in a short time, their management proving unsatisfactory, one Royal E. Whitman, a Lieutenant of the Third Cavalry, U.S.A., was assigned to duty as their agent. Being what is termed a sharp man and of a thrifty turn, he soon saw there was money in the Apache, and lost no time in the practical application of that knowledge, to do which successfully, required outside partners, who were soon found in Tucson. A sutler's store was first started followed by a blacksmith and a butcher shop and a number of strikers chosen in various capacities, ostensibly for the benefit of poor Lo, really "affidavy" and easy-conscience witness men — for the boss — and, as a trite saying goes, hell was fully inaugurated.

The Indians soon commenced plundering and murdering the citizens of Tucson, San Xavier, Tubac, Sonoita, San Pedro and every other settlement within a radius of one hundred miles of old Camp Grant, in the confidence that if they escaped to their reservation, they reached a secure haven. During the winter of 1870–71, these murders and depredations were so numerous as to threaten the abandonment of nearly all the settlements outside of Tucson, especially that of San Pedro, the most numerous and important of all; in the meantime the citizens of Tucson were aroused; meetings were held upon the occurrence of each new murder and outrage; representations were made to Royal Whitman that his Indians were plundering and murdering our people, which he denied, and stood ready to prove by every striker in the reservation that his Indians never left the reservation. Meanwhile the work of death and destruction was kept up with ever-increasing force until the slaughter of Leslie B. Wooster, my former partner, and his wife, on the Santa Cruz, above Tucson, so inflamed the people that an indignation meeting was held at Tucson, a great amount of resoluting and speechifying indulged in, and it was determined to raise a military company at once, for which a paper was drawn up and signers called for, to which eighty-two Americans signed their names. I was one of them, and all hands were to eat up blood-raw every Apache in the land immediately upon the recurrence of a new outrage.

A committee was appointed to visit the Department Commander. General Stoneman, at the time on the Gila near Florence, was interviewed by a committee consisting of S. R. DeLong, J. W. Hopkins, and William S. Oury, the remaining names not now remembered. The result of the conference with General Stoneman was that he had but few troops, and could give no aid; that Tucson had the largest population in the Territory, and gave us to understand that we must protect ourselves. With this cold comfort after a trip of one hundred fifty miles and the loss of a valuable mule, we returned to our constituents, and although no public demonstration was made, at a quiet assemblage of some of our ablest and most substantial citizens, it was resolved that the recommendation of General Stoneman should be adopted, and that to the best of our ability we would endeavor to protect ourselves. A few days afterwards, in the beginning of April, 1871, the arrival of a carrier from San Xavier brought the sad intelligence that the Indians had just made a descent upon that place and had driven off a large number of cattle and horses; the alarm drum (the usual way of collecting our people) was beat — a flaming cartoon carried by a man who accompanied the drummer was displayed with the following inscription: "Injuns — Injuns — Injuns. Big meeting at the court house. Come, everybody; time for action has arrived."

This device had been so frequently resorted to and the result obtained so unsatisfactory that it failed to draw. Meanwhile a party of citizens had saddled their horses, and learning from two San Xavier carriers the direction the marauding Indians had taken, rode off, hoping to intercept them before they reached the Cebadilla Pass. In this they were disappointed, for the Indians had gone into the pass before the pursuing party could meet them. However, the pursuing party found the tracks of the Indians, and came up with a delayed Indian driving the stolen stock on a tired horse. This Indian they killed, and they recovered some stock. The other Indians escaped with the horses and the freshest cattle.

Upon the return of the party to Tucson Mr. William S. Oury went to interview one of them, named Jesús María Elías, and had a long conference with him. (This Mr. Elías was a fine trailer, who could be relied on to follow tracks even over hard ground, through rivers, etc.) This man said to Mr. Oury: "Don Guillermo, I have always been satisfied, and have repeatedly told you that the Camp Grant Indians were the ones that were destroying us. I now have proof positive that the Indian we have just killed is a Camp Grant Indian. If my evidence is not sufficient, I will bring more proof. I have frequently seen him there, and know him well by his having a front tooth out, and as a further proof, when we overtook the Indians they were making a direct course for Camp Grant. Now it devolves upon you as one of the oldest American residents of the county to devise some means of saving us from total ruin which the present state of affairs must invariably lead to if not remedied; see your countrymen, they are the only ones who have money to furnish the supplies necessary to make a formal and effective campaign against our implacable enemies. I know my countrymen, and will vouch that, if arms, ammunition and provisions, however scant, are furnished them, they will be ready at the first call."

Mr. Oury replied: "Don Jesús, for myself I will answer that I will at all times be ready to do my part, and will at once issue a call for the assemblage of my people at the courthouse, when you can publicly state what you have just told me, and some concerted plan can be adopted which may give the desired relief."

With a sad shake of the head Mr. Elías answered: "No, Don Guillermo, for months we have repeatedly held public meetings, at which many patriotic speeches have been made and many glowing resolutions passed; meanwhile our means of subsistance have been rapidly diminishing, and nothing has been accomplished. We cannot resolute the remorseless Apache out of existence. If that could have been done every one of them have been dead long since. Besides, giving publicity to the course we might determine to pursue would surely defeat any plan we might adopt. You are aware that there are wealthy and influential men in this community whose interest it is to have the Indians at Camp Grant left undisturbed, and who would at the first intimation of an intent to inquire seriously into their operations appeal to the military (whose ears they have) and frustrate all our plans and hopes."

Mr. Oury saw at once the force of his arguments, and replied: "Lay out the plan of action, and I will aid you with all the zeal and energy I possess." Mr. Elías then developed the following plan: "You and I will go first to San Xavier, see Francisco, the head Papago there, have him send runners to the various Papago villages notifying them that on the twenty-eighth of April we want them to be at San Xavier early in the morning with all the force they can muster for a campaign against our own, sworn enemy, the Apaches. Francisco will be prepared to give them all a good breakfast on their arrival, and send messages to me at once. This matter being satisfactory we will then return to Tucson. I will see all the Mexicans who may desire to participate in the campaign, and have them all ready to move on the day fixed. You make arrangements with the Americans you can trust, either to take active part in the campaign or render such assistance in supplies, arms, ammunition and horses as will be required to carry out the expedition, and on the day fixed (April 28), news of the arrival of the Papagoes at San Xavier having first been received, all who were to be active participants in the campaign to leave town quietly and singly, to avoid giving alarm, and rendezvous on the Rillito opposite San Xavier, where the Papagoes will be advised to meet us, and where as per arrangement, the arms, ammunition, and provisions will be delivered and distributed. All hands having arrived at the rendezvous, the command to be fully organized by the election of a commander, whom all shall be pledged to obey implicitly. When thus organized the command to march up the Rillito until the trail of the Indians who have committed the recent depredations at San Xavier will be struck; this trail we will follow wherever it may lead, and all the Indians found upon it we will kill if possible."

This is the whole plan of the Camp Grant campaign as proposed by Mr. Elías and concurred in by the narrator.

Mr. Oury continues: "For its successful fulfillment we both went to work with all our energy, he with his countrymen (the Mexicans), I with mine (the Americans), and both together with our auxiliaries, the Papagoes. Early in the morning of April 28, 1871, we received the welcome news of the arrival of the Papagoes at San Xavier, with the notice that after a short rest and feed they would march to a general rendezvous on the Rillito (a small rivulet from north to south and debouching into the Santa Cruz River at Tucson. Soon after Elías gave notice that the Mexican contingent was quietly and singly leaving town for the same destination, and soon after I, having given proper directions to the extremely small contingent of my countrymen, silently and alone took up the line of march to the common rendezvous. By 3 p.m. all the command had arrived, also that which was still more essential to the successful issue of the campaign, to wit: the wagon with the arms, ammunition and provisions — thanks to our old companion, the adjutant-general of the Territory.

"As soon as I was convinced that no further increase was to be expected, I proceeded to take account of stock, with the following result: Papagoes, 92; Mexicans, 48; Americans, 6, in all 146 men good and true. During our short stay at the general rendezvous, a number of pleasantries were indulged in by the different members of the party upon the motley appearance of the troop, and I got a blow squarely in the right eye from an old Mexican neighbor, who said to me: 'Don Guillermo, your countrymen are grand on resoluting and speechifying, but when it comes to action they show up exceedingly thin.' Which, in view of the fact that eighty-two Americans had solemnly pledged themselves to be ready at any moment for the campaign and only six finally showed up was, to say the least, rather humiliating. However, everything was taken pleasantly. Jesús María Elías was elected commander of the expedition, and at 4 p.m. the command was in the saddle, ready for the march. Just here it seemed to me that we had neglected a very important precautionary measure, and I penciled the following note to H. S. Stevens, Tucson: 'Send a party to the Canada del Oro, on the main road from Tucson to Camp Grant, with orders to stop any and all persons going towards Camp Grant until 7 o'clock a.m., of April 30.' This note I gave to the teamster, who had not yet left our camp. He delivered it promptly, and it was at once attended to by Mr. Stevens. But for this precaution our campaign would have resulted in complete failure, from the fact that the absence of so many men from so small a population as Tucson then contained was noted by a person of large influence in the community, at whose urgent demand the military commander at Tucson sent an express of two soldiers with dispatches to Camp Grant. These riders were quietly detained at Canada del Oro, and did not reach that post until it was too late to do us harm. After writing and dispatching the note above referred to, the order 'forward' was given, and the command moved gaily and confidently on its mission.

"About 6 p.m. the trail was struck which we proposed to follow, and the march continued through the Cebadilla Pass and down the slopes along the San Pedro River to the point where the San Xavier party had killed the Indian above referred to, when the order to camp was given, as it was about midnight, the moon going down, and the trail could not be well followed in the dark.

"Just at break of day on the morning of April 29, we rode down into the San Pedro bottom, where our commander determined to remain until nightfall, lest our command should be discovered by roving Indians and alarm given at the ranchería. We had followed all this time the trail of the Indians who had raided San Xavier, and every man in the command was satisfied now it would lead to the reservation. Arrangements were made accordingly. Commander Elías gave orders to march as soon as it was dark, and believing that we were much nearer the Indian ranchería than we really were, and that we would reach its neighborhood by midnight, detailed three men as scouts, whose duty it was, when the command should arrive conveniently near the ranchería, to go ahead and ascertain the exact locality and report to him the result of their reconnaissance, in order to have no guess-work about the actual position of the hostile camp and make our attack a haphazard affair.

"Everything being now ready for the final march, we moved out of the San Pedro Bottom just at dark. It soon became evident that our Captain and all those who thought they knew the distance had made a grave miscalculation, and that instead of its being distant about 16 miles, as estimated, it was nearer 30 miles away, so that, after a continuous march during the whole night, it was near daybreak before we reached the Aravaipa Canyon; therefore, when we did reach it, there was no time left to make the proposed reconnaissance to ascertain the exact location of the Indian camp. This involved the necessity of a change of our original plan of attack. We knew that the ranchería was in the Aravaipa Canyon, somewhere above the post, but the exact distance to it and the situation as to its immediate surroundings nobody knew. We were in a critical position; we were within sight of the post; daylight was approaching, and it was plain that in a very short time we would be discovered either by the Indians or by the sentries of the fort. In either case our expedition would turn out to be an utter failure, but our gallant captain was equal to the emergency. Promptly he gave orders to divide the command into two wings, one to consist of the Papagoes, the other the Mexicans and Americans, and to skirmish up the creek until we should strike the ranchería, approaching it thus on two sides at the same time.

"When the order 'forward' was given, a new difficulty arose, which if it had not been speedily overcome, would have been fatal; the command was now in plain view of the post; the Papagoes had all the time been afraid of military interference with us. I had assured them that no such thing would occur, and vouched for it. It happened that just as the command was halting, I had dropped my canteen from the horn of my saddle, and dismounting to look for it in the dust and semi-darkness, had fallen behind the troop. The Papagoes, not seeing me at the front, when the order forward for the skirmish was given, refused to move inquiring where

Don Guillermo was. Word was immediately passed down the line to me and I galloped to the front and made a motion with my hand, beckoning the Papagoes on. Without a word they bounded forward like deer and the skirmish began, and a better-executed one I never witnessed, even from veteran soldiers. There was not a break in either line from beginning to end of the affair, which covered a distance of nearly four miles before the Indians were struck. They were completely surprised, sleeping in absolute security in their wickiups with only a buck and a squaw as lookouts on a bluff above the ranchería; they were playing cards by a small fire and were both clubbed to death before they could give the alarm.

"The Papagoes attacked the Apaches, in the manner of the Pimas, in their wickiups, with clubs and guns; all who escaped them and took to the bluffs were received and dispatched by the other wing, which occupied a position above them. The attack was so swift and fierce that within half an hour the whole bloody work was ended and not an adult Indian left to tell the tale. Some twenty-eight or thirty small papooses were spared and brought to Tucson as captives. Not a single man of our command was hurt to mar the full measure of our triumph, and at 8 o'clock on the morning of April 30, our tired troops were resting and breakfasting on the borders of the San Pedro, a few miles above the post, in the full satisfaction of a work well done."

The immediate results of this episode were that the farmers of the San Pedro River, who had sought refuge with their families in the town of Tucson, returned to their farms and fields, with their wives and children, to gather their abandoned crops; that in the Sonoita, Santa Cruz, and all other settlements of southern Arizona new life sprang up, confidence was restored, and industry received an impetus that knew no check for many years, until Geronimo started upon his bloody career. In view of these facts, and taking into consideration the terrible provocation the settlers of those regions labored under, seeing no help arriving from anywhere, can you or anybody conscientiously call the killing of the Apaches at old Camp Grant on the morning of April 30, 1871, a "massacre"?

Some efforts were made to bring the participants in the above-described episode to trial, but it was soon discovered that the prosecution would find itself without witnesses, and the matter was dropped.

What kind of a report Lieutenant Whitman sent to Washington about the affair was never made public. At all events, it created some sensation in the Capital, for during the summer, General O. O. Howard was sent to Arizona to investigate the situation and to negotiate, if possible, a permanent peace.

He visited my school with Governor Safford, and witnessed some exercises by the pupils. He paid me the handsome compliment that I was "the right man in the right place," and left some prizes with me to be distributed among the most meritorious pupils. These were delivered to me by his aide-de-Camp, Capt. Wilkinson.

I was present at several conversations between General Howard and Governor Safford. The General mixed freely with the people, and listened attentively to their tales of woe, hardship and losses caused by Apaches, and requested Governor Safford to give him his full cooperation. General Howard desired to do what was right, but it seemed to me that he did not fully appreciate the terrible slaughter of our people, nor the wily cunning and treachery of the Apaches.* Governor Safford invited him to spend two weeks with him, during which they would go and see the desolate homes, the bereaved widows, the fatherless children, the fresh graves, etc. The General said he could not spare the time, but finally consented to send his aide, Captain Wilkinson. With him the Governor traveled two weeks, showing him the desolation caused by the destruction of the Apaches and the sorrow of the survivors of the murdered victims.

General Howard invited representatives of the friendly tribes of Indians and citizens to meet the Apaches at old Camp Grant and endeavor to make peace. My school being then closed for the summer vacation, I accompanied the party as Spanish interpreter for the Mexicans, while one Emanuel acted as interpreter for the Apaches. This latter was a civilized Apache used as a guide and interpreter. At first he was very unwilling to go. He said he had nine marks on the breech of his gun, each one of which was a record of a dead Apache, and he feared they would kill him. Finally, being assured by General Howard and Governor Safford of their personal protection, he consented to go, and rendered very efficient services.

General Crook, who had by this time relieved General Stoneman, was also present at the conference.

The peace council was held on the banks of the San Pedro River near the fort. It was evident to me, as soon as the council opened, that the Apaches were not prepared for peace. One of the first conditions they made was that certain children taken from them by the Papagoes (principally at the Camp Grant massacre, but some previous to that event) should be returned. These children had been sold to Mexicans and had been incorporated into their families, and, to all appearances, were as much thought of and as well treated as their own. These Mexicans had been induced to take the children to Camp Grant as a peace offering. I shall never forget the scene which ensued when these Apache children

---

*Cochise managed to wheedle out of the General a separate reservation for his tribe, which was located in the Chiricahua Mountains, in the very mountain fastness where Cochise retired from his bloody work.

were torn from the arms of their adopted mothers, amid the shrieks of the women and children, and were turned over to the nearly-naked savages. The children knew no other parents than those who had adopted them, and were as much terrified in being torn from their adopted mothers as our children would be. General Crook, who sat beside me, rose hastily from his seat and left the ground, saying quite audibly: "I cannot stand this any longer!"

Tears ran down the cheeks of the old frontiersman. A purse was raised on the spot of one hundred dollars per child, and offered to the Indians if they would allow the children to remain with us; but they replied: "Do you think we are dogs, to sell our own children?"

A sort of a peace was patched up at this conference, but no one had any confidence in its permanency.

Shortly after this I reopened the school, and taught it without interruption until the vacation of the following year.

A WILD GOOSE CHASE

During my last visit home in Tucson, (November 1902), while looking over the contents of an old box stored away in my daughter's trunk room, I came upon some relics of bygone days; namely, two buckskin bags, about ten inches long and four inches wide, to the mouths of which were attached two pairs of strong leather thongs; also a leather-bound memorandum book containing my diary for the years 1871–1874. I instantly remembered that these bags, intended to hold gold dust (here generally called placer gold), had hung for a number of years against a wall of my room under an Apache bow and quiver full of arrows, not so much for ornament as for a warning for all gullible people, inasmuch as these buckskin bags remained empty during and after the greatest wild-goose chase in the annals of Arizona's whole history, reported in my diary as follows.

In the winter and spring of 1872, a man by the name of Miner, a sandy-haired, red-faced Irishman, made his appearance in the northern part of Arizona, and, while at Prescott and Bradshaw, created considerable excitement in his efforts to raise men to accompany him to some rich placer gold diggings he claimed to have discovered some years previously while prospecting this Territory with a company of about thirty men, relating many thrilling encounters with the Apaches while coming into and en route through the country and at the "diggings," as also their marvelous escape, though surrounded, pursued and waylaid and constantly harassed by Indians, until they reached the Colorado Desert, where they lost their mules in a sandstorm. In Miner's own language, "the last

seen of the mules were their ears sticking up through the sand surface."
Miner represented that the "diggin's" were extensive and rich, yielding
from a prospect hole sunk by him sixteen dollars to the pan. Water, timber, grass, and game were abundant, and all Miner asked was enough men
to make it safe and a choice of claims to include his prospect hole. When
asked how many men would be necessary, he gave as his opinion that
three hundred would not be too many, and he would not object to five
hundred or even one thousand, for such was the extent of the placers that
all could get good claims. He was ever careful in all his intercourse with
his interlocutors to conceal the locality of his wonderful discovery, and
no one could reasonably expect such a disclosure. His success in raising
men to go with him was not assured until he met Governor Safford at
Bradshaw, who, on hearing Miner's story, promptly gave him the benefit
of his counsel and support, and among the first steps taken was the one to
advertise through the Arizona and some other papers, requesting all those
wishing to join the enterprise to meet at a certain time at Florence, on the
Gila River.

In pursuance of this notice sometime in the month of July 1872 (my
diary does not give the exact date, but it must have been during the second
week of the month), there assembled at Florence about three hundred
persons. Miner was among the lot. So was I. Hence the buckskin bags. The
school had closed for the long vacation on June 15, time hung heavy on
my hands, and, although I had no more idea about digging for gold than
a butterfly has about beating the big drum of a brass band, I joined the
"outfit," principally because Governor Safford did. Nearly one-half the
number of the assembled crowd were from Yavapai and Maricopa, and the
other half from Pinal and Pima counties.

The formal organization was made at Florence in the field of Colonel
Ruggles, adjoining the town. Four companies were formed; officers elected,
and a commander-in-chief chosen. This position, by general consent, was
given to Governor Safford. At this time, Miner, for the benefit of all and in
their presence, related his story, even to the sandstorm, which greatly
enthused all hands and hastened preparations to make a start — whither
no one but miner knew. And from him we learned that old Camp Grant,
on the San Pedro, was the point from which our final start would be
made, and from there it would take from six to ten days to reach the
place where he had found the gold.

The organization being complete, each company elected its own route
to Grant. All but one chose the old Camp Grant road, and, by making
a dry camp, reached there the second day out. The Prescott company
chose the Gila River route, and was six days in reaching Grant, to the
great annoyance of those in waiting, who were consuming their expensive

rations while lying idle. All being present, two days more were consumed in preparation for the final start. Many added to their outfit sundry tools and implements for use in the mines; even the Governor himself bought an extra burro and loaded it with flour and a twelve-foot crosscut saw; the latter was deemed a profitable investment as well as a necessity, as lumber would be high-priced and the Governor, owning the only saw, would have a monopoly of the lumber market. Saws were in demand, but the Governor had purchased the only one to be obtained at Grant, and the question with many was, What would be the price of lumber, and how much would a rocker cost? (A rocker, sometimes called a cradle, is a primitive wooden concern for washing placer gold.) But no matter, who cared, when a few pans of dirt, as rich as Miner said it was, would pay for it! and, then, the general understanding was that all were to be alike interested in the mines, and no one felt disposed to complain at the prospect of the Governor's getting a fat contract to furnish all the rockers required. So, with the highest expectations harbored, by all except a few, a very few, less sanguine people, we marched from Grant in the afternoon of July 21, and camped on the San Pedro, six miles below, and the next morning bright and early struck out for the "diggin's" with Miner in the lead. We took the cavalry trail leading to San Carlos, and the first two or three days out, the contour of the country enabled Miner to successfully point out or correctly guess how the trail ran; this convinced the Governor and others that Miner knew the country and had really been in it before, and served to inspire confidence in his story.

We learned later that he was following a map drawn by some discharged soldier, and given him in San Francisco. This map contained directions to follow a certain trail which led to Lost Gulch, northwest of Globe, where gold is found, indeed, but not in paying quantities.

Arriving at San Carlos, Miner claimed that his "diggin's" lay northwesterly from that point. There were with us some parties who, years before, had scouted that part of the country with soldiers, and knew that if we took that course, a distance of forty-five miles without water would have to be traversed, and, as many were on foot with only a pack animal, and others were with weak and poor animals, the Governor and others became fearful that in attempting to cover this distance much suffering might ensue, and some, owing to the condition of their stock, might not be able to make it at all. Thus, in order to avoid possible suffering and hardship Miner was asked if it would make any difference if we went up the San Carlos River, and then cross over, by doing which it would only be twenty miles from water to water. On his saying it would not make any difference, we directed our course up the San Carlos River and camped at its headwaters, within six miles of Salt River, and instead of doing what was contemplated, tacking west so as to intersect Miner's trail, we crossed Salt River and wound around until we struck Cherry Creek, skirting the eastern base of the Sierra Ancha Mountains, some forty-five miles north of where the town of Globe now stands, and we finally ascended and camped two days on the extreme summit of these mountains, where we found a plateau of one hundred or more acres of land covered with large pine timber; a mountain stream of cool, clear water, and grass and game quite plenty. This place is said to be a fine potato farm at the present day, producing tubers of large size and the finest flavor. John Dunn, later on a part owner of the celebrated "Silver King" Mine, was the first to bring in a wild turkey, strung on a pole carried by two men. This bird must have weighed fifty pounds, and John's mess was the envy of the camp. The only invited guests at the turkey dinner were Miner and the Governor. Turkey at that time was hardly good enough for Miner, but two days afterward a raw piece of bacon would have been considered too good for him, for it was from the top of this mountain that Miner daily viewed with his field-glass the surrounding country, finally admitting that he knew but little about it, and that, in short, he was lost!

This admission and confession, becoming known, speedily destroyed all confidence and faith in Miner, except on the part of two or three of his special confidants, to whom he had shown his map, declaring it his own handiwork. They claimed in his support that he had been thrown off his track at San Carlos, and blamed the Governor for it. Miner, in his craft and cunning, sought to direct attention from himself to the Governor, and thus escape the vengeance talked of being meted out to him, as about this time a little "necktie" party was strongly talked of. Miner went as far as to threaten the Governor; but on being told that if he hurt a hair of the latter's head, his execution would immediately follow, further trouble of this kind ceased. The final result was a split-up; all talk of hanging Miner ended, and the general conclusion was that any man or set of men that had been fools enough, at the start, to believe Miner . . . ought to be fooled. If the sandstorm was of such violence, how could Miner have withstood it, and how could he have escaped perishing in the desert without means of transportation, water and food, in the midst of the Colorado Desert? The more the affair was discussed the sillier our proceedings appeared to ourselves, and all good-naturedly concluded not to Molest Miner as long as he behaved himself.

Before leaving the mountain we built a monument and christened it "Miner's Folly," and felled a big pine tree to attract attention to it, if any one should come after us in search of Miner's rich "diggin's," to let them know they were on the right trail. On coming down from the mountain we discovered a cave of great natural curiosity, to enter which we had to crawl on our hands and knees some twelve or fifteen feet. It then opened into a large chamber which evidently had been used by the Apaches as a dance hall, for in the center was a circle about the size of a circus ring, plainly marked by oft-repeated treading of feet. There were an east and a west wing adjoining the cave, with stalactites hanging from the roofs like icicles, giving the whole the appearance of a great natural hall. Lower down on Coon Creek, skirting the base of the mountain, we came upon a stone building, one side of which was formed by the cliff or rock, to which it was attached. Inside there was a mine or vein of yellow and red mineral (ochre I think), made useful, no doubt, by the Apaches in beautifying and ornamenting themselves, and their women during their ceremonial dances.

A BRUSH WITH APACHES

On Coon Creek a consultation was held and various propositions considered, which failed to produce harmony or concerted action. In the meantime a Mexican had informed the Prescott party that he could show them gold on Pinto Creek; but Miner, hearing of the Mexican, interviewed him and endeavored to have the Mexican pilot him there; in order that he might, good results being obtained, claim the locality as his "diggin's," and in this way recover his standing. The Mexican refused to desert his Prescott party, who selected ten of their best men and quickly left camp, crossed Salt River and struck out for Pinto Creek, the Mexican acting as guide. Miner, getting wind of this move, selected a like number and followed in hot haste, in the hope of being able to reach Pinto Creek in advance of the other party, "Hundadora" Holmes acting as his guide. The Prescott people, composed of old pioneers, and well-mounted, were able to keep the lead, with Miner, however, in close pursuit at a distance of a few miles only. The advance party ran onto a small band of Apaches, camped in a gulch; they immediately dismounted and prepared to take the Apaches in, and while so engaged, and before the attack, Miner hove in sight and prevented the Indians from being surprised and killed, to the great disappointment of the old-time boys, nearly all of whom had lost friends by the Apaches at one time or another and had had many close calls themselves. Mounting their horses, a steeplechase followed to Pinto Creek, the last four miles of which was very exciting.

Those left behind had started to follow the two advance parties as rapidly as possible. Governor Safford brought up the rear, having been greatly retarded by an accident to one of his men who had shot himself accidentally while in camp on the Sierra Ancha, and who had to be conveyed on a litter. I was with this party, and can truly state that the Governor's care saved the man's life and landed him safely in Florence, where he entirely recovered and left, without even thanking the Governor for his great care and friendship.

All finally reached Pinto Creek without accident, except Captain Rogers (afterward sheriff of Pinal County), whose mule was shot by the Apaches. After prospecting a day or two and only finding a mere "color," the entire party broke up and started for home, having been with Miner fifteen or twenty days in a fruitless search for his placers.

Those from Prescott went north; those from Pima and Pinal started south, leaving only the Salt River people with Miner, about twenty-five in all.

Returning from the search for gold, I went south with the Pima crowd and Governor Safford, and could never again be induced to join a prospecting expedition, although I had the buckskin bags — not even when a little later Governor Safford went to pick up diamonds by the bushel, as will be presently related in the sequel to the gold hunt, as narrated to me by a brother pioneer who belonged to the Salt River party that stayed with Miner and experienced the following adventures. I quote his own words.

"On reaching Pinal camp (later the ranch of Mr. Irion), it was agreed that Miner should take fifteen or twenty men and go back to San Carlos, where he claimed to have been misled, take up his trail, follow it to the "diggin's," and then return to us. They went to the top of Pinal Mountain, where Miner with his field-glasses could see San Carlos, and from this point of the lofty Pinals, claimed that he could see his mountain, where the gold was found by him, and informed us on his return, (which was the next day), that it was distant from Pinal camp only some fourteen miles to the north, and that to get there from where we were, in a direct line, was impossible, owing to the existence of certain box canyons, and that to reach the point desired we would have to go a roundabout way. There was great rejoicing over the fact that all the others had left, and that our party only would enjoy the good fortune of possessing the rich mines.

"Pinal camp had been abandoned only a short time, and there were left behind cracker boxes, stovepipe and nails, much of which we gathered up, put in shape for transportation and packed upon our animals for use in making rockers, when we would reach the mines. The thing was now certain, no longer a delusion, and Miner became once more for a brief period a trump, regaining for the time his lost prestige. Thus in the most hopeful and joyous mood we took our leave of Pinal camp, taking the trail to Picket Post (established in 1871 by George Stoneman), over the Stoneman grade. Miner, just before reaching Picket Post, pretended to recognize the country, and pointed to the Queen Creek Canyon, stating that when first in Arizona, on leaving he came through it. When asked if he brought his mules through it, he answered yes. Some were present who knew the fact that the military had failed to get animals through this canyon, and had to send their stock back, finding that it was all a footman could do to get through. Miner stock once again began to decline. On reaching the Tanks (later on Whitlow's ranch), Miner informed us that the third canyon from our then standpoint was the one leading to the mines, and ascending it about eight miles we would find the place he was in search of. We found the third canyon, and went into camp on its banks about noon time.

"After a hasty dinner, Miner, accompanied by an old man named Pearce, started out on foot, without water or provisions, to explore the canyon. Night and darkness set in and Miner had not returned; fires were built and kept blazing, and signal guns fired at intervals during the night, in the hope of aiding Miner and Pearce safely to reach camp. Daylight came on and no Miner appeared; after breakfast a meeting of the camp was held, in order to consider the situation. Some thought that the two absent ones had been killed by Indians; others that they had lost their way and were unable to find our camp.

"A few sanguine ones believed Miner had found the gold and would return loaded down with the pure yellow stuff that would astonish us all and bid us rejoice. We waited until noon, arranging in the meantime for a picked lot of men to go in search of the missing ones, to take up and follow their tracks until found, or, if killed, bury their bodies. About the time a start was to be made, Miner and Pearce came into camp, hungry and dejected, utter disappointment stamped on their countenances, not having found anything. They had tried to retrace their footsteps, got lost, and camped out all night. Miner said the next canyon was the one. Some asserted that the next canyon was the one through which the Salt River flowed, Miner earnestly contending that it was not. To settle the matter we sent men the next day to examine and report, Miner accompanying the party. It proved to be the Salt River. This being so, the Miner expedition terminated there and then. It consumed in all about a month's time from its beginning until it 'fizzled' out. Miner was permitted to follow in the rear of the Salt River people en route for home, unmolested until he assumed to direct the route to be taken. This was too much for the sadly-deluded party; Mr. Miner was quietly but impressively informed that if he spoke another word he would be hanged to the first tree in sight."

Miner got safely out of the country and back to San Francisco. The general opinion was then, and is now, that in no other country would Miner have escaped hanging. Notwithstanding the just indignation of those he had so wantonly and persistently duped, he was permitted to leave unmolested and unhurt by reason of the good nature and forebearance characteristic of the people of Arizona.

I personally had at no time any faith or confidence in the truth of Miner's story, offering from the very beginning to sell out all interest for an old hen and chickens, in anything he might show us, barring what we might accidentally find. I was induced to join the expedition under the promise of certain parties that we would first go with Miner, as this trip would take not to exceed ten days from Grant, as stated by him; then, if it proved a failure, they would accompany me to what is now the Globe district. With this previous understanding, after Miner's fruitless trip was ended, a company of eighteen men joined me on a further prospect trip on our own hook. To enable us to do so additional supplies were needed, and in order to obtain these, three men with pack mules went to Florence, the others remaining in camp at the "Tanks," to await our return.

GOVERNOR SAFFORD'S SEARCH FOR DIAMONDS

On reaching Florence we were told that Governor Safford, in company with five or six other men, had gone out to see and locate some rich mines discovered on the Miner trip and not disclosed by the discoverer. On imparting this information on our return from Florence, one of our party sang out: "Diamond's, by God; diamonds, boys!" and then informed us that a rich jewelry firm in San Francisco had sent a man to join the widely-advertised Miner expedition, expressly for the purpose of looking out for diamonds, having learned from geologists that the formations of Arizona were favorable to the existence of diamonds, and that a man was known to have picked up at a point between Camp Grant and San Carlos something shaped like, and in size similar, to a small hen's egg, all coated over with a lime crustation, which on being sent to San Francisco proved to be a rough diamond.

The result of this information was such that our party wanted then and there to abandon further prospecting and to travel on the double-quick across the country to the diamond fields, beat Safford if possible; if not, then to be there in time along with him, before the excitement should spread farther. But upon being told that the Governor had a week the start, we all agreed to investigate the prospect in the Globe country, spend there a day or two at most, and then hasten to the diamond fields. The impatience of our party was such that on reaching Globe not more than one day was spent there, and that in camp resting up. Gold, silver, and copper mines, situated in that remote part of the country, were things of little value compared with diamonds. So we hastened our departure and traveled continuously until we reached and camped on the diamond fields, which were plainly visible and readily recognized from the fact that Governor Safford's party had built small stone corrals, within which we found piled-up bushels of the supposed rough diamonds of all sizes and shapes. All we had to do was to load our mules with diamonds, which we were invited to pick up with the greatest liberality, and be off for Florence, happy in the thought that at last our trip had not been in vain, and that each had enough diamonds to insure his happiness and comfort during the remainder of his life. Our wives and sweethearts were princely [sic.] endowed, and great was our rejoicing until we reached Florence and ascertained that the supposed diamonds were worthless limestone crystals of no value whatever. Thus finally ended the Miner expedition as found on record in the hall of the Historical Society of Arizona Pioneers.

Governor Safford and myself remained friends until the changes in our lives brought about a separation. The election succeeding his term elected a Democratic delegate to Congress from Arizona; a Democratic governor was appointed, and Governor Safford went to Florida, where he established a banking business and became very wealthy. I met him a few times in after years, but never felt inclined to mention to him either Miner's expedition, or the cross-cut saw or placer "diggin's" — much less diamonds.

I RESIGN AS TEACHER

After the Governor, who was ex-officio superintendent of the public schools of the Territory, had returned from his diamond expedition I went to interview him for the purpose of laying before him the fact that the mental strain sustained by one man teaching so large a number of boys of all ages and all degrees of both knowledge and ignorance, and this in one and the same room, was too great to bear, and I proposed one of these two alternatives: Either the board of trustees should rent a smaller room for the youngest children and hire an assistant teacher to attend to their tuition, or to raise my salary from $125 to $150 per month, in which case I would employ an assistant at my own expense.

The Governor thought that either of these propositions was reasonable, and advised me to communicate them in writing to the board of trustees, stating that he would indorse said communication. I lost no time in attending to the matter, and soon received a request to be present at the next meeting of the board. The trustees expressed themselves in very complimentary terms with regard to my work, but said that the school funds did not permit any additional expense; that the American population was steadily increasing, and that they had been requested by many parents to employ female teachers ("school ma'ms," they called them) regularly trained for the purpose, and that they could procure the services of two ladies as described for the amount of my salary. Thereupon I tendered my resignation, and when the school reopened in September the two female teachers were on hand, and a hard task they found awaiting them. They soon perceived that about the first requisite toward successful teaching of these Mexican boys was a knowledge of their pupil's language, and they started to take lessons from me at once.

In the meantime I had been offered by the district judge and district attorney the position of interpretor and translator of the U. S. Court and District Court (later on called County Court) of the First Judicial District of Arizona, and had accepted the position, and when court opened in September I was in my place.

Inasmuch as about seven-eighths of the population consisted of Spanish-speaking people who knew nothing of the English language, there was a great deal of interpreting to be done in court, and many documents to be translated, and during court time I was kept very much occupied. For many ludicrous incidents which occurred, principally in the questions and answers passed between lawyers and the more or less ignorant Mexican witnesses, I shall relate a few only. The reader must bear in mind that the unsophisticated Mexican witnesses of the lower classes were for the most part overawed by the majesty of the court upon their very entrance, and that they were easily intimidated and befogged by any lawyer who attempted to browbeat them. And such lawyers there were and are to this day in plenty, and not only in Arizona. Add to this that the class of Mexicans I speak of had very little idea to exact time and measured distances, and my readers will readily understand that interrogations like the following were of frequent occurrence:

District Attorney: "You say you saw the shot fired?"
Witness: "I did."
 D. A.: "How far were you away from the man who was shot?"
Witness: ¿Quien sabe?" (who knows?).
(This expression is in universal use in Mexico. One will hardly ever here the expression "No se" (I do not know), which it really means to imply.)
D. A.: "Where you two yards distant, or three, or four?"
Witness: "That was about it. I think."
D. A.: "Or were you twenty yards away?"
Witness: "That also may be; I think it was."
Or the following:
D. A.: "What time of day was it when the shooting took place?"
Witness: ¿Quien sabe?" (who knows).

D. A.: "Was it in the morning or in the evening?"

Witness: "It must have been in the morning."

D. A.: "About what hour?"

Witness: "Well, the sun was about four yards high" (meaning above the horizon).

I shall never forget the absolute misery depicted upon the face of a culprit who was brought before the court to plead guilty or not guilty to a charge of murder. In those days the indictments found by the grand jury and drawn up by the district attorney read about like this: "The Territory of Arizona versus A. B. — Murder in the first degree. In this, that the said A. B. on or about September 20, 1872, in the town of Tubac, County of Pima, did, with a pistol, then and there held in his right hand, said pistol being then and there loaded with powder and ball, inflict upon one M. N., by discharging said pistol, then and there loaded as aforesaid, held in his right hand, as aforesaid, a deadly wound in the region of the stomach of said M. N., said wound being produced by the ball from the said pistol as aforesaid, from which wound the said M. N. died on September 4, 1872. All this against the peace and dignity of the commonwealth of the Territory of Arizona."

When I was asked to translate this document to the delinquent, a very ignorant half-breed, I requested permission of the judge to state the simple fact of the accusation to the accused, as he would never follow or be able to understand the language used in the indictment. The district attorney, however, interposed and insisted that I should read and translate the rigmarole, word for word.

Of course I had to obey. I translated slowly, now and then glancing upon the countenance of the accused, which became paler and paler, while his hair began to stand erect. As I proceeded he began to look like a monument of imbecility and blank endeavor, and when I had finished he cried out, while big tears flowed down his cheeks, with a trembling voice: "Good God, have I done all that?"

I remember one trial, the result of which gave everyone present a great deal of pleasure, besides furnishing much fun and causing much merriment. It completely nonplussed and demolished one of those browbeating, meddling pettifoggers who go around stirring up strife and litigation where peace and harmony reign. This trial, however, not involving a value greater than $175, was held before the lower or police court. The case was this: A man named Walker had hired a saddle horse from the recently-established livery stable of the town, in order to attend to some business at the San Pedro crossing, distant from the town about fifty-five miles. He returned on the following day about 4 p.m., and delivered his

264 / John Spring's Arizona

horse at the stable in apparently good and sound condition. During the forepart of the night the horse died from cause unknown.

Now this man Walker was a man of considerable means. A few days later one of those pettifogging sharks went to interview the keeper of the livery stable, and tried to induce him to bring suit against Walker for damages in the sum of $175, alleging that he, the lawyer, knew the employe of the livery stable well; that he was a simple, foolish Irishman, and that he could make him say anything upon the witness stand toward proving that the horse died in consequence of being ridden by Walker. At last the livery man was overpersuaded and the suit was filed.

When it came to trial the lawyer demanded a jury, which he used every means to select in the manner best calculated for his interests. The livery man himself had stipulated that he should not be called to testify, as he had discovered nothing wrong with the horse upon its return.

The "simple, foolish" Irishman was placed on the stand and asked if he knew Walker, the defendant, to which he replied in the affirmative.

The lawyer followed up his interrogatory:

Question: "How long have you known him?"

Answer: "About four years."

Question: "Have you ever seen him on horseback?"

Answer: "Frequently."

Question: "How does he ride?"

Answer: "How does he ride? A-straddle, of course."

(Titter in the audience; lawyer's face turning red.)

Question: "That is not what I mean. Does he ride slow or fast?"

Answer (With a drawl.): "Well now, that depends, you see. If he has a fast horse, he would probably go fast; while, if he has a slow horse, he would naturally go slow."

(Pronounced laughter in the audience; lawyer getting "hot.")

Question: (With forefinger pointed at witness.) "You must not trifle with this Court; remember, you are under oath. I will ask you again. Is the defendant Walker a fast or slow rider?"

Answer (very calmly and deliberately): "Well now, Judge, let me explain. If this here Walker is out with a party that travels slow like, he will ride slow. If they ride fast he will naturally go fast to keep up with him."

(More laughter in court).

Question: (With perfect fury): "You know very well that is not what I mean. How does Walker ride when he is alone?"

Answer (With perfect calm): "When he is alone? I was never with him when he was alone."

(Uncontrollable laughter in court. Case dismissed.)

TRIAL OF MAJOR DUFFIELD

During the month of October a very exciting scene was enacted in court, a scene characteristic of the wild and dangerous days in Arizona. It was the trial of the much-feared Major Duffield, mentioned in a former chapter. The fight between him and Maish had been passed upon, but later on he had openly challenged Maish to fight a duel, which in the Howell Code (the then law statutes of Arizona) came within the jurisdiction of the higher court.

When the old major was asked to stand up to have the indictment read to him the district attorney, a very bright lawyer, named McCaffrey, stepped forth and asked the clerk to defer his reading for a moment. He then addressed the court with the request that before the proceedings should begin, Major Duffield should be disarmed. No weapons were visible upon the person of the Major, but the whole community knew full well that he carried never less than four loaded pistols and a dirk or dagger with him hidden in his clothing. The district attorney had no sooner finished uttering his request when Duffield whipped out two Colt's revolvers pointing one straight at the Judge and the other at the Sheriff, saying: "The first man who touches me, falls dead." While he stood thus, the district attorney deftly stepped up behind him with a Derringer pistol, which he placed against his backbone and pulled the trigger. The cap snapped. Fortunately for McCaffrey, Duffield in his excitement and keeping the judge and sheriff covered, never saw or felt the attempt to undo him or else there would have been a dead district attorney in the courtroom. Well, the situation was rather embarrassing. The judge, however, although he had turned somewhat pale at first, soon resumed his presence of mind. He addressed Duffield thus: "Mr. Duffield, you are under bonds until your trial is over; I shall postpone this case until 1 o'clock p.m. on this day, when you will appear here again, and I warn you now to appear before this Court without any arms whatsoever, visible or hidden; you may now retire."

As soon as Duffield had left, the judge ordered all the officers of the court and all men drawn as members of the trial to put in appearance at 1 o'clock p.m., each man to come armed with a pistol or rifle, which they were to carry openly.

When the Court opened at the stated hour the people therein assembled looked more like a body of minutemen than anything else. When Duffield arrived and the court was declared open he walked up to the bar of the judge and stated on honor that he was completely disarmed, offering to divest himself of his clothing in order to give ocular proof of the truth of his assertion. Whether he had been overawed by the judge's order to the assembled court, which of course had been communicated to him by friends, or whether he had taken good advice from a well-meaning counselor, I do not know. At all events, the trial proceeded without any further violence or interruption. In consideration of his age he was not sentenced to confinement, but had to pay a very heavy fine and give bonds in the sum of $1,000 to keep the peace for the period of one year.

While for a time at least the depredations of the hostile Indians had almost entirely ceased in southern Arizona, principally on account of the chastisement inflicted upon the old Camp Grant or Es-ki-men-sin tribe by the citizens and Papagoes, this very security had attracted a large increase in the population of Tucson of that undesirable element known variously as "rounders," "footpads," and bad men of every description, who sought the isolation of Arizona as a refuge from pursuing justice.

Tucson is situated within eighty miles of the Mexican boundary, so that a criminal mounted on a swift horse could reach the latter in about twelve hours. If he had no mount he could easily reach the state of Sonora by following the Santa Cruz River during the night and hiding by day in the dense undergrowth on the river banks. The numerous Mexican murderers and thieves who had committed crimes in their country could pursue the same course, reversing the route.

Arizona had no Rangers in those days, like Texas, for instance. Sheriffs and their deputies were few and far apart; the treaty of extradition between the United States and Mexico unfortunately reads that "criminals may be exchanged between the two Nations upon the demand of either." (I think it still reads thus.) An American criminal, especially when he had money, could consider himself safe so far as extradition was concerned as soon as he reached the "line," unless indeed he should fall into the hands of Mexican bandits, in which case he had no more trouble ever after of any kind. The Mexican authorities, glad to be rid of their worst element, hardly ever demanded the delivery of one of their countrymen from the Governor of Arizona, and frequently disregarded the demands on our side for escaped malefactors, either averring that they could not be found or refusing downright to give them up. The unsettled state of the Mexican Republic in those days, and especially in the ever-recurring State revolutions in Sonora, was of course the principal cause of this unfortunate state of affairs, which allowed a continual stream of murderers and robbers to flow hither and thither.

It will therefore be readily understood that the town of Tucson, now an incorporated city with two regular policemen and a constable for the precinct, harbored many shady characters, and quite frequently its population awoke to find a dead man in the street, sometimes killed over night while seeking his habitation in the then unlighted streets, sometimes also, and this quite frequently, killed in a brawl over cards or women in a bar-room or dance-house, when his body would be simply dragged some distance away and abandoned. As everybody kept firearms in their houses, housebreaking was very rare.

At last a crime was committed of such an atrocious nature that the whole population was shocked to such a degree as to awaken them to the realization that something must be done, quick and sure, to intimidate the criminal element, which was in little fear of the tardily (if ever) administered hand of justice in the courts, and of the absolutely insecure jail.

In the fall of 1872, one Vicente Hernandez located with his wife in Tucson, and soon after established near the southern edge of the town in what is now South Meyer Street, a store of general merchandise, adding thereto somewhat later the business of a pawnbroker. Nearly all Mexicans being inveterate gamblers and nearly all, even the poorest of their women, possessing some jewels of gold or silver, this latter branch of the business was very remunerative, and Hernandez was soon well underway to become, if not a wealthy, still, a well-situated man. I will here observe that Mexicans of the lower classes will pay heavy interest on a small debt for years, rather than pay the debt itself, for the simple reason that the amount of interest paid is always smaller than the amount borrowed, for the payment of which they generally await a "windfall" which very often never comes, that might enable them to liquidate the indebtedness. I have known a Mexican teamster who owned his own wagon and team, and whose wife took in washing and ironing, who during a sickness in the family had borrowed ten dollars from a wealthy countryman, promising to pay a weekly interest of one dollar. Sure enough, every Saturday evening he went to pay his interest, and if he failed to do so the lender would send a reminder and collect it. These proceedings had gone on for two years and two weeks, in fact, till the borrower told me of it. Of course, a settlement was speedily effected. I also knew a woman who had borrowed four dollars, giving as a pledge her heavy gold earrings. She paid eighty cents interest every Saturday for over a year.

To return to our story. According to Mexican custom, which obtains to this day, of giving the store a name, Hernandez had named his business *Las Piedras Negras* (the black stones) and put up a sign accordingly. He came from New Mexico, where he had made the acquaintance of the Zeckendorfs, now, as then, the principal merchants of Tucson, who, knowing him to be an honest and industrious man and a person of gentlemanly appearance and manners withal, advanced him a good stock of merchandise to begin business with. Mrs. Hernandez was a lovely young wife of about thirty years of age, very pretty, refined and charitable, qualities which soon made her beloved by rich and poor.

Their business was carried on in the same house in which they lived; it was a rather long adobe house, of which the store and pawnbroker shop occupied about twenty-four by fourteen feet in width. Two doors led into this establishment, one fronting on the street and the other upon a vacant lot. Windows there were none. A door led from the store through a partition wall into the adjoining living-room, which was parlor and sleeping room in one, being about twenty feet long. At the end opposite to the store there was a door, the only one in the whole rear wall, which led into the corral or yard, where, about ten yards to the rear of the house, was situated a small kitchen, in which the only help employed by Hernandez, a young Indian girl, sometimes slept. In the middle of the wall, running back along a side street, there was a small window protected by upright wooden bars. From the rear corner of this wall an unfinished adobe wall ran around the lot, inclosing it completely up to the outer rear corner of the store. This corral wall was only about five feet high, and a person looking over it could see into the livingroom, provided that its rear door was open. My wife had met Mrs. Hernandez several times, as they both belonged to the Woman's Association for Mutual Benevolence, which had been started in those early days on account of much disease and poverty being prevalent among the lowly Mexicans, and from these meetings had sprung up an intimate friendship between the two. Hernandez and myself were on very friendly terms also, and the two families were in consequence on visiting terms not only, but we had all four a real affection for each other.

When the long court vacation began in June, 1872, which was also the beginning of the school vacation, the well-situated heads of families requested and strenuously urged me to open a private school for boys during the three months' vacation. The board of trustees of the public school kindly placed at my service for the purpose their school room and desks, and thus I taught once more upon the former premises, although not in the government's employ. . . . On account of the extremely hot weather during that season, I had reduced the hours to only four per diem with the acquiescence of the parents, who remunerated me most liberally for my services.

Thus came the third day of August, 1873. I was just leaving the schoolhouse and had put the key in my pocket about 11 o'clock a.m., when I noticed considerable excitement in the street, several people shouting to each other and all within sight running towards the southern end of the city. Among the crowd hastening in that direction I recognized Mr. Appel, the deputy sheriff; I was soon by his side, and asked him the cause of all this commotion. He was an intimate friend of mine, and one of his sons, now a lawyer in Los Angeles, was one of my pupils. He said that the sheriff's office had just received notice that during the previous night the Piedras Negras store had been broken into and the Hernandez people murdered; that the sheriff was temporarily absent on duty in the country. Within a few minutes we reached the house of the unfortunate people; it was already surrounded by a big crowd of men, women, and children seeking access into the building. The front and side doors were still locked, but the rear door leading into the yard stood wide open, and through it we could see inside, where many people had gathered, to gaze upon the ghastly scene which there presented itself to their eyes.

Fortunately the justice of the peace arrived immediately after us. Taking in the situation at a glance, he appointed forthwith two stout men as acting or deputy constables, and we proceeded to clear the house, stationing one man at the door, who should cause all persons to step over and not upon the door sill, where we had noticed two plain imprints of bloody feet. As soon as we had succeeded in clearing the premises, we proceeded to investigate the situation. It was a most horrible spectacle we beheld. Evidently, it being in the hight [sic.] of the summer season, Hernandez and wife had followed the universal custom of abandoning their regular bed, where the mattresses then available were too hot to bear, and had spread upon the floor a large Mexican mat called "petate," covered with a sheet only, upon which they would lie cool, if hard, using another sheet as covering. This bedding had, as the situation of the mat still showed, been spread near the rear door, which was probably left wide open or partly open, to admit air into the poorly-ventilated room. Hernandez's body lay about four feet from this door, the lower part of his body being wrapped in the folds of the much-crumpled-up sheet that had served as a covering. Near him lay a heavy club, roughly made of the knotty mesquite wood prevalent thereabouts. The upper or thick part of the club showed a coagulated mass of blood, brains, and hair. The skull was fractured in several places, and brains had oozed out. A deep cut with a sharp, large knife had severed his jugular vein, and several other cuts about the region of the heart showed that he, being a very powerful man, had probably made many spasmodic movements before he became quite still, and that these additional cuts were intended to hasten his death. His whole body and face were besmeared and bespattered with blood.

The body of the wife lay about in the middle of the room, covered by a long night-robe only. Her skull was also fractured; but she had only one knife cut, severing the jugular vein. Several bloody tracks made by bare feet led through the partition door into the store, where bloody fingermarks were discovered upon the counter, on the money drawer and some other places. The goods upon the shelves were disturbed but little, but the money drawer and the receptacle holding the pawned jewelry were empty. Mr. Wm. Zeckendorf, who was thoroughly familiar with the status of the whole business, stated that there were many pistols missing and a valuable new saddle and bridle. He examined the cash-book, which was posted up to date, which showed that upon retiring the cash on hand in the drawer or till was $37. No large sums were ever kept in the store, but were delivered and locked up in the safe of Zeckendorf Bros., as fast as they accumulated.

From all appearances, putting one and one together, as the saying is, we came to the conclusion that the crime could not have been committed by less than two men, of which the man handling the club must have been a powerful individual, judging from the force of the blows. It was also natural to suppose that some one was employed to act as watch against possible passers-by and incidentally to prevent the Indian girl sleeping perhaps that night in the kitchen near by, from giving the alarm; should she be awakened by the possible outcries of the victims. We surmised (correctly as we found when the facts were developed) that a watch thus employed would be stationed at or upon that part of the corral wall which immediately adjoined the upper end of the living-room, in whose upper corner the sleepers lay. Hence could be seen everything around the building except the immediate front of it, but people reaching this part of the front street could be seen approaching it from either direction. Over this part of the wall you could also see into the interior of the Hernandez living room, through the rear door, watch the proceedings of the assassins and send the note of alarm if it became necessary. We further surmised that the crime was perpetrated in this manner: That the two (or more) assassins first ascertained if the Hernandez people were asleep. This they could readily do, as the rear door was undoubtedly open to admit air. Then they entered noiselessly and immediately proceeded to knock the man senseless, whereupon they knifed him; the lady, awakened by the blows dealt out to her husband, jumped up and ran toward the middle of the room where the man with the club reached her and knocked her into insensibility, keeping her down till the other with the knife had done with her husband and come to sever her jugular vein. Then they entered the store and began sacking their booty, for which purpose they had lighted a new candle; from the burnt or absent part of which we calculated that they must have remained in the store nearly half an hour.

As we were clearing out the premises of people, my attention was attracted by somebody saying in Spanish: "Let us see now if these American smarties will discover the criminals." I turned toward the speaker, and saw that he was an ill-looking, thin, yellow, small, unwashed Mexican with the appearance of a sick cornstalk and all the "ingredients" of a despicable "sneak" stamped clearly upon him.

It was evident that the robbers had found the key of the rear door sticking in the lock, for they had locked this door upon leaving the premises, and thrown the key away; it was found later in the corral behind the kitchen. The Indian girl had slept that night at the house of a sick relative. When she arrived in the morning she began, as usual, to attend to her culinary duties. At first she took no alarm at the protracted non-appearance of her employers, as it frequently happened that her mistress was out late at night attending a social party, in which case Hernandez always waited until she rose, before he sat down to breakfast. But when the sun rose higher and higher and neither her master nor mistress put in an appearance and the store remained closed, she hesitatingly sought the house of some neighbors and communicated to them her feeling that something was wrong in the house. The neighbors congregated with other neighbors, the matter was discussed, much time was lost, until finally the keeper of a small store and liquor shop, instead of notifying the authorities, took it upon himself to break into the rear door, with the result as described.

By this time the hour had reached 11 a.m., which gave the assassins, taking about midnight as the probable hour of the criminals' nefarious work, from ten to eleven hours in which they could have put themselves far away from immediate pursuit. The premises around the house had been trampled over by many hundred feet, and the idea, therefore, of seeking for their tracks when leaving the house, was out of the question.

The sheriff, who returned from the country about noon, immediately appointed six deputies who could use every endeavor toward apprehending the perpetrators of the atrocious crime. The murdered people having been respected and beloved by young and old of every nationality, nearly every one constituted himself for the time being a policeman or detective. More than twenty men, among them the best trailers of the community, set out on horseback in all directions to cut off the criminals, if they had become fugitives, from reaching the frontier.

The principal citizens, to the number of about thirty, formed a committee of public safety, hired men to assist in the search for the murderers, promising large rewards for their discovery and apprehension, and pledging themselves to stand by each other "whatever might be the outcome of the business." It was tacitly understood that if the assassins were apprehended, the judicial authorities would for the time being be deprived of their power and the criminals would be, after a careful examination and unquestionable proofs as to their guilt having been obtained, tried and sentenced by the people, which the said committee represented. Much as I have always been opposed to violence of any kind, except, of course, legitimate warfare, I joined that committee and stood by its decisions and helped to execute them to the end. The chairman of the committee was Mr. Wm. Zeckendorf.

Towards the evening of that day a Mexican washer-woman entered a small grocery of the town to purchase some sugar and coffee, in payment of which she offered several of those small, oblong pieces of paper, officially known in those days of greenbacks as fractional currency and, by the people at large, at least on the Pacific coast, irreverently designated as shinplasters. Two of these paper quarters bore spots very much resembling those produced by the touch of bloody hands, or rather fingertips. Now it was generally known that considerable of this fractional currency had been in the money drawer of the Piedras Negras store. The woman was detained in conversation by the grocery man while his boy went for Mr. Zeckendorf. He was promptly on hand, and requested the woman to accompany him to his office on Main Street, where he managed to hide the Sheriff behind a small partition wall. The woman, who lived in a small shack on the bank of the river, half a mile from town, had as yet heard nothing of the murder, but had, after finishing her day's work, come to the store in search of the groceries without holding any conversation whatsoever on her way. Mr. Zeckendorf, who knew her personally, engaged her in conversation as to her children, etc., and gradually led up to the question whence she had obtained the money with which she paid for the groceries. I think she was offered a drink of mescal. Quite without suspicion as to the importance of her narrative, she began to relate that the money was given her by a woman living in a shack in her vicinity on the river. Her tongue once loosened, she went on to talk, being adroitly questioned by her interlocutor, about that woman who, she said, lived with a rather handsome, nearly white, young man called Sahuaripa; that the said Sahuaripa had acted rather strangely during the night after he had returned at a late hour, or rather early morning hour; that soon after arriving home he had asked for clean clothing, had gone into the river and bathed and washed himself, had put on the clothes, but failed to bring back the soiled ones; that then he had lain down; but kept tossing on his bed, rising now and then, lighting a candle, examining his feet and hands, and again returning to the river to wash them. When daylight appeared he had given the woman some money, about four or five dollars among which were the paper quarters that she, the narrator, had brought to town. Mr. Zeckendorf made the woman a small present, and, cautioning her against mentioning their conversation to anybody, dismissed her.

Less than one hour afterward, Sahuaripa was in the jail, loaded with heavy chains and guarded by four of our committee. Later on, after the street had become emptied of people, we took him to the house of the

Hernandez and began to compare his feet and hands with the bloody tracks and marks left on the floor and counter. Some of them were without question made by himself. From the moment that he saw that his feet and fingers fitted exactly into the signs left by him, he weakened. He was young still, and not a hardened criminal. We then led him to the bodies, which had been handsomely prepared for their last resting place by order of Mr. Zeckendorf immediately after the coroner's inquest was over (the verdict was delayed for 24 hours). We uncovered the faces of the murdered couple and asked Sahuaripa if he would swear by the holy cross (the Mexican oath) that had had no hand in the killing of the two victims before him. He shuddered, and trembling visibly, said: "For God's sake, lead me away; I will tell you everything."

When we returned with him to the jail, he forthwith began his confession of the crime the perpetration of which had taken place almost exactly in the manner we had surmised from appearances. His accomplice, really the concocter of the whole plan and leader in its execution, was one Cordoba, a half-Indian from Sonora. He had handled the club, upon which Sahuaripa gave the death wounds with a butcher knife purchased by him at a hardware store he indicated, and then sharpened upon a flat stone on the edge of the river. One Fiehi was taken into the plot to stand guard, or rather sit watching upon the low wall adjoining the living room of the Hernandez. A fourth man was taken into the conspiracy, but he had weakened and failed to put in an appearance at the important last moment.

Sahuaripa told us that neither Cordoba nor Fiehi had left town, inasmuch as they had not yet divided their booty, except the cash, of which each received one third. He told us exactly the spot where they had buried the jewelry, pistols, and saddle, and all these things were found and unearthed during the night by members of our committee. He also told us where Cordoba and Fiehi generally lived, and where they would probably be found at the present hour (about 11 p.m.). Cordoba was found, as indicated, in a gambling saloon. He was a rather short man, but powerfully built, with a very dark complexion, being about one-half or three-quarters Opata Indian. At first he tried to resist arrest, but was soon overpowered and taken to jail. Fiehi was found in his more than modest habitation, near the Papago village, on the outskirts of the town, where he was occupied in getting rid of his plunder in a game of cancan.

Cordoba was also taken to the house of the murdered people and his foot being placed upon the bloody tracks on the doorsill and his hand upon the marks of the door-frame he ceased the violent protestations of his innocence in which he had at first indulged. Fiehi enveloped himself in a complete state of stolid silence and misery. The money in the pockets of each, considering the expenditures made by them during the day, showed that their division of the cash spoils had been fair and equal.

As there was no question whatever as to the guilt of our three prisoners, who were all heavily chained and whom we guarded personally, we notified them that they must prepare for death, abandoning all hope there and then of escape through trickery of lawyers, or insecurity of the jail, as we, the committee representing the people of Tucson, would surely hang them during the forenoon of fourth of April. Upon being asked if they desired a priest to take their confession and give them his spiritual advice, Sahuaripa and Fiehi availed themselves of the father's good offices; Cordoba persisted in sullen silence, and treated the priest with disdain. My astonishment, when Fiehi had been brought to the jail, where I was one of the watchers, was considerable when I discovered that he was the self-same fellow who had remarked at noon while the people were ordered away from the scene of the crime: "Let us see now if these American smarties will discover the criminals."

Loud and long sounded the bells of the church during the morning hours of that fourth of April, 1873, while the funeral procession, bearing the remains of the murdered couple to their last resting place, wound its slow and solemn march through the streets of Tucson, while the ten men selected by the thirty as a committee of execution prepared the gallows in front of the court house, which formed one side of a large, open space, in Mexican towns generally called the "plaza." Two strong posts forked at the top had been firmly fixed into the ground; and from fork to fork there lay a stout piece of timber with four ropes dangling from it. Four, because there happened to be a twice-convicted murderer, an American named Willis, in the jail, under sentence of death by the regularly appointed Court. The Committee of Thirty decided that he should suffer the penalty of death then and there, as he had escaped punishment for his first crime through legal technicalities and had nearly made good his escape from the insecure jail after being sentenced, for his second most atrocious murder committed in cold blood, to be hanged. His coffin had already been prepared, and stood in the jail yard, but a reprieve had postponed his legal execution.

The whole population, excepting only the lame, blind, and bedridden sick, had accompanied the remains of the Hernandez couple to the cemetery, and when the funeral rites were ended and the graves covered up, this whole multitude wended its way, as if by command or guided by an unseen power, toward the plaza, in the middle of which a small tribune had been erected. Upon its platform presently appeared Mr. Zeckendorf and addressed the assembled crowd. He made a full statement of the crime as committed, and enumerated in detail all the evidence the committee had obtained, acting without haste, but with prudence and care, until the full guilt of the three arrested men was proven beyond any reasonable doubt. He dwelt upon the unsettled state of the country, the unsafety of the jail, the slowness and uncertainty of the judicial proceedings and the ease with which escaped prisoners could forever disappear across the frontier. He concluded his remarks, which had been listened to in perfect silence, with the words: "I now ask you, the people of Tucson here assembled, what punishment have the murderers deserved?"

"Death!" sounded from a thousand voices. Mr. Mariano Molina, a prominent Mexican citizen of the town, then ascended to the tribune and addressed his countrymen in their language, using about the same terms as his predecessor. Again came the question: "What shall we do with these assassins? What say you the Mexican people of Tucson?"

"Que mueran!" (they must die) again sounded from that vast multitude. Mr. Zeckendorf then gave the signal from the tribune to the Committee of Execution at the jail door. Two wagons which had been held ready near by were drawn under the cross pole of the gallows, the delinquents were brought out, hoisted upon the vehicles, two upon each, and their slings placed about their necks.

At this state of affairs, Cordoba, who had weakened somewhat, or at least had lost much of his bravado during the last half hour, requested to be heard, as he wished to confess a few previous murders committed by him some years before, one at Yuma, the other in the Salt River country. However, as he made long introductory remarks, some one in the crowd cried out: "Hasten, make an end, the military are coming from the fort!" Upon this the wagons were quickly pulled forward from under the feet of the condemned men, and they hung in air. As we had left the heavy chains on their feet in order to expedite their dying and thus reduce their death struggles, nothing was perceptible of their agony except a few shivers that ran through their bodies. Their faces had been covered by black calico caps. During the execution perfect stillness reigned all over the plaza, where fully two thousand people were assembled. The only sound faintly perceptible was a humming as of many bees; it proceeded from the Mexican women reading under their breath the Mass for the Dead.

At 4 o'clock in the afternoon the bodies were taken down. The sheriff and his deputies, who had disappeared, as well as the judge and district attorney, from the town since early morning, had returned. A coroner's jury was called to set upon the case, and rendered the verdict that the four criminals came to their death by hanging at the hands of the population of Tucson, and that said hanging was justifiable.

The result of this verdict was, of course, a decided *nolle prosequi* from the district attorney.

The immediate consequence of this lynching, probably the most methodical and orderly undertaking of the kind that ever took place anywhere, was a clearing out of town by many individuals appertaining to what is generally designated as the undesirable hoodlum element; neither was there another murder perpetrated for many years thereafter within the town of Tucson.

While preparations were being made in 1876 in Tucson for the centennial celebration of our Independence, the Committee of Arrangements requested that I write and deliver the historical oration upon that occasion, and furnish a copy to be filed in the Library of Congress, where all such productions were to be preserved, and I acceded.

My wife had been suffering for some time with rheumatism and as her heart had always been weak, her physician advised me to take her into Sonora, Mex., where at Ymuris, a small town on the Sonora River, near the larger town of Magdalena, on the same river, there is a hot spring said to be beneficial to those who bathe in it. I began preparations for the trip, my brother-in-law offering a good two-horse team and spacious wagon with canvas cover and his own services as driver. My mother-in-law, as good and kind an old lady as ever lived, and my wife's elder sister, Refugio, were also to accompany us. Four mounted and well-armed men were hired as escort to protect us, until we should reach our destination.

Zeckendorf Bros., the largest commercial establishment of the Territory at the time, was then contemplating a dissolution of co-partnership. The brothers had large amounts due them in Sonora and asked me to undertake collection of those debts. I promised that I would try. They gave me bills amounting to about $25,000, with the necessary power in writing, certified to by the Mexican consul at Tucson.

On the evening before my departure, which was on July 10, 1876, an attorney of Tucson came to me with a proposition which at first appeared very singular. He said: "If you possibly can, after giving due attention to your wife's condition, go to Hermosillo, I wish you would hunt up in the archives there a land grant or title deed given and signed by King Philip VII of Spain. If you do not find such a document there, you will have to go to Ures, the Capital, where you will find undoubtedly one or more. Be sure that you have before you a genuine, bona fide document. Arrange for permission to translate such deed, or deeds if you find several, and to have them photographed." He handed me a considerable sum of money and added: "Be sure that you obtain a genuine document and a good photograph; spare no money; I will hand you a like sum if you return successful."

Our trip to Ymuris was accomplished in four days. We crossed the frontier where Nogales now stands. A customs house inspector stopped us for a few moments, inquiring into our business, took a look into the wagon, and said : "Está bien, paren!" (It is all right: pass!)

Of course, I had not expected to find a hotel ready to receive us at the hot springs, but still I thought I could reasonably expect some place of shelter near, as my informants had written that there was plenty accommodation to be found at Ymuris for any number of persons. The town of Ymuris was situated upon the top of a high, steep, rocky hill, a full mile distant from the spring, which was in the valley. I rented a small adobe building, which I proceeded to make habitable. This was a matter of necessity, as my wife's affliction had assumed grave proportions; her lower limbs being useless, so that she had to be carried to and from the springs for the first two days. After three or four days we began to perceive decided improvement in her condition, and before the end of one month her health was completely restored, and she returned with her mother, brother and sister to her children at Tucson, and I made ready to proceed to Hermosillo to attend to the business entrusted to me.

As far as the collection of bills was concerned, my efforts were, if not entirely futile, very far from successful. The man does not live who, coming from another country, has ever succeeded in collecting moneys due in Sonora, in any sum worthy of mention.

With the land-grant business I had better success. The Capital was being moved from Ures to Hermosillo at the time of my arrival. After I had examined the documents on hand among those archives that had already made the transit to Hermosillo, and had not found what I needed, I interrogated a state official as to the nature of the documents remaining at Ures, and learned that the document I was looking for was there, locked up in a strong box. After a very "private and intimate" interview with this gentleman, he gave me a letter to the secretary of the governor, and advised me to take a good photographer with me from Hermosillo.

On August 20 I entered the diligencía (stagecoach) for Ures, and after a galloping ride reached the latter place in the night of the twenty-first. The secretary of the governor received me in the most polite manner, and readily granted my requests. The document was quickly found, carefully translated, and then photographed upon eight separate plates. Fortunately it was a grant of land made by King Philip VII of Spain to a person of meritorious services in subduing hostile Indians and furthering the development of the country then called New Spain; fortunately, I say, because I discovered later the object in view for obtaining the photo-

graphs, when I saw them in the Courts of Arizona, before whom one
Reevis claimed the so-called Peralta grant, which embraced the best
lands from nine miles above Tucson to and embracing the town site of
the present city of Phoenix. The document offered in evidence by Reevis
on behalf of his wife, whose maiden name was Peralta, purported to have
been issued to an ancestor in direct line of this woman, for services rendered in the manner above described, by King Philip VII, at the same
time bestowing upon the grantee Peralta a title of nobility — "Baron of
the Colorados."

Later on, before a court in New Mexico, these photographs were
instrumental in proving the deception practiced by Reevis in presenting
his fraudulent title deed or land grant, and he received a sentence of ten
years in the State's prison.

ADVENTURES OF DOCTOR THORNE

The secretary of the Governor was a highly educated gentleman,
with the polite and elegant manners of the old school, and he extended
to me the hospitality of his house.

It was at the hospitable board of the Governor's secretary that I had
the good fortune to meet a gentleman with whom I had long desired to
become acquainted, knowing that he was one of the very few white people
who had lived among the Apaches in their wild state, and could therefore
give reliable information as to them, their habits, home life, and perhaps
of the inner life.

This gentleman was Doctor Thorne, then a resident of Casa Blanca,
three miles above Socorro, New Mexico. He was visiting Sonora, and had
called at the Governor's office. I requested the doctor to relate his adventures of early days. He complied very willingly. My diary, in which the
main features of his narrative were recorded at the time, shows that this
meeting occurred on August 22, 1876, and the story is as follows:

"You know that the Gadsden treaty went into active effect in 1854.
Before that, all of Arizona belonged to Mexico, and the Apaches had
been hostile to the Mexicans ever since 1846. In 1852, I was one of a
party of seven Georgians who left Marysville, Cal., by the southern overland route, to go to New Orleans. We first proceeded to San Diego, and
there recruited our stock and put in good order our ambulance and
wagon, in which we journeyed the long, tedious and dangerous trip across
the deserts. We reached Yuma without experiencing any adventure or
mishap worthy of note, and remained there a week. We sold our wagon
there, and upon a bright morning in early spring, we resumed our route
with the ambulance and six horses, making easy stages eastward.

"I had come prepared for sickness and accidents, and my medicine chest and surgical instruments were always convenient and in perfect order and condition. We were well aware of the danger incurred in entering the Apache country, but trusted to good luck to escape the vigilance of the hostiles.

"Our last camp was made at Gila Bend, and the following day promised us safety, for we were gradually approaching the friendly Maricopas and Pimas; every mile lessened the chance of being attacked by the roaming Apaches. It was then late in the afternoon, and we were yet a long distance from Maricopa Wells, when we were suddenly 'jumped' by the Indians. It came like a clap of thunder from a clear sky and the surprise was absolute.

"At the first shot the driver dropped the reins and fell forward, dead. The horses became frightened, and in turning abruptly around upset the ambulance; the front wheels became uncoupled, and when I extricated myself from the fallen vehicle I saw some of the Indians making off with the horses. The Indians gave us no time for defense; we were disarmed in a moment and then they took me and one of my companions, named Brown, in their midst and urged us forward in a northerly direction. Everything was done so quickly that I had not even time to ascertain the fate of the remaining members of our party. I think, however, that they were killed then and there, perhaps from the first fire. As to us two, we had no doubt that we should be subjected to horrible torture.

"After dark a halt was made; we were stripped of our clothing and forced to march until near daybreak, when we reached a stream, probably the Gila River. Here we camped, hidden in the dense bushes, securely secreted, during the entire day. The Indians evidently feared discovery by the Maricopas, and were not anxious for battle with superior numbers.

"At night we crossed the river and took an easterly course, traveling two days, when we came to a stream of sparkling, clean water, whose borders were timbered with cottonwoods. In this grove we camped. The Indians made a big fire and by signal smoke informed the scattered members of the tribe where they were located. Three or four days later Indians began to arrive from all directions with their squaws and children.

"In the meantime there was an Indian boy in camp with a broken knee-cap from a recent wound, who made a great deal of fuss while a squaw was dressing the wound. I told an Indian who spoke the Spanish language tolerably well, that I could cure that boy. The Indian repeated my words to his chief, who sent one of his sub-chiefs, who spoke Spanish, to bring me before him. The chief questioned me as to my ability to cure the wound. I told him that the leg would have to be amputated to save the boy's life, as gangrene had already set in about the knee-cap; that

I could amputate the leg without causing the boy any pain if he (the chief) had in his possession what was carried in the ambulance, meaning, of course, my medicine chest and case of instruments. The Chief arose and talked earnestly to the Indians about him, and in less than an hour every article taken from the ambulance, even to the bridles and pieces of the reins and harness, was arranged in a semi-circle before me. I gathered up all of my own effects, finding my pocket case and instruments undisturbed. On the following day I administered chloroform to the boy, and amputated the injured limb. To the great surprise and wonder of the Indians gathered about to witness the operation, the nervous and troublesome lad never moved a muscle while under the knife. This remarkable feat at once raised me in the estimation of the Indians to the exalted station of supernatural being, and old Chief Pedro immediately ordered his followers to dress my feet, which were much cut up and blistered from the long walk over rocks and rough ground. He also caused me to be provided with clothing; he had a shade built of willows close to his own habitation for my exclusive use, and had meat cooked for me. The Chief even told me that all my wants, as far as in his power lay, should be supplied; that he would not allow his men to either torture or kill me, provided I made no attempt to escape. He then appointed a strong twelve-year-old boy as my personal follower or servant. The boy accompanied me henceforth in all my walks about the camp and beyond its limits; but I soon discovered that all my movements and doings were faithfully reported to the chief daily, and that the boy was as much a spy as servant. As he followed me like my own shadow and was very swift of foot, an attempt to escape on my part would have been sheer suicidal folly.

"I asked the Indians what had become of my co-operative, Brown, from whom we had parted company the first night after our capture, together with a part of the original attacking party. They pointed to the west and said they had all gone to join another band.

"We remained in this camp, supposed to be about at the mouth of the Verde River, about a month, then we began moving from camp to camp from time to time, always in an easterly direction, and over a big range of mountains. During the summer of 1852, we remained in the mountains. In the fall we went into the valley where another stream emptied into Salt River — on the north side — and remained there all Winter. The boy servant and the amputated boy were my constant companions. I taught them to speak English and Spanish, and they taught me the Apache language, which is exceedingly simple, but on account of its many guttural and hissing sounds not easy of pronunciation for us.

"The following spring, summer and winter were passed at another camp about two days travel to the eastward, on a river or large creek. In

Santa Ana 1896.

Felicidad !

—Courtesy Mrs. Tony Urias

A card made by John Spring for his daughter Ana María, in honor of her saint's day, *el dia de Santa Ana,* or "the day of St. Anne," July 26, 1896.

the region between that stream and the White Mountains we spent four years. The Indians roamed about an area of perhaps one hundred miles square during that time. We returned to the first big mountain we had crossed after the boy's leg was amputated, to bury one of their chiefs who had died there. Then all the Indians moved out of that mountain to another high mountain farther east, having a superstition that death in a camp portends misfortune. In this mountain we made a permanent camp.

"One day I went out hunting with my two youthful companions, with bows and arrows, and the boy with the willow leg I had made for him, accidentally stepped into a crevice and broke it. The Indians thought this to be a bad omen, and at once moved camp eastward, one day's travel, and camped in a cottonwood flat, where they planted beans. At this camp the running waters of the Salt River could be heard at night. I went out hunting — the only pastime we had in fair weather — almost every day with one of my usual companions, and on one of these trips the boy picked up a nugget of gold from the bare bedrock in a wash, west of some small, very red hills. At this place there might have been perhaps $5,000 in gold nuggets in sight. By that time I had become so disgusted with the Indians and my life among them that I evaded all contact with them whenever possible, and I told the boy that the nugget was of no account. The young Indian replied that it was good, and that his people could procure powder and caps with nothing else. I told him to throw it away, that it was of no value, and walked away, apparently unconcerned; but from that time forward I took close observations of the surrounding country, in order that I might recognize the place again if ever I obtained my freedom.

"After I had resided with the Indians nearly seven years, the Apaches and Navajos made a treaty of peace between the tribes, and the Indians with whom I dwelt journeyed to the eastern side of the Mogollon Mountains to participate in the grand ratification of peace, and to complete its conditions. The Navajos were to give the Apaches eight hundred sheep for the return of some of their squaws held in captivity, and to forever remain at peace. The meeting was a pleasant one and the exchange was fully completed, when, to make the event more memorable, a vast quantity of teswin was brewed, and the Indians all got drunk and began fighting. The Navajos succeeded in overcoming the Apaches and taking away from them the sheep just delivered. In the confusion of the melee I succeeded in making good my escape to the Navajos, who left me full liberty to go whenever I desired. I made my way to Cuvero, a little town near Fort Wingate, N.M., and to civilization. I settled afterwards at my present place of residence, Casa Blanca, near Sonora.,

"I made several efforts to find the place where I saw the gold, and bankrupted myself on two different occasions in outfitting expeditions

Continuing a lifelong interest in art, John Spring painted this floral piece in Hampton, Virginia, during his later years, to send to his "darling grandchild," Ana Barreda, in Tucson on her birthday, October 17, 1908.

at Soccoro to find it. The first time I became snowblind in the Mogollon range of mountains, and had to be taken home; on the second attempt the party became disgusted because I could not find the White Mountains, and would proceed no further. Some of the old Mexicans in the party contended that they had already gone close to the borders of California, and turned back when we reached Cibicu Creek."

Being questioned as to the treatment the Apaches inflicted upon their prisoners, Dr. Thorne said that although he had seen much plunder brought into camp from time to time by roving bands, he had never in the seven years seen a male prisoner brought in, either white or Indian. The Apaches take no adult male prisoners. The few squaws and children that were captured were not made to suffer any ill-treatment, were soon embodied in the tribe, and lived among them as members of the families to whom they were assigned.

Questioned as to the manner of living of the savages, Dr. Thorne had nothing to relate that has not already been stated in a former chapter. As to the inner life (the doctor smiled at my expression), he simply stated that they had none; that their whole mind-power was concentrated upon a mass of superstitious omens, to counteract which the men indulged from time to time in dances consisting of going round and round in a circle while they slapped their thighs with their open hands, to a sort of rhythmic measure beaten out on a crude drum, accompanied by rattles made of hollowed gourds partly filled with pebbles.

LEGEND OF ARIZONA NATURAL BRIDGE

"They have, however," resumed the doctor, "many traditions and legends, among which there is one that I have heard the old men repeat again and again to the listening youngsters. It is connected with the well-known Natural Bridge in Arizona, which spans Pine Creek, a mountain tributary of the Salt River, and in an air line is about sixty miles from Phoenix, the direction being northeast. The scenic beauty of this natural wonder is unsurpassed on the Pacific coast. The bridge spans the precipitous walls of the mountain torrent, 170 feet above the water; it is 80 feet in length across, and varies in width up and down the stream from 300 to 400 feet. The limestone walls rise from the water's edge in architectural symmetry to the span above, forming a perfect arch, festooned with stalactites of varying sizes and fantastic shapes.

"This bridge, the Apaches say, once formed the lower barrier of a crystal-like mountain lake, the waters of which broke gently over it and formed a magnificent waterfall. The lake was inhabited by a monster of great size and power, whom only a few of the Apaches ever saw in its mountain home; but while they feared, they also revered this mountain monarch, to whom they attributed their immunity from invasion by the Comanches and other warlike tribes to the north and east. It lived upon deer, antelope, and other animals which, apprehensive of no danger, came to the lake to drink; it was also fed with large quantities of fish brought by the hawks whom it commanded; caught, and carried from the creek below to satiate its delicate taste.

"Large numbers of these fishhawks were constantly employed in this duty, and their weird shrieks and exulting outcries contributed in a great degree towards repelling the superstitious Indians from making any very close investigations of the lake, while the surrounding mountains were given up directly to the control and uses of this enormous animal. This latter is described by the medicine man of the tribe whose crude drawings assist in giving a faint idea of the form of the monster, as having been over two hundred feet in length, with the head and neck of a serpent, the pectoral fins of a very large fish, the legs and body of an immense Gila monster, terminating in a double tail, jointed and flexible like that of a scorpion, but having affixed at the two ends very large and sharp-pointed arrowheads.

"The head of this monster was flat like that of the rattlesnake, but the jaws were not so heavy, and a sharp-pointed crown projected above the intersection of the neck, like the horned toad of Arizona. In addition to the two eyes of the snake, a large eye was in the middle of the forehead, and added ferocity to the appearance of the serpent. Its head was about fourteen feet long and ten feet wide, while the neck, the forepart of which was covered with long red-brown hair, was fully ninety feet in length. The tails were at least seventy feet long, and independent of each other, churning the waters into foam when the animal was excited. The lower part of the neck, the entire body, legs and tails, were covered with heavy scales, an impenetrable armor.

"The Apaches deny having been exclusively a mountain tribe at that remote period, and deny that they occupied their whole time in hunting and fighting; but claim that they occupied all the valleys of Southern Arizona and tilled the soil. The products of the field were exchanged for the game brought to them by the highlandmen, and all were as one family, living in harmony. Quan-i-wah-le, ruling chief of the Apaches, had his camp on the banks of Salt River, a short distance above its junction with the Gila. According to the tradition he was very fond of fish, and being ingenious had a dam constructed to prevent their ascending the river further, and to better enable the squaws to capture them.

"Without warning or previous rains a tremendous flood came down the Salt River, sweeping away the Indian tepees for many miles on either side of that stream, drowning thousands of people, as well as the greater portion of the livestock they possessed, and utterly destroying their irrigating canals. The flood passed away as suddenly as it had come, and while the people wondered much, and mourned deeply their losses of kindred and property, they could not account for the mysterious freshet, and set about repairing the damage as best they could. While these repairs were going forward, a squaw who had been down the river fishing came back and told the Apaches that she had seen the Mountain Lake monster; that it had devoured one horse before her eyes and had attacked another one before she was out of sight. The woman was immediately taken in charge for being a witch. The council decided that she was indeed bewitched, and having become a sorceress was the guilty cause of all the suffering that had befallen the tribe. She was ordered to be tortured and burned that night. The entire tribe was made happy by the opportunity offered to appease the wrath of the Great Spirit; but a dusty and perspiring runner came from the camp at Yah-k-ni-yel, a sub-chief, located with his people in the Pinto Mountains, distant ten to twelve miles from the Natural Bridge, the nearest point to it at which the Apaches ventured to live. He told them that three days before, the Indians there felt the earth shake and heard a mighty roaring in the direction of Mountain Lake; that after waiting two days warriors were sent to ascertain the cause of the disturbance. The messengers found that a mighty hole had been wrought in the barrier of solid rock, that the water had vanished, and the monster had disappeared. The news caused general consternation, and the pleasure of torturing a fellow-being to death was postponed. Three squaws told that while searching for wood with which to burn the witch, they had seen two of their companions seized and devoured by the great serpent. Through fear of being themselves burned as witches, they would have said nothing, had not the runner arrived. The council then decided to send a band of warriors to determine whether or not the monster was indeed in the neighborhood; but the search proved unnecessary. That night a stampede of horses and the unearthly cries of those in pain, mingled with the horrifying, angry snorts of the monster, left no doubt, and the Apaches fled to the mountains.

"When a place of safety was reached a meeting of the sub-chiefs was held, and it being found that old Quan-i-wah-le had endangered the entire race by his gluttonous desire to capture and eat all the fish in Salt River, depriving the great Water Spirit of his share, and causing him to break forth from his mountain prison in anger and revenge, it was ordered that he be deposed. Yah-k-ni-gel, being supposed to be in the good graces of the Monster, from the proximity he had long occupied to him, was selected to succeed the fallen chieftain, and he immediately ordered that no Apache tribe should thereafter reside in the valleys of the Arizona, under penalty of a war of extermination. Obedience to this order is the reason, the medicine men allege, why the Apache Indians never afterwards made their homes anywhere else than in the mountains, although, as the legend runs, the Water Serpent lived in he Salt River Valley but one year longer, when, finding it too warm and the water too shallow, he went down the Colorado River and into the Gulf of California.

"Be it here also recorded that under no circumstances or conditions can the Apache Indians be induced to catch, handle or taste fish in any form whatever, while it is highly relished as food by all the other tribes of Arizona."

I said good-by to the kind secretary and Dr. Thorne, and returned to Hermosillo to wind up my business. Here I found a letter from Mr. William Zeckendorf urging my return, as he had formed a new partnership in the general merchandise business with Mr. Staab, a merchant from Santa Fe, New Mexico, and they wished to engage me as bookkeeper in a new house to be established at Tucson, to which place I proceeded.

Mr. Staab had already begun shipping goods from New York; our storerooms were ready to receive them and I opened the new books for the firm of Zeckendorf and Staab. The nearest railway station to Tucson was then at Brownsville, Tex., and nearly all the goods received from there were brought in prairie schooners drawn by twelve mules each. When the bales of goods were opened they were found to contain numberless fleas. These, however, disappeared within a few days, probably died of heat. With the exception of these imported short-lived jumpers I have never seen a flea or bedbug in southern Arizona, and am now convinced that the pests which bothered us so much on our first trip to Santa Cruz at the San Rafael ranch must have been small red ants, which prevail all over the County to the great detriment of gardens and orchards.

I continued in the employ of Zeckendorf & Staab until 1880, when the firm was dissolved.

RUINED BY PEACE AND PLENTY

During these three years the whole Territory, and especially the southern part of it, had made steady progress, principally by the introduction of the cattle industry and the discovery of valuable silver and copper mines. While farther towards the north the towns of Globe and Flagstaff had been called into life, the rich mine known as Silver King had been opened near Florence, on the Gila River. The rich copper mines of Clifton caused the birth of that town. Along the upper Gila the agricultural lands, brought under irrigation, brought into existence the towns of Safford and Solomonville. Very rich silver mines were discovered at the place now called Tombstone, which caused the erection of several smelting works along the San Pedro River, and called into being the small towns of Charleston and Contention on its borders. Nogales and the now very flourishing town of Bisbee, with its almost limitless rich copper veins, were established.

But that which had been predicted by many farseeing men had come to pass, namely the increase in crime by highwaymen who rendered trading insecure, now that they were no longer afraid of roving Apaches. For these latter kept remarkably quiet at San Carlos, except when they held one of their tizwin sprees, and on which occasions they would often engage in fight and not infrequently would kill each other. Sometimes a small band of malcontents would break out from the reservation, commit a murder or two, and return with their plunder to the protection of the Stars and Stripes proudly waving over the San Carlos Agency. But after the civil authorities had caught, tried and hanged a few of them, they became very cautious. Even Geronimo, who at the death of the old Chief Cochise in 1876, had been selected by the tribe of the Chiracahuas to be their captain, kept very quiet on his separate reservation in the Chiricahua Mountains.

Mexican bandits, however, infested the country to a great extent. Their main object seemed to be the stealing and driving off into their country of the best stock, especially horses, and as those were kept on every mail station on the California route, and these mail stations were far apart, frequently in absolutely isolated regions, the latter became the objective points of the robbers' boldest efforts. At Mission Camp Station they killed four men and outraged a woman, after torturing her nearly to death to make her disclose the hiding place of a large sum of money which they supposed to be upon the premises. At Blue Water Station, about fifty-seven miles west of Tucson, they killed the station-keeper, his wife, and three-year-old child and drove off six horses.

These crimes were generally committed with a nice calculation as to the probable length of time before discovery. Discovery was usually from twenty-four hours to three or four days after the outrage. Often the victims were found only when the next bi-weekly stage came upon the spot. By this time the perpetrators of the outrage would be across the frontier. As we have seen, extradition was altogether precarious, and every attempt towards it involved great expense.

These two cases referred to are only example of many like outrages.

We had no lack of American "roughs and toughs" either. There was a highwayman who called himself Bradley, whose personal courage we cannot help but admire, much as we may deplore and despise his transgressions of the law. This man held up the stage all alone, twice in one week, within seventeen miles of Tucson, and only one mile from the mail station called Point of Mountain. The place selected by him was a sandy, rather wide, wash, which the stage had to cross at a very slow gait. Dense underbrush was growing on both sides of the road and to the very edge of it. He stepped out from the brush and ordered the driver and passengers to dismount and line up along the road and hold up their hands, keeping covered with his gun. For one moment he would turn his head to the rear and say in a loud voice towards the bushes: "You fellows, there, look out; shoot the first _____ _____ that makes a move." Then he would order the driver to bring the mail pouch and deposit it on the ground, as well as Wells-Fargo Co.'s Express box. After going through the pockets of his prisoners he would order them to mount into the vehicle and give the driver the word to go ahead, with the caution that he was watched and had better attend strictly to his business and keep going.

When, three days later, the same maneuver was repeated, at the same spot, by the same man, the authorities "got a move on." Trailers were sent out to follow the man's tracks. These led from the point of attack through the brush to a small cottonwood tree, where the robber had evidently tied his horse, which must have been a large American animal to judge from the size of the hoof-tracks. The horse was shod all around, but had shed the shoe of his left hind foot. This circumstance greatly assisted in following the trail, which led to Tucson, wound around the eastern outskirts of the city, and was finally lost in the Santa Cruz River about one mile above or south of the town. The river here had a sandy bottom for a stretch of about two miles, the water being nowhere, a few deeper holes excepted, over one or two feet deep. The river could therefore be easily crossed and recrossed, and the tracks made would soon be obliterated by the flow of the water. The search for tracks was therefore abandoned at dark of the first day. On the following day our best trailer arrived from his ranch and took the matter in hand, and soon picked up the trail. The tracks led to the house of one Lawrence, who kept cows, whose milk he daily took to town for sale. Mr. Elías, the trailer, returned to town in a roundabout way and reported to the authorities. The milkman, Lawrence, happened to be in town, and was easily found. He was buying a saddle and some provisions, which he said, when questioned, were for Bradley, to whom he was to deliver them that night about midnight at a certain spot in the dense mesquite grove about three miles from town. A posse of sheriff's officers ambushed the robber, guided by Lawrence, and when we shot him he fell crying to Lawrence. "Oh, you _____ _____ you have given me away!" Then he must have felt that he was wounded unto death, for his voice was very weak, though still distinct, when he next spoke: "I am dying; I will pray till I die."

The incipient cattle industry brought, of course, a great number of cowboys into the country. This class of men have been slandered as to reputation, which if we believe some producers of cheap eastern literature, was painted in very dark colors. I have always found them to be a free, open-hearted, manly class of fellows, any one of whom would unhesitatingly risk his life in the defense of a woman, or, for that matter, of anyone in need of assistance. It is true that sometimes, after payday, they would over-indulge in "booze," visit a small town in a body, persist in riding into the saloons and take their drinks on horseback, fire off their pistols promiscuously, and "paint the town red" generally.

Their chief amusement in town was to get hold of an Easterner, unused to the wild ways of the Woolly West, whom in their jargon, they would designate as a "tenderfoot." To him they would relate the most improbable stories of their adventures; of terrific combats with Indians; of hairbreadth escapes; of fierce fights with mad cattle and unbroken mustangs. They would often persist in treating and making their victim drink with them, *nolens volens*. If the latter showed himself good-natured, the cowboys would treat him liberally, but if he proved surly and uncompanionable, his treatment was apt to be rather rough. Wicked men are never liberal, and the cowboys are the most liberal class of men I have ever met. I remember one incident I witnessed in the small town of Charleston, on the San Pedro River. The railroad had just been completed to Benson, and a preacher had arrived in the town by the Benson stage, probably the first who came to exhort this wild community to amend their ways. This man wore black clothes; he was very thin and tall, and wore a high black silk hat that immediately became the target of a dozen cowboys. Within five minutes that hat was perforated by half a dozen pistol bullets. The people laughed, the preacher as much as anybody. Then he disappeared into a store, whence he presently came out with a new hat on his head; this time a flat one with a low crown. He walked up to the cowboys and said pleasantly: "Boys, please don't try it on this hat; my skull reaches to the top; and, besides, I have no money to buy another." The absolute fearlessness of this man not only astonished the cowboys exceedingly, but filled them with respect for the preacher. They took him into their midst and requested him to take just one drink with them. This he did, and then invited them to assemble upon the hotel porch at 7 p.m., when he would address a few remarks to all present and the cowboys all put in an appearance. The sermon was short. In simple words he preached about the inexhaustible love of God for all his creatures; he spoke to them of their faraway mothers at whose knees they had learned their first prayers, and closed his speech with a simple prayer. When he passed the hat around for traveling expenses, it was filled to the brim with silver coins, for the most part contributed by the cowboys. This was, of course, in the early days, from about 1876 to 1883. During that period there had started a feud between two clans or factions whose principal rendezvous was at Tombstone. I do not remember what the original cause of this bitter feud was between the Earps and Clantons, which latter were assisted by the Stillwells; but I know that, first and last, about twenty men lost their lives in the numberless fights that took place between them, sometimes in the streets of Tombstone. Here it was that I witnessed an incident that speaks strongly for the cool courage and presence of mind of these frontiersmen: I was standing in front of Billicke's Hotel, in the main street of Tombstone. Near me stood a man dressed like a cowboy, a clean-limbed, weather-tanned man with remarkably handsome features and fearless steel-gray eyes. He was intently watching two men who were coming down the street toward the hotel, engaged in apparently serious conversation which made them forget their surroundings. When they had arrived within about four feet of the hotel entrance, the cowboy near me whipped out a Colt's revolver and pointing it straight at one of the newcomers said: "I've got you this time, Bill." (This was called "to get the drop on a man.") The threatened individual looked up, and then glancing at the cocked pistol leveled at his heart, said with smiling lips and without the least quiver in his voice: "I see you have got me dead; but you had better put a cap on your pistol; it won't shoot that way!" The aggressor brought his pistol back to look at the nipple. But that moment was enough. In that fraction of a second the assailed man had his pistol out, fired, and the other fell dead.

CAPTURED IN MEXICO

During the month of May, 1881, my wife's old complaint returned with renewed force. At first we tried bathing in the warm springs emanating from the Rincon Mountains about eighteen miles northeast of Tucson, but soon found that no benefit was to be derived from them. Zeckendorf & Staab had closed their business, as before stated, and I was employed as bookkeeper in the grocery store of A. Goodman. Seeing that no relief was to be found from the medicines prescribed by three different physicians, I made up my mind to take my wife once more to the hot springs of Ymuris. My younger brother-in-law furnished a four-mule team, and a commodious wagon was prepared to receive the patient, with whom we started, accompanied by two of her elder sisters, on June 4, taking the route leading to Santa Cruz. By this time a new administration of the custom houses had been established, and from it much trouble resulted. Laws that had existed for twelve years had not been enforced and I knew nothing about them until I found myself consequently in a sad plight, for the punishment of my neglect of formalities was confiscation of our whole outfit. The inspector accompanied me to the wagon, and when he saw my wife whose sickness had made fast progress from day to day, her heart being by this time affected, the milk of human kindness within him stirred him into generous leniency.

"My duty would really be," he said, "to make you return to the principal office at the Palamita, to make there your declaration and to obtain the permit to cross the frontier. I see, however, that the condition of your wife is such as to render any further delay dangerous, and you must hurry to the hot springs at Ymuris. There you can leave your wife with her attendants and proceed with the wagon and mules seven miles farther and report to the Chief Inspector's office at Magdalena to whom I shall send a report of the matter by a mounted guard, in whose charge you must consider yourself, or at least your property."

"Then we are really under arrest?" said I.

"Well, call it so if you will." answered the inspector. "Your person does not cut much of a figure in the matter, but your mules and wagon, harness, and bridles, you must certainly consider as 'Embargados' " (lawfully under attachment).

Within half an hour the mounted guard carrying the Inspector's report to the chief officer at Magdalena arrived, armed with carbine and revolver, and we started, reaching the town of Ymuris about dark of the third day. Here I was horrorstruck by the information that the healthgiving hot spring in the valley below was no longer in existence, because the owner of the field upon whose borders the spring was situated had constructed an irrigating ditch passing directly through the hot spring and rendering it forever useless.

This was the death-blow to all our hopes for my wife's recovery. By this time she was very sick indeed, and unconscious the greater part of the time. Hearing that a certain Dr. Brown, a fine physician who held a diploma of the best medical faculty of Vienna, Austria, happened to be in Magdalena, (I had met him before in Tucson and his son had been one of my pupils), I gave my brother-in-law a letter for him containing the request that he would come to see my wife, with whom I stayed while my brother-in-law proceeded with wagon and team, always under guard, to report to the custom house at Magdalena. Fortunately it turned out that an uncle of my wife happened to be the prefect of that District and although he could not interefere directly with the federal authorities, who controlled the customs, he rendered us such good service through his influence that our bonds were accepted for the return of our wagon and team within thirty days.

On the following day Dr. Brown arrived. A short examination of my wife's condition convinced him that she was beyond all help. He said that she would in all probability not outlive a week, and that we had better remain where we were in reasonably comfortable quarters, instead of being overcome by her demise on the road in hot weather then prevailing. She died four days later on the very day that our lamented President Garfield was shot by Guiteau in Washington, and her remains were deposited in the cemetery at Ymuris. Three days later we returned to Tucson.

Very soon after my return I met a man in the street who had been with us during the "Miner expedition." I invited him to my house, where we had a long talk, during which he informed me that he had quit mining and was then a cowpuncher on the HC ranch up north. "Have you heard of our Fourth of July celebration?" he asked. I answered in the negative. "Well," said he, "I must tell you that most remarkable incident. You know Hank and Yank, the inseparables: they lived hereabouts for four years previous to going up North." I knew the two men very well and he began his story, which will make my readers acquainted with two of the previously-mentioned four men whom I know to have been in the clutches of the Apaches and who have escaped from them unharmed.

The region bordering on the Colorado River on the west, on the Grand Canyon on the north and traversed by the Southern Pacific on the south, has at all times offered rich and continuous grazing. The pursuit of this industry had, however, been handicapped in the early days of Arizona by constant depredations of the Apaches, too frequently accompanied by bloodshed. In the beginning of the 80's the cattlemen, seeing that the reservation and Indian Agency at San Carlos had become a fixture, and contributed to a great extent toward keeping the Apaches within certain boundary, had introduced large herds upon the ranges lying south of the "Rim," so called on account of its forming the southern limit of the Mogollon range of mountains. It is well known that the Indians were more afraid of three cowboys than of ten soldiers. Small marauding bands of these Indians, as well as those living upon the White Mountain Reservation, near Fort Bowie (formerly Cochise's but after 1876, Geronimo's band), would slip out secretly from the reservation and commit all the deviltry that opportunity offered. It is also said, and I believe, has been proven in several instances, that small parties of Apaches were granted a short leave of absence by manner of a written pass signed by the Indian Agent, ostensibly in order to hunt deer and antelope, which game was then very plentiful all over that region, and that such small bands did not always limit their exploits to the legitimate object for which the pass was given.

The cowboys are nothing if not brave; in fact, it would seem that fear has for them only an abstract meaning, and is not known by them in its concrete form. A general outbreak from San Carlos, it is true, was not an infrequent occurrence in those days, and might be expected at almost any time until the Chiricahua Apaches were captured by General Miles and incontinently sent far away from their mountain fastnesses and the theater of their murderous raids. Whenever such an outbreak occurred, or was expected from appearances, according to the principle that "coming events cast their shadows before," the cattlemen and their cowboys were generally prepared to meet all contingencies; this the Apaches knew, and would invariably direct their flight southward, into the Mexican state of Sonora, where they had many hiding places in the mountain fastnesses of the Sierra Madre.

A COWBOY FOURTH

The Fourth of July, 1881, was coming on, and the cowboys along and south of the "Rim" passed the word along from ranch to ranch that a meeting would be held on a certain day in May, at a central location called Walnut Grove, for the purpose of taking concerted steps toward holding a grand celebration of the nation's anniversary of independence. This call was attended to with great alacrity all along the line, and early in June things began to take shape. Cowboys are proverbially active, and prefer at all times quick work to lengthy deliberations.

The place selected for the celebration was that shady Walnut Grove, through which runs a babbling brook of mountain water, clear as crystal. Three committees were appointed to take charge of the business at hand; one on finance, that took charge of the contributions and disbursements; another on arrangements, which took in hand the management of the program, including ceremonies and refreshments, and a third, called the Committee of Invitations, among which were several Mexican *vaqueros,* with families, who undertook to induce a large contingent of dark-eyed señoritas to grace the occasion by their presence. The general program included, besides "speechifying and the reading of the Declaration of Independence," a barbecue, horse racing, lariating and tying of steer, "bronco busting," (the breaking in of a theretofore unridden mustang), a dance in the evening, and a grand "finale," consisting in the letting off of fireworks of every description.

The contributions were opened on the spot and dropped into the committee hat with a liberality known to and practised only by that free-and-easy-going fraternity. The feminine contingent, besides promising a liberal supply of tizwin, tamales, enchiladas, and other Mexican delicacies, began at once the preparation of bunting and flags, for which the material was easily obtained from the store of the Indian trader at San Carlos and at Holbrook, the recently-established town and railway station on the Southern Pacific route. The Committee of Arrangements prepared a list of assorted liquid refreshments, canned goods, sweetmeats, and fireworks, and sent it to Tucson, with request that the goods be shipped, without fail, to reach Holbrook not later than July 1.

The most active members of this latter community were the two cowboys mentioned above, employed by the HC ranch, as they would express it; they were called Hank and Yank, respectively, and were men of splendid physique and undaunted daring, with which they united many sociable qualities. They were fast friends, or, in their vernacular, chums, clinging to one another with that inseparable companionship and mutual devotion which is supposed to have existed between Damon and Pythias of old.

The danger of encountering hostile Apaches while abroad was at all times much reduced by traveling during the night; therefore, when Hank and Yank received notice from the freight agent at Holbrook that their "stuff" had arrived, they procured a Studebaker wagon and two stout mules, with which they drove to the railway station, a distance of about forty miles, during the night of May 31. They rested their team during the following day, with the intention of starting with their load toward nightfall. It would seem, however, that the royal game of poker with perhaps other inducements, retarded their start, and it was well toward midnight when they pulled out from Holbrook. A ten-gallon keg of whisky constituted one package of the freight, several boxes of sweet wine, intended for the ladies, and twelve boxes of assorted fireworks of Chinese manufacture, packed in light and thin board cases completed the load. Hank and Yank sat side by side upon the high wagon seat, their revolvers in their belts, their rifles within reach. When morning dawned they were still about twenty miles from their destination; they were traveling slowly at the time, not only on account of the steep grade they were ascending, but also because they were upon the partly sandy, partly rocky ground of a small and narrow canyon, a branch of the long and dark Devil's Canyon.

Suddenly the mules made a tremendous jump to the right, the wagon struck a big rock, and the shock precipitated the two men from their high perch to the rocks below. At the same time they heard some shots fired in their immediate vicinity, and the fearful Apache yell, well known by its peculiar "tremolo." Being knocked almost senseless from the violence of their fall, they could not realize at once what was doing, and before they had time to think at all, the Apaches were upon them, four or five to each, and had them tied hand and foot, upon which they were dumped into the wagon. Neither of them had been wounded, because the sudden fright of the mules had thwarted the aim of the Indians. The animals had either suddenly scented the Apaches coming around a turn in the road, or perhaps had seen one moving in the bushes along the edge of the narrow road.

(It is firmly believed along the frontier that a mule will scent an Apache quicker and farther than does any other animal.)

The inseparables were thrown in the wagon like so much freight, while their captors, who had succeeded in righting the running-gear and partly quieting the snorting and trembling mules, were driving the team like fury, leaving the main road as soon as practicable and taking a westerly direction over the hills.

It must have been about 9 o'clock in the morning when the party came to a stop in a small kettle-shaped depression surrounded on three sides by high cliffs. Here the Apaches unloaded the wagon and unhitched the mules laying the prisoners upon the ground. Now, there are two things that the Apaches are very fond of — liquor and mule meat. Two of them forthwith proceeded to kill a mule by cutting its throat, while others gathered some dry sticks and made a fire; they had matches as well as the modern kind of flint and fuse apparatus sold in the stores of mining camps. Others began to overhaul the unloaded stores, and, of course, immediately took possession of the whisky keg, which announced its contents by its exhalations. They smelled of it by turns, with plain indications of joyful anticipation. With an old bayonet one of them carried at the point of a maguey stick as a lance, they knocked in the stopper of the faucet hole. An Apache will drink liquor regardless of circumstances, simply because he cannot resist the temptation and has not the moral stamina for moderation. A general "drunk" was therefore soon under way. They drank from a gourd at first, but having discovered a saucepan among the unloaded articles, they kept that filled and passed it around. One of them approached the prisoners and offered them a piece of half-cooked meat; but neither Hank nor Yank had any appetite just then. Upon this, after having examined their bonds, found securely tied, the Indians left their prisoners in peace. Of course, they knew what would be their lot when they would reach the ranchería and its squaws, to whom they would be turned over for torture.

The liquor, recklessly imbibed, soon began to tell upon the captors. They became more and more hilarious, and acted like a lot of fools. They had opened the boxes of fireworks, had taken them probably for a kind of fancy candy, had broken some of the red sticks (Roman candles) and tried to eat them; but promptly abandoned that undertaking. Some had fastened bunches of firecrackers around their ankles, wrists and necks, in imitation of the anklets, wristlets and necklaces they adorn themselves with during their ceremonial festivities at which they dance. One had managed to fasten upon his head a wheel made of powder-filled cylinders, and wore it as a headdress. Hank said afterward that "the monkeyshines these fellows cut with that apparatus would have made a dead man laugh."

Gradually the reaction set in; being now very drunk, some indeed "dead" drunk, they lost control over their motions, and those that could still assume an upright position (there were only three such) staggered helplessly about, hugging a wine bottle.

In their drunken condition the Apaches allowed the fire to grow larger than if they had been in a sober state. Hank and Yank were lying side by side, about eight feet from the fire, and with their feet toward it, and the boxes of fireworks, nearly all of which had been opened, were piled in a promiscuous heap between the prisoners and the fire. Behind them was the slaughtered mule, about which were strewn some of the Indians' knives. Hank had taken in the situation; he began to wriggle and slide toward the pile of fireworks. When he thought he was near enough, he whispered to Yank: "Old boy, now or never; say a prayer quick and watch me; roll backward toward the knives as soon as I 'shoot;' then we make for the mule, the live one over at yon tree." Yank understood at once.

With all the strength Hank could muster, he doubled his legs well up and then shot them forth like a catapult against the pile of fireworks, which fell in a promiscuous heap upon the fire. The highly inflammable material became at once a mass of sparks, communicating themselves from package to package, and created a pandemonium surpassing, at least in variety, that of Dante's Inferno. The rushing hither and thither of leaping fiery frogs, the crackling of bunches upon bunches of fire-crackers, the whirring of wheels and whirligigs, the popping of Roman candles, from which issued a multitude of variegated stars, the hissing of rockets flying everywhere, and the fearful detonations of the so-called Japanese bombs, were enough to frighten an army. Some Apaches were so completely drunk that they never woke up, but had to be pulled upon their feet by the others; those who could still move were sobered all at once, found their legs, and ran off like people pursued by the evil one, as fast as they could, to escape from this incomprehensible "bad medicine."

Hank and Yank lost no time. They each soon had a knife between their teeth and severed their ropes. In another moment they were at the tree untying the mule, which was making frantic efforts to free himself;

they mounted upon him and soon gained ground upon which they recognized their bearings.

On the following day some of the canned stuff and sundry other articles were recovered by a party sent out for that purpose, guided by Hank.

The celebration took place, perhaps in not so luxuriously festive a manner as intended and provided for, but still to the satisfaction of everybody there. The joy at Hank's and Yank's escape made everybody forget the consequences of the mishap. These two men were, of course, the lions of the occasion; they had to dance with every woman upon the premises regardless of age and looks. Hank had to make a speech, in which he related the minutest details of his adventure. His closing remarks were: "I tell you, ladies and gentlemen, them fireworks went off beautiful; they were the most all-fired, sixteen-horse-power, double-bottom, copper-headed and brass-riveted free show anybody ever seen anywhar. I only regretted that I could not stay to see the going off of the spread eagle in red, white and blue lights which I had specially ordered. But that box had not been opened, and lay at the bottom; it must have gone off last. You see, I could not stop till that box got lit, as I had a pressing desire to join the ladies in the dance!"

I returned from Ymuris during the latter part of July, and went to see my employer, Mr. Goodman. He had employed another bookkeeper in my stead during the meantime. However, he told me, strictly in confidence, that he would be glad to employ me again, if he thought that he could "stand the press," by which expression he meant, if he would be able to meet his indebtedness. In the hope that his business would go on increasing as it had begun, he had bought a lot and was then building quite an extensive store, while formerly he had carried on his business in a rented place. He had underestimated the expense involved in the new building, and felt himself now financially crippled and was being hard pushed by his creditors. About this time the mercantile trade at Tucson had already begun to decrease. One reason for this was that the merchants of Tucson had begun to refuse credit, with few exceptions, to the small stores in Sonora who had heretofore purchased their supplies from them. Neither were the cash transactions as extensive as they had been. From 1876 to 1881, the Mexican dollars had been brought over the line in very large amounts, and taken by the Tucson merchants at par. Now their value had decreased, and they were accepted only at a discount of 25 per cent. The town of Nogales sprang up, being built upon the very frontier line which divided it into an American and Mexican town, large stores being promptly erected on either side. For many years one could buy much cheaper in Nogales than in Tucson, on account of the thirty miles free zone which the Mexican Government had established south of and adjoining Nogales.

There was still another reason which kept many Mexican purchasers away from Tucson, and this was, to our shame be it said, the bad faith practiced by a few merchants when dealing with Mexican smugglers.

Soon after my return I found that I was in a serious predicament with regard to my four children, the eldest of whom was a girl only nine years of age. The others were respectively seven (a boy), five, and three years, all now motherless. The younger of my wife's sisters, who had accompanied me to Ymuris on the last trip, as well as my good, kind mother-in-law, were perfectly willing to take charge of my household, but the two sons of the old lady had also to be provided for in a household apart, as neither of them was married. In almost any other country my sister-in-law could have acted as my housekeeper, but in a Mexican community the thought could not be entertained for a moment that a single woman not a blood relation to a man should live in his house. Therefore, knowing that she would make an excellent mother for my children, I proposed marriage to her and she became my wife. I never regretted this step, as she has ever since been to me a good, kind companion and an equally good mother to my offspring.

I was not particularly anxious to enter anybody's employ at that time, as I had already entered the field of literature. I was the Arizona correspondent of the *Illinois Staatszeitung,* and wrote a weekly story for its Sunday supplement; also, several articles for the *Globus,* an ethnological journal issued at Brunswick, Germany, and several descriptive articles of travel in Mexico for the *Journal des Voyages,* published at Paris, France. These different languages never proved any serious obstacle to me, because in the high schools and colleges of Switzerland, foreign languages are taught and learned in such a manner as to stay with you for life.

However, my brother-in-law, Mr. A. Levin, who was the owner of the Park Brewery and its adjoining small park, kept pressing me to take charge of the preparations and subsequently to run the Saint Augustine Feast, which would begin on Aug. 29.

This, however, requires an explanation.

The children of the orthodox Catholic parents (the mothers are almost without exception such) of any Mexican population receive, as a rule, at their baptism as Christian name the name of the saint as indicated by the calendar of the Catholic Church. Thus, one born on June 24 (St. John Baptist), would receive the name John, if a boy, and the name Jane, if a girl. (Juan and Juana respectively.) To this name there is generally added that of the godfather and godmother. This latter relation is taken by them much more seriously than with us, and the godmother of a girl must be very poor, indeed, if she does not manage to procure for her godchild's first communion, at the age of twelve or thirteen, a new white muslin dress and a veil of Swiss muslin, upon which a crown or wreath of flowers is fastened. Mexicans care very little about their birthdays, and very seldom make a family feast of it. But when the saint's day, as marked in the calendar, comes around, the respective namesakes prepare for the hospitable reception of their friends, and not infrequently an impromptu dance is gotten up on these occasions. The young swains who have sweethearts will engage a number of musicians and give the maidens a serenade under their windows about midnight on the preceding day.

All the Spanish missions, presidios (garrison towns), hamlets, and convents were put under the special protection of one particular saint, who was supposed to be the patron and guardian of the place.

The particular saint whose protection the town of Tucson was supposed to enjoy is St. Augustine, whose day falls upon the twenty-ninth of August. As late as 1870, the feast celebrated in honor of this patron saint was mainly of a religious nature. High Mass was sung, a procession went around, and all the Agostins and Agostinas kept open house. But gradually there developed from these beginnings, principally with the advent of the American drinking bars and gambling houses, the holding of a feast, which, little by little, from year to year, increased in volume and durance, until in 1881 it had assumed the character of a three weeks' — well, let us say "spree." When I reached Tucson in 1866, the Feast of St. Augustine lasted only two days, and the only popular amusements then in vogue upon the church plaza was a little gambling, principally at the simple game of "monte," upon a common pine table, and dancing by the rabble under a shed constructed upon the center of the plaza.

But early in 1871 the church plaza was found too small; and the feast was moved to the much larger courthouse plaza. The city then, in order to derive some benefit from the proceedings, which at that time extended over a full week, sold on August 1 at public auction the privilege of occupying the plaza for the term of ten days, to the highest bidder. This man then began to lay off his ground, and sold the privilege of erecting booths for drinking-bars, gambling-tables, fruit, candy, lemonade and cigar-stands by the front or square foot. Several restaurants, principally offering the quite palatable Mexican dishes, were also opened.

AN ANNUAL GAMBLE

On August 28, in the evening, the ball was sent a-rolling. I could never understand, and cannot now, how it came about that the population of any town could keep up a feast of that kind for three weeks. The fact, however, remains that night after night the people of Tucson came upon the feast grounds, ate Mexican and American dishes, drank liquor and gambled. Stately matrons accompanied by their husbands and children would sit by the hour around the Chusa tables and bet pores o' nones (odd or even) for quarters, half dollars, dollars, half-eagles, eagles, and double eagles. This game is little known in the United States. I think it originated in Mexico, or perhaps old Spain; at all events, the Chusa tables were at all times surrounded by a multitude of people, the Americans liking the game and patronizing it fully as much as the Mexicans.

I have seen many people of the best standing in the community playing at this game by the hour, and it seems that no one lost any social prestige or smirched his or her reputation by indulging in it.

The faro, rouge et noir, roulette, monte, and dice tables were also well patronized, principally by miners, cowboys, etc.; but here, also, many respectable citizens who would not dream of investing a five-cent piece in a game of chance during the remainder of the year, became gamblers *pro tem.* There were at least twenty drinking-bars upon the premises, besides innumerable ice-cream, fruit, candy, lemonade, and cigar-stands, not to mention the occasional quacks with their Indian medicines, etc.

In the middle of the square stood a wooden platform, an improvement on the earth floor, and here the rabble danced as of yore, and to the same music and tones that I had first heard twelve years before. In fact, the music, which was for years produced by the same Papago Indians upon their home-made fiddles, consisted of only two distinguishable tunes or airs. One did service for polka, schottisch, waltz, and quadrilles by simply adapting its "tempo" to the faster or slower movements of each dance. The other was the so-called *"pascola,"* a distinctly Papago dance. What these native musicians lacked in tuneful accomplishments they made up by perseverance, for they daily played those two tunes continuously from 4 p.m. until long after midnight, during the nineteen days that the feast lasted. Upon the platform only the low-class Mexicans, half-breeds, and Indians danced, and only women of questionable (or rather unquestionable) reputation. This feast of 1881 proved very profitable to us, but it was the last that was gotten up in such grand style. The railroad having now reached our town, the large circuses included Tucson in their visiting lists, as also did many dramatic companies and minstrels, and the St. Augustine Feast gradually became a thing of the past.

When I returned from a trip along the coast in the Spring of 1882, my wife informed me that one Mr. Pierre Charouleau had called at my house repeatedly and had left word that he wished to see me on urgent business immediately after my return.

This man was a Frenchman, a native of the neighborhood of Toulouse. He was then about forty-five years of age, a cooper, a good, easy-going man, but very illiterate. The greater part of his life he had spent in South and Central America, and had accumulated there a small capital.

His aunt, a very sharp and thrifty business woman of advanced age, had come to Tucson in the early sixties from Acapulco; she brought some money with her and established at once a pawnbroker shop, where she charged 20 per cent per week on moneys advanced upon portable property, and from 5 to 10 per cent upon money loaned on real estate. Thus she prospered financially, and was soon the owner of many lots and houses, which steadily increased in value. When, about 1873, she concluded to retire from business, she sent for two nephews, the above-mentioned Pierre, another named Jean, a youngster who had been in Bourbaki's army in the Franco-German war of 1870-'71, and who was then living with his family near Toulouse, France.

The two nephews arrived at Tucson at nearly the same time, and the old lady proceeded forthwith to make over her real estate to them, Pierre receiving by far the large and more valuable part of it. Pierre's wife, a fine Spanish woman, whom he had brought with him from Guatemala, died soon after their arrival, and in the following year he married a French woman in Sonora. It was soon after that he engaged me.

Mr. Charouleau, with whom I had been acquainted ever since he reached the town of Tucson, had a fine place in the range and after the business was dissentangled he invited me to go there for a rest and a hunt.

About the beginning of June we had finished. The proposed rest was taken at the Catalina ranch, which was situated about thirty-seven miles from Tucson upon a plateau, whence a beautiful view of the surrounding mountains was obtainable. The house contained four rooms and a kitchen, all well furnished and appointed, because Madame used them sometimes for weeks during the extreme summer heat, as a summer resort for herself and daughters. I knew that Mr. Charouleau was a good hunter, and that he was a sure shot and had killed several bears during the preceding seasons. He kept at this place a number of rifles and shotguns, as the whole surrounding country was populated with game of every kind — the mesa lands with deer and antelope, the course of the creek with valley quails, the higher regions with bears and mountain lions, while turkeys, doves, hares, rabbits and mountain quails were also quite numerous.

I have roamed a good deal over the mountains of southern Arizona, but have never seen there a grizzly bear; nor have I known one reliable man who has. The cinnamon and the black bear, however, are very common, nearly all the year round, and I believe that they hibernate, if at all, for a very short period only. They live principally on berries during the Summer, perhaps also on cactus fruit. Small game they can catch in plenty, and when hunger presses them very hard, they will occasionally capture and devour a small calf or a sheep from the numberless herds grazing all over the hills and in the mountain gorges.

The most destructive quadruped, however, was then and is now the American mountain lion, called in the Middle and Eastern States panthers. These large cats kill and devour many calves and colts, notwithstanding that quite frequently the mares, especially, defend their colts with great courage and fury. I have seen at the ranch of my Mexican brother-in-law several mares that had been fearfully scratched and torn by mountain lions while defending their colts, and also several cows, although these latter do not fight for their offspring with the energy displayed by the mares.

Near this ranch a mountain lion broke into the calf pen of a neighboring ranch and killed within a few minutes five calves by biting them through their jugular vein, and would probably have killed more if the noise caused by the commotion in the pen had not awakened the rancher and brought him to the rescue.

A premium of $25 is paid by nearly every county of the Territory for the scalp of a mountain lion, and several men follow their destruction as a means of living. As this big cat never devours an animal completely at one meal, but returns to eat it after a while, their destruction by poisoning has been attempted frequently, but almost invariably with poor success, as the scent of the lion is incredibly acute and he will at once run off from his prey, the moment he scents the touch of human hand upon it. Besides, if poisoned, he does not die at once, but hides in a cave inaccessible to man. The female mountain lion, as well as the wildcat, will, before going on a hunting expedition, carefully hide her young, the latter not unfrequently carrying them into a deep depression made by the forks of a large tree.

Upon a fine morning in June, Mr. Charouleau pronounced himself ready for hunting, the majordomo having reported fresh bear tracks found on the previous evening, leading into a canyon halfway up the mountain. We mounted immediately, taking with us a herder experienced in tracking and a very strong, though ill-trained dog, supposed to be a cross between a wolfhound and bulldog. The majordomo led the way, which soon entered the foothills and thence took us higher and higher towards the base of the mountains, where we crossed several canyons rich in verdure. After we had ascended to a hight [sic.] of about 2,500 feet from the house (4,900 above sea-level); the majordomo showed us the tracks, and then having urgent duties elsewhere left us. The dog did not at first scent the tracks, which were, however, so distinct that we easily followed them. They led into a deep canyon, widening and leading toward the mountain-side. We followed the bear for about two miles until we arrived at a place where the sides of the canyon were easily accessible; the tracks led to the right and upwards to a level space about two hundred yards wide, when we came to a smaller canyon, into which we descended, finding that the tracks again led upwards toward the mountain. In a sandy place we found a spot hollowed out as by a large body that had lain there recently. Evidently the game we were after had rested here for some time, and probably left the place that morning. The dog now showed interest in the chase, sniffed eagerly around the spot, and took up the trail of his own volition. Fearing that he would start forward beyond our call, we tied him to a line held by our herder. The tracks were now quite fresh, and we dismounted, tying our horses to a scrub oak. This canyon was overgrown with many bushes around which our way wended; many of them were junipers, and we could plainly observe the spots where the bear had torn off small branches from time to time. At length the dog gave tongue and made a bound forward. He was released and shot forward like an arrow.

An instant afterwards he returned to us howling, with a broken paw and bloody ears. At the same time there emerged from a clump of bushes about one hundred yards ahead of us a dark body, evidently a full-sized cinnamon or black bear. Out of courtesy Mr. Charouleau gave me the first shot. The bear was in full retreat, and offered therefore to us his rear for a target. I took aim quickly, while he traversed an open space between the bushes, and fired. We heard the thud of the bullet upon flesh distinctly, and saw the bear give a shake. But he did not stop. For a short time we could not see him, as he had entered a thicket growing well up towards the ridge on our right, but we could at all times guess pretty close where he was by the noise he made forcing his way through the brush and the rocks that came tumbling down the side of the ridge. Soon he emerged from the thicket and stood for a moment in plain view, looking down at us. While doing so he turned sideways and showed a plain dark silhouette against the light-gray rocks behind him. Before I was ready to take aim, Charouleau took advantage of this auspicious instant and sent a bullet behind the bear's left shoulder straight into his heart. He made a sort of leap that brought him standing upon his hind legs, but for a moment only. Presently he fell over on his side and rolled down the ridge until stopped by a group of young trees, where we found him dead. The distance traversed by Charouleau's bullet was about two hundred fifty yards. The bear was a fine male specimen of his race, although the skin might have been in better condition for a rug or buggy robe. My bullet had struck him in the thickest part of the buttock and had therefore not disabled him.

During the following day we rested from our fatiguing tramp. I felt somewhat sore over my useless shot at the bear, although under the circumstances the best hunter could probably not have hit a vital spot, unless his bullet broke the backbone just under the hump between the shoulders. At all events, I made up my mind that I would furnish a succulent breakfast for the next day, to consist of tender quail that abounded along the creek. For this purpose I carefully cleaned and loaded a fine shotgun, with the intention of starting on my errand before day break. We all slept on cots in front of the house, under the porch, which ran along the whole front of the building. Towards midnight we were awakened by the clatter of hoofs. A rider approached and halted in front of the porch, calling for Don Pedro (Monsieur Pierre). He was one of the latter's Mexican herders, all of whom had orders to report forthwith all signs and tracks of large game observed while on their rounds. This man stated that towards nightfall a lion had emerged from a mountain gorge, and seized a fat young calf, with which he had run off into a wooded hollow. The moon had come up about that time; he had followed cautiously upon the course of the robber, had seen him bite the calf's neck through and devour part of it, after which he (the lion) had carefully hidden the carcass in a cave-like hollow to which he (the herder) could easily find his way. That the lion would without doubt return to his prey for breakfast, and if we mounted quickly we should in all probability be able to reach the place in good time and kill the marauder.

Such an opportunity could not be neglected. We saddled up at once and armed ourselves. The majordomo, who had arrived from the range during the evening and slept at the house, readily consented to go with us. He and Don Pedro armed themselves with rifles, while the Mexican herder and myself carried carbines; all had, of course, revolvers. The herder led us over hill and dale for at least three hours, during which our plans of campaign were thoroughly discussed and arranged. About 3 o'clock a.m., while the moon was shining full, we dismounted, descended into the riverbed and followed it up over and between boulders until we came into a sort of kettle-shaped depression surrounded by a grove of cottonwood trees that stood up high above the surrounding dense bushes. In the middle of this kettle there lay apparently a small heap of twigs, branches, and leaves, surrounded by rocks scattered about in irregular groups. Although we could plainly see this heap in the rays of the moon which penetrated freely through the trees, we failed to discover the dead calf or any sign of it. Our herder, however, protested that it was hidden there. As he knew almost to a certainty from which direction the lion would come, he posted us in a semicircle, distant about seventy-five yards from the heap, in such a manner that the wind, which was blowing with some force, would come directly against us. We each found a hiding place, where we crouched under cover to our ears and awaited the panther.

Just at break of day the lion appeared. He came down a gulch and walked in the most deliberate manner straight toward the hiding place of his prey. Arriving there he halted, looked carefully around, and sniffed the air. My heart beat so that I seemed to hear it; while I looked with all the intensity I was capable of upon that splendid animal, standing out in the full moonlight, motionless for a few moments with the exception of its tail, the curved end gently swaying from side to side. Presently he crouched down before the heap of twigs and began to uncover it; then he reached with his right fore paw deep into the carcass; the the herder cried: *"Fuego!"* (fire). The almost simultaneous report of our four guns reverbrated through the groves. We saw the lion make a high jump into the air and then fall heavily to the ground, where he twisted himself in spasmodic motions for about five minutes, when he lay still. All cats die proverbially hard, and the herder, who had hunted these animals previously on different occasions, and who knew "their tricks and their manners," would not allow us to approach the carcass until he had sent a bullet through its skull from a distance of a few feet. At this the apparently dead animal made one more heave, as if trying to rise, but fell back, when one more spasmodic stretching movement and a visible shiver passing through his body indicated that he was dead indeed. All four shots had hit their mark, two making fatal wounds, one breaking the backbone and one penetrating the heart. The animal was a full-grown male lion in the prime of life.

We killed no more large game during our stay at the ranch, where we remained three weeks longer, but always had a surplus of quail, rabbits, turkeys, and doves, until our stomachs became so surfeited with game that a rasher of bacon seemed to us a royal feast.

In the spring of 1883, Chatto, a sub-chief of the Chiricahua Indians, left the reservation with a band of his followers and went up the Gila River by way of Clifton, killing seven men in the vicinity of that town and five more in the Mayflower mining district, farther east. This latter outrage was committed March 26. On the following day, about 10 o'clock a.m., Judge McComa, his wife and little son, Charley, were murdered by this band while traveling in a vehicle to Shakespere, where the Judge intended to leave his family while he went to Las Cruces, N.M., to attend the United States Court. They had just left Thompson's Canyon behind them, which was the pass leading out of the Burro Mountains, and emerged upon the open plain. Growing by the roadside were walnut trees and hackberry and other bushes. It was behind a cluster of these, about twenty-five feet from the road, on the right side as the Judge was traveling, that Chatto and twenty-nine Indians lay in wait.

When the judge and family were nearly opposite them, the Indians fired and shot down the off-wheeler of the team and wounded the Judge. He ran about sixty yards before he fell. The red devils then gave a wild whoop and a rush, and Mrs. McComa and her son were made captives. Then there followed a horrible scene the details of which my pen must not describe. It was fully related afterward by the perpetrators whom General Crook refused to deliver to the civil authorities. The person of the unfortunate lady was violated in the most brutal manner; her clothes were dragged from her body, which was torn and scratched most horribly. When her life was almost tortured out, they beat the back of her head until her brains oozed out; then they broke off branches of the elder bushes and thrust them deep into her body.

The judge's body was riddled by bullets, and not a stitch of clothing was left upon it. Little Charley was never heard of afterward.

After my return to town with Mr. Charouleau I had taken up the occupation of bookkeeper, keeping the accounts of a wholesale liquor store, a grocery store and a fruit store, respectively, giving at the same time many private lessons in bookkeeping to young clerks, Spanish lessons to Americans, being also frequently called upon to render services as interpreter and to translate documents for parties in litigation.

In the summer of 1883 and during a short period in 1884 and 1885 I revisited Hermosillo, and in the latter year the city of Guadalajara, in order to take copies of documents deposited in those cities. The attorneys of Tucson saw the time approaching when the United States would appoint a land court, which would definitely settle the validity or invalidity of certain Spanish and Mexican land grants or charters embracing immense tracts in what afterward became United States territory.

The lawyers representing American claimants of grants which had been purchased by them engaged me to go to the Capital of Sonora and copy for them such documents as they thought necessary in their respective cases, and to have my copies certified to by the Secretary of State. The documents I went to copy were generally kept in a stone safe thickly cemented and safely shut in by a heavy iron door fastened by three enormous padlocks attached to strong iron bars.

MEXICAN MURDER TRIAL

In Hermosillo I looked up Mr. Jose Sermino, a cousin of my mother-in-law. As she had informed me, I found him an oldish gentleman of good education and courteous manners, a judge in the Superior Court which consisted of three members. This court, with the exception of two months in the hight [sic.] of summer, was in session daily from 9 a.m. to 12 m.

Upon the invitation of my distant but friendly relative, I visited the court while in session, and witnessed the trial of a half-breed who had stabbed his wife so seriously that she died of her wounds after a month. The trial was very short, not occupying over an hour. Jury there was none. It would be a foolish institution in a country seven-eighths of whose population consists of Indians. The district attorney (*licensiado del estado*) made a plain statement of facts and introduced his witnesses. The attorney appointed for the defense by the Court then made his statement and introduced two witnesses, who testified to "great provocation" for the fatal act. No cross-examination of witnesses by either attorney was allowed. The presiding judge asked such questions of the witnesses on both sides as he thought necessary to further elucidate the case, and then gave each attorney ten minutes for his final statement, the prosecution leading.

It was evident to me from the presiding judge's conduct of the trial and his intelligent interrogatory of the witnesses that he was well learned in the law and a very sensible man. As soon as the defense had closed the final argument, the chief justice opened the statutes, laid his forefinger upon a paragraph, and showed the place to his two associates. They both nodded their heads in sign of assent. The prisoner was ordered to stand up and receive sentence. This latter read: "Ten years state's prison."

When the court adjourned Mr. Sermino invited me to dine with him at his house. During the after-dinner conversation it occurred to me to ask where the state prison was located.

"Well," began my host, "it is really a very peculiar institution; one the like of which you have probably never seen."

"What are its peculiar features?" I asked, "and where does it stand?"

"It does not often stand long on one place; it moves about quite frequently," said the judge.

"Who moves it, and what for?" I asked again, forgetting my grammar in my astonishment.

"It moves itself; it walks! See here, my boy; today is Friday. On the day after tomorrow be here at 9 o'clock a.m. sharp, and you will see our state prison walk by this house; I will therefore say no more now."

Of course I was promptly on hand, and the matter was explained.

The sound of a drum, rapidly approaching, brought us to the door, in front of which passing through the middle of the street, there marched about fifty unarmed men all clothed alike in cheap cotton garments rather soiled. Each carried under his arm a bundle of clean clothing. One thing quite noticeable about them was their very short hair (an almost unknown feature in that country), upon which stood a shako as white as snow, carrying in front a large brass number 6, giving to many of them, especially the undersized ones, a strong resemblance to an oversized monkey, for nearly all of them were very dark-featured. On either side of this contingent there walked upon the sidewalks two commissioned and about ten non-commissioned officers of the regular Mexican army. Each one of them carried a revolver on the full cock in his right hand which hung by his side; six regulars with loaded rifles walked at the head and six at the rear of the procession.

As soon as they had passed our door the judge said: "This is our state prison going to the river to take a bath." Then he gave me the further explanation that, not having a state's prison as yet, the sentence of a criminal sending him for a number of years to said establishment was actually docketed in these words, but really meant that he was to be enrolled in sixth battalion of state troops, in which battalion the discipline was as rigorous as in any prison. Here the delinquent had to perform for the period of his sentence all manner of work, being always strictly guarded by the regulars, as I had seen. They had to police the streets, repair the public highways, keep the public buildings in order, as well as the parks, etc.

"Then they never carry arms?" said I.

"Oh, yes. When troops are needed to quell an Indian outbreak or to follow a murdering and robbing band into the mountains, the Pelones always have to go."

(This word "pelones" means the "shorn ones," from the fact that upon entering this prison battalion their hair is cropped as short as possible and maintained in that state.)

"How can you trust a lot of criminals with firearms and ammunition?" I asked.

"Well," said the Judge, "you see, there are always regular troops with them, and their officers have the right to shoot on the spot the first one who makes a threatening move in the wrong direction. They render very good services in an Indian campaign against Apaches; they travel far and fast on very little food, and never seem to shirk a fight. If one of them shows great bravery or performs a feat of special valor before the enemy he is pardoned forthwith."

The next year news reached Hermosillo that the Pelones forming the greater part of the garrison at Enseñada, the nearest frontier town in Sonora to the American boundary line, had rebelled, arming themselves with the rifles of the regulars constituting their guard; had exterminated the latter, and taken themselves to the mountains.

The institution of Pelones is now abolished.

A REBUKED SAINT

One day during the month of July, Mr. Sermino, who had insisted that I should quit the hotel where I stopped and become his guest during the remainder of my stay, said to me after breakfast: *"Primo mío* (my dear cousin), if you have the time and inclination to see something quite interesting, you must rise very early to-morrow morning and start for the fields below the *pueblito* (the little town of Seris situated directly opposite the city of Hermosillo, across the then dry Sonora River), and witness the punishing of San Ysidro (St. Ysador or Isidor). This saint is supposed to have particular charge of the farming population; he is the patron saint of agriculture, as was the goddess Ceres for the old Romans. I was informed that from the first of that month the people had formed processions every morning very early, as had been the custom for unnumbered years, and, headed by the priest, walked to the fields, gardens and orchards, then extremely dry, marching around them, the while singing, and praying for the rains which are usually expected about St. John's Day (June 24). Two weeks having then elapsed since the praying was begun, and no rains having fallen, nor yet any signs pointing toward a speedy fulfilment of their desire and answer to their prayers, they have resolved to begin a series of punishments to be inflicted upon the statue of figurehead of San Ysidro standing in the chapel of the agricultural town of Seris. The priest is, of course, not present, at these performances, fearing perhaps that part of the punishment might fall upon him! "Go there about daybreak," said Mr. Sermino; "you can take my horse, but remain an indifferent spectator, and do not interfere in anything you may see; neither must you indulge in mirth, for these people take that matter very seriously."

I had heard the expression "punishing the saint" somewhere previously, and by actively rummaging memory's old chests, I remembered an old Mexican lady whom I had frequently visited during my marriageable age, she having two beautiful and good girls. This old lady was called Doña Concha, an abbreviation for Concepción, and she had a picture of a female person called Sta. Concepción. One morning I had found that picture turned with its face to the wall, and upon inquiring the reason was informed by the old lady that her patron saint had failed to respond to her most earnest prayers for a certain occurrence to happen, and was now under punishment in the manner indicated.

The judge's remarks had excited my curiosity not a little, and I saddled my host's horse, rode away, and arrived in the fields just in time to see a long procession of people, fully three-fourths of whom were women, form a circle around a tree, under the branches of which I could see the figure of a person dressed in white muslin and adorned with glittering tinsel. A man in a wide-brimmed straw hat seemed to admonish this mute and immovable statue, which was the ornamented manikin representing San Ysidro in the church of Seris, giving it from time to time severe lashes across its back. Then they all returned with it to the chapel.

The judge, to whom I reported the results of my excursion, advised me to go again on the following day, and yet again the next to see the thing out. On the following day I went somewhat earlier, tied my horse to a tree distant from the scene of action, and was thus enabled to find a place in the front rank around the dummy, which was set up as before. After a short consultation between the leaders of the procession, which consisted entirely of poor, ignorant, and illiterate field laborers, it was resolved that the figure should be hanged by the neck to an overhanging branch of the tree and stripped of all its finery, lace, and ornamental trinkets. This was done, and the culprit saint was left hanging. No rain appearing yet, another procession started on the succeeding day. They took the despoiled saint from the tree and taking hold of the rope around his neck, dragged him to a muddy irrigating ditch, threw him into it and dragged him thus for about a hundred yards, while the lowest of the rabble apostrophised him with epithets I will abstain from repeating. Then they brought him back to the tree and fastened him anew to the branch where he looked very forlorn indeed, being now but a mass of muddy and frazzled shreds. During all these performances I thought at times that I must be dreaming; I almost had to pinch myself to make sure that I was really awake and living in the year of our Lord, 1884 and not in the Middle Ages. On the third of August, the rain came: torrents of rain. The river filled its bed, the irrigating ditches resumed their functions, the trees, bushes, orchards, gardens, and fields revived and San Ysidro was cut down from the tree, reinstated in his old place in the chapel and once more dressed up in fine linen and adorned with tinsel.

Along the western edge of the city of Hermosillo (the beautiful), the capital of the Mexican state of Sonora, runs a long, narrow street called *la calle del Carmel,* or Carmen (Carmel Street), beginning at the northern end where the church or chapel of that name stands. Directly from the outer edge of this street there rises an elevation which extends nearly the whole length of the street, attaining a hight [sic.] of almost four hundred feet. It is evidently the result of volcanic eruption, being composed entirely of lava rocks that give forth the metallic sound inherent in all such formations. It is completely bare of vegetation, except in a few fissures or cracks where the decay of ages has formed a little soil.

The whole mountain is one mass of rock whose surface is cut up into innumerable caverns, cavities, fissures, and cracks, surrounded at every side by small peaks, projections, boulders, and rocks of all sizes and shapes, thus making the ascent to the top quite a laborious task.

This rocky hill is known far and wide as *el cerro de las campanas* (the mountain of the bells), because from it there issue from time to time the most wonderful and variegated sounds imaginable, changing in strength of tone and nature of sound, from resemblance to bells rung at a distance to such as would be produced by a church organ played very softly or listened to from the outside of a church. Again, at times, especially when a light ocean breeze comes up from the Gulf of California, the music of the mountain seems to be that of a flute, at intervals weakening into a soft murmur not unlike that produced by a jew's-harp, distant and softly played. When there is no wind from any direction the mountain remains mute.

I had visited Hermosillo on several occasions before 1884, on business as well as for pleasure, and had repeatedly heard these mysterious sounds; but had neglected to inquire into their cause or their origin. As I was now making a lengthy stay, with no urgent business that required a speedy return, I resolved to solve the mystery. Many were the questions I put to inhabitants of the city, of all classes, but without success. The old residents considered the sounds a matter of course, having heard them from their infancy; later arrivals had become accustomed to them also, and the latest had either not found time to give the matter any thought, or, if so, had given it up as an unsolvable riddle. I could find nobody who seemed to be interested in the matter, seriously or lightly, until I brought the subject up in the presence of the judge, who remarked: "I do not believe that you will find in the whole city a single person who takes any interest in the matter or thinks it worth while to do so. You see, scientific research is not in our line; in the first place we are too indolent to ascend that mountain to investigate its secrets; and in the second place we have heretofore been kept pretty busy with revolutions. However, now that you have brought the matter up I remember that there exists a Yaqui Indian who used to tell a wonderful tale about the mountain. I think you will find him upon the farm of an old Frenchman, Monsieur Tait."

I found Mr. Tait. The Yaqui, he said, was still with him. He called him *el Chino* (the curly one), and spoke of him in most laudatory terms.

(It is customary in Mexico to give a surname to anyone whose exterior affords the facility of applying a distinguishing attribute. In a family where all are dark-complexioned save one, this one will of a certainty be called *el guero* (the light-complexioned one), and in case of the circumstances being reversed, the exceptional one will be called *el negro* (the black one) or *el trigueño* (the dark one).

A ride of nearly an hour's duration across the Sonora River and through the outskirts of the small town of Seris brought us to the cultivated fields where recently San Ysidro had been maltreated, and eventually to the farm of Mr. Tait. The Yaqui was sent for, and soon made his appearance. He was a man of middle-age. His features indicated intellectuality. He spoke Spanish quite fluently, although with that peculiar aberration from grammar characteristic of all Yaquis, which consists in placing almost invariably the masculine definite article "el" before a feminine noun, and vice versa.

"Ah, Señor, what I know about this *cerro* and its *voces* (voices) is wonderful; but I do not like to tell it, because the people often make fun of it. But I know it to be true, as true as the sun, the moon, the stars, the rain, and whatever else we can see with our eyes. My father was killed by Apaches, when a young man, in the Sierra Madre, and I was reared by my grandfather, who was a direct descendant of many, many generations of *caciques* (chiefs). He told me the story himself over and over again, as he had it from his ancestors, and surely it is true — it is — it is!"

A YAQUI LEGEND

"You see the mountain over yonder whence the sounds come. It is only a vast heap of rocks now; but it was once, long, long ago, a beautiful green hill, and all about and around it the hills and valleys were green with trees and pasture, gemmed with beautiful flowers. The rains were more frequent then, and the river was never dry. Our nation was rich and powerful — as numerous as the grains of sand down by the shore of the gulf. It occupied the whole country from the Pimería Alta (Arizona in the North) down to the sea. Large herds of cattle were grazing everywhere, and silver was as plenty as brass and iron are now with your mighty people. Our Montezuma was a great warrior, very tall and muscular, with eyes like a hawk; no other man could string his bow, none could wield his lance; his shield was of pure silver and shone like the moon at full. He lived on the top of the mountain. In front of his house there hung between two posts a large dirk of beaten silver, and when he struck it with his clenched fist, the sounds it gave forth reverberated over hills and dales to a great distance and caused his chiefs to assemble around him; for the whole country was subject to him. There was no more powerful chief than Takahuitl, who was our Montezuma at the time I speak of. His subjects were well organized into large and small bodies, for warfare, and he could assemble an immense fighting force in a very short time. Around his palace on the hill were many smaller houses where his women lived, with their servants.

"Powerful though our nation was, we had an ememy who would often encroach upon our lands, drive away our herds, and at times even succeed in carrying away some of our women and children. My grandfather called this hostile nation Comanches, and said that many, many years ago those men came for the first time, mounted upon animals swift as the wind. At first they had only a few, later more and more; and at last they all came mounted in large swarms like so many big bees. This made them much swifter than our men, especially on level ground, and although we could and did fight them successfully man to man, we could not follow up or pursue with good results.

"At last a party of these Comanches suddenly swept down the river from the Primería Alta, and, between the present site of the town of Magdalena and this place, attacked a pueblo of our people, taking the inhabitants completely by surprise. They killed nearly all the men, carried off the women, children, and cattle and destroyed the houses, crops and other property. When a runner came to Takahuitl with the sad news, the Montezuma was overcome by a great fury and swore by the Great Sungod that he would have revenge.

"Loud and long sounded the calls from the dirk on the green mountain; fast and far flew the runners to summon the bravest and fleetest warriors of the nation. An expedition was quickly organized consisting of great numbers of the best warriors, as Takahuitl intended to penetrate into the very heart of the Comanche country, to recapture the prisoners and to retaliate in full for all the indignities and depredations our people had suffered for many years. In order that the home government of the nation should be carried on in an orderly manner, the chief's brother, rendered incapable for warfare by having a leg crushed in a fight with a bear, was appointed to rule during the absence of the Montezuma, which was expected to last an unusually long period.

"Long and weary for those remaining at home, were the days of waiting, and full of anxiety, doubt, and fear. Upon the roof of the chief's house stood a watchtower, whence the lookout scanned the horizon to the east and north for signs of an approaching war party. A bright fire was kept ablaze upon the top of the tower, from dark till dawn, as a signal for the returning warriors. Nearly three months had elapsed, when the dirk upon the mountain gave the signal of alarm, and again, and yet again. The vice-chief and his followers rushed out to the watch tower and saw — saw they aright? They saw three Comanches coming at full speed directly towards them. Comanches they must be, for they were on the swift animals of that people. Nearer and nearer they came, and now their persons could be distinguished, their headdresses and their armament. There were none of the white feathers of the Comanches upon their heads, upon which the straight eagle and hawk quills stood boldly upright. Approaching swiftly they then raised their lances high, struck with their shafts the glittering centerpieces of thin rawhide shields, and uttered the far-sounding war cry of triumph of the Yaquis. Presently they were at the foot of the hill, were ascending it, and now they dismounted in the midst of their brethren.

"Ay, Señor, the good news they brought! Takahuitl had followed the trail of the marauders from the Sonora River without ceasing; day and night. Game was plenty everywhere. The fastest runners followed the tracks of the hostile body ahead of our war party, showing by signal fires at night their whereabouts and indicating the route to be pursued. Then they would rest a few hours until the main body should come in sight, when they were off again. The Comanches, now aware of pursuit, fled from our greater force. To the farthest east of the Pimería Alta the Yaquis thus pursued the Comanches, whose horses could not bear the strain. At last, when approaching the great river, the enemy, completely exhausted, was forced to make a stand and give battle. We outnumbered them greatly, notwithstanding the fact that many of our men, whose strength was overtaxed by the long, rapid and ceaseless pursuit, had fallen behind. The short bows of the Comanches shot neither as far, as strong, nor as sure as our long bows. The combat was short. The marauding Comanches were nearly exterminated; our women and children were nearly all recaptured, and we took many animals from them.

"There was great rejoicing on that day all over the nation, runners being sent out to the remotest parts to carry the glad tidings.

"When, a few days later, the war party returned there was feasting without end. The fifty prisoners were distributed among the chief men, who took them into their families as servants.

"To the lot of Takahuitl there fell a beautiful maiden just budding into womanhood; lithe as a willow wand, with long, dark tresses, large, liquid eyes, at one moment full of fire, at the other reflecting a melancholy languor. The tribe called her Lotumaia (morning glory), she was so fresh, so lovely. As Takahuitl's first wife, Tetemaka, a woman of already advanced years, looked upon her with disfavor, the Montezuma lodged her in a house apart, with an old woman as attendant. She was not required to do any menial work. Material was furnished her to manufacture moccasins, baskets and headdresses, an occupation which seemed to suit her. Takahuitl would often visit her and listen to the plaintive songs of her nation.

"More and more did the Montezuma spend of his leisure time with the beautiful flower, his captive. He would sit near her by the hour and teach her the language of our nation. By the light of the moon he would walk with her over the green hills and down to the river, where they would chat and sing together under the trees. As he had swift animals now, they would ride together from place to place, drinking love from one another's eyes (for he would carry her in front of him on the same horse). All these doings were either observed by the now furiously jealous Tetemeka or reported to her by her spies.

"Then came a day of sadness and unspeakable woe. Takahuitl had been out hunting for two days and, contrary to all previous custom, had returned without game. Lotumaia had also been absent, nobody knew where, during the greater part of this period, but had returned early that afternoon and had buried herself at once in her lodge. Soon after nightfall the Montezuma returned, tired, hungry and thirsty. He sat down upon a bundle of deer skins before the door of Tetemeka's lodge and called to the woman to bring something for him to eat. His bow and lance stood against the wall near him. Servants appeared, placing before him some dry bread and a gourd of water. Incensed at this treatment, he called for his wife. She reluctantly stepped out of the door and faced him. Upon his request to be served with better food he received from her the sullen answer: "Poor food to a poor huntsman." At this moment Lotumaia, who had appeared from another direction, stepped forth and set before her lord and lover a savory stew of lamb's meat. He addressed her, beginning: 'Sweet one, how much kinder is your heart than that of my —'

"He had not time to say more. Like a fury sent by the evil spirit himself the jealous wife had seized the chief's lance and buried it deep into the heart of the Comanche maiden, who fell dead, reaching her little hand towards Takahuitl, who threw himself upon her expiring form and pulled out the murderous spear.

"At the same instant a tremendous roar shook the air as if a thousand whirlwinds had centered upon the top of the hill; the mountain began to heave hither and thither like the angry ocean down in the bay during a storm; the watchtower tumbled down, the houses shook and the earth opened wide in many places; vivid lightning seemed to shoot from the earth, crackling fires and sulphurous fumes emanated from numberless fissures, amid tremendous peals of thunder, and in a few minutes the beautiful green hill became the heap of stones that you see now.

"But the voices, ay, the voices! Have you heard those soft, long-drawn, deep tones which the northwind carries to us down here? Well, that is the voice of Takahuitl calling to his Lotumaia. And have you noticed the sweet, bell-like strains which vibrate far over the city when the gentle southwind reaches us from the bay? That is the voice of Lotumaia answering the call of her beloved. The great commotion and upheaval of the mountain has separated their bodies, but their souls live, calling to each other.

"This, Señor," ended the Yaqui, "is the true story of the mountain of the bells and the origin of its sounds. But our glorious nation, once so powerful, will never more attain to the glory and power it enjoyed under the great Takahuitl."

PROGRESSIVE FARMER

Mr. Tait's house, orchard, gardens, and fields were certainly a model establishment of its kind in that country, where I saw thousands of cattle grazing on the hills and could not obtain a pint of milk anywhere during the day, after milking-time, and never an ounce of butter! He had a cool cellar built upon the northside of a rock, or, rather, two cellars; one for a dairy and one where he made wine from the grapes of his vineyard. He raised, besides, sugarcane, tobacco, all kinds of fruits and vegetables, horses, mules, donkeys, swine, sheep, and innumerable fowls.

Mr. Tait being a widower, his son's wife, a farmer's daughter from the south of France, was the head of the household, a very numerous one, if we include the farmhands and house servants. Everything in and about the house and whole establishment bore the appearance of order combined with comfort. Upon Mr. Tait's invitation I visited him during several afternoons and spent many a pleasant hour with the family and walking under the orange trees, shooting the numerous woodpeckers that made a speciality of pecking the choicest oranges.

These woodpeckers are very pretty birds with a plumage speckled like that of a guinea fowl, and a bright red patch upon their heads. The Mexicans call this bird "carpintew" (carpenter), on account of the repeated loud knocks he gives.

It was during one of these bird-shooting walks in the orange orchard that I over-heard one morning two female voices in what seemed to be a very animated conversation interrupted from time to time by great sobs and crying fits. Desiring to discover the cause of the distress I investigated and discovered beyond the hedge two young Mexican women washing clothes, and I heard one confide to the other that she had allowed herself to be seduced by a Mexican dandy called Manuel, who now, breaking his promise, refused to marry her. She threw her arms about the neck of the other and wept hysterically.

"I would give him *toloache,* I would, I would," responded the other with a firmness and decision altogether unusual in the character of the ever-docile and humble Mexican woman.

Not caring to be a witness to an intimate conversation of this nature, but puzzled about "give him *toloache,*" I went to the house and asked Mr. Tait, Jr., what was the meaning of *toloache.*

"Why," said he, "you see it every day; it is that large plant with big leaves and large white flowers that you find around here almost everywhere in damp places, especially along the borders of ditches. Come, I will show it to you," and he pointed to a plant which I immediately recognized as *datura nicotiana,* the well-known Jamestown weed, generally called all over the United States "Jimson weed."

I related to him what I had seen over the hedge and also that part of the conversation I had overhead.

"Oh," said he, "I understand. That was undoubtedly poor little Conchita; so she is a victim of that skalawag Manuel. With his guitar and love songs and his beautiful eyes he has turned the heads of half the young girls hereabouts. Poor child, she is barely sixteen, and has no mother!"

"Well," said I, "where does the *toloache* come in — the Jimson weed, you know?"

"Ah, of course," he answered. "This plant contains a narcotic poison, which seems to increase in strength the further south the plant grows. The seed capsule is the seat of its strength. It happens quite often in Mexico that a woman, first seduced and then abandoned by her lover, boils a few of these seed capsules and gives the liquid thus obtained to her faithless swain to drink, of course, without his knowledge. This is most easily done at a dance or feast or social gathering. If the *toloache* tea is strong enough, and it generally is, the effect is swift and terrible. The man's brain becomes affected within an hour to such an extent that he becomes quite irresponsible and develops a strong tendency to do violence upon himself; his first impulse seems to be to isolate himself.

"You see, the girl has no redress by the law; if she has no father or brother, who might take her part, and either cause the faithless lover to marry or support her and their offspring, she takes her revenge in her own hands; but generally not before the man begins to neglect her and takes up with another girl. This seems to be the case with Conchita now, and that skalawag Manuel had better look out for himself.

The following day was Saturday. In the afternoon several of the farmhands came to the house and obtained from Mrs. Tait mescal, wine, and cigarets, stating that they were going to have a dance that night in the storehouse or at the lower end of the farm.

On the following day we all were sitting at breakfast in the open hallway of the house, when there appeared at the front opening the figure of Manuel; but he was no longer the clean dandy with the laughing eyes and mirthful voice. His appearance was shocking; his clothes were torn, he was besmirched with mud and he seemed to stare into vacancy with eyeballs double their usual size, protruding from their sockets. He stopped but a moment, waved his hand toward us and with a hoarse, hasty "Adiós, todos!" (good-by, all) he was off as fast as he could run.

"*Toloache*, by _____!" said Mr. Tait; "hurry, boys! after him!" His son and myself sprang from our seats. Mr. Tait, Jr., seizing a lariat from a peg in the wall, and followed the fugitive, who took the direction of the river. He ran in a straight line towards a cliff overhanging a deep place where a rapid current existed. He stopped for nothing; he jumped over the numerous nopal cactus like a deer, tramping down the smaller creosote bushes and leaping over ditches. He left us far behind. After about ten minutes we heard a cry that penetrated shrilly the stillness of the beautiful Sabbath morning.

In the afternoon some laborers discovered and brought to the hut of Manuel his body, which they had fished out of the water nearly a mile below the cliff.

Mr. Tait gave the body decent burial. Three months later I received a letter in Tucson from Mr. Tait, Jr., stating that they had laid the remains of Conchita beside Manuel's, she having died after giving birth to a male child, whom they (the Taits) had legally adopted.

SONORA SCHOOLS ORGANIZED

In the fall of 1884, the new Palace of the Governor was finished and thrown open for occupancy at Hermosillo. Previously I had met one Mr. Bonillas, then mayor of the town of Magdalena. This gentleman had been, thirteen years before, my best pupil by far in the public school at Tucson. By him I was introduced to Governor Ramón Corral, of the state of Sonora, who asked me if I would be willing to established the public schools of Sonora in accordance with the school system of Switzerland, which I agreed to do, and from January 1, till the end of May, I was occupied in that task. The two principal objections urged in Mexico against the American school system were co-education of the sexes and the long vacations occurring between two school terms. Co-education could not be thought of, for reasons previously dwelt upon, and the latter I overcame by making the whole year a school year with four weeks' vacation during the hight [sic.] of summer, three weeks during the fall and two weeks during the holidays embracing Christmas and New Year, the teachers to receive their salaries during the entire year unabridged by reason of vacations.

In May, 1885, I returned to Arizona.

INDEX

Apache Indians
  Oatman massacre, 20, 43–44
  Cochise, 51
  attacks: on Camp Wallen, 56–57; on mail rider at Mowry Mines, 96; in Huachuca Pass, 121; on Spring's party, 131; on Tubac merchants at Sonoita Creek, 184–186; on Mexicans at Los Nogales, 187–188; on Spring near Calabazas, 198; on Wooster, 237
  peaceful relations with settlers, 52
  Spring's account of causes of Apache wars, 53–55
  pursued by scouting parties from Camp Wallen, 97–102, 121–125
  citizens of Territory petition for aid against, 145–146
  Spring's historical account of, "in war and peace," 148–155
  superstitions and customs, 152–155, 284–287
  atrocities and depredations, 191–192, 245–247, 306–307
  warfare with Pima Indians, 225–227
  Camp Grant massacre, 245–253
  Dr. Thorne's sojourn among, 279–287
  Fourth of July kidnapping, 295–298

Babocomari, 13, 57, 66, 69, 143, 155
biological specimens, Spring's collections, 16–17
Bonillas, Ignacio, 15, 16, 319
botanical descriptions:
  mesquite at Yuma, 40
  agave at Camp Wallen, 79
  barrel cactus, 113–114
  cholla ("silvery yucca"), 232–233
Brichta, Augustus, 15, 144
Brown, W. Harvey, 26, 27, 33, 39, 48–49, 55, 58, 77, 82, 125–127, 129
Buchler, von Steffisburg family, 2–4
Buckalew, Oscar, 96–97
Buehman, Henry, 17
Buttner, A., 59, 103

The text of JOHN SPRING'S ARIZONA was set and composed in Linotype Times Roman by Morneau Typographers in Phoenix. Printing was by Arizona Lithographers of Tucson, on sixty-pound University Eggshell text, with end sheets of Andorra. The book was bound by the Roswell Bookbinding Company of Phoenix in Columbia Riverside Chambray, RVC 3731. Erwin Acuntius was the designer.